REPUTATION MANAGEMENT

Reputation Management is a how-to guide for students and professionals, as well as CEOs and other leaders. It rests on the premise that reputation can be measured, monitored, and managed. Organized by corporate communication units including media relations, employee communication, government relations, and investor relations, the book provides a field-tested guide to corporate reputation problems such as leaked memos, unfair treatment by the press, and negative rumors, and focuses on practical solutions. Each chapter is fleshed out with real-world experience of the authors and contributors, who come from a wide range of professional corporate communication backgrounds.

This updated 2nd edition of *Reputation Management* features:

- **Two new chapters on social media and public relations consulting**
- **Textbox features** relating key communication theories to the practice of public relations and corporate communication
- Expanded coverage of **global issues**
- **New and updated examples** throughout
- **New companion Web site**, featuring lecture materials for instructors and extensive learning resources for students and professionals at: **www.routledge.com/textbooks/doorley**

John Doorley, former Head of Corporate Communications for Merck & Co. Inc., is Academic Director and Clinical Assistant Professor of the M.S. in Public Relations and Corporate Communication program at New York University, School of Continuing and Professional Studies.

Helio Fred Garcia is President of Logos Consulting Group. He is an Adjunct Professor in the Executive MBA program of New York University's Stern School of Business, and teaches courses in NYU's M.S. in Public Relations and Corporate Communication program at the university's School of Continuing and Professional Studies. He is the author of *Crisis Communications* (AAAA Publications, 1999).

REPUTATION MANAGEMENT

2ND EDITION

The Key to Successful Public Relations and Corporate Communication

John Doorley
and
Helio Fred Garcia

First published 2007 by Routledge

Second edition published 2011
by Routledge
711 Third Avenue, 8th floor, New York, NY 10017

Simultaneously published in the UK
by Routledge
2 Park Square, Milton Park, Abingdon, Oxon OX14 4RN

Routledge is an imprint of the Taylor & Francis Group, an informa business

© 2011 Taylor & Francis

Typeset in Bembo and Zurich by Prepress Projects Ltd, Perth, UK
Printed and bound in the United States of America on acid-free paper by Edwards
Brothers, Inc.

Library of Congress Cataloging in Publication Data
A catalog record has been requested for this book.

ISBN13: 978-0-415-80184-3 (hbk)
ISBN13: 978-0-415-80185-0 (pbk)
ISBN13: 978-0-203-87686-2 (ebk)

TABLE OF CONTENTS

6 Government Relations   164
By Ed Ingle

7 Community Relations   188

PREFACE

Public Relations is the management of communication and relationships between an organization and its publics. It is also the selling of ideas, policies, products and services through often uncontrolled media and two-way communication that complement or replace the controlled media and often one-way communication of advertising.

— Doorley and Garcia

■ ■ ■

This definition is built on the seminal, 10-word definition by Grunig and Hunt—"the management of communication between an organization and its publics."[1]

Corporate and organizational communication: The centralized management of communication on behalf of the organization; the function is a critical contributor to an organization's reputation—and thereby its competitiveness, productivity, and financial success. It is a subset of public relations.

— Doorley and Garcia

This book on public relations and corporate and organizational communication is grounded on the simple premise that everything communicators do should be respectful of, if not geared toward, the long-term interests of the organization. Organizations that manage their reputations well benefit not just in so-called soft, feel-good ways, but in quantifiable, bottom-line ways as well. Organizations that ignore the reputational effects of their actions pay the consequences over the long term, as the rash of business scandals since 2002 has shown. And the consequences range from soft, embarrassing ones to dissolution of the organization.

This book is unique because:

- It covers each of the major disciplines in the field of corporate and organizational communication, bridging real-world practice with communication theory and history.
- It covers the field from the perspective of reputation management, and provides a new framework for managing reputation into the future.
- Each chapter was written by someone who has practiced the craft successfully at a high level.
- The authors cite personal experiences, including both successes and failures.
- Each of the chapters includes some history and theory, real-world, how-to information, and the perspective of a practitioner other than the chapter's author. Each chapter concludes with best practices, resources for further study, and questions for further discussion.

It is our hope that this book will help advance the practice of public relations and corporate and organizational communication by helping practitioners and students become more knowledgeable about the history, theory, and practice of their craft. Ours is not a primer—for example, we do not show readers how to write a press release. Our book presumes a basic knowledge of communication theory and practice appropriate to professional communicators, executives, and students at the advanced undergraduate or graduate levels. There are good basic public relations and communication texts on the market. What we have tried to produce is a how-to book, based on solid academic principles and written by leaders from the communication professions—a book that addresses communication problems and opportunities in a thoughtful, thoroughgoing, practical way.

> What we have tried to produce is a how-to book, based on solid academic principles and written by leaders from the communication professions.

This book is a team project. John and Fred have collaborated on the entire book, and have shared responsibility for drafting individual chapters. John has taken the lead in drafting the chapters on "Reputation Management," "Media Relations," and "Community Relations," and has done much of the liaison and editing work with outside authors. Fred has taken the lead in drafting the chapters on "Communication Ethics," "Investor Relations," "Issues Management," "Crisis Management," and "Challenges and Opportunities." John wrote the proposal for the book and secured the agreement with the publisher.

We have also sought the help of several prominent practitioners whose perspectives and experiences complement ours. These contributions come in two forms: authorship or coauthorship of individual chapters, and contributions of sidebars or case studies within chapters.

To keep clear who wrote what, the chapters written by John and Fred have no author attribution at the beginning of the chapter; each chapter written by a contributor begins with the contributor's byline.

ILLUSTRATIONS

When we were working on the first edition, we thought it would be nice to retain a student, and, long story short, we found Julie Osborn, a graduate student in the Center for Advanced Digital Applications Program in New York University's School of Continuing and Professional Studies. Lucky us! Julie's work, though Jules Pfeiffer-like, is original, sometimes humorous, always engaging. Since our first edition was published in 2007, Julie has earned her graduate degree and landed a job with George Lucas (the *Star Wars* Lucas). Lucky George! It was Julie who conceived Mr. ProCom and Ms. ProCom. But then the question became: which person to use with which chapter? Being quite the serious professional communicators ourselves, we pondered the media relations challenges, the looming issues to manage. Should we prepare a crisis communication contingency plan? In the end, we decided to have Ms. ProCom adorn the cover of each of the 14 chapters of the first edition and all 15 of this edition. Why? Perhaps because we have a few more male contributors in our book than female;

perhaps because women communicators now have a population edge in the PR profession, or perhaps because Fred and John found Ms. ProCom to be better company. In any case, we show them working together here—teamwork, it is called, which entails picking each other up every now and then. And if any of this is upsetting to anyone anywhere—well, we simply have no comment!

STRUCTURE OF THE BOOK

Chapter 1 includes "The Ten Precepts of Reputation Management," with the tenth stipulating that reputation should be managed like any other asset—that is, in a strategic way. The rest of the chapter includes a new, copyrighted framework for implementing comprehensive reputation management. It is remarkable, but very few organizations approach reputation management in a comprehensive way, as they would any other asset; in fact, most organizations do not know what their reputations are worth. Corporate communication professionals should make it their business to understand the value of reputation, and ways to support, enhance, and measure it. Chapter 1 also includes a discussion of the Pushmi-Pullyu syndrome, whose schizophrenic tug has been felt by every communication professional.

> Chapter 1 also includes a discussion of the Pushmi-Pullyu syndrome, whose schizophrenic tug has been felt by every communication professional.

Chapter 2 focuses on ethics. The subject is up front in the book, right where it belongs. The ethical practice of communication is neither an oxymoron nor an afterthought, but should be an integral part of practicing the craft. And it has a tangible effect on reputation. Failure to keep ethical issues always in mind can cause predictable, negative consequences. At New York University's Center for Marketing, whose students are working professionals, Fred used to teach communication ethics in the fall semester and crisis communication in the spring semester. Students invariably wanted to discuss the same case studies in both semesters; they noticed a meaningful overlap in companies with ethical challenges and crises. That led some students to note: "Better pay attention during fall or you'll be quite busy in the spring." This chapter includes general principles of communication ethics, the normative standards of behavior embodied in the codes of ethics of major professional organizations, accounts of recent scandals in communication ethics, and two historical sidebars showing that such ethical issues have been part of professional communication for many, many years.

Chapters 3–13 are organized according to the corporate and organizational communication disciplines (for example, media relations, organizational communication, and government relations), or around issues or functions that protect reputation (such as corporate responsibility, issues management, and crisis communication).

Chapter 14 is a new chapter on Public Relations Consulting. We are honored to have Lou Capozzi as the author of this chapter, and the reader will quickly appreciate why we say that. Each of the first 14 chapters begins with a true anecdote that reflects the essence of the chapter.

Chapter 15 looks ahead, and frames criteria for the successful practice of public relations and corporate and organizational communication in the future. It also describes ways to enhance the credibility of the communication function among senior leaders. It provides a framework for thinking strategically about the impact of communication, and on assuring that all the organizational communication functions are aligned not only with each other but also with the bigger enterprise.

We hope that students and professional communicators will find the personal, anecdotal approach an interesting and informative complement to other books in the field, most of which take a third-person, definitional approach. This book should also be helpful to people—from managers to CEOs—who supervise or work with professional communicators. Communication is not rocket science, but it is not easy either, and it can make or break an organization, perhaps faster than any other function.

> Communication is not rocket science, but it is not easy either, and it can make or break an organization, perhaps faster than any other function.

Today, those who communicate on behalf of institutions have greater power than ever before, because communication media are both more powerful and more widespread than ever. And professional communicators are under greater pressure to use their power in the right and responsible way to meet the pressing requirements of laws and regulations, corporate and organizational governance, and a more vigilant society. Paradoxically, pressures to compromise the forthrightness standard are also becoming greater in this increasingly competitive and fast-paced world.

In order for organizations to build solid, sustainable reputations and avoid the kinds of scandals that have recently affected so many of them, organizational communication, like organizational performance, must be proficient and ethical, because communication and performance are major components of reputation. An organization must speak with all its constituencies with one voice that is highly trained and true. It is our hope that those with a stake in corporate and organizational communication, as well as students and aspiring communicators, will find in this book sound, ethical communication principles and practices that they can believe in and adhere to over the long term.

YOU SAY COMMUNICATIONS ...
WE SAY COMMUNICATION

This is a stylistic point, of course, but some logic can be brought to the discussion. Most academics label their disciplines and their courses as singular. They are professors of communication, and they teach organizational communication, intercultural communication, and so on. On the other hand, practitioners most often use the plural, and they work in departments of corporate communications, employee communications, and so on. We're afraid the academics have it. Communication covers the entire spectrum. It is a discipline, like art or language, and is therefore singular. And to label it and think of it as singular is to help elevate what is too often perceived as tactical—for example, issuing press releases and publishing newsletters. Most unabridged dictionaries make only a few exceptions to the use of communication as singular. They refer to the various means of sending messages as plural, so that radio, television, telephones, and the Internet are communications media. And they refer to multiple messages as communications. In the 1980s, when Fred headed "communications" for a large investment bank, he was often approached by bankers who wanted to add a phone extension or install a computer. "Communications" sounds like the phone company.

> We're afraid the academics have it.

This book will go with logic, and the unabridged dictionaries, and use communication. We will use the plural only in referring to the media, and to the titles of practitioners and the names of their departments, because that is how practitioners usually refer to themselves. Everywhere else, it will be communication.

John Doorley and Helio Fred Garcia

ACKNOWLEDGMENTS

This book would not have been possible without the active support and encouragement of many people in addition to the two primary authors and all of the contributors. We wish to thank all those who have supported us, our work, and the book. We wish in particular to thank our editors at the venerable publisher Routledge, Taylor & Francis Group, Matthew Byrnie, Nicole Solano, and Alfred Symons, for their steady hands in helping us shape a book that would be valuable to both the professional and academic audiences.

We wish also to take a moment, individually, to acknowledge and thank those who have helped each of us in our task.

JOHN DOORLEY'S ACKNOWLEDGMENTS

To Carole Doorley, with love and gratitude.

To these executives, former executives, and friends who have done the profession of public relations proud by communicating strategically, ethically, and very successfully over the years. I appreciate your reading the various iterations of the manuscript, the fervent discussions, and the insights Fred and I could not have brought by ourselves.

Albert D. Angel	Randy Poe
Mike Atieh	Robert Pellet
John Baruch	Richard D. Trabert
Kenneth P. Berkowitz	Paul Verbinnen
Rich Coyle	

To these communication scholars for their encouragement, editing, and scholarly insights:

Boston College:
Edmund M. Burke (recently deceased)

New York University:
William E. Burrows
Lou Capozzi
Helen Ostrowski
Fraser Seitel

Purdue University:
Stacey Connaughton

Rutgers University:
Todd Hunt
James Katz
Brent D. Ruben

*University of California
Santa Barbara*:
Ronald Rice

University of Missouri:
Donald Ranly

Western Michigan University:
Maureen Taylor

To Lisa Ryan and Jim Masuga of Heyman Associates for helping to recruit contributors and coauthors. To Michael Cushny of NYU for sending us Julie Osborn, our illustrator.

To the following family, friends, and colleagues for their logistical, proofreading, editing and moral suppport: Carole Doorley, Jonathan Doorley, Nanci Doorley, Clark Landale, Madeline Najdzin, Nick Kornick, Dr. Charles P. Yezbak, Alice Yezbak, and Sam and Jean Davis.

HELIO FRED GARCIA'S ACKNOWLEDGMENTS

Much of the content of the chapters I drafted was honed over nearly three decades of advising clients and more than two decades of teaching students, mostly at NYU. I thank those clients and students whose insights and challenges allowed me to grapple with the issues distilled here.

I thank my partners and colleagues at Logos Consulting Group and the Logos Institute for Crisis Management & Executive Leadership, especially Barbara Greene, Anthony Ewing, Laurel Hart, Oxana Trush, and Adam Tiouririne. They helped frame much of the content and provided invaluable support and insight. Elizabeth Jacques did much of the research for Fred's chapters and copyedited much of the first edition's manuscript. I thank her for the care she showed in helping make the manuscript more effective. Lisa Wagner of ArtTech Web designed the graphics in the ethics, issues, crisis, and challenges chapters, and I thank her for helping to make complex ideas easy to grasp.

Finally, I wish to thank the three women in my life: My wife, Laurel Garcia Colvin, and our children, Katie and Juliana. They tolerated my burying myself in research, writing, teaching, and client service, and my too-frequent absences, and always welcomed me home.

ABOUT THE AUTHORS

This book is written and edited from the perspective of communicators who have done it and taught it.

■ ■ ■

JOHN DOORLEY

In 2008 and 2009, John led the team of Communication and Public Relations leaders who, working for and with the Public Affairs and Corporate Communication Department at Johnson & Johnson, built and launched ACCEL—the Academy for Communication Excellence and Leadership. Perhaps one of industry's most ambitious professional development programs, ACCEL is focused on optimizing the link between the Communication function, the Corporation and its 200+ businesses around the world.

Since 2005, John has also served as academic director of the M.S. degree in public relations and corporate communication at New York University, a program he founded in 2005, and one that has been recognized by the prestigious *PR Week* Awards as the nation's number one academic program in the field. His proudest accomplishments there, he says, are the "faculty we have recruited, the students we are training and the contributions we are making to the validation of public relations as a social science."

From 1987 until 2000, when he began his teaching career at Rutgers University, he was head of corporate communication at Merck, which often ended up on just about every "most admired" list, usually at the top.

And while John won't play the rooster taking credit for the dawn, he will accept some credit for the company's accomplishments on the communication front.

At Merck, he: led many policy initiatives for the company and the healthcare industry, most notably in AIDS, healthcare reform and managed care; directed the company's communication programs for each of its business development initiatives, including acquisitions and joint ventures; earned the Merck Chairman's Award, the company's rarely-bestowed, top honor; and his Corporate Communication team was named "The Best Corporate Communications Department" by a leading trade publication. He developed the proposal and led the group advocating publishing of the Merck Manual Home Edition, now available in two million homes.

Before joining Merck, he was the chief speech writer for the CEO of Hoffmann-La Roche Inc. His work in reputation management has been covered in *PR Week* and *O'Dwyer's Public Relations News*, as well as in academic journals, and *PR News* called him a "luminary on reputation management." He holds a bachelor of science degree in biology from St. Vincent College and a master of arts in journalism from NYU. John has won numerous writing awards, has been recognized by the New Jersey Governor's Office for his pro bono work with pediatric cancer patients, and received the Award For Outstanding Service from NYU's School of Continuing and Professional Studies. John can be reached at johndoorley@aol.com.

HELIO FRED GARCIA

Helio Fred Garcia is the president and founder of the crisis management firm Logos Consulting Group, and is the executive director of The Logos Institute for Crisis Management & Executive Leadership. He is widely regarded as a leading expert in crisis management and crisis communication.

Fred is a coach, counselor, teacher, writer, and speaker. Since 1980 he has advised and coached leaders of some of the largest and best-known companies and organizations in the world. In addition to serving North American clients, Fred has had an active international practice, advising clients in Europe, Asia, Africa, Latin America, the Middle East, and Australia.

In the 1980s Fred worked at several of the leading public relations firms, and served as head of public relations for a global investment bank and for a large public accounting firm. In the 1990s Fred headed the crisis practice of a leading national strategic communication consulting firm. He founded Logos in 2002.

Fred is an adjunct associate professor of management and communication at New York University, where he has taught since 1988. He teaches crisis management in the Executive MBA program of the Stern School of Business. He teaches courses in communication strategy and in communication ethics, law, and regulation in the Masters in Corporate Communication program in the School of Continuing and Professional Studies. He has received the school's awards for teaching excellence and for outstanding service.

Fred is also on the adjunct faculty of the Starr King School for the Ministry—Graduate Theological Union in Berkeley, CA, where he teaches a seminar on religious leadership for social change. He is a frequent guest lecturer at the Wharton School of Business of the University of Pennsylvania, the U.S. Marine Corps Command and Staff College, the Center for Security Studies of the Swiss Federal Institute of Technology, and other universities.

In addition to working with John on *Reputation Management*, Fred is the author of the two-volume book *Crisis Communications*, published by AAAA Publications in 1999. He was technical editor and editorial advisor for *The Complete Idiot's Guide to Business Presentations* (Alpha, 1997).

His article "Effective Leadership Response to Crisis," which appeared in the January/February 2006 issue of the peer-reviewed journal *Strategy & Leadership*, won the Highly Commended Award at the Emerald Literati Network 2007 Awards for Excellence. Fred is accredited by the Public Relations Society of America, and received the Society's New York Chapter's Philip Dorf Award for mentoring.

Fred has an MA in philosophy from Columbia University, and studied classical Greek language and literature in the Greek Institute of the City University of New York Graduate Center. He has a BA with honors in politics and philosophy from New York University, where he was elected to Phi Beta Kappa. He received an honorary doctorate in Humane Letters from Mount Saint Mary College.

ABOUT THE CONTRIBUTORS

Chapter Contributor Biographies

Unless otherwise specified, the chapters were authored by John Doorley and Helio Fred Garcia. The other authors' biographies follow, in chapter order:

Chapter 4, Social Media, by Laurel Hart, partner, Logos Consulting Group

Laurel Hart   Laurel Hart is a partner at the crisis management and communication firm Logos Consulting Group, where she helps clients, both corporate and nonprofit, understand the evolution of social media and its relationship to organizational communication, reputation, and crisis. She has worked in the communication field since 2000, and prior to joining Logos, worked for companies and nonprofits in Seattle and New York City. Laurel is an adjunct instructor at NYU, and teaches a course on social media in the Master's in Public Relations and Corporate Communications program. She has also been a regular guest lecturer at the Wharton School of Business of the University of Pennsylvania. She has a BA in English from Colby College and an MS in Public Relations and Corporate Communications from NYU.

Chapter 5, Organizational Communication, by the authors with significant input from Jeff Grimshaw and Tanya Mann, partners, MGStrategy

Jeff Grimshaw   Jeff Grimshaw, a partner in MGStrategy, is an expert in accelerating accountability and alignment. Over two decades, he has helped hundreds of leaders across dozens of Fortune 500 companies deliver the results on which they've staked their reputations. Jeff is also Senior Advisor, Leadership Solutions at stickK. com, helping leaders apply powerful insights from behavioral economics to improve performance. With rogue POW/MIA activist Paul Pinkerton, Jeff co-founded Paul's Kids Vietnam Children's Charity, which helps orphans, poor children, and children with disabilities.

Tanya Mann   Tanya Mann is a Philadelphia-based management consultant and partner in MGStrategy. She advises clients on internal communication, organizational change, and leadership development. Tanya has worked with Yale University, Kaiser

Permanente, the Children's Hospital of Philadelphia, IBM, EMD Chemicals, Merrill Lynch, Independence Blue Cross, Texas Folklife Resources, and the Washington Redskins, among others. She helps create lasting infrastructure through collaboration with those closest to the work and alignment to leadership strategy, with a hefty concentration on discipline and adherence to process. Tanya earned a bachelor's degree in communication studies and a master's degree in interpersonal communication, both from the University of Texas at Austin.

Chapter 6, Government Relations, by Ed Ingle, managing director of government affairs, Microsoft Corporation

Ed Ingle Ed Ingle is managing director of government affairs at Microsoft Corporation and has over twenty-five years of public policy and political experience. He previously served in the White House as a senior aide to President George W. Bush. Ed was a consultant for twelve years with the Wexler & Walker government relations firm (owned by WPP Group plc), where he lobbied Congress and the Executive Branch on behalf of corporate clients. He served in the Reagan White House Office of Management and Budget from 1985 to 1989. Ed has a bachelor's degree in journalism/public relations from the University of Tennessee, and a master's in public administration and policy from Indiana University.

Chapter 8, Investor Relations, by the authors and Eugene Donati

Eugene Donati Eugene Donati is an assistant professor of advertising and public relations at The City College, City University of New York. His research interests include the communication of financial and scientific information and the role of public relations in public policy formulation. He is also an adjunct professor at New York University, where he teaches investor relations and public affairs. Gene is a graduate of the Universities of Toronto and Pittsburgh and the American University, Washington. He began his thirty-year public relations career as a press secretary on Capitol Hill and, later, was managing director at the consulting firm Clark & Weinstock, New York.

Chapter 9, Global Corporate Communication, by Lynn Appelbaum, APR, associate professor, The City College of New York, Gail S. Belmuth, vice president of global corporate communications, International Flavors & Fragrances Inc., and Katja Schroeder, president, Expedition PR, LLC

Lynn Appelbaum Lynn Appelbaum is a professor at The City College of New York (CCNY), where she is program director for the Public Relations and Advertising specialization in the Department of Media & Communication Arts. She has taught at CCNY since 1993. Prior to her academic career, Lynn practiced PR for fifteen years during which time she managed media relations for NBC News's "Today." She served as public affairs director for Cooper Union, and as marketing director of Merkin Concert Hall in Manhattan. She has consulted for several New York Metropolitan organizations, including Lighthouse International and The New York Public Library. Lynn has conducted and presented her findings of a major research study of diversity in public relations. She was elected to the board of directors of The Public Relations Society of America (2008-10) and serves on the board of the Public Relations Society of America-New York (PRSA-NY) chapter, which honored her with the chapter's Dorf Mentoring Award. She has written about mentoring in the PRSA's *Strategist* and about crisis communication in PRSA's *Tactics*.

Gail S. Belmuth Gail S. Belmuth, former vice president of global corporate communications, International Flavors & Fragrances Inc, has twenty years of global corporate communication and international political consulting experience. Currently on hiatus to raise her daughter, Gail has held senior positions in corporations and communications agencies including Burson-Marsteller and Banner McBride and has run her own consulting practice. Former clients include Unilever, Textron, Cemex, the National Cable Television Association, the governments of Russia, Kazakhstan, Bolivia, El Salvador, and Panama, and a presidential candidate in Columbia. Gail graduated Phi Beta Kappa, magna cum laude from Brown University with a degree in Russian Studies. She completed post-graduate work at Leningrad State University.

Katja Schroeder Katja Schroeder has helped multinational companies develop and maintain their corporate reputation in North America, Europe and Asia-Pacific. She led award-winning campaigns on the agency side for B2B and consumer companies of all sizes. In 2009, Katja founded Expedition PR, a boutique agency that focuses on connecting emerging global players and technologies with their markets. Katja holds both a Master in Information and Communication Sciences from Sorbonne in Paris, France, and a Master of Arts in Communication from Free University in Berlin, Germany, as well as Diploma in European Public Relations. She is fluent in German, English and French and has basic knowledge of Spanish, Urdu and Mandarin.

Chapter 10, Integrated Communication, by Timothy P. McMahon, principal, McMahon Marketing LLC

Timothy P. McMahon Timothy P. McMahon is a management consultant at McMahon Marketing LLC. He is also a visiting professor at St. Joseph University Haub School of Business in Philadelphia. He has taught at Elon University and New York University. From 1997 to 2003, Tim headed corporate marketing and communication at ConAgra Foods, Inc., a Fortune 100 company at the time. Before that, he founded and managed an award-winning advertising and public relations firm for a dozen years. He has also headed national advertising for Pizza Hut, Inc. and was the founding marketing director for Godfather's Pizza, Inc., the fastest-growing restaurant chain in the country. Tim holds a Ph.D. from Gonzaga University, an MA from Seton Hall University, and a bachelor's from the University of Nebraska at Omaha. Tim's research interests include organizational performance and social media.

Chapter 13, Corporate Responsibility, by Anthony P. Ewing

Anthony P. Ewing   Anthony P. Ewing is a lawyer, consultant and teacher. As a partner at Logos Consulting Group, Anthony counsels executives on corporate responsibility, crisis management and communication strategy. Anthony has helped companies to engage stakeholders, define corporate human rights standards and implement compliance programs and partnerships. Anthony teaches a graduate seminar on business and human rights at Columbia Law School. He has served as an independent corporate responsibility expert for the International Labor Organization and is a member of the United Nations Global Compact Human Rights Working Group. Anthony holds a BA in Political Science from Yale University and a law degree from Columbia University.

Chapter 14, Public Relations Consulting, Louis Capozzi, retired CEO of Manning, Selvage & Lee

Louis Capozzi   Louis Capozzi retired after a forty-year career in public relations and corporate communications. He was CEO of Manning, Selvage & Lee, one of the world's largest public relations consulting firms, and before that was vice president of corporate communications at Aetna. He earlier held senior communications positions in both corporations and consulting firms. A graduate of New York University in journalism/marketing, Lou holds an MBA from the Bernard Baruch Graduate School of Business.

Sidebar Contributor Biographies

Lee Aase   Lee Aase is director of the Mayo Clinic Center for Social Media, a first-of-its-kind social media center focused on healthcare, which builds on Mayo Clinic's leadership among health care providers in adopting social media tools. By night, Lee is Chancellor of Social Media University, Global (SMUG), a free online higher education institution that provides practical, hands-on training in social media for lifelong learners. Prior to joining Mayo Clinic in 2000, Lee spent more than a decade in political and government communications at the local, state and federal level. He received his BS in Political Science from Mankato (Minn.) State University in 1986.

Kenneth P. Berkowitz   Kenneth P. Berkowitz, a graduate of Brooklyn Law School with a master's degree in trade regulation law from NYU Graduate School of Law, had a unique position at Hoffmann-La Roche Inc. USA, a major healthcare products company, based in Basel, Switzerland. As vice president of public and regulatory affairs and drug safety, his responsibilities included virtually the entire corporate communications and public affairs spectrum as well as drug regulatory and safety issues. He is now a healthcare industry consultant and a recognized expert in the regulation and marketing of prescription medicines.

Sandra Boyette   Sandra Boyette is senior advisor to the president of Wake Forest University. Prior to that appointment, she was Wake Forest's vice president for public affairs, and then vice president for university advancement. She is a graduate of the University of North Carolina–Charlotte, holds a master's degree in education from Converse College, and earned her MBA at Wake Forest.

Barbara M. Burns   Barbara M. Burns, APR, Fellow of the International Public Relations Association (IPRA), heads up BBA Communications, Inc, a New York City consultancy specializing in international practice. Barbara is the 2001 recipient of the PRSA Atlas Award for Lifetime Achievement in International Public Relations. She is president-elect of the PRSA New York chapter, and serves as the UN representative in New York for IPRA.

Steve Doyal   Steve Doyal is senior vice president of public affairs and communications for Hallmark Cards, Inc. A thirty-year communicator at Hallmark, Steve leads the company's corporate communications, public relations, and government affairs functions. He also is responsible for reputation management and crisis preparedness, and serves on the company's ethics committee. He is a graduate of the University of Missouri School of Journalism and is a trustee of the University of Missouri-Kansas City and Baker University.

T.A. Fassburg   Terry Fassburg recently retired from the post of vice president, brand & corporate communications, for Philips Electronics North America after over thirty years of senior level communications experience with Fortune 20 companies. He also served in senior communications roles at PepsiCo, Frito-Lay, Seagram, General Foods, Ogilvy, Grey Advertising and Burson-Marsteller.

Ernie Grigg   Ernie Grigg, the book's editorial and research assistant, is a freelance corporate communications writer with experience working mostly for nonprofit organizations. In the private sector, he has worked on advertising campaigns by some of America's most successful start-up companies. He is also an adjunct instructor and guest lecturer in NYU's graduate program for Public Relations and Corporate Communications.

Mark Hass   Mark Hass joined Edelman in January 2010 assuming leadership of one of China's largest PR firms with two brands – Edelman and Pegasus – and more than 165 employees. With offices in Beijing, Shanghai and Guangzhou, Edelman and

Pegasus in China represents Anheuser-Busch, BMW, China Unicom, The Carlyle Group, General Electric, Johnson & Johnson, Nike, PepsiCo, Pfizer, Shell, Starbucks, and Wal-Mart. The former CEO of MS&L Worldwide, Mark has three decades of experience as a journalist, entrepreneur and communications professional. He is based in Beijing.

James E. Lukaszewski   James E. Lukaszewski, ABC, APR, Fellow PRSA, is chairman of The Lukaszewski Group. Jim advises senior management on crisis communication, conflict, confrontation and contention reduction including employee and community relationship recovery. For more information, visit his firm's Web site at http://www.e911.com or his blog http://www.e911.com/crisisgurublog.html.

Maril MacDonald   Maril MacDonald is a nationally recognized leader in communications and strategy execution. She is the immediate past president of the Arthur W. Page Society and continues to serve on the Executive Committee of the Board of Directors. Previously, Maril held leadership positions spanning operations, communications, and human resources with International Truck and Engine Corporation, Bayer USA Inc., The Standard Oil Company / British Petroleum and a Cleveland-based public relations firm. *PR Week* has named her one of the top 25 leaders in the industry, and one of the "50 Most Powerful Women in PR." Maril serves as a Trustee for the Institute of Public Relations, and she serves on the Georgetown University Master Of Professional Studies Strategic PR Communications Advisory Council.

Raleigh Mayer   Raleigh Mayer, principal at Raleigh Mayer Consulting, is an executive development advisor and coach, as well as speaker, specializing in helping business professionals build powerful presence and gravitas. A frequent lecturer at Columbia University's MBA programs, Raleigh also serves as a coach for NYU's Stern School of Business and a women's leadership lecturer at Barnard College. She has been an adjunct professor of marketing and management at NYU for fifteen years. In her previous position as vice president and spokesperson for the New York City Marathon, Raleigh was instrumental in the exponential growth and development of the event. Raleigh is currently a senior fellow at the Logos Institute for Crisis Management and Executive Leadership, a senior associate with Benchmark Communications, Inc., and a career-development advisor for the Association of Executive Search Consultants.

Julie M. Osborn   Julie M. Osborn is currently happy at work at Lucasfilm Animation, run by George Lucas of Star Wars fame, in northern California – her dream job! She received her BA in Studio Art with a minor in Japanese from the University of California, San Diego. Afterward, she moved to New York for a change of pace at NYU's School of Continuing and Professional Studies, where she received an MS in Digital Imaging and Design. While there, she met one of the authors, John Doorley, and happily accepted the challenge of illustrating this book.

Tony Plohoros   Tony Plohoros heads 6 Degrees Communications, a full-service communications firm specializing in the healthcare sector. He has accumulated a track record of superior results as a strategist, company spokesperson, marketer and counselor to senior management over nearly twenty years in several industries. In addition, Tony is an adjunct professor at New York University's MS in Public Relations and Communications program, where he teaches Media Relations. Tony earned an MBA in strategy and marketing at NYU's Stern School of Business, and a BA in Public Relations at Syracuse University's Newhouse School of Communications.

Bonnie Rothenstein Bonnie Rothenstein is the head of Enterprise Mobility Communications at SAP AG, responsible for all internal and external communications supporting SAP's leadership in mobility. With more than fifteen years of international corporate and agency experience, Bonnie has a proven track record of managing crisis communications and creating award-winning communication campaigns for Fortune 500 companies. Her strategic communications campaigns have been recognized with numerous PR awards, including Gold and Silver SABREs, and International PR Association Golden World Awards.

Jay Rubin Jay Rubin is a public relations writer, a presentation skills trainer, and a corporate communication consultant to some of America's best-known companies. An adjunct faculty member at New York University, he teaches graduate students in the Public Relations and Corporate Communication program at the School of Continuing and Professional Studies and undergraduates at the Leonard N. Stern School of Business.

Gary Sheffer Gary Sheffer oversees external and internal communications and provides strategic communications advice to GE executives on a full range of corporate reputation issues. In his public affairs role, Gary works with stakeholders to foster understanding of GE policies and businesses. Gary joined GE in 1999 after seventeen years in journalism and government communications. For ten years, Gary served as a press aide to two New York governors. He previously was a newspaper reporter and editor, earning several writing and reporting awards. Gary earned a BA in English from Siena College in Loudonville, New York and today serves on its associate board of trustees. He also is a trustee of the Institute for Public Relations and is a member of the advisory board for Columbia's University's master's program in strategic communication. Gary also serves on the boards of several associations for communications professionals, including the Wisemen, the Seminar, and the Arthur W. Page Society.

Judy Voss Judy Voss is director of professional development for the Public Relations Society of America, the world's largest organization for public relations professionals. She provides direction and support for PRSA's mainstream seminars and teleseminars. She is heavily involved in building, managing and presenting the PRSA annual International Conference. Previously she has held communications positions with both for-profit and non-profit organizations including the American Hospital Association, Perkin-Elmer and Woodhead Industries, Inc. She earned her bachelor's degree from Northwestern University in Chicago, majoring in communications, and earned her Accreditation in Public Relations designation in spring 2003.

REPUTATION MANAGEMENT

Character is like a tree and reputation like its shadow. The shadow is what we think of it; the tree is the real thing.

— *Abraham Lincoln*

1 REPUTATION MANAGEMENT

■ ■ ■

In 1998 Abercrombie & Fitch published a back-to-school catalog with a section advocating that college students drink creatively, rather than just participate in the standard beer binge. The section, headed "Drinking 101," contained recipes for the Woo-Woo, the Beach Hemorrhage, and other potent mixtures. The organization Mothers Against Drunk Driving was irate. Within days, NBC's Today Show was set to interview MADD's president, but the clothing company refused to send a spokesperson (issuing just a brief statement). The question is: Should the company have sent a spokesperson?[1]

When that question is asked of communication or PR majors (this book's co-author John Doorley has done this with many classes) most students say yes; often the teacher is the only dissenter. The reason for dissent: The company had not formulated any policy expressing embarrassment, let alone shame, and there was no commitment to mitigate the damage—for example, recall the catalog and help wage responsibility-in-drinking campaigns. Most college students are not of drinking age, and the company appeared to care little about the health of the people who wear their clothing. What could the spokesperson have said, in lieu of repudiation and correction, that would not have made the matter worse? For as Will Rogers was fond of saying: "When you find yourself in a hole, the first thing to do is stop digging."

Eventually, of course, the company had to issue statements and provide stickers for existing catalogs that advocated responsibility in drinking. MADD and most PR observers agreed it was too little too late.

It turns out that A & F has published catalogs for its young audiences with nude models and been criticized for not featuring people of color. The company discontinued its 2003 "Christmas Field Guide" catalog after it caused more controversy over the sexually explicit nature of several articles. Since then, A & F has launched a slightly more responsible version of the catalog in Europe, but slogans on its products have offended many different groups in the United States. A sample list of boycotters includes Asian American groups, women's organizations, Christian schools, the State of West Virginia, and USA Gymnastics.

However, it seems that A & F is not concerned about its reputation with older audiences, believing perhaps that the younger audiences will not care about the social issues and may even want their clothing all the more. One has to hand it to the company: it is a bold marketing strategy, and a very risky reputation strategy, especially over the long term. Creating demand is one thing, but alienating the people who pay the bills, as well as groups that devote their lives to a cause, is another. (By the way, what is the name of that organization of mothers that almost single-handedly forced the United States government into the nationwide drinking-age limit of 21?)

■ ■ ■

Shakespeare called it "the purest treasure mortal times afford." Men have fought duels and killed for it. Companies and other institutions have succeeded or failed because of it. Warren Buffett said: "If you lose dollars for the firm by bad decisions, I will be very understanding. If you lose reputation for the firm, I will be ruthless." It seems that Mr. Buffett was paraphrasing Othello: "He who steals my purse steals trash … but he that filches from me my good name … makes me poor indeed."[2]

The business scandals of the first years of the twenty-first century demonstrated how important it is to build, maintain, and defend reputation. The scandals spread to nonprofits, government, universities, and sports, and the public seemed to tire of the press reports. But fatigue did not convey immunity, so people demanded change: tougher laws, more governance, and greater accountability. At the same time, academic researchers and public relations professionals intensified efforts to quantify and manage reputation, heretofore thought of as an intangible asset.

Reputation scholar Charles Fombrun, professor emeritus, Stern School of Business, New York University, an editor-in-chief of the journal *Corporate Reputation Review*, defines reputation as the sum of the images the various constituencies have of an organization.[3]

John Doorley and Fred Garcia (this book's coauthors) accept that definition but also like their own—which leads us to:

**Reputation = Sum of Images =
Performance + Behavior + Communication**

This definition helps make it clear that performance and behavior, as well as communication, are critical components of reputation.

REPUTATIONAL CAPITAL

Just as people develop social capital that helps them build relationships and careers, corporations and other organizations develop reputational capital that helps them build relationships and grow their organizations.

A good reputation has both intangible and tangible benefits. It is important for stakeholders, from customers to employees to consumer advocates, to feel good about an organization, and it is important to build a good reputation to sustain an organization through the tough times. But a reputation is worth much more than that. Companies with the better reputations attract more and better candidates for employment, pay less for supplies, gain essentially free press coverage that is worth as much if not more than advertising, and accrue other benefits that actually contribute to profits.

Reputation adds value to the actual worth of a company—that is, market capitalization (the number of shares outstanding times the price per share) is often greater than just the book value or liquidation value of assets. The reputation component of market capitalization, reputational capital, is a concept closely related to "goodwill," and it is worth many billions of dollars in many large corporations. It has a value in not-for-profits, government, and universities as well. For instance, a good reputation helps a university attract students and donors.

Although CEOs agree that reputation has a value—is an asset—few firms actually treat it as such. Few companies or nonprofits take a rigorous, quantifiable approach to reputation management—measuring, monitoring, and managing reputation assets and liabilities—yet such an approach is intrinsic to the concept of asset management. Most organizations have no idea what their reputations are worth, yet reasonable measurements can be agreed upon and taken. Most companies do not have a system in place for regular, periodic accountability on variations in reputation, yet without such a system opportunities will be missed and problems will become magnified. Measurement, acknowledgment, and planning make possible proactive behaviors and communications to take advantage of reputational opportunities and minimize problems—thereby building reputational capital.

> Although CEOs agree that reputation has a value—is an asset—few firms actually treat it as such.

The formula $R = P + B + C$ applies to the reputations of individuals as well as organizations. Within a period of weeks in the late summer of 2009, four Americans behaved badly in an extraordinary way in public: tennis great Serena Williams threatened and verbally assailed a judge at the U.S. Open; Kanye West jumped on stage at the MTV Video Music Awards to wrest the microphone from one artist because he thought another deserved the VMA; Michael Jordan retraced decades-old interpersonal squabbles at his induction into the Basketball Hall of Fame; and Congressman Joe Wilson of North Carolina yelled, "You lie" when U.S. President Obama was addressing a joint session of Congress in what is usually a reverential forum. At the same time, in other countries, leaders like Prime Minister Berlusconi of Italy continued to demonstrate that inappropriate behavior seems to have no limits.

> At the same time, in other countries, leaders like Prime Minister Berlusconi of Italy continued to demonstrate that inappropriate behavior seems to have no limits.

The formula demonstrates that reputation is cumulative. So when a famous individual behaves badly, he or she cannot generally make up for it with a press conference, no matter how sincere or eloquent the apology. Similarly with organizations, communication is not enough to right a wrong. A reputation is built on performance, behavior and communication and it can generally be repaired only by working on all three aspects.

IDENTITY

To reputation scholars like Fombrun, "identity" is the raison d'être of an organization. It is, simply, what the organization stands for above all else. To distinguish this concept from other uses of the term (such as corporate identity programs that try to position the company in a particular way through all its communications and graphic vehicles), Paul Verbinnen of Citigate Sard Verbinnen coined the term "intrinsic identity." (We use that term in this book.)

> "Identity" is the raison d'être of an organization. It is, simply, what the organization stands for above all else.

Of course organizations, like individuals, have multiple identities. Research by George Cheney of the University of Colorado, in *Rhetoric in an Organizational Society: Managing Multiple Identities*, is consistent with the proposition that multiple identities need not pose any conflicts, as long as there is a clear, dominant identity.[4] Johnson & Johnson, for example, seeks not just to develop, make, and market quality healthcare products for patients, it also seeks profits large enough to attract shareholders, reward employees, and stoke research. But the commitment to serving patients and the healthcare community, as expressed in the company's credo and demonstrated in the response to the Tylenol® tampering crises in 1982 and 1986, has clearly been the dominant identity over the years.

Other companies, such as the venerable General Electric and the relative upstart Starbucks, have each stayed true to a dominant identity: respectively developing and marketing consumer and technology products of the highest quality, and employing the best people to obtain, market, and sell quality coffee and collateral products in a warm and welcoming venue. Starbucks is not at all embarrassed to proclaim the ideals of mutually beneficial and profitable relationships with employees and communities. A description of its 2009 ad campaign on the Starbucks blog says, "value today has new meaning. It's not about what's cheapest—it's about what's best—for [consumers], their families, their communities and the world around them."[5]

Other organizations, sadly and notably, have recently failed to stay true to the dominant identities that made them successful:

Lehman Brothers

Lehman Brothers was one of the oldest and most respected investment banks in the United States. After posting record high earnings in 2007, the bank firmly entrenched itself in the following year's subprime mortgage crisis caused by bad mortgage loans and borrowers defaulting on payments. Lehman folded, resulting in the largest bankruptcy filing in U.S. history. An exchange of e-mails disclosed by the House Oversight Committee reveals one major cause of the collapse. A memo from managers suggested that top executives forgo their 2008 multimillion dollar bonuses. The e-mail said, "It would send a strong message to both employees and investors that management is not shirking accountability for recent performance."[6] The Lehman executive committee dismissed the memo as a joke, and CEO Dick Fuld even told his top people not to "worry." Throughout its history, Lehman had a reputation for making values-driven decisions. But when subprime mortgages presented the opportunity to earn large amounts of money quickly, the Lehman executives ignored those values and lost in the end.

> But when subprime mortgages presented the opportunity to earn large amounts of money quickly, the Lehman executives ignored those values and lost in the end.

The Catholic Church

The scandals over the sexual abuse of young children by some priests, which came to light starting in the Boston Archdiocese in 2002, were shocking and horrible enough. Catholics and non-Catholics recognized that evil could exist anywhere. But what drove many Catholics away from the church was the cover-up by the church hierarchy, from bishops to cardinals. In numerous instances, they knowingly sent offending priests to other parishes without telling the legal authorities or the people in the new parish, leaving the priests free to commit the same crimes over and over. The average priest believes he exists to give spiritual and emotional guidance to the people in his parish, but many of the bishops and cardinals forgot that raison d'etre; instead, they believed they had to protect the church's image at all cost.

In his first public statement as Boston's new archbishop, Sean P. O'Malley made explicit reference to the need to return to the Church's intrinsic identity:

> We can only hope that the bitter medicine we have had to take to remedy our mismanagement of the problem of sexual abuse will prove beneficial, making all of us more aware of the dreadful consequences of this crime and more vigilant and effective in eradicating this evil from our midst. How we ultimately deal with the present crisis in our Church will do much to define us as Catholics of the future. If we do not flee from the cross of pain and humiliation, if we stand firm in who we are and what we stand for, if we work together, hierarchy, priests, religious and laity, to live our faith and fulfill our mission, then we will be a stronger and a holier Church.[7]

Many believe that Pope John Paul II did not do enough to recognize the victims of these crimes, and from a public relations standpoint, he did not. The pope attempted to minimize the issue with general statements and expected his American bishops to manage the problem. His successor, Pope Benedict XVI, understood that this strategy was not working. In almost every public appearance during his first papal trip to the U.S. in 2008, he acknowledged the horror of the incidents and he encouraged victims and others alienated by the scandals to find comfort in their faith. He publicly apologized. In Washington, D.C., Pope Benedict met privately with victims from the Archdiocese of Boston. He vowed to fix the problem, and he assured the victims that he understood the problem on an emotional level.[8]

The New York Times

To its credit, *The New York Times* broke the story itself in a front-page exposé on May 11, 2003. Reporter Jayson Blair had plagiarized content from other newspapers, had fabricated whole stories, and had invented scenes for stories that appeared in the paper, including major front-page ones over a period of years. There were warning signs bold and numerous enough to have stopped him early on, but the top editors ignored them. Why did the people charged with seeing that the country's "newspaper of record," the one that exists to report "all the news that's fit to print," publish the unfit? An explanation that makes sense is that one of the paper's other identities—including its commitment to affirmative action (Blair is African American) and a desire not to rock the boat about a reporter thought to be a favorite of the executive editor—superseded, in this case, its commitment to quality. So while the paper can be proud of its various identities, it cannot be anything but humbled by its failure to live up to its commitment to quality journalism, above all else.

In the wake of the Blair scandal, *The Times* has reaffirmed its commitment to its intrinsic identity, and has established numerous structures, including a public editor and a standards editor, to try to assure that it is not distracted from its mission again.

It is important for employees to understand and be committed to the organization's dominant intrinsic identity. For example, if the CEO truly believes the organization is committed above all else to quality products, but the average sales person believes the dominant identity is the sales quota, there exists a prescription for disaster. For in difficult times, what the employees believe the organization stands for will determine what they will do, just as surely as it did with Blair and the church.

> For in difficult times, what the employees believe the organization stands for will determine what they will do.

Another benefit of a clear identity is that it can drive behavior, performance, and communication, as it should. Then internal and external constituencies will all understand what the organization is about.

CAN REPUTATION BE MEASURED?

Fombrun maintains that reputational capital is the difference, averaged over time, between market capitalization and the liquidation value of assets. Many chief financial officers disagree with that formula, believing that the difference overstates the value of reputational capital. But even those CFOs agree that much of that difference is reputational capital. The more common approach to measuring reputation is to take comparative measures against similar organizations. The annual *Fortune* magazine survey of the World's Most Admired Companies is among the most widely known and respected by both industry leaders and academics. But it surveys only three constituencies: senior executives, (outside) board members, and securities analysts. A more comprehensive approach would include surveying all the major constituencies, including employees, customers, and the press.

Another is the Harris-Fombrun Reputation Quotient (by Harris Interactive in association with Charles Fombrun). It evaluates reputation among "multiple audiences," according to twenty attributes that are grouped into what are referred to as "dimensions of reputation": products and services; financial performance; workplace environment; social responsibility; vision and leadership; and emotional appeal. The results of that survey are widely covered by the press.

CAN REPUTATION BE MANAGED?

There are many organizations with "reputation management" in their names and their number has increased markedly since the Sarbanes-Oxley Act became law in the wake of U.S. corporate scandals. Yet most of them are actually reputation measurement organizations that offer little in the way of reputation management. There are many conferences on reputation management, yet they too focus on measurement or only on specific parts of reputation management, such as crisis communication. They do not produce a plan or a document that aims to manage reputation as other assets are managed—including the pluses and the negatives associated with any asset.

Some academics believe that reputation can be managed, while others believe it cannot be. While more research in the field of reputation management is needed, the pro-management body of academic literature is certainly as strong as the contrary studies, if not stronger. And one thing is certain, as recent business scandals have demonstrated in the sharpest relief: reputations can surely be mismanaged, and in many cases, not managed at all. There is a clear need for a new approach that will help companies and other organizations measure, monitor, and manage their reputations, and the factors that contribute to reputation, organization-wide, over the long term.

"INTANGIBLE ASSET"—THE WRONG PERSPECTIVE

The reason most organizations do not have formal programs to manage reputation is that they view it as something "soft"—intangible. Yet as nebulous as reputation can seem, it has real, tangible value (dollars, for example) that can be measured. So the historical view of reputation as an intangible asset is the wrong approach. Moreover, such a view is analogous to that of some parents who say they need not be that concerned about their young children's character, because "they will be influenced by their peers anyway when they become teenagers." Such laissez-faire-ism—whether in parenting children or organizations—is a prescription for disaster, as recent history has clearly demonstrated.

> So the historical view of reputation as an intangible asset is the wrong approach.

Like all other assets—a building or a product, for example—reputation has its liability side. So any reputation management plan has to measure, monitor, and establish a plan for managing both the reputation assets and vulnerabilities/liabilities. The important thing is to have a plan. If the following is not an ancient proverb, it should be: "If you don't know where you're going, any road will take you there." And you might end up in the wrong place.

So a major question for leaders of organizations is: Can reputation be managed? It follows that those who believe it can be managed—perhaps not totally, but which asset can be?—must establish a plan to do so, as they would for any other asset.

IT'S ALL ABOUT BUILDING THE RELATIONSHIP

By Kenneth P. Berkowitz, Esq.

A critical first step in reputation management, it seems to me, is the building and cultivation of relationships with key constituencies. Show me a successful PR practitioner or lobbyist, and I will show you someone who has developed strong individual relationships and cultivates them in a planned, concerted way on an ongoing basis. Building and maintaining relationships, as is true of reputation, should be viewed as a full-time effort.

The best way to establish a relationship is to understand that it must benefit both parties—in this case, the organization as well as other constituencies, the government including regulatory agencies, news media, customers, suppliers, employees, and other important constituencies including bloggers and other social media contacts as possible.

It should come as no surprise, therefore, that a critical first step is to identify the critical constituencies of the organization. Practitioners should then identify or, as necessary, conduct research to determine the constituency's needs and then use that information for the benefit of both parties, what the academics call the "two-way symmetrical" model (Media Relations, Chapter 3). What often happens is that PR departments do the research and then try to exploit it for the organization's benefit alone ("two-way unsymmetrical"); this seldom proves a productive strategy over the long run. And once an established relationship "sours," it may prove to be unsalvageable.

Along those lines, relationships have to have a degree of unselfishness in order for the parties to be respectful of each other. It's a dot-connected world—word gets around. And a PR practitioner or company lobbyist cannot afford just to disconnect from a relationship when it becomes unproductive: for example, when the reporter retires or a legislator loses an election, or when the constituency acts against the interest of the organization.

Disagreement must be anticipated, as one can never expect both parties to be in agreement on all issues. So that this aspect of relationship management is not viewed as "soft" and static or unmanageable, formal strategies and objectives should be established and monitored. The strategies and objectives should also force practitioners to go out and meet face-to-face on an ongoing basis with their constituencies, which is a hard thing even for some public relations people and lobbyists to initiate. You almost need to treat your constituencies as sales people would treat their customers. Here are five such strategies that I have encouraged my colleagues to implement over the years:

1   Target key areas that really matter to your organization. Public relations practitioners and lobbyists have to focus first on areas where the organization has business or other interests, particularly areas where they can make a difference. It does little good to try to meet with reporters at each of the one hundred top dailies, or to establish relationships with every congressional or state legislative staffer (and remember that staff can be as important as the elected official). While you need to target the capitals (Brussels, Washington, and the state capitals, for example), absolutely do not forget the communities where the organization has a large business, factory, distribution facility, or employee base. A more

challenging need today is to try to be aware of and establish some contact or relationships with bloggers or social media sites.

2   Target the leaders but do not stop there. This can be a very difficult challenge unless you have sufficient resources at your disposal. Research can identify who the thought leaders are within particular constituencies and who or what influences their views on issues. Seek to cultivate relationships with as many of them and/or their staffs as possible. But do not stop here; instead, identify others (individuals or organizations) who may have important roles to play. And remember, do not limit yourself to one political party. Had you just focused on Republicans in the Bush or Reagan years, you would have paid the price when the Democrats took control.

3   Identify the emerging players. Who are the up-and-coming staffers and journalists (or even bloggers), for example? A particularly good time to establish relationships is when a new official is elected or a staff member or reporter comes on board. PR practitioners who cultivate those people before they become major players can hope to establish strong relationships before anyone else even tries to. Once the staffer or journalist reaches the top, stand in line.

4   Use your organizational resources. Work with key groups in your organization so that you have all the necessary data and facts at your disposal depending on the particular issues. Do not be fearful of bringing your experts to meet with constituencies. While preparation is critical, it is often the expert that reporters or governmental representatives would appreciate meeting with on an issue. It does not undermine your relationship, but should strengthen the other party's view of you and your organization. At the same time, make sure that you are always kept in the "loop."

5   Always be the first to tell the "news" to your constituency—particularly if it is bad news. This is very important in maintaining strong relationships and credibility. Once a person has heard from others, it becomes extremely difficult to change views or opinions and could undermine existing relationships. The U.S. healthcare industry, which I have always been proud to be a member of, is embroiled in controversy over healthcare reform, pricing, access, and other significant issues. Never before has the industry faced such grave challenges. Yet few industries produce the societal benefits the healthcare industry does. If the U.S. industry is to continue to lead the world in the discovery, development, and marketing of medicines and other healthcare products, we must rebuild our reputation. And if we are going to succeed we have to build stronger and more productive relationships with all our constituencies. One relationship at a time.

■ ■ ■

COMPREHENSIVE REPUTATION MANAGEMENT

"Comprehensive Reputation Management" provides a formal framework for managing reputation (copyright 2003, John Doorley). It is one way for an organization to get its arms around this asset, and a way to manage reputation problems, vulnerabilities, and opportunities. It has been vetted before the leadership of the Conference Board, many industry leaders and CEOs, numerous academic

> It is one way for an organization to get its arms around this asset, and a way to manage reputation problems, vulnerabilities, and opportunities.

researchers, and heads of corporate communications at thirty major companies. Paul Verbinnen and Rich Coyle of Sard Verbinnen made significant contributions.

> **Comprehensive Reputation Management =**
> A long-term strategy for measuring, auditing, and managing an organization's reputation as an asset.
>
> Comprehensive Reputation Management
> is to reputation what risk management is to other assets

This strategy results in the management of an organization's intrinsic identity (what it stands for) and external images, giving an organization a methodology for working to bring the two together. The Comprehensive Reputation Management methodology is applied to the major areas of an organization—for example, finance, human resources, investor relations, manufacturing, marketing, and public affairs. Each area gets involved in a process that is a way of approaching total reputation management—(performance and behavior) + communication—and is distinct from brand management (the marketing value of a name) or corporate identity programs (which usually boil down to institutional advertising).

These are the six major components of Comprehensive Reputation Management:

Comprehensive Reputation Management

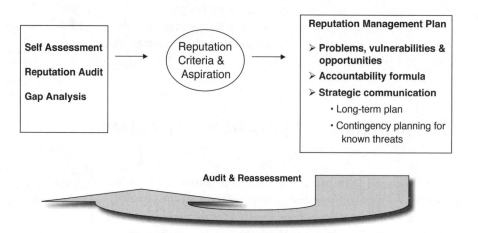

Figure 1.1

1. *Customized Reputation Template*

The measurement tool begins with a basic template that is then customized for each organization. In some cases, the organization may simply want to improve its ranking in an established poll, such as *Fortune* magazine's, which is based on eight criteria or attributes: innovativeness, quality of management, employee talent, financial soundness, use of corporate assets, long-term assets, long-term investment value, social responsibility, and quality of products/services. Certain of the financial measures may be more important to some companies than to others, as might be environmental performance and community relations (under "social responsibility") and so on.

Reputation Criteria: Basic Template for Comprehensive Reputation Management program includes:

- Innovation
- Quality of management
- Employee talent
- Financial performance
- Social responsibility
- Product quality
- Communicativeness (transparency)
- Governance
- Integrity (responsibility, reliability, credibility, trustworthiness)

The first six are the time-tested *Fortune* criteria, with the three financial measures collapsed to one. Communicativeness is part of the template because there has now been more work done to demonstrate the link between an organization's transparency and its reputation. (See reference to Corporate Reputation Review paper in the Best Corporate Communication Strategy section, later in this chapter.) Governance is listed because it is now, especially post Sarbanes-Oxley, an important part of the reputation mix. Integrity is this model's way of encompassing the four character traits that research by Fombrun and others has shown to have a direct effect on reputation: responsibility, reliability, credibility, and trustworthiness.

The basic template can then be customized for the particular organization, and the resultant customized template becomes senior management's acknowledgment of which reputation factors are most important. The customized template becomes the tool for measuring changes in reputational capital. The template can also be customized by constituency, because different constituencies care more about different attributes.

2. *Reputation Audits of Internal and External Constituencies*

One audit assesses what employees believe to be the intrinsic identity (what the organization stands for) and compares that with what senior leadership believes the intrinsic identity to be. The gap between the two views is analyzed and a plan (part of the Reputation Management Plan) to converge them is created. A second audit measures how external constituencies view the organization, and the sum of those constituency images constitutes reputation. The gap between identity and reputation is analyzed, and a plan (part of the Reputation Management Plan) to converge the two is created.

3. *Reputational Capital Goals*

Goals are established for performance within an industry group, for example, or versus competitors. For example, a company might establish a goal of moving up into the top quartile of its industry sector. Progress toward that goal can then be measured, monitored, and managed.

4. *An Accountability Formula*

This is based on changes in reputation measured against the customized template. If the organization is slipping according to one reputation attribute (for example, communicativeness) particular departments, such as public relations, can be given the responsibility of correcting that impression through proactive communication initiatives.

5. *A Reputation Management Plan*

This is the deliverable that the Comprehensive Reputation Management process produces. It is a strategic performance (behavior) and communication plan for convergence of identity and reputation—a plan to move the images the various constituencies hold about the organization closer to the intrinsic identity. The very act of having to list their reputational assets and liabilities helps the various units focus on reputation management. The Reputation Management Plan includes: a summary of the internal and external audits; measures of reputational capital; a statement of reputation challenges and potential problem areas by company or organizational unit; the respective goals and opportunities; and corporate or organizational message strategies. With objectives, strategies, timelines, and so forth, the Reputation Management Plan becomes a strategic guide for units of the organization to follow, short—and long—term.

6. *Annual Follow-Up Audit and Assessment according to the Standards in the Reputation Management Plan*

CONFUSING COMMUNICATION WITH PERFORMANCE AND BEHAVIOR

Pushmi-pullyu

In Kurt Eichenwald's Conspiracy of Fools, Enron CEO Kenneth Lay proclaims to his public relations officer Mark Palmer, not long before the collapse of the company: "The reason we can't right the ship is we're not doing a good job in dealing with the press."[9] In other words, Lay saw a communication problem, not a performance or behavior problem. On the other hand, a major article about professional basketball in *The New York Times Magazine* of February 13, 2005, maintained that the National Basketball Association does not have a "drug problem or a thug problem (or a PR problem)." Instead, the players, despite their unprecedented athleticism, do not play with teamwork, the way the sport used to be played. "It has a basketball problem."

In the contest between the steak and the sizzle the steak will, inevitably, prove more important.

Or, as in Enron's case, the sizzle will always evaporate. Wendy's television commercial from the 1980s, "Where's the beef?" said it best.

In *The Story of Doctor Dolittle*, by renowned children's author Hugh Lofting, the good doctor comes across a mythical, rare animal in Africa. It is a llama-like creature with one head at the front, where it would normally be, and one at the base of its spine, and it is called Pushmi-pullyu. "Lord save us," cries the duck. "How does it make up its mind?"[10]

The **Pushmi-pullyu metaphor** (devised by John Baruch, LittD, former CEO of Reed & Carnrick) is a fitting one to represent the problem that public relations and corporate communication practitioners face: the confusion of behavior or performance with communication—of the substantive issue with the communication about it. While the communication objectives and strategies should always be in synch with the business objectives and strategies, they are distinct. Communication cannot make a bad product good, at least over the long run. Of course it can make a good or fair product seem worse, as it did with the Exxon Valdez crisis in 1989. (Many observers agreed that Exxon did a pretty good job operationally in cleaning up the oil spill, but the communications were a disaster.) In 2006, the mishandling of communication regarding the hunting accident involving Vice President Dick Cheney clearly made the matter worse, and played right into the hands of the press and its insatiable appetite for sensationalism.

Pushmi-pullyu is a syndrome that explains the generations-old lament of corporate and organizational communicators about their lack of a "seat at the table." The reason this has been a problem, of course, is that, too often, an organization develops an ill-advised product or position, or takes such an action, and then asks the communications group to justify it. The performance/behavior head is turning in one direction and saying one thing, and then it expects the communication head to turn and speak in a different direction.

Reframing the Problem

In 2002, this book's coauthor Fred Garcia was called into a company to consult on what the communication people called a "*Fortune* magazine problem." They said *Fortune* was working on a story about the company's chairman, a flamboyant, politically connected executive who had borrowed millions of dollars from the company to support a lavish lifestyle. The chairman's business and political enemies were pointing to the lifestyle, and to other personal foibles and business failures, and the company's stock was suffering. Investors and analysts were asking questions but getting no satisfactory answers. It seemed like the worst mix of Enron, Tyco, and WorldCom. Company leadership was also concerned that the weakening stock price could lead to a hostile takeover.

Fred asked the company leadership what would happen if *Fortune* magazine should be persuaded not to run a story: would the problem be solved? They acknowledged that they would still be as vulnerable to takeover and to critics' capitalizing on the company's weakness in other ways. "You don't have a *Fortune* magazine problem," Fred told them, "you have a governance problem." He met with the general counsel and several board members. They discussed various scenarios under which they could remedy the company's weaknesses. Regardless of the scenario, one thing was consistent: success required the chairman to resign and to repay his loans to the company. The only meaningful question was timing: could he leave before the company suffered more harm, or would he resist, leading to calls by shareholders and others for his resignation, declines in the stock price, and eventually his ouster? Given the alternatives, the Board persuaded the chairman to leave quickly. He resigned within two weeks, and repaid his loan. The company's stock price rebounded. There was no takeover. And no *Fortune* article.

The solution to the struggle represented by the Pushmi-pullyu metaphor—the solution to the push and pull of substance and communication—is to have the entire organization behave and communicate as one.

THE EDELMAN PUBLIC ENGAGEMENT MODEL

In 2008, Richard Edelman, the president and CEO of Edelman, the world's largest independent public relations firm, delivered the inaugural Grunig Lecture, sponsored by the Institute for Public Relations, at the University of Maryland. He spoke about a communication model—of which he is the most notable advocate—called the Public Engagement Model. The address came almost 25 years after Professor Jim Grunig of the University of Maryland coauthored with Professor Todd Hunt of Rutgers University the four models explained on page 82 of this text.

Given Mr. Edelman's perhaps unparalleled success in public relations, it is wise to take special note of the model he helped pioneer. For context, he believes that public relations is more than just a tool for communicating decisions. Organizations should—and will, he maintains—incorporate the discipline into business strategy and policy.

As proof that communication strategy needs reassessing, he cites several trends he thinks will permanently influence business practices: the collapse of financial institutions, the rise of government regulation, the disappearing line between mainstream and new media, the dispersion of authority, and the growing expectations for social responsibility in the private sector.

The public engagement model, which will deftly handle these trends and the new professional environment they create, has four attributes.

1   Democratic and decentralized. As opposed to the "top-down" pyramid approach of making and communicating decisions, public engagement relies on a sphere of cross-influence. Organizations establish key messages and introduce a conversation that allows all interested parties to participate, adapt, and influence. A good example is the 2008 Obama presidential campaign, which gave five million volunteers the autonomy to contact voters, attract funds, and communicate through social media. By receiving a stake in the organization's goals, the public becomes excited about its products and services.

2   Inform the conversation. Public relations has historically relied on one-way communication of researched messages delivered through the media. Mr. Edelman's public engagement model requires organizations to become resources on particular areas of expertise. In addition to engaging the media, an organization can post information on its Web site, host virtual and physical discussion forums, create wikis and blogs, and publish reports and speeches. The emphasis is on facilitating a dialogue about the subject rather than focusing on a few tested messages.

3   Engagement with influencers of all types. Academic or professional credentials no longer dictate who is influential. Personal experience or passion for the subject can validate a person as an influencer. A campaign that educates a specific section of the population, which consequently spreads the message to wider audiences, communicates more effectively than a single credentialed spokesperson dictating to the public. In 2008, Johnson & Johnson's Family Health Institute in China correctly guessed that mothers were the perfect vehicles to promote its new programs addressing unmet needs in China's healthcare system. Every family consults Dr. Mom, so in targeting mothers, J&J earned a reputation as a healthcare company that cares.

4   Reputation is built on policy and communication. Organizations must put their stated standards into practice. Policy and communication have to be congruent or an organization is "destined to fail." Edelman often discusses this element of public engagement in terms of corporate social responsibility. He suggests that the private sector partner with the social sector in making decisions and gathering support from the public. Unilever promoted its laundry detergent through the "Dirt is Good" campaign. Together with nonprofits focused on obesity and youth, the company encouraged children to stay healthy through playing outside and "getting dirty." By going beyond consumer need, the global campaign aligned with the company's mission and increased its market share.

Richard Edelman, "Public Engagement," *Richard Edelman 6 A.M.*, October 30, 2008, http://www.edelman.com/speak_up/blog/archives/2008/10/public_engageme.html.

■■■

REPUTATION MIS-MANAGEMENT: LESSONS FROM THE FINANCIAL CRISIS

The causes and effects of the Great Recession of the last years of the first decade of the new millennium were many and, admittedly, complex—including, arcane financial instruments, and massive greed on the part of not just bankers and business leaders but average consumers as well. Data have been compiled, analyzed, peer reviewed and published. The tomes already published will be followed by Ph.D. theses, Pulitzer Prize winning series, and bestsellers.

Out of this morass of facts and theories has emerged a consensus that the seminal causes were with the real estate industry and the banks, who often collaborated to sell property to people who could be expected to pay for it only if the value of property continued to rise. With American consumers leading the way—spurred on by government policies that fostered home ownership with or without the ability to pay—the cycle of profligate lending and spending spread worldwide. When property values leveled off and then plunged, so too did the worldwide economy.

While it is true that the financial instruments that accompanied this cycle were novel and complex, and while it is true that the greed that arose was

> The complicit parties, from consumers to banks to governments to regulatory agencies, failed to live up to the intrinsic identities that had served them well over the ages.

novel in its creativity and pervasiveness, there is a simplicity to be found in the story that explains how it happened and how a similar catastrophe might be prevented from happening again. And for professional communicators, the lesson to be learned is only partly one of communication. For in the final analysis, the complicit parties, from consumers to banks to governments to regulatory agencies, failed to live up to the intrinsic identities that had served them well over the ages. And they failed to protect their reputations, by failing to protect the component parts.

Reputation = Performance (P) + Behavior (B) + Communication (C)

The Performance Failure

When property values and other economic indicators fell, the reputations of the real estate and banking industries fell, and then, as was inevitable, business overall. In its 2008 Reputation Quotient Report, Harris Interactive reports that Americans have an extremely low opinion of banks. According to the survey, the financial services sector has such little public support that even the tobacco industry enjoys a better reputation.[11]

The Behavior Failure

Leading up to the collapse, when the economy was on the ascent, executive compensation continued to rise. It became a caricature of unfairness, viewed much like outsized pay to top athletes, except that consumers often felt they had no recourse, could not even withhold the price of a ticket to the game. Even though executive compensation outpaced by far the rate of growth in wages for average workers, the protests were not strong enough to force more moderate executive pay practices based on performance.

As people started to lose money and jobs, leading business figures seemed unaware of public sentiment. Witness the infamous jet rides of the Detroit auto executives to the Congressional hearings in November 2009.

The Communication Failure

Were the Detroit corporate communicators consulted before the CEOs took their private jets to Washington? Were they consulted over the decades of collapse of an industry that had once led the United States economy and the world? Were they just seen as communicators, whereas they should have been involved in the performance and behavior considerations as well?

Of course many industries lost reputation during the financial crisis. In general, the closer the consumer connection, the greater the loss—to wit, energy, apparel, food, and retail in general.

It will be interesting to see how the professional communicators in the U.S. fare with the major healthcare reform initiatives that will continue well beyond 2010. Can the pharmaceutical company communicators convince their stakeholders that the industry supports reform, not only because it will bring new customers but also because it is good for society? Can the health insurance industry communicators convince their stakeholders that they support expanded insurance coverage not only because it will bring new customers but because what is good for the insurance industry is good for society?

In his September 2009 speech on the anniversary of the Lehman collapse, President Obama praised community banks for "being responsible lenders [and] doing the right thing."[12] During the early months of the financial crisis, banks with assets of less than $5 billion outperformed their larger competitors in nearly every measure important to stakeholders. While it is still too early to make definitive conclusions about the economic mess, analysts are closely monitoring the practices of small banks. Even after accepting money from the Troubled Asset Relief Program (TARP) because the government deemed them too big to fail, a number of the larger institutions remain at a collective low point. On the other hand, many of the small banks, which simply rely on maintaining accountability and making sensible business decisions, are weathering the crisis with relative ease.

The investment bank Goldman Sachs accepted $10 billion in TARP funds in October 2008, but paid it back with interest in June 2009 as soon as the U.S. government would allow repayment. During the worst months of the Great Recession, Goldman reported positive earnings results that were much better than the other major investment banks. It seemed that the better Goldman performed the more criticism it received from journalists, bloggers and the traditional media. In 2009, major exposés appeared in *Vanity Fair*, *New York* magazine and *Rolling Stone*, among others, criticizing the firm for relentless profiteering and perpetuating all of the major market bubbles in the last century and a half. It was called, "a great vampire squid wrapped around the face of humanity."[13]

But Goldman leadership views reputation through a different lens. The *New York Times*'s DealBook blog reported that, during an August 2009 meeting with a CreditSights analyst, Goldman executives claimed that the "negative image of the firm portrayed in the popular press had not damaged its franchise with its institutional clients nor adversely impacted its funding levels, liquidity access or stock valuation." The analyst said that, "Goldman Sachs's view is that it must keep striving to deliver value for its shareholders and doing what it thinks is in the best interests of the firm in spite of some recent negative press in the media." Goldman's own perspective considers the views of securities analysts, Goldman customers, and others to whom financial performance is the major criterion.

But if one views reputation as singular, the way most reputation scholars do—that is, an organization, or an individual, has just one reputation, which is the sum of the views of all its stakeholders—then the company leadership should not be so sanguine. For example, its executive bonuses seem way out of bounds to most people. Goldman, despite its remarkable strengths, has been tarred by the same brush that painted the entire investment banking industry.

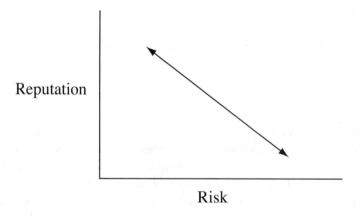

Figure 1.2   *Tom Matteini is president of Jeffrey & Foster, a small printing company that has held its own for 60 years against the behemoths—in the New York City market no less. He conceived this chart: "Actions that put at risk what you stand for— with us it's printing quality, reliability, and competitive pricing—inevitably lower reputation. But you have to be willing to lose some of the bids and some revenue. Sometimes, you just cannot compete on price."*

The Identity Failure

For centuries, banks made loans only to people who had enough resources and income to repay them. What banks stood for, simply, was soundness in lending and investing. In the late 1980s, one bank after another started making unsecured loans on the prospect that the properties offered as collateral would appreciate. Often, the banks sold the dangerous loans to other banks, absolving the original lender of vulnerability—for a while. The practice became so lucrative that too many banks felt they could not pass it up. Smart consumers—who had always stood for hard work and living thriftily—bought into the illusion that they could live in a house they could not afford.

> Smart consumers—who had always stood for hard work and living thriftily-- bought into the illusion that they could live in a house they could not afford.

THE TEN PRECEPTS OF REPUTATION MANAGEMENT

These precepts are meant to help professionals who spend their workdays communicating on behalf of organizations. Because the precepts are intended to help with reputation management, they have as much to do with performance and behavior as with communication. These precepts are the same ones the authors listed in the 1st edition, with some new examples for currency. We ask the reader to review them to see how well they have stood the tests of the financial crises and other reputational challenges that have occurred since the 1st edition.

> We ask the reader to review them to see how well they have stood the tests of the financial crises and other reputational challenges that have occurred since the 1st edition.

1. *Know and honor your organization's intrinsic identity.*

Jim Burke, the CEO of Johnson & Johnson during the Tylenol® tampering cases of 1982 and 1986, said he deserved little credit for the extensive product recalls, which were undertaken at much risk to the franchise and the finances of the company. He explained that the company credo—its intrinsic identity—puts the health of the patient first. That credo begins: "We believe that our first responsibility is to the doctors, nurses, and patients, to mothers and fathers, and all others who use our products and services."[14] When a company acts always in ways that reflect its first responsibility to the people who use its product, and people are dying after using its product, the decision to pull its product is an easy one.

The Johnson & Johnson case stands in stark contrast to the sexual abuse scandal in the Catholic Church, where bishops put what they perceived to be the interest of the organization above the emotional and spiritual well-being of the people they exist to help. Of course organizations have multiple identities (for example, quality products and competitive profitability), but as George Cheney and other researchers have demonstrated, the identities must be compatible, and one must be dominant. That dominant, or intrinsic, identity must be clear to the members of the organization. It is what the

> That dominant, or intrinsic, identity must be clear to the members of the organization. It is what the organization stands for, and it will often determine what the employees will do as a first resort, in good times and bad.

organization stands for, and it will often determine what the employees will do as a first resort, in good times and bad.

2. *Know and honor your constituents.*

The American Red Cross, among the most successful and highly regarded charities in U.S. history, had good intentions when it decided to withhold from the families of the victims of 9/11 some of the monies donated for them. The fund had generated an overwhelmingly generous response, and the leadership of the Red Cross reasoned that not all the monies were needed by the families, and that it would be prudent to save some to help when future disasters, man- and God-made, strike. Donors were outraged, and a major crisis ensued.

The moral: do not presume to know the will of your constituents, and do not presume that good intentions alone are sufficient to protect against criticism that the organization is acting against the interests of its key constituents.

3. *Build the safeguards strong and durable, for they are the infrastructure of a strong reputation.*

Former U.S. Federal Reserve Chairman Alan Greenspan maintains that greed was the root cause of most of the recent business scandals, but he acknowledges that weakened safeguards let the greed flourish. Two stories illustrate this point. According to the U.S. Securities and Exchange Commission, the misuse of company funds by the Rigas family at Adelphia Communications represents "one of the most extensive financial frauds ever to take place at a public company." Not only did the internal controls—from company lawyers to accountants to the board of directors—fail to function, the external ones—from auditors to bankers to regulators—did as well. Likewise, former Wall Street financier Bernard Madoff pleaded guilty to 11 federal crimes tied to charges that he defrauded his clients of $65 billion in a Ponzi scheme. In spite of several SEC investigations and red flags raised by analysts and competitors, Madoff's operation remained intact for 20 years. According to reports, authorities only made cursory investigations into his business practices and usually in search of specific offences. The moral: strong, efficient safeguards, internal and external, are in an organization's best interests.

4. *Beware the conflict of interest, for it can mortally wound your organization.*

Few firms in history had better reputations than Arthur Andersen, and a statue of the company namesake and founder stood tall at the company's training facility as a reminder of what he stood for: the meticulous and rigorous auditing and reporting of a client's finances. Andersen's primary duty was to the shareholders of companies whose books it audited. But by 2001 Andersen's imperative to boost revenues and profits had eroded structures intended to assure the independence of auditors. Andersen allowed itself to act in its own short-term interest and against the interests of its clients' shareholders. The compromising of audit standards and auditor independence was discussed publicly within and outside the firm for years before the damage became apparent and severe.

After the Enron/Andersen scandal broke in late 2001 and early 2002, a committee of some of society's most respected leaders, including former U.S. Federal Reserve Chairman Paul Volker and former Merck CEO P. Roy Vagelos, was convened to save it. But by then the firm's intrinsic identity—meticulous, honest auditing— had already been so compromised that the core had been ruined; Andersen was convicted of a crime and soon closed its doors. The conviction was later reversed, but by then the firm had gone out of business and thousands of employees had lost their jobs.

Paul Volker once said that it is only the people or organizations that have not accomplished very much who could be free of all potential conflicts. Nevertheless, the test for labelling something as a major conflict of interest might be as simple as the one used by U.S. Supreme Court Justice Potter Stewart to label pornography: it may be hard to define, but you know it when you see it.

5. *Beware of the " CEO Disease," because there is no treatment for it.*

It is the same malady the Greek gods said destroyed so many tragic figures, and it is called hubris. Chief executives command tremendous incomes, power, and prestige. Thousands of employees almost genuflect when they walk by, and powerful people from all sectors of society treat them with deference. It must be difficult not to fall into certain traps, such as wanting to be surrounded by employees who always agree with them. Ask anyone who has worked in corporate communication for a long time: There is a "CEO Disease" (and heads of governments, nonprofits, and universities are not immune).

One of the manifestations of hubris is an inability to see that a looming problem requires immediate attention. Many CEOs mishandle initial phases of a crisis out of either arrogance or willful blindness, caused by a misplaced sense of invincibility. The outcome is otherwise manageable crises that result, ultimately and after much hardship, in the CEO's ouster. The year 2004 saw more forced CEO turnover than any year since such statistics have been compiled. According to the consulting firm Booz & Company's annual CEO succession survey, the "giant sucking sound heard in the business world during 2004 was the extraction of chief executives from seats of power ... The first quarter of 2005 brought headline-generating forced successions at Disney, Hewlett-Packard, Boeing, and AIG, linked to shareholder dissatisfaction, scandal, or both."[15] The trend continued until the beginnings of the most recent recession, when further Booz surveys discovered that "the nature of the recession is leading boards of directors of Western companies to stick with the leaders they know." However, government intervention and market volatility, as well as performance, can determine CEO turnover in the new economic climate.

6. *Beware of organizational myopia, for it will obscure the long-term view.*

Especially during times of crisis, organizations tend to focus on the short term. It's part of the corporate and organization condition, and not falling into that trap is one of the lessons of crisis management (Chapter 12). Sometimes organizations are given plenty of advance notice of issues looming large, but few heed the warning signs.

7. *Be slow to forgive an action or inaction that hurts reputation.*

Warren Buffett said it best to a group of Salomon Brothers managers after a 1991 trading scandal hit the bank in which he had an interest. The quote, at the beginning of this chapter, bears repeating: "If you lose dollars for the firm by bad decisions, I will be very understanding. If you lose reputation for the firm, I will be ruthless."

8. *Do not lie.*

People tell lies, most of which are small and harmless, and some of which may even be good things ("Honey, do I look heavy in this dress?"). Similarly, organizations are not always completely forthcoming with information and, indeed, that is sometimes a very good thing (Media Relations, Chapter 3). But lying is of course a slippery slope, eventually dragging the organization into a deep hole from which there is no extrication. Organizations can often get away with lying for a while, but that's all. Sometimes, efforts to mislead have significant adverse consequences, a lesson learned by President Nixon with Watergate, President Clinton in the Monica Lewinsky scandal, and by Martha Stewart, who was prosecuted, convicted, and imprisoned for lying to law enforcement officers.

9. *Dance with the one that "brung" you.*

This aphorism, popular within sports teams, applies to organizations as well as individuals. By the fall of 2000, it was becoming clear that Firestone tires were leading to traffic accidents, and many of them were on the Ford Explorer. Bridgestone-Firestone blamed Ford and vice versa. A business and public relations crisis ensued, and in May 2001 the two companies severed their business relationship that had endured for almost one hundred years. Most analysts agreed that the crisis was compounded by the lack of cooperation, and although the relationship was later revived, the damage had been done. Likewise, it is not uncommon today for a firm that is downsizing to give pink slips to employees, and then have a security guard publicly usher them to the gate—even those employees with excellent, long-term records. Thankfully, however, many other companies take monumental initiatives to be loyal to their employees, customers, and other constituencies. Aaron Feurstein, owner of Malden Mills in Lawrence, Massachusetts, was able to retain all his employees after a fire destroyed his factory in 1995. He said he would simply not abandon his employees, and quoted from the Torah, or Jewish Law: "He is poor and needy, whether he be thy brethren or a stranger." Similarly, a family-owned company based near Stuttgart, Germany, that employs 8000 people manufacturing laser tools for the automobile industry had been able to avoid any layoffs (at least through the end of 2009), despite the downturn in the German and worldwide economy. "The responsibility I have for our employees is what is dearest to my heart," Nicola Leibinger-Kammuller, the family member who heads the company, told *The New York Times*. "It's not the family wealth. It's not our standing with the public."[16]

> A family-owned company based near Stuttgart, Germany, that employs 8000 people manufacturing laser tools for the automobile industry had been able to avoid any layoffs.

10. *Reputation is an asset and must be managed like any other asset.*

Reputation is intangible, but it has great, tangible value (worth many billions of dollars in large corporations, for instance). It is therefore an asset. Failure to acknowledge reputation as an asset can be self-fulfilling. By ignoring reputation and factors that harm or help it, companies often behave and communicate in ways that cause harm to the reputation. Successful stewardship of reputation not only protects against the downside, but can affirmatively enhance the enterprise value of an organization. Because the component parts of reputation (performance/behavior and communication) can be managed, one should devise a strategy and plan to measure, audit, and manage it on an ongoing basis.

**Reputation = Sum of Images =
Performance + Behavior + Communication**

SAFEGUARDING A BRAND: GENERAL ELECTRIC

By Gary Sheffer

Communication and public affairs professionals are confronting daunting challenges. Macro economic and social forces are thwarting our efforts to protect and enhance the reputations of individuals and institutions.

The biggest obstacle we face: a disintegration of public trust in America's business leaders. Admittedly, since the dawn of commerce, "The Businessman" has been criticized. But today, the public cynicism and anger generated by contemporary business villains—from Wall Street CEOs to convicted Ponzi-scheme practitioners—has created an environment in which conventional assumptions about the motives of business people have been almost completely reversed: It used to be that most businessmen and women were presumed honest, with a few exceptions. Today, there's an assumption that most business executives are corrupt; and the burden of dis-proof rests squarely on executives' shoulders.

At GE, we are redoubling our efforts to safeguard a brand it took 131 years to build. To that end, the communications and professionals inside our company are taking the following steps:

- *We're redefining performance* by bringing the outside world into our company. At GE, this translates into an increased emphasis on engagement with investors, for without results we cannot exist. We have also increased alignment with social interests, because without public trust and support we cannot endure.

- ***We're running our reputation like a campaign,*** with the same intensity and rapid-response strategies employed by political pros. Inside GE, we call it "Campaign GE," a way of rallying ourselves around our goals: to help GE win by telling the GE story in a compelling, persuasive manner to build trust and create commercial opportunities.
- ***We're getting into the news business.*** In October 2008, we launched GE Reports, a no-frills company news source that disseminates the facts about GE. At first, its goal was to respond to market misinformation and speculation about GE. Today, it's an online "media outlet" where we break news about the company. It has quickly become one of the most trafficked corporate Web sites, with about 4,000 visitors daily.
- ***We're expanding our public affairs capability.*** Since the economic crash of 2008, government's presence in the business world has increased dramatically. New government regulation and legislation is certain. As a result, we've added people worldwide to interface with government and other external stakeholders.

■■■

REPUTATION MANAGEMENT: THE BEST CORPORATE COMMUNICATION STRATEGY

The remaining chapters of this book flow from a discussion of ethics (Chapter 2), to a discussion of approaches to working with the various corporate communication constituencies (Chapters 3–10), to ways of handling certain major responsibilities (Chapters 11–14), to the challenges facing those who seek to build a career in corporate and organizational communication (Chapter 15).

The premise of Chapter 1—that reputation can be measured, monitored, and managed—begs for the adoption by corporate communications departments of a long-term strategy of reputation management, customized for the particular constituencies, and in synch with an intrinsic identity that the entire organization understands and believes in. A growing body of scholarship shows links between reputation and business performance, and the ability of public relations, particularly corporate communications, to impact reputation. Such studies include:

> A growing body of scholarship shows links between reputation and business performance, and the ability of public relations, particularly corporate communication, to impact reputation.

- *Harvard Business Review*, "Reputation and its Risks," Eccles, et al., 2007. "This article provides a framework for proactively managing reputational risks. It explains the factors that affect the levels of such risks and then explores how a company can sufficiently quantify and control them." The authors of this article maintain, unlike the positions taken by the authors of most articles on reputation management, that corporate communication is not the best department to oversee the reputation management process, since corporate communication has too large an interest in communication. But as the formula for reputation given in this chapter illustrates, communication is just one of the three components of reputation (along with performance and behaviour). Another weakness with this HBR article is that it focuses exclusively on the risks to reputation, with never a mention of the fact that reputation management calls for capitalizing on the positive aspects of reputation as well as minimizing the risks.

- *Journal of Public Relations Research*, "Measuring the economic value of public relations," Yungwook Kim, 2001. "This study established a two-step model to measure the economic value of public relations by testing two relationships: the impact on reputation as a goal of public relations, and the economic impact of reputation on companies' bottom lines." The study showed a positive causal relationship between public relations and reputation, and a positive causal relationship between reputation and revenue.

- *Southern Economic Journal*, "A latent structure approach to measuring reputation," Quagrainie et al., 2003. "The study provides estimates of reputation as a dynamic latent variable that is determined by price premiums and market data." It showed a positive effect between reputation and the prices a company can charge.

- *Corporate Communications*, "Measuring corporate reputation," Bradford, Stewart Lewis, 2001. "This paper considers how corporate reputation is most influenced by the actions of an organization rather than a successful (or otherwise) PR campaign, and how a communication strategy can best influence reputation." The paper established that it is important to measure and manage reputation by constituency.

- *Corporate Reputation Review*, "The concept and measurement of corporate reputation ...," de la Fuente Sabate et al., Winter 2003. "This paper ... leads us to a new definition of corporate reputation, one that not only introduces the perceptions of how the firm behaves towards its stakeholders, but also takes into account the degree of transparency with which the firm develops relations with them." The paper established that information transparency (communicativeness) affects reputation and the ability to do business. Positive reputations have a positive effect on a company's ability to do business.

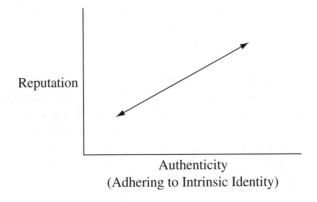

Reputation

Authenticity
(Adhering to Intrinsic Identity)

Figure 1.3

Since reputation is the sum of performance/behavior and communication, an effective corporate communication strategy must be that inclusive. As with individuals, the relationships an organization has will succeed or fail based on performance/behavior and communication. In other words, relationships must be sound and aggressively fostered. Such a strategy can ensure that the organization moves forward, avoiding the Pushmi-Pullyu Syndrome and the reputation pitfalls.

THE EXPANDED REPUTATION FORMULA

Ray Jordan, vice president of public affairs and corporate communication at Johnson & Johnson, told authors Doorley and Garcia that he believes professional communicators should understand the reputation formula first postulated in the first edition of this book: $R = P + B + C$. But he challenged us to include a consideration of intrinsic identity: "Isn't it always true that what an organization stands for, and how well it lives up to that standard, will significantly affect its reputation."

So we took up that charge, starting with the word "authenticity," which the Arthur W. Page Society calls the "coin of the realm for successful corporations and for those (including the communication officers) who lead them." In its 2007 report, *The Authentic Enterprise* (see Sidebar article in this chapter), the Page Society states that any corporation that wants to establish a distinctive brand (reputation) must, "more than ever before, be grounded in a sure sense of what defines it—why it exists, what it stands for and what differentiates it in a marketplace of customers, investors and workers."

To be authentic is to have "integrity" and it follows then that a failure to live up to what one stands for is a failure of integrity or authenticity. The word integrity is linked with being whole, or undivided, which explains why everything inevitably falls apart once integrity or authenticity fails. "Once you lose integrity," John Haldeman said of his role in the Watergate scandal, "the rest is easy." Put more positively, an organization's reputation will be in direct proportion to its authenticity.

The Authenticity factor (Af)—the authors' response to Ray Jordan's challenge—is the indicator of how well an organization (or person) lives up to its intrinsic identity. When there is authenticity, the organization is whole, undiminished. On the other hand, when integrity or authenticity fails, the Authenticity factor is a fraction. The organization is divided, and its reputation will decline, because it will be a fraction of the sum of $P + B + C$.

It is not important to try to assign numbers to the factors in the following equation. What is important for communicators and other leaders to understand is that reputation depends on each of the factors. Therefore, reputation can only be managed by managing all the components in the equation. Communicators, in order to do their jobs, need that "seat at the table," need to be involved not just in the communication.

After much thought, research and peer review, we got back to Ray Jordan with the following formula:

> **Reputation = (Performance + Behavior + Communication) × Authenticity factor**
> **R = (P + B + C) × Af**

Ray thought it represents a "step forward—it has simplicity and applicability."

THE AUTHENTIC ENTERPRISE: EXECUTIVE SUMMARY

A task force of the Arthur W. Page Society set out to examine the evolving role of the senior communications executive in 21st-century business. As our team pursued its mission, we found ourselves confronting phenomena that go far beyond the future of public relations. The relevance of these phenomena was confirmed in a new study, commissioned for this report, in which we surveyed chief executive officers on their perceptions of how their own jobs are being reshaped.

Businesses and institutions today are facing a rapidly changing landscape:

- the emergence of a new digital information commons;
- the reality of a global economy; and
- the appearance and empowerment of myriad new stakeholders.

Together, these forces have created a global playing field of unprecedented transparency and radically democratized access to information production, dissemination and consumption. They are overturning the corporation's traditional ability to segment audiences and messages and to manage how it wishes to be perceived. Today the corporation's relationship with one constituency is readily visible to all constituencies, who are multiplying in number and growing in sophistication. Further, some of these new players are not legitimate stakeholders at all, but rather simply adversarial or even malicious. At the same time, powerful new possibilities are being opened up for the corporation to reach genuine stakeholders, to advance its policy interests, to build its brand and enhance its reputation.

In such an environment, the corporation that wants to establish a distinctive brand and achieve long-term success must, more than ever before, be grounded in a sure sense of what defines it—why it exists, what it stands for and what differentiates it in a marketplace of customers, investors, and workers. Those definitions—call them values, principles, beliefs, mission, purpose or value proposition—must dictate consistent behavior and actions.

In a word, authenticity will be the coin of the realm for successful corporation and for those who lead them. But when we describe the emerging business model as "the authentic enterprise," two important caveats are necessary. The first is that we are not suggesting that business of the past were somehow inauthentic. Rather, it is the general arena of judgment and differentiation that has changed—and changed fundamentally. That in turn requires a corresponding change in how the corporation operates. Its actions and reputation, which used to be safeguarded by a cadre of professionalized functions, are now the responsibility of everyone in the enterprise. What used to be controlled within the company's "four walls" is now spread across multiple partners, communities and individuals around the globe.

This implies that companies must think in different ways about the roles of senior management and the responsibilities of all employees. In our study, CEOs described the need for their companies to capitalize on the new realities. Many of the changes required involve stakeholder relationships and public perceptions, so CEOs are looking for their Chief Communications Officers to take a more strategic and interactive role within the senior leadership of the company. And because the authentic enterprise requires a highly coordinated approach across marketing, human resources, legal, finance and other corporate functions, as well as line management, more than ever, leaders will need to hone their collaboration skills.

■■■

SYSTEMS THEORY

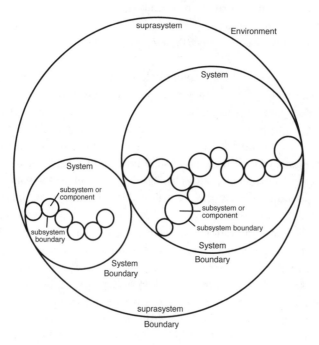

Figure 1.4

SYSTEMS THEORY

Communication is the means by which an organization functions, and it is axiomatic that the better the communication the more productive the organization. That proposition is supported by communication theories, most notably in the case of corporate communication by General Systems Theory. It provides a communication framework which conceives of organizations as living things composed of interrelated components or parts. It provides a way of thinking of an organization not as an amalgam of distinct, seemingly unrelated disciplines, such as finance, customer service, or research, but rather as a whole that comprises components bound together by certain commonalities. As a system, the organization is part of a community that is part of other communities and they all interact, wittingly or unwittingly, in a planned or unplanned way. Systems theory can help communicators and leaders of organizations adopt a working philosophy that communication is the only way to unity and synergy within the organization, and to openness and harmony with systems (for instance, publics) in the environment outside the organization.

"One of the fundamental concepts of General Systems Theory can be traced to Aristotle," explains Rutgers University Communication Professor Brent Ruben, "who said in *Politics* that a state is composed of villages, which are in turn made up of households, which contain families.[17] Conceiving of entities in terms of wholes and interrelated parts is a basic concept in the general system framework of today."

The modern-day father of systems theory in organizational communication was Ludwig von Bertanffly, who conducted his research in the 1950s and 1960s. He was influenced by researchers who were working at the time to identify and express the generalities that tie the scientific disciplines together, so that biology and physics, for example, could be viewed in an interrelated way, rather than as separate, highly specialized fields. For example, cybernetics, which can produce a self-regulated machine that can perform functions greater than any part could, represents a specific application in the physical sciences; Gestalt psychology, which approaches psychotherapy from the perspective of the whole person, including the diverse systems of which he is a part, as opposed to an analytical approach, represents an application in psychotherapy.

Within the communication framework of systems theory, an organization can be pictured as a series of systems and subsystems within a supra system (see Figure 1.4). For example, a company could be pictured as a system, the departments as subsystems, and the particular industry as the supra system that functions within the environment of society. Of course, each supra system, system, and subsystem has a boundary and contains components (individuals). The boundaries are porous, opening subsystems to systems to supra systems to the environment. Subsystems and components are identified by the processes they perform. (Systems figure reproduced with the permission of Ruben, Gibson et al. of Rutgers University.)

Systems theory provides a framework for organizational communication based on the following properties and principles common to all systems. The properties and principles have implications for all communication enterprises, with employee communication, media relations, government relations, investor relations, and community relations being among the most obvious:

- Just as in a **biological system** where information flows from one cell to another, information in an organization flows across the borders in what theorists like Professor Ruben call the "metabolism of information." It follows that the more effective the communication, the more productive the organization.

- No part of a system, no person within an organization, can exist by himself or herself. This is the theoretical basis for tearing down the "silos," which became a theme throughout industry in the 1990s.

- Systems are dynamic. Feedback, from one component to another and with the environment, is essential. Implications for dialogue and engagement are clear in communication enterprises ranging from classroom learning to employee communication. The old communication model of sender-receiver may work for thinking in terms of transferring information; it is not helpful for understanding more complex processes involved with attitudes and behavior.

- Participation in the system is mandatory. One cannot not communicate. (That is the phrase attributed to communication scholars Watzlawick, Beavin, and Jackson.[18]) Engagement is essential.

- Human communication systems are "open systems." As opposed to closed, self-contained systems, which, for example, produce predictable chemical reactions in a test tube, the reactions of the things that go into an open system cannot be precisely calculated in advance; that is, the output cannot be calculated from the input. The open system has properties distinct from its parts; the total, therefore, is not equal to the sum of the parts.

- There are generalities that tie the parts together but one must be careful here. To say something meaningful about the whole—for example, the employee audience—is to omit specifics about the parts. "The key is to find the optimum degree of generality," Professor Ruben states. The implications for audience segmentation (internal or external audiences) are clear.

- The environments within and surrounding the supra system, systems, and subsystems shape those parts, and the reverse is true as well. Likewise, the environment shapes the individual's view of reality, and the individual actually shapes the environment. That is, the environments of a company (everything from the physical and cultural environments within and around the company to the country in which the company is based) shape the employees and vice versa. This point illustrates the great potential of communication.

"The systems approach," Professor Ruben states, "has been a particularly useful foundation for what may be thought of as the quality approach to organizations. The dominant metaphor for the Quality School is team, which relies on communication for success." Sports metaphors about teamwork may be clichéd, but they have solid foundation in theory as well as practice.

> Systems Theory: A framework that supports many of the principles expressed in the following chapters.

Professor Ruben: "Communication is the lifeblood of human systems. It is the means through which leadership functions, the mechanism by which parts relate to one another, the process by which systems relate and adapt to their environments. In organizations, quality and effective multidirectional communication go hand in hand."

■ ■ ■

BEST PRACTICES: REPUTATION MANAGEMENT

1   Understand and value the components of reputation, including integrity, governance, and communicativeness (transparency).

2   Establish a formal mechanism periodically to monitor, measure and manage reputation.

3   Establish a formal mechanism—for example, a regularly scheduled meeting of senior officers, or a "Reputation Management Plan"—to manage reputation on an ongoing basis. The very act of establishing and adhering to a formal mechanism clearly expresses leadership's commitment to protecting the reputation asset.

4   A formal mechanism (for example, a Reputation Management Plan) can help your organization converge brand reputation and the broader corporate reputation with intrinsic identity (what the organization stands for).

RESOURCES FOR FURTHER STUDY

Alsop, Ronald J., *The 18 Immutable Laws of Corporate Reputation*, *A Wall Street Journal Book* (New York: Free Press, 2004).

Argenti, Paul, *Corporate Communication* (Dartmouth University, The Amos Tuck School of Business Administration: McGraw-Hill, 1998).

The Corporate Communication Institute at Fairleigh Dickinson University.

The Corporate Reputation, an electronic newsletter by Peter Firestein, president of Global Strategic Communications Inc., at http://www.firesteinco.com/reputation.

Corporate Reputation Review: An International Journal, Henry Stewart Publications.

Schultz, Majken, et al., *The Expressive Organization: Linking Identity, Reputation and the Corporate Brand* (London: Oxford University Press, 2000).

Fombrun, Charles J., *Reputation: Realizing Value from the Corporate Brand* (Boston: Harvard Business School Press, 1996).

The Institute of Public Relations, http://www.ipr.org.uk/reputation.

Chris Matthews, *Life's A Campaign: What Politics Has Taught Me About Friendship, Rivalry, Reputation and Success* (New York: Random House, 2007).

Measurement of "intangible assets." Refer to the work of Professor Baruch Lev of New York University, the Stern School, http://www.stern.nyu.edu/~blev/main.html - 9k.

Morley, Michael, *How to Manage Your Global Reputation: A Guide to the Dynamics of International Public Relations* (New York: New York University Press, 2002).

Morley, Michael, *The Global Corporate Brand Book* (London: Palgrave Macmillan, 2009).

Ross, Leslie Gaines, *CEO Capital: A Guide to Building CEO Reputation and Company Success* (New York: John Wiley & Sons, 2003).

Schultz, Majken, Hatch, Mary Jo, and Holten, Mogens (eds.), *Larsen* (New York: Oxford University Press, 2000).

The Authentic Enterprise, Arthur W. Page Society, 2007, http://www.awpagesociety.com.

QUESTIONS FOR FURTHER DISCUSSION

1   Why do you think *The New York Times* was for so long blind to reporter Jayson Blair's plagiarism and fabrications?

2   Why is it that most by far of the organizations that claim to provide reputation management services are really selling reputation measurement? Do they really not know the difference?

3   Can you think of examples of the Pushmi-pullyu syndrome in your organization? Should that animal, exciting though it may be to watch, ever be permitted to exist in an organization?

4   Are companies whose products largely share the company name (Coca-Cola, Johnson & Johnson, etc.) at an advantage or disadvantage in terms of reputation management?

5   Is it easier to manage the reputation of an organization in a free or totalitarian society?

6   During the Great Recession, many great enterprises collapsed—including: Fannie Mae, Freddie Mac, Lehman Brothers, Bear Stearns, AIG, General Motors, Chrysler and scores of banks. Is it an oversimplification to say it all happened because of a failure to manage reputation?

7   Arcane fields like physics, economics and chemistry build stature and credibility by offering formulas—for example, if you mix these chemicals together, the following result will occur. Why do you think there are so few formulas (for instance, $R = Af \times P + B + C$) in public relations and corporate communication?

8   Public relations is an emerging social science. Draw some similarities and lessons from other social sciences.

Management is doing things right; leadership is doing the right things.

— *Peter F. Drucker*

2 ETHICS AND COMMUNICATION

■ ■ ■

Scott McClellan hadn't even begun his new job, but he knew it would be a challenge.

McClellan, deputy press secretary to President George W. Bush since the president took office in January, 2001, had just been promoted to succeed press secretary Ari Fleisher, in July, 2003. The U.S. had invaded Iraq in March, ostensibly to prevent Saddam Hussein from being able to use weapons of mass destruction. In the run-up to the war, senior administration officials had warned of the grave consequences of leaving Hussein in power, including assertions that "the smoking gun may well be a mushroom cloud."

Just before McClellan took the top spokesperson job, *The New York Times* had published an op-ed by former ambassador Joseph C. Wilson IV, who had been dispatched by the U.S. government to investigate concerns that the African nation of Niger may have provided uranium to Iraq. The op-ed took exception to a statement President Bush had made in his 2003 State of the Union address, suggesting that there was credible evidence that Niger had provided materials to Iraq that could be used to make nuclear weapons. Wilson noted that his 2002 trip concluded that the concerns were unfounded; that Niger did not have such a capacity. It noted that Wilson was convinced that the White House had been so informed. He further concluded that the administration had twisted the intelligence to exaggerate the Iraqi threat.

According to McClellan, in his 2008 book *What Happened: Inside the Bush White House and Washington's Culture of Deception*, "To defend itself against the accusations of deliberate dishonesty leveled by Joe Wilson, Vice President (Richard) Cheney and his staff were leading a White House effort to discredit Joe Wilson himself." Wilson's article had appeared on July 6. On July 14, conservative pundit Robert Novak authored a column about how Wilson's trip had come about and what it concluded. It ended with "Wilson never worked for the CIA, but his wife, Valerie Plame, is an agent, an operative on weapons of mass destruction. Two senior administration officials told me that Wilson's wife suggested sending him to Niger to investigate [the report about uranium]."

As it happens, Wilson's wife was indeed a CIA agent, working under cover—in particular, under non-official cover, meaning that she posed as a business person, not a member of an embassy staff. Revealing the identity of a covert CIA agent is a crime. Novak's column provoked a firestorm of criticism, and ultimately led to an investigation by a special prosecutor.

As McClellan began his press secretary duties, the media was focused on questions about who leaked Plame's identity. By October, the emerging narrative in the Washington press was that the White House had deliberately blown [Plame's] cover. Administration officials had anonymously leaked her identity to reporters in order to punish (at worst) or discredit (at best) her husband, who was publicly alleging that the administration had misled the country into a war in Iraq. News stories suggested that White House aides had disclosed Plame's identity to at least five reporters. A concerted effort to disclose her identity would have meant that the officials involved, knowingly or not, had leaked classified national security information.

McClellan spoke directly to the two senior-most aides in the White House: Karl Rove, President Bush's closest advisor, and Lewis "Scooter" Libby, Vice President Cheney's chief of staff. Both denied any role (for themselves or their bosses), in the outing of Plame's identity. Confident in their assurances, McClellan addressed the October 10 press briefing with this definitive statement: "I spoke with those individuals, as I pointed out, and those individuals assured me they were not involved in this, and that's where it stands.'"

McClellan would later write:

> The public assurances I provided that October 10 would be my final statements from the podium denying that Rove and Libby had been involved in the outing of a covert CIA official, and my final comments on any other matters which might be part of the criminal investigation that the leak of Plame's name had already spawned.
>
> There was just one problem. What I said was not true.
>
> I had unknowingly passed along false information. And five of the highest ranking officials in the administration were involved in my doing so: Rove, Libby, Vice President Cheney, the president's chief of staff Andrew Card, and the president himself.
>
> For my next two years as press secretary, the false words I uttered at Friday's briefing would stand as the official White House position on the Plame case. Little did I know at the time that what I said, and the pervasive deceit underlying it, would be my undoing as the president's chief spokesman.
>
> I had allowed myself to be deceived into unknowingly passing along a falsehood. It would ultimately prove fatal to my ability to serve the president effectively.
>
> I didn't learn that what I'd said was untrue until the media began to find it out almost two years later. Neither, I believe, did President Bush. He too had been deceived, and therefore became unwittingly

involved in deceiving. But the top White House officials who knew the truth—including Rove, Libby, and possibly Vice President Cheney—allowed me, even encouraged me, to repeat a lie.

McClellan discovered the hard way a constant reality of public relations. Communication takes place in a climate of belief. Effective persuasion over time requires not merely truthfulness but intentionality about truthfulness.

> Communication takes place in a climate of belief. Effective persuasion over time requires not merely truthfulness but intentionality about truthfulness.

Public relations professionals in particular are subject to severe consequences of conveying falsehoods, whether intentionally lying or, like McClellan, unintentionally passing along false information. But public relations professionals who are seen to lie or to be unconcerned with the truth often find themselves marginalized by the media, and by other stakeholders. Trust can plummet when stakeholders discover they have been treated dishonestly.

Public relations professionals' occupational hazard is that clients, bosses, and even journalists will sometimes be dishonest with them in pursuit of their own goals. But it's the PR people whose credibility suffers when the lie is discovered. The challenge of professional public relations is dealing with truth, falsity, and ambiguity, and managing through the muddle with integrity.

> The challenge of professional public relations is dealing with truth, falsity, and ambiguity, and managing through the muddle with integrity.

■ ■ ■

INTRODUCTION: WHY ETHICS MATTERS

The ethical practice of corporate communication and public relations is a given for many professional communicators.

But to much of the outside world there is something vaguely unethical about the entire enterprise. Such phrases as "just PR" or "spin" suggest that people see a meaningful difference between truthful and candid discussion and the kinds of activities that professional communicators are thought to engage in.

> Communication ethics: normative standard of behavior that govern the practice of public relations with integrity.

This has been a perennial concern for practitioners of the craft—from the roots of professional communication in the fourth century BC through the formative years of the modern practice of public relations in the twentieth century AD, to the present.

The irony is that most professional communicators not only practice ethically but deliberately want to do so. And many corporations, learning the lessons of Enron, WorldCom, Andersen, and other celebrated corporate scandals of 2001–2, now recognize that inattention to ethical issues exposes them to far worse consequences than they may have previously understood.

Inattention to ethics risks significant harm to reputation and to other important intangible corporate assets—including employee morale and productivity, demand for a company's products, confidence in a company's executives, and stock price performance. Ethical lapses also lead directly to changes in senior leadership of a company. Inattention to ethics and the consequences of unethical behavior, as evidenced in the collapse of Enron, Andersen, and other well-known companies, can even affect an organization's ability to survive.

WHAT IS ETHICS?

Despite a general desire to practice corporate communication ethically, many professional communicators have only a passing knowledge of ethics and the way ethical standards have evolved in business generally and in the professional practice of communication in particular.

> Individuals and companies often get into ethically murky situations because they confuse ethics with morality, legality, etiquette, or aesthetics – that is, they confuse actions with motives, crimes, politeness, or feelings.

Individuals and companies often get into ethically murky situations because they confuse ethics with morality, legality, etiquette, or aesthetics—that is, they confuse actions with motives, crimes, politeness, or feelings.

Many people associate the word "ethics" with some sense of morality, and often use the words "ethics" and "morality" interchangeably. And although there is a high degree of overlap between the words, they mean different things and should not be confused. Ethics concerns behavior—what people do—and the behavior at issue is often public.

"Morality" concerns motivation—why people do things. And because morality involves intention and attitudes, it is generally within the realm of personal conscience, and is typically private. Sometimes morality drives ethics; that is, sometimes personal conscience leads to admirable public behavior. But sometimes the admirable public behavior takes place for other reasons.

Although some people might wish that all actions be done for the right reasons, from an ethical perspective motives are less important than the actual behaviors. Take a simple example: lying. As an ethical issue, it is a matter of indifference whether people refuse to lie because they are afraid of getting caught, because they have become habituated to not lie, or because of a strong moral commitment to honesty. From an ethical perspective, a person who doesn't lie—for whatever reason—is behaving ethically. Similarly, someone who lies for benevolent reasons—for example, from a desire not to hurt someone's feelings—commits an ethical offense. It doesn't matter that the motive was positive, even that the motive was moral. All that matters in such a case is that the lie—the public behavior—is unethical.

The same applies in the corporate world. It is more important that a company insist on ethical behavior by its employees than that it do so for some moral reason. Some companies' leaders are genuinely driven by a moral desire to practice business ethically—to do what's right. Others are driven by a desire to avoid the distraction and costs associated with ethical lapses. And some insist on ethical behavior because they know that having and policing a strong code of ethics protects them under U.S. federal sentencing guidelines should they or their employees be convicted of a crime. But the motive for a company's behavior is less important than recognizing that its behavior is acceptable or unacceptable. And because morality is a private matter, it is often difficult to discern a company's, or an individual's, true motive. Sometimes people and companies act from a mixture of both moral and practical motives.

Ethics is also often confused with legality; unethical behavior with illegal behavior. In broad overview, morality, ethics, and the law are part of a continuum of sometimes overlapping considerations. Take again, for example, lying—telling a deliberate untruth with the intention of deceiving. Lying can be seen to be a moral failing. Lying to someone in a business context can be seen to be an ethical lapse, the violation of a codified or implied rule stating that people in business not lie to each other. And in some circumstances—such as lying under oath or to a criminal investigator—lying may trigger legal action. In the Valerie Plame example that began the chapter, Lewis "Scooter" Libby, the vice president's chief of staff, was convicted of lying under oath to investigators. Libby's lying could be considered a moral lapse, and it may also have been an ethical lapse. But he was prosecuted, convicted, and sentenced to prison not for moral or ethical lapses but for violation of the criminal law. (President Bush later commuted Libby's sentence.)

It may be useful to think of morality, ethics, and legality as three circles of a Venn Diagram (see Figure 2.1), with some overlap among the three areas, but each a distinct set of issues with its own distinct worldviews, considerations, and consequences.

Sometimes people compartmentalize the three, and fail to recognize that the violation of one of these may also be a violation of others. For example, in 2002 it became widely known that many Catholic priests in the U.S. had sexually abused children,

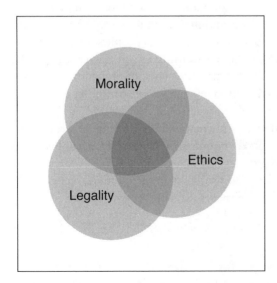

Figure 2.1

and that the bishops who ran the Church in the U.S. had known about the problems for years and had done little to stop the abuse.

Abusing children was clearly immoral—in the vocabulary of the Church, a sin. And it was also a clear violation of priests' own codes of ethics, particularly their vows of celibacy and a duty to protect the vulnerable from abuse by those in power. But what seemed to be unaddressed was the fact that such behavior is also a crime. Before the scandals became widely known in 2002 few Catholic priests had been prosecuted; afterward many were, including some of the most notorious abusers. Now some dioceses have established zero-tolerance policies, including recognition that allegations of abuse should be turned over to law enforcement authorities for investigation and prosecution.

Sometimes legal and ethical duties conflict: for example, the ethical duty to maintain confidentiality—such as a reporter's promise to keep the identity of a source secret—and the legal duty to answer questions when testifying under oath in a trial or in a grand jury investigation. In 2005 the U.S. Supreme Court refused to consider an appellate ruling that journalists could not refuse to identify their sources to a grand jury investigating the Plame leak. As a result, a *New York Times* reporter, Judith Miller, went to jail rather than violate her promise—described by her and *The New York Times* as an ethical obligation—to protect the identity of her source.

Similarly, some actions may be perfectly legal but also unethical, such as representing two companies with conflicting interests. While such client relationships may violate ethical standards, unless there is a contractual prohibition against such a relationship the law is generally silent about them.

It is also common for people to confuse ethics with etiquette: what is polite. For example, some people consider it impolite to criticize others. So they sometimes withhold criticism, or even tell a "white lie"—that is, an innocent untruth not intended to deceive, but to flatter—in order to avoid giving offense. While this kind of behavior is often seen to be admirable, the conflict between etiquette and ethics often comes into full focus when a desire to avoid offense leads to more than an innocent untruth, but to a full-blown lie—that is, a deliberate untruth intended to deceive. Often the duty to be truthful conflicts with the desire to be polite, and ethical people sometimes need to tell hard truths to others; failure to tell those hard truths may be seen as unethical. More significantly, because ethics refer to habitual behaviors, the default to etiquette over ethics can habituate someone to default to politeness over truthfulness, leading to inadvertent ethical lapses.

Similarly, ethics is often confused with aesthetics: what is pleasurable. People say things that make them and others feel good, regardless of the underlying truthfulness of the statement. Or they avoid saying things that may be unpalatable to them or to their audiences. Like etiquette, the desire to feel good and help others feel good is often admirable, but can lead to habitual behaviors that conflict with ethical duties.

Ethics as Habits

The English word "ethics" comes from the ancient Greek word that translates into the English word "habits." The word began to take on its current meaning when it was used by the Greek philosopher Aristotle (c. 384 to 322 BC) in his book *The Nichomachean Ethics*, which describes habitual behaviors that lead to happiness. He noted that we are what we habitually do.

Over the years "ethics" has come to mean habitual behaviors that are appropriate in certain circumstances. So ethics consists of the behaviors that are habitually practiced by an individual and, collectively, by a group of individuals. As individuals form groups that serve particular purposes, they establish formal or informal codes of conduct to govern relations among themselves and between their group and other groups. Over time these codes of conduct describe socially acceptable patterns of behaviors.

> We are what we habitually do.

It is useful to keep the word "habits" in mind when discussing ethics, because ethics describe behaviors that are repeated over time and that therefore become unconscious. As an ethical issue it is a matter of indifference whether an individual refuses to lie because of fear of getting caught or because of a strong commitment to morality. But as an individual becomes habituated over time to avoid lying, the original motive may be forgotten. Someone who initially refuses to lie because of fear of the consequences may, over time, become habituated to not lie—even when there are no likely negative consequences. In other words, the behavior becomes habitual.

Similarly, it can be risky to permit suspect behaviors, even when the reasons are defensible, because over time these suspect behaviors may become habits: so someone who lies in certain circumstances may be habituated to lie in others, and it becomes more and more likely that such a person will lie as a first resort.

Codes of Ethics and Normative Standards of Behavior

One reason groups develop formal ethical rules is to establish normative standards for behavior that can then become habitual among members of the group. Such rules are an ordinary part of social interaction.

> Professional societies developed their own codes of professional behavior, establishing behaviors that are required, permitted, and forbidden among their members.

Over the years, and especially in the twentieth century, professional societies developed their own codes of professional behavior, establishing behaviors that are required, permitted, and forbidden among their members. So doctors in the U.S. are bound by the *Code of Medical Ethics* of the American Medical Association; lawyers by the *Code of Professional Responsibility* of the American Bar Association; accountants by the *Code of Professional Conduct* of the American Institute of Certified Public Accountants, and so forth.

In the 1920s, Edward L. Bernays, the first professional communicator to call himself a "public relations counselor," called for a code of ethics to govern the behavior of the emerging profession of public relations:

> In the 1920s, Edward L. Bernays called for a code of ethics to govern the behavior of the emerging profession of public relations.

> The profession of public relations counsel is developing for itself an ethical code which compares favorably with that

governing the legal and medical professions. In part, this code is forced upon the public relations counsel by the very conditions of his work. While recognizing, just as the lawyer does, that everyone has a right to present his case in its best light, he nevertheless refuses a client whom he believes to be dishonest, a product which he believes to be fraudulent, or a cause which he believes to be antisocial.[1]

In that very description of the choices a practitioner makes, Bernays previewed some of the ethical challenges facing public relations practitioners in the twenty-first century. Today the Public Relations Society of America's *Member Code of Ethics*, the International Association of Business Communicators' *Code of Ethics for Professional Communicators*, and the International Public Relations Association's *Code of Athens* (named for the city where the code was ratified), set standards by which their member practioners are expected to abide.

ETHICS AND PROFESSIONAL COMMUNICATION

Most professional communicators are not members of industry associations, and most associations do not have corporate members. So technically most professional communicators are not bound by such industry codes of conduct. Further, membership of these associations is voluntary and is not a requirement for most jobs in corporate and organizational communication. And the codes provide little in the way of enforcement. The maximum penalty for being found to have violated the code is removal from the association, an association that many communicators do not belong to in the first place. The enforcement is nothing like an attorney being disbarred for violating the legal profession's code of ethics and losing his or her license to practice law. Some people argue that removal from a voluntary organization that doesn't affect employment is not a sufficient penalty to deter unethical behavior, and that therefore such codes are meaningless.

> Because codes are normative, they provide standards that both members and non-members can use as guides for effective action.

But because the codes are normative, they provide standards that both members and non-members can use as guides for effective action. Clients and others can compare any given behavior to one of the codes to determine whether it's appropriate. In other words, regardless of the strength of the sanctions involved, the descriptions of normative behavior provide value by setting standards against which any individual's, group's, or company's behavior can be evaluated.

Indeed, the International Association of Business Communicators (IABC) "encourages the widest possible communication about its Code," publishes the code in several languages, and grants permission to any individual or organization to copy and incorporate all or part of its code into personal or corporate codes (with attribution to IABC).

As members and non-members of various professional associations adapt their behaviors to these groups' normative standards, and the behaviors become habitual, they establish even stronger norms. Violations of the code, by non-members who are subject to no disciplinary procedures, nevertheless can be recognized as inappropriate, and as aberrations from the professional practice of communication.[2]

International Association of Business Communicators Code of Ethics for Professional Communicators

The International Association of Business Communicators' *Code of Ethics for Professional Communicators* offers three overarching rules:

- First, that members of IABC "engage only in communication that is not only legal but also ethical and sensitive to cultural values and beliefs"
- Second, that they "engage in truthful, accurate, and fair communication"
- And third, that they adhere to the articles of the *Code* itself.

The IABC *Code*, in turn, consists of 12 normative statements, each describing the behavior of professional communicators. These include:

> Professional communicators disseminate accurate information and promptly correct any erroneous communication for which they might be responsible…
> Professional communicators give credit for unique expressions borrowed from others and identify sources and purposes of all information disseminated to the public…
> Professional communicators do not accept gifts or payments for professional services from anyone other than a client or employer.[3]

The complete *IABC Code of Ethics for Professional Communicators* may be found at http://www.iabc.com/members/joining/code.htm.

Public Relations Society of America Member Code of Ethics

After a significant ethics scandal in the early 1990s (see Case Study on Citizens for a Free Kuwait), the Public Relations Society of America (PRSA) came under sharp criticism. The Association was criticized for not taking a position in the public discussion of communication ethics during the scandal, and for having a code that was difficult to follow, not particularly helpful to individual practitioners, and out of date.

The PRSA's Board of Ethics and Professional Standards, which led the revision of the code in the late 1990s, recast the code to emphasize the standards that apply to the professional practice of public relations.[4] This Board focused on the fact that the most effective codes are normative, and can therefore serve as guides to the ethical practice of the craft as a whole, not just to the Association's members.

The new *Member Code of Ethics* was prepared by the PRSA Board of Ethics and Professional Standards, which consisted of nine senior public relations practitioners.

They were assisted by the Ethics Resource Council, a Washington-based ethics consulting organization. The Ethics Board convened a series of discussions with members in 1998 and 1999, leading to the launch of the new *Code* in 2000.[5] In their introduction to the new *Code*, the authors note that "the primary obligation of membership in the Public Relations Society of America is the ethical practice of public relations," and observe that the new *Code* "is a way for each member of our society to daily reaffirm a commitment to ethical professional activities and decisions."[6]

Unlike the prior code (and unlike several other associations' codes, including IABC's) the new PRSA *Member Code* also includes examples of behaviors that would be considered unethical, providing more concrete guidance to members and others of what would be considered inappropriate behavior. It not only lists required and forbidden behaviors in the abstract; it demonstrates by example and analogy the kinds of behaviors that are inappropriate, making it more likely that proper behaviors will be habituated, that improper behaviors will be avoided, and that practitioners will find the *Code* useful as a guide to the real-world practice of professional communication.

> The PRSA *Member Code* includes examples of behaviors that would be considered unethical.

The PRSA *Member Code of Ethics* consists of three parts: *Values*, *Provisions*, and a *Pledge*:

- *Member Statement of Professional Values*. These values, each of which is defined with several bullet points, include Advocacy, Honesty, Expertise, Independence, Loyalty, and Fairness. They provide a conceptual framework for the ethical practice of public relations.
- *PRSA Code Provisions*. For each provision there is a plain English description, a statement of intent, guidelines, and examples of improper conduct.

  For example, the *Principle* Disclosure of Information is described as follows: "Open communication fosters informed decision making in a democratic society." Its *Intent* is described as "to build trust with the public by revealing all information needed for responsible decision making."

  The guidelines include:

  > Be honest and accurate in all communications. Act promptly to correct erroneous communications for which the member is responsible. Investigate the truthfulness and accuracy of information released on behalf of those represented. Reveal the sponsors for causes and interests represented.[7]

  The *Examples of Improper Conduct Under this Provision* section includes the following: "A member deceives the public by employing people to pose as volunteers to speak at public hearings."[8]
- *Pledge*, which each member signs, that affirms his or her commitment to, among other things, "conduct myself professionally, with truth, accuracy, fairness, and responsibility to the public."[9]

The complete PRSA *Member Code of Ethics* can be found at: http://www.prsa.org/_About/ethics/index.asp?ident=eth1.

International Public Relations Association Code of Athens

The International Public Relations Association (IPRA)'s *Code*, drafted in Athens in 1968, begins with several *Considerations*, including the observation that "the use of the techniques enabling them to come simultaneously into contact with millions of people gives Public Relations practitioners a power that has to be restrained by the observance of a strict moral code." The *Code* then includes 13 clauses, each framed in the imperative mood, describing things a member shall do, and shall refrain from doing.

For example, one of the three *Endeavors* says that a member shall endeavor "To conduct himself/herself always and in all circumstances in such a manner as to deserve and secure the confidence of those with whom he/she comes into contact." One of three *Undertakings* says that a member shall undertake "To carry out his/her undertakings and commitments which shall always be so worded as to avoid any misunderstanding ..." And two of the four clauses describing forbidden behaviors require that members refrain from both "subordinating the truth to other requirements" and "circulating information which is not based on established and ascertainable fact."

The complete IPRA *Code of Athens* may be found at http://www.ipra.org/aboutipra/aboutipra.htm.

These three association codes of ethics describe, each in its own way, normative standards of behavior for professional communicators around the world. Although the specific provisions apply directly only to members of the respective organizations, they create a framework for understanding appropriate standards of conduct for all professional communicators. And although there are variations among the codes, they are generally consistent in broad overview and collectively serve as useful benchmarks against which to assess the typical ethical challenges that professional communicators face.

> Although the specific provisions apply directly only to members of the respective organizations, they create a framework for understanding appropriate standards of conduct for all professional communicators.

ETHICS OF COMMUNICATING

In broad terms, ethics of communication fall into four categories:

1. Ethics inherent to communicating, usually involving truthfulness and transparency.
2. Ethics of running any kind of organization.
3. Ethics of representation.
4. Helping clients and employers behave ethically.

> Ethics inherent to communicating involves behaviors one engages in that are intrinsic to the process of shaping public opinion by means of communication.

Ethics inherent to communicating involves behaviors one engages in that are intrinsic to the process of shaping public opinion by means of communication.

Effective communication starts with a climate of belief, and credibility is the strongest asset a professional communicator may have. Most of the ethical questions relating to the practice of communication involve credibility in one way or another. The most significant issues of credibility involve truthfulness and falsity of communication, and disclosure of the client or cause on whose behalf a communication is being made.

Some critics of professional communication assert that the very idea of public relations is itself unethical, and use words such as "propaganda" and "spin" to suggest that such activities are inherently misleading. Public relations critics John Stauber and Sheldon Rampton assert that the business of public relations represents a significant social problem. They claim that

> Today's PR industry is related to democracy in the same way that prostitution is related to sex. When practiced voluntarily for love, both can exemplify human communication at its best. When they are bought and sold, however, they are transformed into something hidden and sordid.[10]

Stauber is executive director, and Rampton is research director, of the Center for Media and Democracy, which publishes *PR Watch*, dedicated to investigative reporting on the PR industry. In their 1995 book *Toxic Sludge is Good for You: Lies, Damn Lies and the Public Relations Industry*, Stauber and Rampton attribute sinister motive to the practice of public relations:

> Public relations exists to manufacture the necessary illusions that bridge the gap between the dream and reality of American society ... If the PR industry were *only* based on "lies and damn lies," it might be easier to see through its deceptions. But PR's cunning half-truths and "spins" appeal to us and work on us because they come from us, from the constant plumbing of the social mind by surveys, opinion polls, focus groups, and information gathered as we apply for bank loans, purchase goods with credit cards, place birth announcements in newspapers, vote, and make phone calls.[11]

Stauber and Rampton particularly object to press releases, video news releases, and other techniques common to the practice of public relations that involve providing information to journalists for their consideration and publication.

While Stauber and Rampton acknowledge that not every instance of public relations practice is by itself illegitimate, they also argue that the craft is more often used in the service of illegitimate corporate gain:

> Citizens and individual PR practitioners can use ethical public relations techniques to right social wrongs, clean up the environment, promote minority rights, protect working people, and make communities better. But we consider it an illusion to imagine that PR is a "neutral" technology that can simply be adopted uncritically to achieve socially responsible ends.[12]

But a close look at many of the arguments used by Stauber, Rampton, and other critics shows them to be oversimplifications of the corporate communication process, to project to the entire profession the unethical behavior of a small number of people, to confuse criticism of PR with the practices of journalism, or to use PR as a foil in the service of a political agenda—in Stauber's and Rampton's case the argument that it benefits large corporations at the expense of ordinary people. Indeed, the introduction to *Toxic Sludge is Good for You*, by journalist Mark Dowie, lays out the political agenda of the book:

> A single public relations professional with access to the media, a basic understanding of mass psychology, and a fistful of dollars can unleash in society forces that make permanent winners out of otherwise-evident losers—whether they be products, politicians, corporations, or ideas. This is an awesome power we give to an industry that gravitates to wealth, offers surplus power and influence to those who need it least, and operates largely beyond public view.[13]

In particular, much of the criticism also seems to blend critique of the practice of corporate communications and public relations with criticism of journalists' reliance on PR's work product.

> Much criticism also seems to blend critique of the practice of corporate communications and public relations with criticism of journalists' reliance on PR's work product.

Are Press Releases Unethical?

For example, some critics of public relations and corporate communication point to the tools used to communicate—especially press releases, video news releases, and related hand-outs that are provided to the news media—and suggest that these very tools are somehow sinister and misleading.

But most of the tools are neither. Press releases are corporate announcements written in the style of a newspaper story that a news organization may choose to use or not use. Some press releases are printed verbatim in newspapers; some are excerpted. Many press releases serve simply as a starting point from which a reporter will write his or her own story, often lifting language or quotes from the press release. Among the criticisms of press releases is the observation that quotes lifted from a release convey to the reader of the news story the impression that the reporter actually spoke to the person quoted. The suggestion is that using the quote misleads readers, giving a false impression that the reporter spoke with the newsmaker.

But a close review of such practices suggests that if there is an ethical issue, or a credibility issue, inherent in such practices, the ethical challenge is on the part of the news organization. News organizations are certainly free to ignore a press release, and many press releases are never printed in news media. News organizations are also free to supplement a release with their own reporting, including speaking with the person quoted in the release. They are also free to label the quote in such a way that lets a reader know that the quote came from a press release. Such formulations include "in a statement the company said ..." or "in an announcement Mr. so-and-so said ..."

From a professional communicator's perspective, the ethical duty is different: to assure that the announcement genuinely represents the point of view of the client on whose behalf it is distributed; that the source of the information is clearly and accurately identified, and that there are no deliberate falsehoods in the text of the release. So long as these ethical duties are met, the communication is generally considered ethical. All three professional association codes of ethics—IABC's, PRSA's, and IPRA's, require that all communication—including news releases and related materials—be truthful and that the source of the communication be clearly identified.

One of the counterarguments to the suggestion that press releases by their very nature are unethical is to note that often press releases are required by law and regulation. For example, under U.S. laws and regulations governing corporate disclosure in the securities markets (see Chapter 8, Investor Relations), companies whose stock is publicly traded are required to issue press releases to the media and investment community describing their financial performance and other significant news. In fact, a significant percentage of business news is the routine excerpting of such corporate press releases.

The same regulations that require press releases as a financial disclosure device also establish standards for accuracy and truthfulness of such communications. In general, these announcements may not be "materially misleading" or contain "material omissions": that is, they must be accurate and complete. Releasing deliberately inaccurate or incomplete information may be considered securities fraud, and companies and individuals may be subject to civil or criminal penalties. Releasing information known by the communicator to be false or misleading is also a breach of ethics.

Are Video News Releases Unethical?

Video news releases (VNRs) are the broadcast equivalent of print news releases. Some video news releases are simply edited footage of a news event, such as a speech, presentation, testimony, or meeting, provided to television networks in much the same way as a press release. News organizations can choose whether to use any, part, or all of such video footage as part of their larger reporting on a story. Some VNRs are packaged to resemble local television news stories, including tightly scripted voice-overs, well-edited graphics, and compelling images. Television stations are free to use or not use such video news releases as they choose, including editing the footage to add their own reporting, interviews, or images.

Stauber and Rampton argue that VNRs are unethical because, among other things, they take advantage of news organizations' limited resources:

> Canned news and industry-supplied "experts" are effective because they appeal to budget-conscious news organizations. When a TV news show airs a video news release, the PR firm that produced the segment pays for all the costs of scripting, filming, and editing. Likewise, PR-supplied experts enable reporters to produce authentic-sounding stories with a minimum of time and effort. The public rarely notices the self-serving bias that creeps into the news along with these subtle subsidies.[14]

In 2005, ten years after Sheldon and Rampton's book appeared, VNRs were again in the news. The U.S. government and several public relations firms retained by U.S. government agencies were severely criticized for distributing video news releases that gave the impression that they were objective news reports that happened to promote government programs. Some of the criticism was that the VNRs deliberately mischaracterized the identity of the party on whose behalf the VNR was issued. But much of the criticism focused on the very idea of a VNR.

This scandal triggered renewed criticism of such news practices. *The New York Times* reported that at least 20 U.S. government agencies, including the Census Bureau and Department of Defense, had distributed hundreds of video news releases in the previous few years. "Many were broadcast on local stations across the country without any acknowledgement of the government's role in their production."[15]

In response to the 2005 VNR criticisms, the U.S. Federal Communication Commission warned broadcast and cable news organizations, according to *Reuters*, "to properly identify the source of video news releases that some government agencies have circulated through commercial TV outlets despite criticism. Congressional investigators earlier this year concluded that repackaged news stories created by the Office of National Drug Control Policy constituted covert propaganda."[16]

One of the FCC's Commissioners told *Reuters*, "People in this country have a right to know where their news is coming from, but it's getting almost impossible to know. Everyone understands that a story cannot be judged without knowing its source, but increasingly the source goes unreported."[17]

The scandal also prompted the Radio-Television News Directors Association (RTNDA), citing its own *Code of Ethics and Professional Conduct*, to remind its members of their duties:

> News managers and producers should clearly disclose the origin of information and label all material provided by corporate or other non-editorial sources. For example, graphics could denote "Mercy Hospital video" and the reporter or anchor script could also acknowledge it by stating, "This operating room video was provided by Mercy Hospital."[18]

RTNDA also directed its members to subject VNRs to the same news standards as they do their own work:

> News managers and producers should determine if interviews provided with video/audio releases follow the same standards regarding conflicts of interest as used in the newsroom. For instance, some releases might contain interviews where subjects and interviewers are employed by the same organization. Consider whether tough questions were asked and if the subject was properly questioned.[19]

PR Watch published an article by Rampton addressing the 2005 VNR scandals. Rampton made two points: first, that use of VNRs isn't limited to government, and second that VNRs and other communication tools are illegitimate: "In fact, corporate public relations is the biggest single source of video news releases, just as corporate PR is the biggest single source of other types of PR that pollute the media ecosystem."[20]

Rampton's critique, while colorful, isn't particularly helpful to professional communicators. In fact, both the FCC's and RTNDA's discussions of the controversy focused on disclosure of the source of the news as the key ethical issue, and place the burden and the ethical criticism rightly on journalists. That is, to the degree there are ethical issues inherent in VNRs, they are primarily issues affecting journalists' use of the VNRs and their disclosure of the source of the content. From a professional communicator's perspective, the ethical standards regarding a VNR are the same as those regarding a print news release: the source of the material should be clearly identified by the communicator, and the content should be accurate and truthful. If these standards are met, the VNR generally passes ethical muster.

Corrupting the Channels of Communication

One ethical concern facing professional communicators is the integrity of the channels of communication, particularly regarding the independence of news organizations and news commentators. The integrity of the communication process is impaired by, among other things, payments to reporters, so that their interest in providing objective coverage is or appears to be compromised. This includes providing bribes, inappropriate favors, hiring relatives, and otherwise mingling the reporter's private interests with those of a professional communicator's client or employer.

The PRSA *Member Code of Ethics* specifically calls for members to "maintain the integrity of relationships with the media, government officials, and the public."

In early 2005 *USA Today* reported that the prominent conservative commentator and columnist Armstrong Williams had received $240,000 from a public relations firm working for the U.S. Department of Education to promote the Department's initiatives on Williams' television program.[21] A firestorm of controversy ensued. As a result of the disclosure, *Tribune Media Services*, which syndicated Williams' column, dropped the columnist, saying,

> Accepting compensation in any form from an entity that serves as the subject of his weekly newspaper columns creates, at the very least, the appearance of a conflict of interest. Under these circumstances, readers may well ask themselves if the views expressed in his columns are his own, or whether they have been purchased by a third party.[22]

The U.S. Department of Education initially defended its payments to Mr. Williams as legal, but after significant criticism the outgoing Secretary of Education, Rod Paige, said, "All of this has been reviewed and is legal. However, I am sorry that there are perceptions and allegations of ethical lapses."[23]

As the Williams controversy became public it was also learned that syndicated columnist Maggie Gallagher had promoted the Administration's "healthy marriage" initiative while receiving $21,500 from the U.S. Department of Health and Human Services.

At a press conference President George W. Bush was asked about the accumulation of scandals involving VNRs and payments to columnists. He replied, "All our Cabinet secretaries must realize that we will not be paying… commentators to advance our agenda. Our agenda ought to be able to stand on its own initiative."[24]

The PRSA's *Member Code of Ethics* offers guidance on less dramatic, but potentially equally challenging, ethical choices. In its *Examples of Inappropriate Conduct* under its *Free Flow of Information* provision, the *Code* offers two cases of inappropriate behavior: "A member representing a ski manufacturer gives a pair of expensive racing skis to a sports magazine columnist, to influence the columnist to write favorable articles about the product. A member entertains a government official beyond legal limits and/or in violation of government reporting requirements."[25]

Front Groups

Another challenge to the integrity of the communication process is the establishment of "front groups," or organizations that purport to have a certain, usually public purpose, but that in fact are acting on behalf of an undisclosed interest.

Citizens for a Free Kuwait (see Case Study, below) is the most notorious example in recent memory, but is hardly the only such group. At the same time as the Kuwait story was in the news in the early 1990s, Greenpeace criticized a Washington PR firm for what it called a "phony citizens group," to lobby against increased fuel efficiency standards. The group, called "The Coalition for Vehicle Choice," was funded by the major automobile manufacturers.

Ironically, Edward L. Bernays, who in the 1920s called for a code of ethics for public relations, was a master of creating front groups. It all started in 1913 when Bernays, just out of college, was working at a medical magazine called *Medical Review of Reviews*. Bernays published a review of a play called *Damaged Goods*, which dealt with the effects of syphilis. The play violated social taboos against discussion of sexually transmitted diseases. Bernays persuaded Richard Bennett, a popular New York actor who wanted to produce the play, to let Bernays underwrite the production. According to his biographer, Bernays realized that in order to create interest in *Damaged Goods* Bernays needed

> to transform the controversy into a cause, and recruit backers who already were public role models. The twenty-one-year-old editor formed a Medical Review of Reviews Sociological Fund Committee, then attracted members with an artful appeal that played on Bennett's reputation as an artist as well as the worthiness of battling prudishness.[26]

Bernays needed to transform the controversy into a cause.

Committee members included John D. Rockefeller, Jr., Mr. and Mrs. Franklin D. Roosevelt, and Mrs. William K. Vanderbilt, Sr. Rockefeller offered a typical endorsement: "The evils that spring from prostitution cannot be understood until frank discussion of them has been made possible."[27]

Despite weak reviews, *Damaged Goods* was a big success, and sold out in New York. It then went to Washington, where it was performed for Supreme Court justices, members of Congress, and members of the Administration. Bernays' biographer says that using a third-party group of luminaries to lend credibility to a commercial or political cause became Bernays' preferred method of operating.

> Using a third-party group of luminaries to lend credibility to a commercial or political cause became Bernays' preferred method of operating.

This was the first time [Bernays] or anyone else had assembled such a distinguished front group. And its success ensured not only that he would use this technique repeatedly but also that it would continue to be employed today, when it takes a detective to unmask the interests behind such innocuous-sounding groups as the Safe Energy Communication Council (antinuclear), the Eagle Alliance (pronuclear), and the Coalition Against Regressive Taxation (trucking industry).[28]

In the 1940s Bernays was retained by Mack Trucks to help recover market share in freight hauling from railroads. He devised an extensive campaign to improve the quality of interstate highways to make shipping cargo by truck more feasible. And he created a number of front groups, including Trucking Information Service, the Trucking Service Bureau, and Better Living Through Increased Highway Transportation, which in turn created state chapters to run local campaigns to influence members of Congress. Bernays was successful, and in 1950 Congress approved $556 million in new highway construction funds, and in 1952 increased the funding level to $652 million. The U.S. interstate highway system remains the living beneficiary of Bernays' campaign, which also set the standard for contemporary lobbying and political action committees.[29]

Today front groups that purport to represent one interest but actually serve a hidden interest are violations of most ethical standards, which require disclosure of the interests on whose behalf communication is taking place. PRSA's new *Member Code of Ethics* specifically requires identification of the ultimate beneficiary of any front group. It requires that a member "reveal the sponsors for causes and interests represented." Its *Examples of Improper Conduct Under This Provision* includes this clause: "Front Groups: A member implements 'grass roots' campaigns of letter-writing campaigns to legislators on behalf of undisclosed interest groups."[30]

> Front groups that purport to represent one interest but actually serve a hidden interest are violations of most ethical standards.

ETHICS OF RUNNING AN ORGANIZATION

Professional communicators need also to abide by ethical standards that apply to any professional situations. These are ethical situations that any organization might face, involving mostly the interpersonal relationships between the organization and its employees, customers, business partners, and other companies.

> Professional communicators need also to abide by ethical standards that apply to any professional situations.

Some of the particular ethical duties include:

Confidentiality

Professional communicators are often in a position to know things before the general public, and sometimes also to know information that should never be revealed because they include trade secrets, personal information about fellow employees, or other proprietary information.

Under U.S. securities law and regulations there are strict prohibitions about revealing "material non-public information" or to disclose selectively. So professional communicators are sometimes subjected to legal and regulatory requirements to keep secrets. (See Chapter 8, Investor Relations, for more detail.)

Sometimes professional communicators are bound by contractual obligations to keep certain information confidential. But even absent legal, regulatory, or contractual requirements, professional communicators may also be required to maintain confidences for ethical reasons. For example, the PRSA *Member Code of Ethics* has an entire provision on *Safeguarding Confidences*. The *Intent* of the principle is "to protect the privacy rights of clients, organizations, and individuals by safeguarding confidential information." The *Guidelines* require that members "safeguard the confidences and privacy rights of present, former, and prospective clients and employees. Protect privileged, confidential, or insider information gained from a client or organization." In *Examples of Improper Conduct Under This Provision* the *Code* notes "a member changes jobs, takes confidential information, and uses that information in the new position to the detriment of the former employer."[31]

Similarly, the IABC *Code of Ethics for Professional Communicators* contains two articles on the subject: "Professional communicators protect confidential information and … do not use confidential information gained as the result of professional activities for personal benefit."[32]

Conflicts of Interest

One of the persistent ethical challenges for professional communicators involves conflicts of interest. Sometimes the conflict is between the individual and his or her employer or client, such as when a professional communicator receives payment from an entity whose interest may be opposed to the communicator's employer or client.

The PRSA *Member Code of Ethics* has a provision on *Conflicts of Interests* that includes two guidelines on such personal/professional conflicts, saying that a member shall "act in the best interests of a client or employer, even subordinating the member's personal interests," and "avoid actions and circumstances that may appear to compromise good business judgment or create a conflict between personal and professional interests." The *Code* lists as an *Example of Improper Conduct Under This Provision* the following: "The member fails to disclose that he or she has a strong financial interest in a client's chief competitor."[33]

Similarly, the IABC *Code of Ethics for Professional Communicators* contains an article that says "Professional communicators do not accept undisclosed gifts or payments for professional services from anyone other than a client or employer."[34]

Sometimes the conflict arises from a professional communicator having as clients two organizations whose interests are in conflict.

Note, however, that simply representing two competing companies does not necessarily result in a conflict of interest. For example, two competitors may have a common interest in legislation, and each could use the services of a government relations professional seeking to influence legislation that would benefit the clients' industry as a whole, and therefore both clients. Similarly, a communicator may represent two competing companies for different functions; for example, doing internal communications for client A, and government relations for client B.

> Simply representing two competing companies does not necessarily result in a conflict of interest.

Many professional communicators have significant expertise in a particular industry, and represent more than two companies who compete with each other. Some companies require exclusivity from their communication advisors, and usually pay a premium for that exclusivity. But others recognize that they ultimately benefit from an advisor with significant industry expertise.

One way to manage such multi-client relationships is full disclosure to all parties of the various relationships. The assumption is that there is no conflict if each party is aware of the various relationships.

> One way to manage multi-client relationships is full disclosure to all parties of the various relationships.

The PRSA *Member Code of Ethics* requires members to "disclose promptly any existing or potential conflict of interest to affected clients or organizations," and to "encourage clients and customers to determine if a conflict exists after notifying all affected parties."[35]

Similarly, the IABC *Code of Ethics for Professional Communicators* says that professional communicators "do not represent conflicting or competing interests without written consent of those involved."[36]

In any event, representing more than one company in a given industry or representing competing companies underscores the need for professional communicators to maintain strict confidentiality of client proprietary information, so as not to deliberately or inadvertently reveal to one company the business plans, strategies, staffing, sales volume, or similar sensitive data of another such company.

Ethics of Routine Business Relationships

Professional communicators are bound by the same ethical standards as other professionals, including fair treatment of customers, business partners, and employees. Routine business ethics challenges, such as accurate billing, paying employees for hours worked, providing safe workplaces, and adhering to legal and regulatory requirements, apply to professional communicators as they do to employees in other industries.

Sometimes the ethical challenges of professional communicators in routine business matters cast the profession in a negative light. For example, at the same time in 2005 that the public relations industry was being criticized for VNRs and for paying columnists to support clients' policies, a public relations firm in Los Angeles was found to have overbilled its client the City of Los Angeles and had also billed the

City for work not performed. After an investigation the public relations firm agreed to a settlement with the City of Los Angeles valued at $5.7 million, and apologized to the citizens and city officials of Los Angeles,[37] and a firm executive pleaded guilty to fraud.[38]

In a similar ethics and legal crisis, two former senior executives of the advertising agency Ogilvy & Mather Worldwide were convicted in 2004 of ordering employees to alter time sheets, resulting in overbilling their client, the U.S. Office of National Drug Control Policy. In 2005 both were sentenced to more than a year in prison and were fined. U.S. Federal District Judge Richard Berman further ordered the more senior executive, Shona Seifert, as part of her sentence, to write a code of ethics that could be used by the advertising industry to prevent such billing practices in the future.[39]

ETHICS OF REPRESENTATION

One area that provokes much discussion and disagreement is the question of representation; the suggestion that there may be something ethically suspect about working with certain clients or companies. Where should professional communicators draw the line? Are there whole categories of companies, industries, products, causes, and people that a professional communicator should refuse to help?

The PRSA *Member Code of Ethics* says that PR professionals "provide a voice in the marketplace of ideas, facts, and viewpoints to aid informed public debate," and that they "respect all opinions and support the right of free expression."[40] Some might interpret these statements of professional values as providing justification to representing all interests, however personally offensive, dishonest, distasteful, or ethically suspect those interests may be. Others suggest that just because all parties may be equally entitled to representation, there is no duty on any given practitioner to agree to work with any given client.

> One area that provokes much discussion and disagreement is the question of representation; the suggestion that there may be something ethically suspect about working with certain clients or companies.

As Edward L. Bernays pointed out in 1928,

> While recognizing, just as the lawyer does, that everyone has a right to present his case in its best light, [a professional communicator] nevertheless refuses a client whom he believes to be dishonest, a product which he believes to be fraudulent, or a cause which he believes to be antisocial.[41]

In practice many professional communicators, and the firms that hire them, understand that whether to work with a given client is often a matter of personal choice. The IABC *Code of Ethics for Professional Communicators* makes such a choice explicit: "Professional communicators refrain from taking part in any undertaking which the communicator considers to be unethical."[42] The IPRA *Code of Athens* has a similar provision, requiring that members refrain from "taking part in any venture or undertaking which is unethical or dishonest or capable of impairing human dignity and integrity."[43] And the PRSA *Member Code of Ethics* does require that members "decline representation of clients or organizations that urge or require actions contrary to this Code."[44]

Such activities could include not just the ethics of communication and the ethics of running a business, but also the nature of the organization for which the communicator would work.

Among the industry categories that are often cited by practitioners as causing concern are:

- Tobacco companies
- Individuals or companies accused or convicted of a crime
- Companies that harm the environment
- Companies that use animals in medical experiments
- Foreign governments whose policies are thought to be repressive or contrary to a practitioner's national government's interests
- The military, especially in time of war
- Manufacturers of handguns or other weapons
- Chemical companies
- Pharmaceutical companies
- Alcohol beverage companies
- Causes that advocate policies contrary to a communicator's own values, religious beliefs, or political views
- Companies with abusive workplace practices, or that employ child, prison, or slave labor
- Companies based in countries with poor records of human rights, financial fraud, or political oppression.

The list could continue for quite a while, and some PR firms have affirmative policies specifying the industry sectors for which they will or will not work.

Some communicators differentiate between the company they work for and that company's parent. For example, in the U.S. for some time tobacco companies also owned food-processing companies, and communicators who would never promote tobacco had no difficulty working for the food processors that were owned by tobacco companies. Others saw no difference between working for a benign division of a company they found objectionable and promoting the objectionable product, and avoided such companies altogether.

Sensitivities change over time. For example, in the 1980s fur companies and nuclear energy companies were considered by some communicators to be objectionable. In the 1990s companies that tested products on animals were often seen to be controversial, as were the countries of China, Indonesia, and Turkey.

Edward L. Bernays, over the course of a long career, saw his own sensitivities change. In the 1920s and 1930s he was an ardent promoter of tobacco companies, and is credited with making it socially acceptable for women to smoke in public. Bernays' biographer, Larry Tye, notes that Bernays shifted his views as the science became clearer:

When the surgeon general and other medical authorities released incontrovertible evidence of the dangers of smoking, Bernays used his talents of persuasion to help undo the addictions he'd help build. In 1964 he unveiled a bold and detailed plan to transform smoking into "an antisocial action which no self-respecting person carries on in the presence of others."[45]

Beyond categories such as industry sector or national policy, some representation choices concern the character of the individuals. Several PR firms routinely require prospective clients who are rumored to be involved in organized crime to pay for independent private investigations of their activities to validate the prospects' claims that they had been falsely accused.

One common concern about representation is helping governments rally public support for a war. In a CBS *60 Minutes* program about the Citizens for a Free Kuwait controversy (see Case Study, below), correspondent Morley Safer summed up this view: "The troubling part of the story is the belief by the public relations industry that, with enough access, enough money, and knowing which buttons to push, war can be marketed, just like soft drinks and toothpaste."[46]

A close look at the history of public relations, however, shows that mobilizing public opinion has been an integral part of the U.S. going to war (in every war except Vietnam, in which the U.S. government made only half-hearted efforts to mobilize public opinion). From Committees of Correspondence in the American Revolution, to war cries such as "Remember the Maine!" in the Spanish–American War, to the use of sophisticated public relations techniques and embedded journalists in the war with Iraq that began in 2003, professional communicators have been active in most U.S. military operations. Edward L. Bernays himself practiced his craft on behalf of U.S. involvement in World War I and World War II.

Professional communicators who work with the military argue that there is nothing inherently suspect about working for a military operation, including during a war, but note that they continue to be bound by the usual ethical requirements, including the duty to communicate honestly and accurately. John R. MacArthur, who revealed the Citizens for a Free Kuwait controversy (see Case Study, below) and whose book examines ethical failings of both the news media and the public relations industry, notes that truth is often a casualty of war:

> In modern wars, exaggerated or manufactured enemy atrocities have frequently played an important part in the cause of boosting war fever at home... Slaughtered and mutilated Belgian babies were a tremendous propaganda triumph for the Allies [in World War I]. In retrospect, the success of these manufactured stories possessed ominous implications for future wars, especially the one to liberate Kuwait.[47]

Every professional communicator, as part of his or her ethical development, needs to reflect on the kinds of companies, causes, people, and circumstances that cause ethical concern, and be ready to make

Every professional communicator, as part of his or her ethical development, needs to reflect on the kinds of companies, causes, people, and circumstances that cause ethical concern, and be ready to make decisions on whether to represent such causes or not.

decisions on whether to represent such causes or not. The three criteria to consider in making such a decision are:

- Who is the client? Is there anything inherent in the client's identity that is objectionable:
    E.g., convicted felon, etc.
- What does the client do? Is the client's industry sector objectionable?
    E.g., tobacco, firearms, etc.
- What does the client want you to do? For example, is there a difference between marketing the client's product and helping it develop effective internal communications, or outreach to communities?

HELPING COMPANIES BEHAVE ETHICALLY

The corporate scandals of the 2000s demonstrated that a company's ethical lapses can cause significant harm to reputation, operations, morale, customer demand, stock price, and in some cases even a company's survival. Often ethical slippage is a leading indicator—a kind of early warning—of legal problems. From Enron to Andersen to the Roman Catholic Church, ethical lapses that were apparent to insiders and observers were ignored by organizations' leaders, only to re-emerge in criminal conviction, civil penalties, and in Enron's and Andersen's cases, corporate death.

> Increasingly, corporate communication departments are seen as the conscience of a company, and play an important role in helping a company behave ethically. Recognizing the relationship between ethical lapses and reputational harm, many companies now see commitment to ethics as an integral part of managing their reputation and preserving the value of the company's intangible assets.

Increasingly, corporate communication departments are seen as the conscience of a company, and play an important role in helping a company behave ethically. Recognizing the relationship between ethical lapses and reputational harm, many companies now see commitment to ethics as an integral part of managing their reputation and preserving the value of the company's intangible assets.

On a more practical level, U.S. Federal Sentencing Guidelines, which set rules for punishment for corporate crimes, mandate that companies with strong ethics codes, training programs, and compliance procedures can be subjected to less severe penalties if they should be convicted of certain crimes.

Sometimes the professional communicator's ethics role is informal, helping the company navigate day-to-day communication decisions in an ethical way.

Sometimes the corporate communicator's ethics role is paired with the company's program of corporate social responsibility (see Chapter 13, Corporate Responsibility). And sometimes the corporate communicator's role is paired with the company's own code of ethics.

Some companies have robust ethics codes and training programs. For example, General Electric's Code, called *Integrity: The Spirit & Letter of Our Commitment*, runs for 35 pages. It starts with a single page GE Code of Conduct, which requires that GE people obey laws and regulations, be honest, fair and trustworthy, avoid conflicts of interest between work and personal affairs, foster an atmosphere of fair employment practices, strive to create a safe workplace and protect the environment, and sustain a culture in which ethical conduct is recognized.[48] The balance of the document provides extensive procedures for implementing the code.

Sometimes companies overhaul their codes following ethical lapses. For example, from 2002 to 2004 The Boeing Co. suffered reputational harm through a series of scandals involving the recruitment of Pentagon officials for senior positions in the company while these officials were still overseeing Boeing and other defense contractors for the government. Eventually Boeing's chief executive officer, Phil Condit, was forced to leave the company. He was replaced by retired vice chairman Harry Stonecipher, who promptly instituted a revised *Code of Conduct*. The new single-page *Code* includes the following sentence: "Employees will not engage in conduct or activity that may raise questions as to the company's honesty, impartiality, reputation, or otherwise cause embarrassment to the company."[49] It also requires that employees promptly report any unethical conduct.

Ironically, soon after implementing the *Code*, Mr. Stonecipher conducted a romantic affair with a female subordinate. A fellow employee, following the Code's requirements, reported his suspicions to the company's board, which promptly investigated. Mr. Stonecipher was fired for violating his own code.

Commentators noted that the Board's dismissal of their new CEO demonstrated that the *Code* worked and that the company took ethics seriously. The *Seattle Post-Intelligencer* quoted University of Washington business professor Jonathan Karpoff saying that Boeing reacted so dramatically to the CEO's affair because of its recent ethical challenges. "'Everyone's on pins and needles when it comes to manipulating the numbers, but now it's spreading out to all aspects of a firm's leadership—especially in light of the lapses Boeing has been involved in over the years,' Karpoff said." The newspaper also quoted Kirk Johnson, vice president at ethics consulting firm Integrity Interactive Corp., saying "This story demonstrates that ethics programs work, and that they do have teeth."[50]

Some companies' commitment to ethics is triggered by a series of ethical scandals that impair their ability to do business effectively. For example, in 2004 Japanese banking regulators revoked Citigroup Private Bank's license to operate in Japan. Citigroup's chief executive officer, Charles Prince, formally apologized to the regulators, including participating in a seven-second ceremonial bow. A photograph of Mr. Prince bowing before regulators appeared in newspapers around the world on October 26, 2004.

Citigroup's Japan problems were just the latest ethical challenge in a series of mishaps over several years. Citigroup was involved in financing Enron, WorldCom, and Parmalat, each of which was found to have committed financial fraud. Its European traders were implicated in a controversial trading strategy named "Dr. Evil," although the company was later cleared of wrongdoing in that strategy. And it had been implicated in scandals involving the independence of its research analysts.

In March 2005, Mr. Prince announced a new ethics initiative, telling *The Wall Street Journal* that the project would consume "at least half his executive time and energy over the next several years." He told the newspaper, "This is job one. If I don't own this, I don't think it will succeed."[51] Mr. Prince specifically linked the ethics initiative to restoration of Citigroup's reputation, saying it was intended to make Citigroup the most respected financial-services company.

Mr. Prince recognized that even the best ethics code won't protect a company's reputation if the company's culture isn't responsive to ethical considerations and ethical responsibilities.

Indeed, Enron Corp., which has become synonymous with corporate corruption, had a 65-page ethics code that included all the usual requirements and prohibitions that highly respected companies' codes contain. These include four core Values: Respect, Integrity, Communication, and Excellence.

An elaboration of the Respect value is particularly ironic, given Enron's ultimate demise: "We treat others as we would like to be treated ourselves. We do not tolerate abusive or disrespectful treatment. Ruthlessness, callousness, and arrogance don't belong here."[52]

An introductory letter to the code from Kenneth L. Lay, chairman and chief executive officer of Enron, said,

> We want to be proud of Enron and to know that it enjoys a reputation for fairness and honesty and that it is respected. Gaining such respect is one aim of our advertising and public relations activities, but no matter how effective they may be, Enron's reputation depends on its people, on you and me. Let's keep that reputation high.[53]

The letter was dated July 1, 2000. Less than two years later Enron was out of business, brought down by a series of ethical and legal shortfalls.

Another company to go out of business in the wake of the Enron scandal was Enron's auditor, Arthur Andersen. The firm went out of business just six months after it emerged as inextricably linked to the Enron scandal, following its conviction for obstruction of justice. But a close look at the firm in the years before the scandal shows that the Enron entanglements were a symptom of a much larger problem, particularly an inattention to the ethical standards that had helped propel Andersen to the heights of respectability and profitability.

Barbara Ley Toffler, formerly a professor of ethics at the Harvard Business School, and presently a professor at Columbia University's Business School, ran Arthur Andersen's Ethics & Responsible Business Practices consulting group. After the firm's demise in 2002, she wrote a book diagnosing the root causes of the firm's collapse. She writes that:

> Arthur Andersen was a great and venerable American brand that had, over the course of the twentieth century, become a global symbol of strength and solidity … In my years working at Arthur Andersen, I came to believe that the white-shoed accounting firm known for its legions of trained, loyal, honest professionals—a place that once had the respect, envy, and admiration of everyone in Corporate America—had lost its way. The accountants and the consultants forgot what it meant to be accountable. The fall of Arthur Andersen, I believe, was no murder. It was a suicide, set in motion long before there was ever an indictment. Yet while the guilty verdict sealed Andersen's fate, by the time it came it was merely a formality, the last nail in a coffin whose grave had been primed for burial.[54]

Toffler says that her attempts to bring ethical problems to management's attention were rebuffed. She says that it was clear to her—and to anyone who chose to see—that Andersen's culture had shifted powerfully to a short-term focus on profitability at the expense of its core values of independence and client service, to what she termed "billing our brains out," regardless of the value delivered to the client, of unethical entanglements, or of suspect behavior. She describes a culture where every employee who had or might have anything to do with a client had to figure out a way to sell more services to clients, regardless of the client's need. "Some would call this client service—but in my experience it seemed to be more about raping the client than serving it."[55]

Toffler's business was advising clients on ethical business practice, not serving as an in-house ethics officer for her own firm. But internal ethical issues came to her attention, including a partner who she says had taken his and a client's daughters to a New York Yankees game in a limousine, which waited for the entire game, and then took them home. The partner directed that the expenses for the trip be billed to the client as an audit-related expense. She recounts:

> I could find no indication that ethics was ever talked about in any broad way at Arthur Andersen. When I brought up the subject of internal ethics, I was looked at as if I had teleported in from another world … The end result was the continual reinforcement of the idea that it was okay to play with numbers … The laxity of this approach would come back to haunt the Firm later: Billing Our Brains Out or compromising quality was what we all had to do to get ahead—or to keep up.[56]

According to Toffler, "there was simply too much similarity of thought, too much acceptance that the way things were done was the best simply *'because that's the way we do it'* to see that this culture was turning on itself."[57]

She concludes: "I believe strongly that the suicide of Arthur Andersen—and the assault on the investing public's trust—could have been avoided had people paid attention to the danger signs flashing everywhere in the late 1990s."[58]

One of the critical roles of a professional communicator is to serve as an early warning system, for such danger signs. As the entity formally charged with protecting and advancing an organization's reputation, the corporate and organizational communication function needs to be fully engaged in discussions of all of an organization's reputational threats, including the implications of unethical behavior.

One of the critical roles of a professional communicator is to serve as an early warning system for danger signs.

CASE STUDY: HILL & KNOWLTON AND CITIZENS FOR A FREE KUWAIT

The most significant communication ethics scandal of the 1990s concerned the PR firm Hill & Knowlton's work for its client, Citizens for a Free Kuwait. The scandal was triggered by publication of *Second Front:*

Censorship and Propaganda in the Gulf War, by *Harper's Magazine* publisher John R. MacArthur in 1992. Much of the book focused on the U.S. government's management of the media in the 1991 Gulf War, and the media's acquiescence to the government's groundrules. But the revelations about ethically-suspect behavior involving the PR firm and its client set off a firestorm of criticism against the firm and PR in general.

In August, 1990 Iraq invaded Kuwait. In the days that followed Hill & Knowlton undertook a major campaign to mobilize U.S. public opinion to defend Kuwait and go to war with Iraq. Hill & Knowlton was the largest and, by some accounts, the most powerful public relations firm in the world.

Working for an entity it described as "Citizens for a Free Kuwait" (CFK), Hill & Knowlton staged a number of public events that it said represented the interest of private Kuwaiti citizens in the U.S. and Canada. After the war MacArthur called into question the legitimacy of much of Hill & Knowlton's work, including the identity of CFK.

> MacArthur concluded that Citizens for a Free Kuwait was a front group for the government.

Although Hill & Knowlton insisted, both to MacArthur and to the CBS television news magazine *60 Minutes*, that its client was a group of concerned citizens and not the government of Kuwait, MacArthur concluded that Citizens for a Free Kuwait was a front group for the government:

> The "Citizens" part of the organization was a fiction, as was the pretense of being an ordinary nonprofit charity. After the war, when it grudgingly owned up to its true status, CFK reported to the Justice Department receipts of $17,861 from seventy-eight individual U.S. and Canadian contributors, and $11,852,329 from the government of Kuwait.[59]

Jack O'Dwyer, editor of a leading public relations trade newsletter, characterized the veracity of Hill & Knowlton's claim by analogy: "If the manufacturer of a suit that was 99.85% cotton called it a wool suit because it was 0.15% wool, you'd expect the company to be arrested."[60]

The identity of Hill & Knowlton's client was just the starting point in a discussion of systematic ethical wrongdoing. MacArthur further suggested that Hill & Knowlton (H&K) was really doing the bidding of the White House. Craig Fuller, then head of the CFK account and Washington-based President of H&K, had previously served as chief of staff to then-Vice President George H.W. Bush. He left H&K when the scandal broke, and served as chair of President Bush's 1994 Republican National Convention.

What is The Congressional Human Rights Caucus? And Who is Nayirah?

One of the more serious criticisms of H&K's work involved what MacArthur described to *60 Minutes* as the Kuwaiti's and Administration's need for a "defining atrocity."[61] That defining atrocity concerned allegations that the invading Iraqi army had systematically pillaged hospitals in Kuwait, removing dozens (in some reports, hundreds) of premature babies from incubators, leaving them to die on the hospital floors. The most riveting account of the incubator story came from a 15-year-old Kuwaiti girl identified only as Nayirah.

On October 10, 1990 Nayirah testified at a meeting of the Congressional Human Rights Caucus. Although it had the appearance of a full-fledged congressional hearing, in fact it was merely an informal gathering of like-minded members of Congress. MacArthur points out that

> The Human Rights Caucus is not a committee of Congress and therefore it is unencumbered by the legal accoutrements that would make a witness hesitate before he or she lied ... Lying under oath in front of a congressional committee is a crime; lying from under the cover of anonymity to the caucus is merely public relations.[62]

The nature of the caucus and its relationship to H&K and CFK is a critical one. According to MacArthur, the co-chairs of the caucus, Congressman Tom Lantos (C-CA) and Congressman Edward Porter (R-IL), were also co-chairs of the Congressional Human Rights Foundation, whose rent-free offices were in H&K's Washington offices. After the caucus meeting at which Nayirah testified, the Congressional Human Rights Foundation, which had paid for travel and lodging for Congressmen Lantos and Porter, and for their wives, received a $50,000 contribution from CFK.[63]

At the caucus' October 10 meeting, Nayirah was introduced only as a 15-year-old girl with first-hand experience of the events to which she was testifying. Her full identity was withheld, it was said, in order to protect her family in Kuwait from reprisals.

Nayirah, who had been coached by H&K and whose testimony was later included in H&K's press materials about the caucus meeting, told the caucus:

> While I was [at the al-Adan hospital] I saw the Iraqi solders come into the hospital with guns, and go into the room where 15 babies were in incubators. They took the incubators, and left the babies on the cold floor to die.[64]

Nayirah's story, distributed by H&K via video news releases, press releases, and other tools of the trade, was widely covered, and referred to often by President Bush and by members of the U.S. Senate and House of Representatives.

As the U.S. Senate debated a resolution authorizing the U.S. to go to war against Iraq, the babies-pulled-from-incubators story had become the war's defining atrocity. It was mentioned often by President George

H. W. Bush. More significantly, the war resolution passed the U.S. Senate on January 12, 1991 by a five-vote margin; six senators who voted for the resolution referred to the baby incubator story in justifying their vote. MacArthur argues:

> The significance of the baby incubator story in the larger pro- paganda campaign against Saddam Hussein and for the war option cannot be underestimated. Without it, the comparison of Hussein with Hitler loses its luster; to make the case effec- tively, one had to prove Hussein's utter depravity.[65]

After the war ended, MacArthur discovered that Nayirah was no ordinary refugee, and questioned whether her anonymity would have made any difference in protecting her family from reprisals: She was in fact a mem- ber of the Kuwaiti royal family, and the daughter of Kuwait's Ambassador to the United States (and, because CFK was a front group for the Kuwaiti government, the Ambassador was also H&K's client). He further discov- ered that five of the other six Kuwaitis who spoke at the U.N. used false identities. He says that H&K claimed that the fact that the witnesses used false identities had been revealed at the time, but he was unable to find any proof of this. He further notes that several of them were prominent Kuwaitis, whose identity would have been known in Kuwait, including the head of the Kuwaiti Red Crescent. MacArthur muses, "Why would a well- known public health official—even one working for the Kuwaiti govern- ment—need to hide his identity if not to mislead the media and human rights investigators and to make follow-up inquiries more difficult?"[66]

After the war leading human rights organizations—including Amnesty International and Human Rights Watch—went to Kuwait to investigate reports of atrocities, and each concluded that the baby incubator atrocity had never taken place.

Aftermath and Backlash

MacArthur revealed his findings in a *New York Times* op-ed article on January 6, 1992, just before the one-year anniversary of the war. The article, based on his book, was the first salvo in what would be an esca- lating and nearly year-long scandal. Within weeks the criticism included an editorial in *The New York Times* called "Deception on Capitol Hill" and criticism of Hill & Knowlton—and of public relations in general—by *60 Minutes*, ABC *20/20*, *Newsweek*, the *Wall Street Journal*, and the *Washington Post*. *TV Guide*, with a circulation of more than 15 million, ran a story that accused Hill & Knowlton of "systematic manipulation of the news."[67]

Hill & Knowlton defended its work for CFK, and rebutted MacArthur's and the media's criticisms. Thomas E. Eidson, H&K's president and CEO in 1992, defended both the accuracy of Nayirah's testimony and the firm's insistence that it worked for a citizens' group and not for the government of Kuwait.[68]

In the aftermath of the CFK scandal, with H&K's and PR's integrity impeached, the firm became the subject of intense scrutiny about other clients it represented. Soon after the Kuwait story broke H&K was sued for "PR fraud" by creditors of its client, the disgraced Bank of Credit and Commerce International (BCCI), and its work against abortion for the U.S. bishops and for the Church of Scientology was criticized as well. It was also criticized for its work for governments of countries implicated in human rights abuses, including Turkey, Indonesia, and China. It suffered severe decline in staff morale, client defections, and ultimately turnover of most of the people at the top of the company, including nearly every senior person involved with the CFK business.

Inside PR magazine, which published a yearly report card on major public relations firms, assessed the damage to Hill & Knowlton in its July/August 1992 issue:

> What was the greatest PR agency in the world has come to be regarded as a pariah by many prospective employees. Internally, morale is resurgent, but a reputation for petty politics and the controversies of the past two years make H&K in the '90s look about as attractive as Dow [Chemical] in the '70s … Crisis-plagued and battered in the media, new management faces an uphill battle.[69]

Hill & Knowlton's battering in the media served as a proxy for the public relations industry as a whole. Senior PR executives opined that employees of H&K had violated the PRSA *Code of Ethics*, but the PRSA was largely silent on the scandal, creating a vacuum of opinion and leaving the impression that H&K's behavior was acceptable and common PR practice. The PR profession was in crisis, but the industry association seemed paralyzed and either unable or unwilling to take a public stand on the scandal. The board of the PRSA met in New York in late January, but refused invitations to speak with the PR trade media.

> Hill & Knowlton's battering in the media served as a proxy for the public relations industry as a whole.

The controversy severely damaged the reputation of Hill & Knowlton, of the public relations industry, and of the Public Relations Society of America (PRSA), which remained paradoxically silent about the scandal while its members, the media, and critics were calling for it to take a stand on the controversy. Six months after the scandal broke, the chair of the association's "PR for PR Committee" called the PRSA its "own worst enemy."[70]

Six years after the CFK scandal the PRSA began a complete overhaul of its ethics process. The PRSA's new *Member Code of Ethics*, ratified by the society's membership in October 2000, specifically addresses front groups. Its provision on *The Free Flow of Information* says that a member shall "reveal the sponsors for causes and interests represented." Its *Examples of Improper Conduct Under This Provision* include a clause that specifically describes front groups purporting to represent one interest but secretly representing another interest.[71]

And today the PRSA has a mechanism for commenting on ethical issues, in the form of Practice Advisories, that provide standards on ethical issues in the news, and Practice Commentaries, that provide topical comment on ethical behavior.[72]

In the aftermath of the scandal PRSA saw defections from its own ranks, including coauthor Fred Garcia, who at the time was teaching a communication ethics workshop at New York University, and who resigned both from the PRSA and from a leadership position in the association's New York chapter because of the association's mishandling of the ethics issue and its failure to defend the profession.

Over the course of the mid-to-late 1990s Hill & Knowlton recovered, and is again a strong and respected firm. But it lost significant market share, momentum, and clout. And PRSA's multi-year self-assessment recast its *Member Code of Ethics* and became more active in defining and defending the profession.

HISTORICAL PERSPECTIVES ON COMMUNICATION ETHICS

The professional practice of public relations is not a twentieth-century invention. Neither are the ethical challenges facing it. Concern about the integrity of professional communication goes back much farther than 1923, when Edward L. Bernays was worried that people viewed it as some "vaguely defined evil, 'propaganda.'"[73]

> The professional practice of public relations is not a twentieth-century invention. Neither are the ethical challenges facing it.

In fact, professional communication emerged as a profession 2500 years ago. And it was criticized in much the same way that it is now: Those who practiced it were said to care little for the truth.

A careful review of the critique of classical public relations can be helpful in pointing the way to solving the problem of communication ethics in the twenty-first century.

> Professional communication emerged as a profession 2500 years ago.

The historical antecedents of professional communication may be found in fourth century BC Greece. While Plato never used the term "public relations," he had a deep awareness of the importance of crystallizing public opinion, and of the methods and proper uses of persuasion.

Unlike Aristotle, whose *Rhetoric* provides a theoretical construction of oral persuasion, Plato (c. 427 to 346 BC) did not articulate a discrete theory of persuasive communication. But his *Gorgias* provides a sharp criticism of the practice of professional communication in his day, and his *Republic* articulates the appropriate method for shaping public opinion.

Classical Rhetoric

Classical Greece was an oral society. While today most communication is done in print, on television, or on the Internet, in Greece most public discourse was spoken.

But like today, in classical Athens public opinion determined matters both large and small, from whether to build city walls to the appointment of generals to sentences at criminal trials. And also like today, there was a growing demand for expert help to shape public opinion. To meet that demand, a new class of professional persuaders, called rhetoricians, emerged. They called their craft "rhetoric," which Aristotle later defined as "the faculty of discovering the possible means of persuasion in reference to any subject whatever."[74]

> Like today, there was a growing demand for expert help to shape public opinion.

Aristotle differentiated this general persuasive nature of rhetoric from the specific natures of other pursuits:

> This is the function of no other of the arts, each of which is able to instruct and persuade in its own special subject; thus, medicine deals with health and sickness, geometry with the properties of magnitudes, arithmetic with number, and similarly with all the other arts or sciences. But Rhetoric, so to say, appears able to discover the means of persuasion in reference to any given subject.[75]

Rhetoric as a distinct practice emerged in the fifth century BC on the then-Greek island of Sicily. Citing a lost book of Aristotle, the Roman orator Cicero says that following a political upheaval, two enterprising Sicilians, Corax and Tisias, developed a method of instructing others how to argue persuasively, so as to recover property confiscated by the prior regime.[76] Corax, in addition to teaching clients how to argue persuasively and providing them with a set of rules for dealing with difficult questions, also wrote speeches for his clients to deliver in court, and was the author of the first handbook on rhetoric. His pupil Tisias, who also composed a handbook on rhetoric, later became tutor to the great Greek rhetoricians Gorgias, Isocrates, and Lysias.

Rhetoricians should not be confused with other distinguished Greeks who used persuasion as part of other pursuits. Statesmen such as Pericles were powerful speakers, but were primarily engaged in governing. Sophists such as Protagoras used techniques similar to those used by rhetoricians but claimed that their teaching instilled virtue in their pupils. Rhetoricians, on the other hand, were concerned neither with governing nor with instilling virtue. Rather, they provided communications services to those who paid for them. These services were remarkably similar to those offered by modern professional communicators. They included speechwriting, speaking on clients' behalf, and coaching clients how to argue their cases persuasively. This latter service included anticipating difficult questions and framing appropriate answers, similar to modern media training.

By Plato's day rhetoric as a distinct discipline was well established in Greece. The foremost rhetorician was Gorgias of Leontinium in Sicily, who is reputed to have lived 108 years (c. 483 to 375 BC). Gorgias' view of rhetoric differentiated it specifically from other persuasive pursuits such as governing and instilling virtue. Gorgias claimed that his only object was to foster persuasive skills on any subject whatever. Cicero, again citing a lost book of Aristotle, reports that Gorgias further encouraged speakers to exaggerate or extenuate, as the occasion might require.[77]

Plato's Critique

Plato wrote his *Gorgias* in about 387 BC and relates events said to have taken place when Gorgias was in his eighties and at the pinnacle of his influence, around 403 BC. The work, in dialogue form, pits the Platonic protagonist Socrates in argument with Gorgias and Gorgias' disciple Polus regarding the nature of rhetoric.

Socrates and Gorgias agree that, if it is anything, rhetoric is a form of persuasion. Gorgias defines it as

> the ability to persuade with speeches either the judges in the law courts or statesmen in the council-chamber of the commons in the Assembly or any audience at any other meeting that may be held on public affairs.[78]

He agrees with Socrates' further characterization:

> You say that Rhetoric is a producer of persuasion, and has therein its whole business and main consummation.[79]

Socrates begins his critique of rhetoric by securing Gorgias' acknowledgment of the difference between knowledge and belief. While knowledge can only be true, belief can be either true or false. Gorgias further agrees that rhetoric, as a persuasive medium, is not concerned with instilling knowledge:

Socrates: This rhetoric, it seems, is a producer of persuasion for belief, not for instruction in the matter of right and wrong.

Gorgias: Yes.

Socrates: And so the rhetorician's business is not to instruct a law court or other public meeting in matters of right and wrong, but only to make them believe.[80]

Gorgias asserts that the rhetorician will persuade the public on all matters, even when competing for public opinion against experts.

Socrates: Now, do you mean to make him carry conviction to the crowd on all subjects, not by teaching them, but by persuading?

Gorgias:	Certainly, I do.
Socrates:	You were saying just now, you know, that even in the matter of health the [rhetorician] will be more convincing than the doctor.
Gorgias:	Yes, indeed, I was—meaning, to the crowd.
Socrates:	And "to the crowd" means "to the ignorant"? For surely, to those who know, he will not be more convincing than the doctor.
Gorgias:	You are right.
Socrates:	And if he is to be more convincing than the doctor, he thus becomes more convincing than he who knows.
Gorgias:	Certainly.
Socrates:	But he who is not a doctor is surely without knowledge of that whereof the doctor has knowledge.
Gorgias:	Clearly.
Socrates:	So he who does not know will be more convincing to those who do not know than he who knows; supposing the [rhetorician] to be more convincing than the doctor. Is that, or something else, the consequence?
Gorgias:	In this case it does follow.
Socrates:	Then the case is the same in all the other arts for the [rhetorician] and his rhetoric: there is no need to know the truth of actual matters, but one merely needs to have discovered some device of persuasion which will make one appear to those who do not know to know better than those who know.[81]

Pressed by Gorgias and his disciple Polus to provide his own definition of the art of rhetoric, Socrates responds that it is not an art at all:

> It seems to me, then, Gorgias, to be a pursuit that is not a matter of art, but showing a shrewd gallant spirit which has a natural bent with dealing with mankind, and I sum up its existence in the name of flattery.[82]

Asked to elaborate further, Socrates identifies rhetoric as a semblance of a branch of the art of politics.[83] By semblance, he means an unreal image or counterfeit: It uses the same techniques, and vocabulary, and claims to be directed toward the same end.

Socrates elaborates on the nature of such a semblance by analogy. Consider, for example, the health of the body. Maintenance of health, which Socrates calls gymnastic, has a semblance, self-adornment. While gymnastic is concerned with maintaining a body's health, self-adornment is concerned with the appearance of health. Gymnastic strives for a body that is robust and functioning at its best. Self-adornment, on the other hand, strives for a body that appears healthy, without regard to whether it actually is healthy.

Similarly, medicine is concerned with the restoration of health in an ill body. The doctor prescribes the proper foods, herbs, and beverages to be ingested to restore health. The semblance of medicine is cookery, which provides foods, herbs, and beverages that are pleasing to the body without regard to whether they will help restore health. Socrates summarizes:

> Cookery is flattery disguised as medicine; and in just the same manner self-adornment personates gymnastic: with its rascally, deceitful, ignoble, and illiberal nature

it deceives men by forms and colors, polish and dress, so as to make them, in the effort of assuming an extraneous beauty, neglect the native sort that comes through gymnastic.[84]

Socrates asserts that rhetoric, as practiced by Gorgias and his followers, is a semblance of something else, which in this instance he calls justice. "As cookery is to medicine, so rhetoric is to justice."[85]

Socrates' specific objection to rhetoric, it must be noted, is that it is concerned merely with persuasion, without regard to whether those persuaded have received knowledge or merely belief, which may in turn be either true or false.

So, to state his objection more briefly, rhetoric is the semblance of justice because it is concerned with persuasion without regard to whether the beliefs it generates are true or false. We can construct the following matrix for justice (where T=True, F=False, B=Beneficial, H=Harmful).

Justice

T	F
B	H

Rhetoric, on the other hand, is concerned with what is beneficial to the persuader without regard to whether it is true or false. We can construct the following matrix for rhetoric:

Rhetoric

T *or* F
B	H

Notice that Plato's objection is *not* that rhetoric persuades by instilling beliefs that are *necessarily false*. In his analogy, cookery is perfectly capable of providing foods that could restore health; it is merely *unconcerned* with whether its foods restore health or not. Similarly, self-adornment is concerned with providing the body with the appearance of health, even when the body is already healthy. It is unconcerned with whether the body is or is not healthy.

> Plato's objection is not that rhetoric persuades by instilling beliefs that are necessarily false. The objectionable nature of Gorgias' rhetoric is its lack of concern whether its statements are true or false; it would be objectionable even if its statements turned out to be true.

The objectionable nature of Gorgias' rhetoric is its lack of concern whether its statements are true or false; it would be objectionable even if its statements turned out to be true.

Translating this into modern vocabulary, we can create a matrix that helps us understand the ethical use of professional communication: So a modern professional communicator can ground his or her professional judgment on the degree to which he or she promotes statements that are both true and beneficial to his or her client. As a general principle, a professional communicator does not promote statements that are harmful (with the possible exception of disclosure in the investment markets, which may require such communication). But an ethical communicator is concerned with whether his or her statement is true; an unethical communicator isn't necessarily one that deliberately promotes falsehoods, but someone who is unconcerned with whether a statement is true or false. We can construct a similar matrix to differentiate between ethical and unethical communication (where T=True, F=False, B=Beneficial, H=Harmful).

Ethical Communication

T	F
B	H

Ethical communication promotes statements that are both truthful and beneficial to a client.

Unethical Communication

T *or* F
B	H

Unethical communication is concerned with statements that are beneficial, without regard to whether those statements are true or false.

The ethical practice of professional communication is one where the professional communicator deliberately seeks to promote only true and beneficial statements, avoids false statements, and cares about the difference.

Unethical communication is concerned with statements that are beneficial, without regard to whether those statements are true or false. The ethical practice of professional communication is one where the professional communicator deliberately seeks to promote only true and beneficial statements, avoids false statements, and cares about the difference.

■ ■ ■

ETHICAL COMMUNICATION BEST PRACTICES

The ethical practice of public relations requires both a desire to behave ethically and an understanding of ethical issues in professional communication. Here are some of the best practices:

- Understand the letter and spirit of the various industry association codes of ethics, both for communication professionals and for the industries on whose behalf you communicate.

- Recognize that codes of ethics are valuable because they establish normative standards of behavior that become habitual through repetition.

- Understand the difference between ethics, morality, legality, etiquette, and aesthetics.

- Know where you draw the line. Ultimately you need to know what behaviors are acceptable to you and which are unacceptable. If you think this through in advance you'll be better able to navigate ethical challenges when they present themselves.

- Identify likely inadvertent violations of ethics codes before they happen, and call attention to them. Don't argue just on the basis of morality, but on the basis of practical business issues, including the likelihood that the unethical behavior will be discovered, and the negative consequences to the organization if this should be the case.

- When in doubt, seek counsel of more experienced practitioners.

RESOURCES FOR FURTHER STUDY

Council of Public Relations Firms

The Council of Public Relations Firms represents the business of public relations in the United States, and includes more than 100 public relations firms. The Council's members agree to abide by its *Code of Ethics* and *Statements of Principles*. Its overriding principles are that openness and transparency are not only in the public interest, but also necessary tools for meeting clients' objectives. Its Web site is http://www.prfirms.org/who/code.asp.

Ethics Resource Center

The Ethics Resource Center in Washington DC is the oldest not-for-profit association in the United States devoted to organizational ethics. The ERC conducts research, including an extensive National Business Ethics Survey, and publishes a free electronic newsletter, *Ethics Today Online*, http://www.ethics.org/resource/ethics-today.

The Center publishes a number of guides to ethical practice, including *Creating an Workable Company Code of Ethics: A Practical Guide to Identifying and Developing Organizational Standards*. The Center also sponsors character development and ethics courses for educational institutions and for corporate ethics officers. The Center advised the Public Relations Society of America in its overhaul of the PRSA *Member Code of Ethics*. The Ethics Resource Center can be found at http://www.ethics.org.

Global Business Standards Codex

This survey of business ethics standards around the world was conceived by several Harvard Business School scholars and described in detail in the *Harvard Business Review*. See Lynn Paine, Rohit Deshpandé, and Kim Eric Bettcher, "Up to Code: Does Your Company's Code of Conduct Meet World-Class Standards," *Harvard Business Review* (December 2005), p. 122. Reprints can be ordered at http://hbr.org.

International Association of Business Communicators (IABC)

IABC, based in San Francisco, has more than 13,000 members in more than sixty countries. It publishes guides to best practices, and offers professional development programs. The IABC can be found at http://www.iabc.com; its *Code of Ethics for Professional Communicators* can be found at http://www.iabc.com/about/code.htm.

International Public Relations Association (IPRA)

IPRA, based in Surrey, UK, is a membership organization of public relations professionals from nearly a hundred countries. IPRA has more than fifty years of experience in sharing and promoting professional development. IPRA has published several Codes and Charters seeking to provide an ethical framework for its members' professional activities. IPRA can be found at http://ipra.org.

Public Relations Society of America (PRSA)

The PRSA, based in New York City, is the world's largest organization of public relations professionals. It was founded in 1947 and as of 2010 had 21,000 members. The PRSA can be found at http://www.prsa.org; its *Member Code of Ethics* can be found at http://www.prsa.org/AboutPRSA/Ethics/CodeEnglish/index.html.

QUESTIONS FOR FURTHER DISCUSSION

1   What are the differences among morality, ethics, legality, aesthetics, and etiquette as they relate to any particular practice of public relations and corporate communication?

2   Codes of ethics are normative standards of behavior, and as such can be used by individuals or organizations who are not members of the organization that drafts the code. What are some of the other advantages of codes of ethics as normative standards of conduct?

3   Are print and video news releases, by their very nature, unethical? Why or why not?

4   How can a professional communicator resolve conflicting duties? For example, if asked a factual question by a reporter about a sensitive issue, the duty to keep confidences and the duty to be truthful may conflict. What are some of the ways to resolve the apparent conflict?

5   Is there a meaningful difference between public relations and propaganda?

That we teach others how to treat us is as true in press relations as anywhere else.

3 MEDIA RELATIONS

■ ■ ■

In the spring of 1998, an administrative assistant in Merck's Corporate Communications Department tried to fax an eighteen-page, confidential internal memorandum on the planned restructuring of the company's relationship with Astra, the Swedish pharmaceutical firm, to an outside investment banker counseling Merck. The machine jammed and she pushed what she thought was the "redial" button, but inadvertently sent the fax to the *Star Ledger*, New Jersey's largest newspaper. To her credit, she told her boss, John Doorley, immediately, and John knew he had to contact his boss, Ken Frazier, senior vice president and general counsel.

The restructuring of the joint venture that marketed Prilosec for the prevention and treatment of gastroesophageal reflux disease (GERD) was weeks from culmination, and premature disclosure would pose countless communication and regulatory problems, as well as trust issues with Astra. Ken agreed that John would contact Iris Taylor, a reporter at the *Ledger* with whom he had a long-standing, trusting relationship. Ms. Taylor retrieved the fax and returned it to John as requested, promising she would not read it. Although the eighteen pages were coded for confidentiality, a business reporter covering the pharmaceutical industry would have been able to unravel it. The deal, valued at over $3 billion when it was announced weeks later, could have collapsed.[1] It was saved because the Communication Group and other people at Merck, including two CEOs, had invested much time and effort over many years in building a good reputation with that reporter. The relationship meant more to her—and she believed to her newspaper—than an ill-gotten scoop. The company's investment in the relationship, often intangible and hard to quantify, paid off handsomely that day.

■ ■ ■

What each constituency believes and feels about an organization contributes to its reputation. But there is one group that influences every other constituency that matters to a company, a group that can affect the company's reputation quickly and profoundly: the news media.

Media relations is one of the core disciplines in public relations and corporate and organizational communication, and it is often one of the most visible. But it is also one of the most difficult for senior management to understand.

■ ■ ■

THE CASE FOR A CENTRALIZED MEDIA RELATIONS FUNCTION

Media relations consists of all the ways an organization interacts with the news media. These include the ability to build long-term relationships with reporters whose area of responsibility, often called a "beat," includes covering the organization every day. Media relations also includes managing ad hoc contact with reporters who may be calling the company for the first and only time in their careers. Media relations also includes the processes of seeking media coverage and of responding to reporters' requests for interviews or information. And it includes developing procedures to measure, monitor and manage the contact between an organization's employees and reporters. In major organizations including most large companies, the media relations function has major responsibility for social media.

It is neither intuitive nor self-evident that an organization must have a strict policy governing which people can communicate with the media.

An organization should not communicate through the news media until it knows what the facts are, and then only when the organization is prepared to disclose those facts. And it needs to communicate with a single voice.

But to the outside world, it is neither intuitive nor self-evident that an organization must have a strict policy governing which people can communicate with the media about the organization, its activities, products, policies, and positions. Why should the researcher who conducted the breakthrough research for the organization not take the call from the reporter who is inquiring about that research? Why should the chief financial officer or senior accountant not take a phone call about the company's latest sales and earnings press release? Why should any employee not be permitted to express his or her opinion on what is happening at the company?

Outsiders, especially young journalists and young employees (sometimes even including those in the communication department), tend to sense a conflict between forthright communication and managed communication, and they tend to believe that "open and forthright" means "tell everyone everything right away." Yet such a strategy would be irresponsible—in fact, anarchic. And in light of securities regulations, it could also present a company with legal liability and regulatory problems.

To an organization's constituencies, anyone from the organization who speaks about the organization is often seen to be speaking for the organization. But different people speak from different perspectives, using different vocabulary, and based on different levels of knowledge about an issue. The result can be confusion, inaccurate communication, and reputational harm.

When speaking with reporters, it is even more important for communication to be centralized. Reporters, especially when covering breaking news, are often less interested in understanding a complex issue than in harvesting quotes to bring a story to life. The way reporters use quotes is different from the way most constituencies use the information they receive. Speaking with a reporter without knowing how one's words are likely to be used can lead to what are often seen by the person quoted to be misquotes. But in our experience, most instances of a "misquote" are really accurate quotes based on people speaking imprecisely, with limited knowledge, or with little understanding that only one or two sentences—out of dozens or hundreds spoken—would be quoted. Good organizational practice dictates that only people who have been trained to speak effectively with reporters be authorized to do so.

One of the best examples of the consequences of uncoordinated press communication remains, three decades later, the nuclear accident at Three Mile Island. The accident that occurred there on March 28, 1979, was the country's first nuclear accident, and it provoked a torrent of press inquiries.[2] Within minutes, local journalists, including wire service reporters, were on the scene. They interviewed several employees of the Metropolitan Edison utility company who were not fully informed, were not communicating with each other, and were unfamiliar with the utility's plan for corrective action. As a result, the various employees related inconsistent information about what had happened and about what was being done in response. The result was confusion, fear, and the sense that the utility did not know what it was doing. The press coverage, which would have been negative in any case, was made much worse by the perception that the utility was unprepared for such a situation, and that the public was at greater risk than it actually was. What had begun as a manageable situation was turned into a communication disaster by the utility itself, acting in unwitting concert with local journalists, who in many cases had little understanding of science or science writing.

Even when reporters know a company or industry well, it is still important to limit their access to information and people in a company. For example, we have been struck over the years by how individual pharmaceutical researchers viewed the promise of a particular research project differently. If ten scientists were working on a new medicine, seven might think it held little promise, two might be cautiously optimistic, and one might think it was the next penicillin. Allowing reporters random access to any or all of the researchers would present a confusing picture of the therapeutic potential of a given medicine. While robust internal debate can be a good thing, the tendency of the media to oversimplify would lead such a story to be cast as confusion, disagreement, or internal strife, rather than the natural give-and-take of a scientific enterprise.

Unrestricted communication to the news media can cause more than just confusion. It can be irresponsible, and sometimes even illegal. For example, it would be both irresponsible and potentially a violation of securities laws and regulations for an executive prematurely to reveal to a reporter that the company is in negotiations on a potential merger. The very coverage of a merger negotiation would have an adverse impact on the negotiation itself, often limiting the flexibility of one side or the other. Similarly, the securities market's reaction to the news may affect the price of the various companies' stocks as investors buy or sell stock on the news, potentially affecting the economics of the merger. And the news would give competitors, and other potential merger partners, a heads up on what the organization was planning, often triggering reactions on the part of competitors, including a possible bidding war for the company that may be acquired. So premature disclosure could result in the derailment of a merger that appeared to be headed to a successful conclusion. Just as significantly, merger discussions and other material information are subject to strict disclosure rules, and premature or selective disclosure of such negotiations could subject the company or individuals to civil or criminal liability.

Enlightened organizations establish clear guidelines on who can speak to reporters on what topics, maintain press logs for tracking who has spoken to whom, on what topics, what was said, what follow-up is required, and when a story is likely to appear.

ORGANIZING THE MEDIA RELATIONS FUNCTION

Media relations typically resides within a corporate communication function, but it can also reside in other corporate structures, including:

* Marketing
* Product divisions
* Regional offices
* Operating companies
* Investor relations (in the case of the financial media)

In large companies, there is often a breakdown of responsibility, with different people responsible for different kinds of media relations, including:

* Corporate media relations, for articles about the corporation as a whole, including governance issues, industry trends, senior leadership, sales and earnings, and issues affecting the entire corporation.
* Product media relations, sometimes residing with a single person, sometimes with a different person responsible for each product category. These individuals focus on inquiries about, or stories featuring, individual products. These can include the general interest consumer media (newspapers, magazines, television, electronic), or can include industry trade publications.
* Marketing public relations, focusing on initiating coverage of the company, its products, issues, and people. This function often is responsible for creating special events, promotional campaigns, and other opportunities to affirmatively show the company in a positive light.
* Financial media relations, usually coordinated carefully with the investor relations function, responsible for distributing news of interest to the investment community, and in fulfillment of a company's securities law disclosure requirements.
* Operating company/Regional media relations, often a distinct function in each geographic region or company, and often reporting to the management of the region, or the operating company, with a dotted-line reporting responsibility to corporate media relations.

There are many other configurations of the media relations function. The most effective functions are those that fit the strategic and operational needs of their organizations. But to succeed, the function must be well coordinated, regardless of the structure or reporting responsibilities. Many companies manage the coordination by having well-defined policies for who is responsible for which relationships with which kinds of media; who is responsible for handling inquiries on which topics, and the like. They also have frequent, often weekly conference calls with all media relations staff to assure up-to-date understanding of pending stories and developments, and to share insights, resources, or information.

Most companies also have clear policies directing all other employees to refer any press inquiries, on any topic, to certain people in the media relations department.

MEDIA RELATIONS AS A LIGHTNING ROD

Reporters who cover a company or industry speak constantly with industry observers, participants, critics, and supporters. They sometimes develop insights that are even deeper than a company's management may have at any given time. They can serve as an early warning system of trouble ahead. And they are often seen within a company to have an anticompany agenda or bias, even when that is not true.

Journalists will often know about problems in an organization early on. It is important that communicators feel free to pass along to senior management negative comments and questions without fear that management will want to "kill the messenger." And it is important for senior leadership to see these negative comments or questions as possible precursors of trouble ahead, not with the individual reporters but with the business performance or practices in question. In other words, communicators need beware of the Pushmi-Pullyu Syndrome (Chapter 1).

> It is important that communicators feel free to pass along to senior management negative comments and questions without fear that management will want to "kill the messenger."

For example, several years before the accounting scandals about American business broke onto the front pages, several journalists openly questioned the accounting methodologies and inherent conflicts of interests that would bring down major companies in 2002. Similarly, many journalists questioned the independence of Wall Street research for several years before then-New York State Attorney General Elliot Spitzer and the Securities and Exchange Commission forced major Wall Street firms into a financial settlement and structural changes to assure that analysts' opinions are in fact independent of the investment banking agendas of their employers.

At least one thing is certain from the communication post mortem of these business crises: Not enough corporate and organizational communicators listened early on, and few raised their voices internally against negative practices that were clearly wrong and often indefensible.

THE FOUR ACADEMIC MODELS OF PUBLIC RELATIONS

In the seminal public relations text, *Managing Public Relations*, James Grunig and Todd Hunt identified four models that generally guide the communication philosophy of practitioners.[3] We believe it can be helpful for public relations practitioners to examine their own communication philosophies to try to determine which model they generally follow. Although it can be helpful to look at these models in terms of communicating with various constituencies, the models can be especially helpful with media relations. The following definitions of the models, which have stood the test of time, are Grunig's and Hunt's; the commentaries are by Doorley and Garcia.

1   **Press Agent/Publicity Model**. The guiding principle here is to get favorable publicity—not to try to ensure accuracy and truthful reporting. <u>Commentary</u>: This model can place the goals of accuracy and truth in second place to publicity. While this model can produce good results for the client organization, at least over the short term, it can be bad for the various constituencies (for example, the media, customers, employees, and the community). The term "spinning," which came into vogue twenty years after this model was defined, is just another label for it. This is the approach that gives public relations a bad reputation.

2   **Public Information Model**. The focus here is on the communication of objective information, generally without regard to the self-interests of the organization or client for whom the PR person works. <u>Commentary</u>: In theory, the constituency wins. The client organization, often a government agency or nonprofit, can also win. But we would argue that public relations practitioners have a responsibility to advocate for the client, not just to disseminate information. And if the advocacy is up front—that's why organizations have letterhead!—then the advocacy is transparent and ethical.

3   **Two-Way Asymmetric Model**. The PR practitioner conducts research to determine the views of a particular constituency and then uses that information to help achieve the client's objectives. <u>Commentary</u>: The client organization can win, at least over the short term. But the constituency probably loses, and we would argue that this is a myopic and sometimes unethical approach.

4   **Two-Way Symmetric Model.** The PR practitioner conducts research to determine the views of a particular constituency and then uses that information to help achieve the objectives of both the client organization and the constituency. <u>Commentary</u>: This is the approach that will most often produce a win-win outcome. It can be useful in conflict resolution and in any public relations program. It can help address ethical questions, including that of advocacy versus objectivity, by looking at the interests of both the client organization and its constituencies.

■■■

MODERATING EXPECTATIONS

When a story turns out well for the organization, the people interviewed are seen to have done a good job, and they might pass along a brief compliment to the media relations person. If the editors are pleased with the news report, the journalist might thank the media relations person as well.

On the other hand, if the news report turns out badly for the organization, the media relations person will usually take at least a small hit, regardless of how the report arose or the accuracy of it. If the journalist's editors are unhappy with the report, the journalist is generally unhappy with the media relations person because of, for example, inadequate access.

> If the news report turns out badly for the organization, the media relations person will usually take at least a small hit.

To be effective, the media relations professional needs a supportive boss. If he or she does not have a superior who will absorb at least some of the criticism for the bad news reports and take only some of the credit for the good ones, the media relations person might be able to survive for a while. But he or she cannot do the job well over the long term. It is impossible. Polish the resumé. It is time to leave.

The good news is that most heads of public affairs (or whatever function media relations reports into) have the honesty and courage required to support their people. Fortunately for us—John Doorley over the years at Roche and Merck, and coauthor Fred Garcia at two corporations and a number of firms—most of our bosses fell into that category.

One challenge, an occupational hazard, is the tendency of some executives to assume that the media relations professional is an advocate for the news media. Sometimes this is framed as "being on the reporter's side"; sometimes as having "gone native" and caring more about maintaining relationships with reporters than protecting an organization's reputation. Most of the time such criticism misses the mark. The best media relations people are advocates in two directions: they need to clarify and focus the organization's viewpoint for reporters. But they also need to help management better understand what a reporter is up to and whether and why it is in the company's interests to engage with the reporter.

Nevertheless, it is extremely important that the media relations person take substantial responsibility for the news that appears. We have known press relations people who would say, "I don't write the news reports, you know." Our answer to them, assuming they were actively involved in cooperating with the journalist, was: If the article had turned out well, would you be saying the same thing?

One key to effectiveness in media relations is to manage the expectations that company executives have both inflated expectations about positive news or the ability to avoid bad news and negative expectations about a crisis. And it is usually best to put it in writing.

THE JOURNALIST AND THE SPOKESPERSON

In many ways reporters and company spokespeople are similar. They go to many of the same events and conferences, and share interviews with the same important people. They often have similar academic and professional backgrounds—in fact, many media relations professionals began their careers in journalism. Both address (talk or write about) the same subject matter. But their jobs are different. The journalist's job is to write stories that his readers or viewers want to read or watch. The media relations professional's job is to manage the company's engagement with the journalist in ways that ultimately benefit the company, or are, at minimum, fair. The two jobs are not mutually exclusive. In fact, each depends on the other for success. But the jobs are not the same.

So media relations people should try to build good working relationships with journalists, meaning that each party tries to understand and respect the perspective of the other. It means treating each other with dignity and honesty. It means that the media relations person needs to respect the timetable that reporters work under. But it does not mean that the timetable should be the sole driver of a company's response to an inquiry. It means that a spokesperson should deal forthrightly with the journalist, even when they disagree. But it does not mean acquiescing to every request or withholding criticism when it is deserved. And it sometimes means giving the other party the benefit of the doubt, as in the story about the misdirected fax that began this chapter.

Most importantly, building good relationships does not mean that the spokesperson and reporter should conspire with each other as if they were partners in a common enterprise. Often media relations people confuse good working relationships with friendships. While such relationships have much in common with friendships, they are not the same. In fact, friendships can complicate things, mostly by letting down the guard that is often necessary to prevent one party from taking undue advantage of the other.

> Often media relations people confuse good working relationships with friendships.

So journalists and media relations people work on the same projects, but often with completely different perspectives. Journalists are sometimes skeptical and they often see media relations people as impediments. Media relations people sometimes fear the journalist's penchant for bad news or oversimplification. The secret of good media relations is to find the common goal and work toward it together: a timely, fair news report or feature that accomplishes what the reporter wants—a story people are interested in—and that also accomplishes what the spokesperson wants—a story that is fair, and more favorable or less negative than it would have been without his involvement.

FEAR OF THE PRESS

We believe that many media relations people are not very good at their jobs, and that this is so because many of them are afraid of journalists. "Now, please don't quote me on that," is the constant refrain. It's much like a salesperson ending a call with: "Now please don't buy any." Is not the spokesperson who is afraid to speak an oxymoron?

> Is not the spokesperson who is afraid to speak an oxymoron?

Especially in large organizations, there is a danger that media relations people become mere order-takers, responding to press inquiries and helping provide journalists with information, but not necessarily working to change a journalist's perceptions of the organization. And especially in a large organization that receives many press calls daily, there is a tendency for media relations people to see their job as fielding inquiries—catching, rather than initiating coverage, pitching. Sometimes this is for a good reason: because the volume of incoming calls is so high. But sometimes it is inertia or even fear that suppresses a media relations person's appetite for initiating discussions with reporters.

One reason fear develops in media relations people is the constant scrutiny and criticism within an organization of what is stated and not stated in press reports. Senior officials in organizations often react out of all proportion to the slightest problem in a news report. A mistake by the spokesperson is out there for the world to read, see or hear—colleagues, bosses, CEOs, family, friends, and neighbors. The spokesperson begins to doubt his or her ability to synthesize and express a view on behalf of the organization.

Yet the spokesperson is paid to convey certain facts and points of view. While there are times when one should speak "for background," or even "off the record," or indeed not at all, constant pleas for the journalist not to print or broadcast certain information give the journalist another reason to want to ignore the media relations person. After all, the journalist usually wants to speak with someone else in the organization anyway.

Often media relations people are afraid of the media because they are intimidated by the prestige of the institution. For a twenty-five-year-old, or even a forty-year-old, a call from a senior reporter at *The New York Times*, or from a producer at CBS's *60 Minutes* can cause panic or worse. When the stakes are so high, it is easy for media relations people, especially those who are not particularly confident in their own abilities or their stature in their organization, to worry that their own words may come back to haunt them.

Some journalists, especially those with the news organizations that specialize in sensationalist stories, play "Gotcha journalism," hovering over the interview subject like jackals. We have witnessed instances where executives have said something they did not mean to say—statements the journalists knew to be inaccurate and unintended—and the journalists used the misstatements because they buttressed the story angle. And a small number of journalists, like some people in other professions, are simply bad people who will cheat and lie, and they do that by deliberately misquoting someone, and sometimes by inventing quotes or stories outright. We suspect that journalists who have no qualms about such matters are cynics who believe that the people they interview (the rest of the world) are duplicitous and untrustworthy, and that the journalist's dishonesty is therefore necessary to get the truth out to the public.

> Nevertheless, in more than a combined forty years of press relations work with thousands of journalists, we have seen only very few examples of what we perceive to be blatant unfairness.

Nevertheless, in more than a combined forty years of press relations work with thousands of journalists, we have seen only very few examples of what we perceive to be blatant unfairness.

One was on July 29, 1994, when a journalist for *The New York Times*, Gina Kolata, took remarks from an interview John had given her four months earlier on a completely different subject and put it in a page-one article about the possible conflict of interest that Medco, a pharmacy benefits management organization recently acquired by Merck, would henceforth face in handling prescriptions for patients.[4] The powerful last paragraph of the article had the reporter writing: "Mr. Doorley of Merck said critics have to consider the drug industry's point of view. Something has to be done to restore profits." The remarks were not printed as a direct quote but they appeared to have been written to produce that effect. John Doorley had made such remarks—at least remarks to that effect—in an entirely different context, but, when used in the July 29 article, they buttressed the conflict-of-interest theme and made Merck look like it put profits before patients. John and Merck appeared callous and greedy.

The New York Times refused to publish John's letter to the editor, even though he spoke with editors there and explained what had happened. He received a letter, dated August 17, from news editor William Borders: "As to the quotation from you with which the article ended, you don't seem to dispute that you said what she (Kolata) said you said, only the context. I am afraid I cannot agree. There is nothing wrong with using in July a quotation from an interview four months earlier, so long as the context is fair, and in this case I think it is. You were talking about the need for Merck to be more profitable, and certainly the Medco arrangement moves toward that goal."[5]

John subsequently realized that this newspaper would seldom publish letters critical of its journalism (unlike National Public Radio, for example, which broadcasts critical comments every week). In late 2003 *The New York Times* appointed a public editor as one of the mechanisms for assuring high-quality journalism in the wake of a scandal where a reporter (see Jayson Blair, Chapter 1) had been inventing stories. Under pressure from the public editor, *The Times* changed its letters policy, and now sometimes discusses lapses in journalistic standards in its expanded corrections column.

A second incident of journalistic unfairness involved John's colleague, Sharyn Bearse. On October 24, 1995, a reporter for the *Star Ledger*, New Jersey's largest newspaper, phoned Sharyn and asked if it was true that Merck had committed infractions against the Cuban embargo when some of the company's midlevel executives had visited Cuba about a year earlier. Sharyn answered that the Merck employees who visited Cuba did so at the request of the Pan American Health Organization and that they had not violated the embargo. The reporter's call had come out of the blue, precipitated by a surprise Clinton administration press release about Merck's embargo infractions, something the administration officials had said they would not do. But Castro was visiting the United Nations in New York City, and apparently someone in the administration could not pass up an opportunity to criticize "Big Pharma." After Sharyn spoke with the reporter, she and John contacted Merck attorneys who explained that, technically, the Merck employees had violated the embargo—a distinction John and Sharyn had not understood—by having certain chemicals tested at a Cuban laboratory under a routine agreement that nevertheless constituted a contract and was therefore a violation of the embargo.

Sharyn and John agreed she would phone the reporter—it was the Communication Department's policy to correct misstatements and to do so as soon as possible—and tell him that what she had said earlier was not technically correct, and that she would like to amend her statement. The reporter, instead of simply changing Sharyn's statement as most would do, constructed a narrative that made Sharyn look as if she had been duplicitous, rather than simply mistaken. The scenario in the next day's page-one article, headlined "Merck Pays $127,500 in Fines for Cuba Deal," implied that Merck had business plans for Cuba.[6] Lost in the story was the fact that any such business in Cuba would have amounted to a minuscule percentage of Merck's 1995 annual sales of $16.8 billion. But the reporter wove a captivating tale.[7]

However, such journalism is not a reason to be afraid of the press, because it is the exception, not the rule. The press relations person has to begin a relationship with a journalist presuming trustworthiness, just as one should begin other relationships in life that way, both because trusting relationships are more productive and for the sake of one's own sanity and soul. If a particular journalist is untrustworthy or unethical, it will become clear soon enough.

A degree of anxiety can increase performance. It is reasonable and good to be anxious when dealing with journalists because they are human and make mistakes. They sometimes misunderstand what is said or they mistranscribe quotes. And today, in the ever-faster-paced media world, there are more and more opportunities for mistakes.

Another reason for having a healthy degree of anxiety about the press is that every journalist brings a perspective to an assignment. Some are better than others at being objective, but no one can wipe clean the slate of life's experiences, opinions, predilections, and prejudices. A big part of the media relations person's job is to figure out what the journalist's perspective is. If the perspective is favorable and accurate, reinforce it. If it is unfavorable, try to understand why, and then deal with the problems and issues.

Still another reason for healthy anxiety is one's own inadequacies as a spokesperson. How many people can talk with absolute precision for, say, an entire hour? Can one swear, at the end of the interview, that he or she said "appraise" rather than "apprise" or, "Yes, I disagree" rather than, "No, I don't disagree"?

Spokespeople say things ranging from insensitive to inappropriate to dumb. We all do so in our personal discourse, out of carelessness, naiveté or ignorance, sometimes even offending the very people we care most about. Media relations people can say things that are inaccurate or reveal information that should not be revealed. One of the biggest fears of public relations professionals in technology-based companies should be that they might

> Spokespeople say things ranging from insensitive to inappropriate to dumb.

unwittingly reveal something proprietary. The rule most companies follow is: if the information has been presented before a scientific forum published in a scientific journal, it is considered public. But of course few rules are that simple. Sometimes, for example, scientists present information at a sidebar session (a "poster" session) and not in front of the entire conference. Sometimes, a scientist overstates or understates a scientific development and that might not be easily apparent from the transcript.

Similarly, public relations people who work in the financial industry must be acutely aware that everything they say is subject to securities laws and regulations, and has the potential to move markets. Fear of civil and criminal liability has a tendency to focus one's mind, and to make one default to precision or to silence.

THE PRESS' RIGHT TO KNOW

If a journalist does not ask a question in precisely the right words, yet the spokesperson knows what information the journalist is seeking, does the spokesperson have an obligation to give the desired information?

For example, a journalist phones the spokesperson for the publicly owned ABC Company and says: "I understand that Ms. X (a senior officer in the organization) has resigned." The fact is that, as the spokesperson knows, Ms. X will formally resign the next day, but has not done so yet. So the spokesperson answers: "No, that is not true." The journalist failed to phrase the question precisely or broadly enough, and the spokesperson took advantage of that. "Gotcha journalism" in reverse, one might say.

Did this spokesperson handle the matter well? The answer is that it depends on the circumstances. If Ms. X is in line to succeed the CEO, the resignation announcement could be considered "material," meaning that a shareholder or prospective shareholder might buy or sell stock on that information. The spokesperson could not prematurely acknowledge the resignation to that one journalist, because that would constitute selective disclosure and possibly violate securities laws or regulations. Similarly, securities laws prohibit statements that are "materially misleading." Saying, "It's not true that Ms. X has resigned," while technically true when spoken, may no longer be true when the newspaper is published. Such a statement could be seen to be materially misleading. A safer approach would be to avoid commenting on the resignation at all. The story about the resignation would still appear, but without the company's comment, one way or the other.

Such considerations apply when journalists raise questions about rumored business development activities. If a journalist asks: "I understand that you have acquired XYZ company," and the spokesperson knows that the acquisition agreement, while expected soon, has not yet been reached, the spokesperson can answer "No." A better answer might be: "As a matter of policy, ABC company does not comment on rumors about our business (or organization)." This is a particularly effective response if used consistently. The spokesperson can explain to journalists (as well as securities analysts and others who inquire) the reason for the policy: to deny certain rumors but not others is implicitly to confirm the others. Of course when rumors rise to the level where they have a

To deny certain rumors but not others is implicitly to confirm the others.

significant (for example, "material") effect on the organization, a denial or confirmation may have to be issued before the organization would otherwise plan to do so. But that should be a rare exception. Armed with a no-comment-on-rumors policy, the spokesperson need not even make the internal inquiries to determine the truth about the rumor. In fact, he or she should not delay in giving the response: "As a matter of policy, ABC does not comment on rumors."

While the press arguably has the right to ask any question, the press does not have the right to know everything. Reporters often assert that they are proxies for the public at large, and that "the public has a right to know." They often assume that such an argument is persuasive, and in fact sometimes inexperienced media relations people fall into the trap of assuming that the public has some such right. In fact, the public does not have a right to know everything reporters might choose to write about. While companies have disclosure obligations, those obligations are very clearly specified in securities regulations, as is the timing and manner of such disclosure. But there is a big difference between a company's duty to disclose certain kinds of information in a certain manner, and the public's or press' right to know whatever it wants to know.

The press does not have a right to know proprietary information; personal information; information that is not fully developed; or information that might threaten security.

Proprietary Information

Inventions must be patent protected before they can be discussed outside the organization. The trade secret is another valid way of keeping information confidential until the appropriate time for disclosure. If a journalist asks a question about a proprietary matter, it is perfectly acceptable to say, "The matter is proprietary, and we don't discuss proprietary information." The reporter does not have a right to know trade secrets or other appropriately confidential information.

Personal Information

Individuals have the right to protect information that is truly personal and none of the public's business. So, also, do individuals within organizations have the right to protect their personal information. Publicly traded organizations have a duty to disclose some private information about a small number of their senior-most executives (usually, their salary, bonus, and stock holdings). But for most employees their compensation, personnel files, and other work-related personal matters are not public, and should be protected.

When Fred was a spokesperson at a major investment bank in the 1980s, Wall Street compensation was a hot topic, and Fred would frequently be asked about particular executives' compensation. As a matter of policy the bank did not disclose compensation information except for the small number of executives required by law. Fred would often say something like, "As a matter of policy we don't comment on executive compensation." Often reporters would persist, asking to confirm ranges: "Does he make more than $10 million? Does he make less than $20 million?" Fred's reply would persistently be, "That's a question about compensation and we don't comment on employee compensation." With one *Wall Street Journal* reporter, Fred and the reporter had this type of exchange for every salary level from $1 million to $20 million, always with the same response, over a period of a half hour. The reporter later told Fred, "You can't blame me for trying to get you to crack. And besides, I had to be able to tell my editor that I had grilled you on every salary level." The interaction was a kind of dance, with each party knowing precisely what the other would do, but duty-bound to do the dance anyway.

> The interaction was a kind of dance, with each party knowing precisely what the other would do.

Information that Is Not Fully Developed

Even "sure things" fall apart. The train may be moving smoothly along the tracks, but even the conductor does not know with certainty what may be lurking in the tunnel or around the corner. In any case, spokespeople should never acknowledge anything before the organization agrees to the timing. The reasons range from illegality (for example, selective disclosure) to certain unemployment for the spokesperson. And sometimes the premature disclosure of a pending event may prevent the event from happening at all.

Preparation can prevent such problems. If something new is brewing in an organization, the communications people should be brought in early so that the best response can be prepared for the announcement day, and another for the interim period.

Some situations are so difficult that a "no-comment" response or a euphemism is called for. The phrase "no comment" has become, through movies and television programs, a caricature of evasion. And the phrase itself is awkward. Because of the baggage the phrase carries, it can cast a negative impression with both the reporter and with those who read, view, or listen to the story. But there are ample ways of avoiding comment without using that two-word phrase. Among the possibilities are:

* "We don't discuss financial projections."
* "As a matter of policy we don't comment on (rumors/employee matters/investigations, etc.)."
* "It is proprietary."
* "We cannot reveal the identities of the victims until next of kin have been notified."

Even a "no comment" is always better than a lie. The U.S. Supreme Court has ruled that "no-comment statements" are the functional equivalent of silence. But it also ruled that denying a rumor that happened to be true was the functional equivalent of a lie, and held the offending company liable for the lie.

So as a rule, some form of "no-comment" statement, however phrased, is the less bad alternative between inappropriate disclosure of private information and lying.

Some form of no-comment statement is preferable to "was not available for comment," since a big part of the spokesperson's job is to be available.

"Let me check and get back to you" can be a useful response when the spokesperson is caught off guard or unaware. The problem with this response is that the spokesperson has to get back to the journalist, who will expect some enlightenment after an hour or two of grace. It is far better to be prepared with an immediate response.

If the journalist and the spokesperson have a good relationship, the spokesperson will often have to work hard to see that confidentiality concerns do not damage their relationship. For example, if a journalist is hot on the trail of breaking news for three days, and the spokesperson cannot reveal anything until the fourth day, the spokesperson might gain the necessary internal approvals to tell that journalist first on the fourth day or to give him or her a special interview opportunity at the right time.

Security Concerns

Spokespeople have a profound obligation—especially in this day and age—to protect the security of the organization and its people. Yet anecdotal research suggests that most corporations do not train their communication people to guard against lapses that could pose a security threat.

THE PRESS' PENCHANT FOR BAD NEWS

"Does the press have a penchant for bad news?" is a question much like the ones we used to ask as kids about the Pope being Catholic, and the bear doing something in the woods. The answer is yes, and nobody can credibly take another position. "If it bleeds, it leads," is the mantra of local television news directors.

Journalists can argue that their behavior reflects society's desires and the discussion can become arcane, but the answer is still yes—there is a penchant for negative news. Realizing that is important for two reasons:

First, if there is bad news brewing in your organization, the press will probably find out about it and report it, so why not generally address the matter up front? When patents are about to expire on a major product in a technology-based company, for example, the business press covers the matter early and thoroughly. The best way for a company to deal with this is to understand that patent expirations are important and legitimate stories, and be ready with the best answers to such questions as "What will happen to the company's profitability?" Similarly, management turmoil, weak sales, and other negative information will often find its way to reporters before the company is fully ready to discuss it.

Second, the penchant for bad news interferes with coverage of good news, if only because the newshole (that is, the total amount of space in any given print or broadcast story minus the space or time for advertisements) is only so big. The 1988 story of Merck's introduction and donation of Mectizan to prevent and treat river blindness in millions of people is literally one of the greatest stories in history. Yet it proved extremely difficult over the years to get coverage of the story (with some notable exceptions such as the cover story in *The New York Times Magazine* of January 8, 1989).[8]

Journalists would often say that people in the West are not interested in stories about people afflicted with river blindness who live mainly in developing countries in Africa. Yet all one has to do is note how prominent the coverage is of the bad news out of Africa about AIDS, wars, famines, and other horrors. Would not one think that the media would rush to cover the story of a pill (taken just once a year) that prevents or treats a parasitic disease that ravages entire populations, with blindness being only one of the symptoms? As if that were not enough to ensure coverage, the company that discovered and developed the medicine has committed to continuing to donate it to the millions of people who need it for as long as necessary.

After the 1974 resignation of President Richard M. Nixon in the wake of the Watergate scandal, there was an influx of young people into journalism. They were following the example of Carl Bernstein and Bob Woodward, whose dogged pursuit of a "third-rate burglary" resulted in the downfall of the most powerful person in the free world. Romanticized by the movie *All The President's Men*, journalism was seen as a vital mechanism for democratic accountability.

But the thrill of the chase often became the foremost concern of some journalists. In the late 1980s, Fred had lunch with the newly appointed reporter in charge of the investment banking beat at the *Wall Street Journal*. It was a time of turmoil in investment banking, punctuated by insider-trading scandals that served as the basis for the popular movie *Wall Street* with Charlie Sheen. The *Wall Street Journal* had recently won a Pulitzer Prize for its coverage of the scandals. The once-powerful firm Drexel Burnham Lambert ceased to exist, and its charismatic head of junk bonds, Mike Milken, was on his way to jail. During the lunch Fred innocently asked the reporter what his goal was in covering the industry. In all seriousness the reporter said, "My goal is to bring down a major investment bank before I'm thirty." Fred thought the reporter was joking, and asked him, "No, really, what's your goal for your beat?" The reporter, with a straight face, replied, "No, really. That's my goal." After several seconds of awkward silence, Fred asked, "Well, how old are you?" The reporter was twenty-eight, which gave him two years to accomplish his goal.

Sure enough, the reporter wrote story after story that proved to be both very damaging and untrue. Numerous attempts to change his behavior proved unsuccessful. After a while, the only course left was for the chairman of the bank to send a forceful letter to the publisher of the *Wall Street Journal*, describing in great detail the various violations of the *Journal*'s own standards in the reporter's coverage. It worked. The reporter turned his attention to other firms.

While, in the aftermath of Watergate, journalism came to be seen as investigative, over the last three decades—and particularly with the advent of all-news-all-the-time cable news coverage—journalism has morphed into a kind of entertainment medium, with production values and story lines similar to the dramatic features offered on television entertainment programs. Whereas in the "early years" CBS's news division was not considered a profit center, it now has to justify its existence in terms of advertising dollars. The result can be positive: production values and fast-breaking news. But it can also be negative: ignoring important stories for the sake of interesting ones.

In the fall of 2004, just before the presidential election, Fred had the opportunity to speak with Walter Cronkite, the celebrated CBS news anchor from the 1960s and 70s.

Cronkite was once considered the "most trusted man in America." Speaking about his own craft, Mr. Cronkite said that the competition from cable news, and the premium on conflict, had changed his profession in profound and disturbing ways, and deprived the audience of what it needed to make informed decisions about pressing issues.

THE GOOD NEWS ABOUT THE PRESS

Journalists are usually not in the profession for the money, and many of them could do better financially on the "other side," in public relations. They are journalists because they believe in what they are doing and take great pride in it. Most believe that theirs is a noble profession.

Many press relations people, as well as leaders from business, government, and other fields, become jaundiced about journalism. This book's coauthors always felt grateful for journalism, believing that the social, personal, and business freedoms we have could not endure without it. When our clients' story is not being properly reported, we tend to look, first, at the performance of the sender (ourselves) in the classic academic communication model, the message, the channel (in this case the journalist), and then at the other information or attitudes ("noise") that might be causing interference.

Noise
Sender → Message → Channel→ Receiver→ Feedback
Noise

Today, more than ever, journalists need public relations, media relations people. There are fewer journalists doing more work, so they have less time to report and build relationships. Today, more than ever, the media relations person who can be trusted is invaluable.

Of course there is one other piece of potentially good news about the press: They can get very excited about good news from time to time. But new inventions can be oversold, and breakthroughs in basic biomedical research can be headlined cures for cancer. Advice to media relations practitioners: beware of the good hype as well as the bad. We cannot have it both ways.

PRESS RELATIONS FROM A POSITION OF POWER

It is easy to think that journalists hold all the power in the relationship with companies and other organizations, but this is not necessarily the case.

Journalists often ask the questions an organization hopes would not be asked. They are pressing, even threatening: "You know, I am going to cover the story with or without your help, and I believe I already have what I need." The spokesperson feels powerless. The senior-most people in the organization brazenly prescribe responses from afar—"Just stick to the prepared response"—until they get calls from the journalist directly or are about to be interviewed. Then the brazenness collapses into what they would call anxiety but some might call fear.

> Journalists often ask the questions an organization hopes would not be asked.

"Power" often implies something underhanded or Machiavellian, so heads of communications and senior officers in organizations may want to call it "strength" or "influence." But the fact is that a person in a stressful relationship must not feel powerless. Companies and other organizations have the ability to shape the stories that appear about them, but they need to wield that influence responsibly and carefully.

We know of one case where an individual reporter who was grossly unfair to an organization was frozen out of that organization's public relations information chain. Sometimes—rarely—this is necessary, and the journalist may move on to another beat because of a lack of access. But there is a big difference between "black balling" one reporter versus the entire news medium. The most famous instance of the latter was Mobil Oil's 1984 declaration that it would henceforth not communicate in any way with the *Wall Street Journal*.[9]

Again, there is seldom a need even to consider such extreme remedies. But it is critically important for an organization and its spokespeople to realize that it is not powerless in the face of the awesome power of the press.

Day to day, the best way for spokespeople to leverage power is by managing access. Journalists have to go through the communications office to get to the senior officers, and managing access in a fair way will rebound to the credit of the entire organization.

Enduring power in media relations flows from relationships built on fairness, respect, and credibility. One of the keys to power in the relationship with journalists is to be very good at the media relations discipline, knowledgeable about your own industry, and well-versed on what journalists do and why.

SUCCESS IN MEDIA RELATIONS

Everyone in media relations chants the same mantra: success in media relations depends upon building solid relationships with the press. Of course knowing it and doing it are two different things. How to do it? The formula is simple: success as a communicator will be in direct proportion to one's skills as a communicator, one's conviction, the quality of the product, position, or story one is selling to the press, and one's preparedness.

Communication Skills

Communication is one of those things that most people think they are good at. After all, it involves speaking, reading, and writing. Most people have been speaking from the first year or so after they were born, and learned to read and write in first grade.

But true communication skill requires more than just speaking, reading, and writing. It involves using those behaviors to influence the attitudes and behaviors of others. And like any other set of skills, it can become stale and fall into disuse. Effective communicators regularly upgrade their communication skills.

For example, this book's coauthors have both taken numerous writing courses and won writing awards, but we still work hard at improving our craft. Over the years, we would routinely invite writing instructors to hold workshops for our professional staffs, and we would participate ourselves.

Conviction

Journalists are like kids and puppy dogs: if you do not mean what you say, they can smell it. For example, we knew of a young woman in corporate communications for a healthcare company who intellectually accepted the need for animal research of investigational medicines. But she did not have a firm conviction that, while the best tools of science should be mobilized to minimize the number of animals used, some animal studies must be performed before an investigational medicine can be administered to a man, woman, or child. As a result, she was often ineffective in interviews on the topic. It was not a function of knowledge or understanding, but of being able to enthusiastically represent a position.

> Journalists are like kids and puppy dogs: if you do not mean what you say, they can smell it.

Eventually, her superior asked her not to take any more calls about animal research, assuring her that her career would not suffer. There were many other things she could do well, and there were also other people in the group who had enough conviction in the appropriateness of responsible animal testing of medicines to withstand a badgering from any reporter or activist and still hold firm.

Quality of Product or Story

If the thing you are selling to the press is not a page-one story, do not try to get coverage there. If your product or story is not what your organization says it is, the lie or omission will eventually be uncovered. Do not lie. Sounds easy, but it is not. Be willing to stand up in your organization and object to a story line that obscures, blurs, or distorts the truth. Let your uncompromising position be known within the organization—you will not have to blurt it out, because the opportunity to let people know how you feel will come.

Similarly, if you are trying to interest a reporter in a story, you need to package it in ways that get the reporter's attention and make it more likely that the reporter will become the story's champion. This usually requires doing much of the legwork for the reporter before even pitching the story. The general rule of thumb for a major story is that the media relations person needs to do 80 percent of the work on the story, and the reporter will be able to do the other 20 percent. Trying to interest a reporter in a poorly planned, weak, or otherwise uninteresting story is a waste of the reporter's time as well as your own, and can prevent the reporter from seeing the media relations person as a valuable resource.

Preparedness

Be knowledgeable about your organization, and its products, services, and people. Otherwise, you are just an obstacle to the press. Unfortunately, too many media relations people think their job is simply to arrange interviews. There is a time to call upon the experts in your organization to grant interviews, but the communications people should be able to field a significant percentage of incoming calls and be well enough informed to approach a journalist with the basics of a story. If you know what you are talking about—that is, understand your industry, not only your company—journalists will begin to rely on you. When they start calling you for guidance on a story that does not directly involve your organization, you know you have accomplished something. If you have arranged for someone in your organization to be interviewed, make sure he or she is prepared.

THE ART OF THE PITCH

By Raleigh Mayer, Principal of Raleigh Mayer Consulting

Successful pitching to reporters begins with a clear understanding of the outlet, its audience, and the utilization of appropriate tone, timing, and content.

A PITCH IS NOT:

- A high-pressure sales presentation
- Press release text
- Advertising copy
- A plea or solicitation
- A social conversation

A PITCH IS:

- An invitation to cover a story
- A concise, compelling, and customized invitation to interview an expert, preview an event, report on a phenomenon or trend, test a product or service
- An idea for a compelling story, and a road map for how to get the story

SUCCESSFUL PITCHING REQUIRES COMPREHENSIVE KNOWLEDGE OF THE TARGETED MEDIA, INCLUDING:

- Prior and current coverage of your industry
- Style and bias of the outlet
- Format of specific columns, departments, segments
- Preferences and interests of individual journalists

SUCCESSFUL PITCHING REQUIRES COMPREHENSIVE KNOWLEDGE OF YOUR STORY, INCLUDING:

- Answers to basic questions about the event, person, business, market
- How to bring the story to life for readers or viewers
- How to get access to others, including those who are not part of your organization

PITCHING ON PAPER

Lead with:
- Question

JUXTAPOSITION

- Comparison
- Observation
- Riddle

After Lead:
- Support or expand on your claim or theme
- Explain who you are and why you are writing
- Present relevant facts, statistics, or documentation
- Name what you are asking or offering: interview, story, profile, attend event, and so forth
- Conclude with a promise to follow up
- Keep to one page if possible

PITCHING BY E-MAIL:

Make it Compact:
- Put the lead in the subject line
- Condense body copy to one or two paragraphs
- Include contact information in signature
- Do not send attachments unless asked

PITCHING BY PHONE:

- Conduct it conversationally
- Identify yourself clearly
- Deliver the lead and let the reporter respond
- Have prepared message points ready

- Organize your desk so you can concentrate during call
- Give up graciously if the reporter declines or defers pitch
- Thank the reporter for considering it

PITCHING BY VOICE-MAIL:

- Be concise
- Be prepared to leave pitch as voice-mail message
- Give compressed pitch—still powerful, but short
- Leave your name and number at both beginning and end of message
- Do not be careless in leaving message

IF PITCH IS DECLINED:

- Pitch different angle to same reporter
- Pitch same angle to different desk of the same outlet (if relevant)
- Pitch new angle to another section
- Pitch competing reporter at different outlet

AFTER THE STORY APPEARS:

- Keep in contact with reporter
- Update reporter of relevant developments, even if there is no immediate benefit to you
- Deliver next pitch with same level of professionalism as the last one

IF THERE ARE ERRORS:

- Let the reporter know, politely, of the errors
- Do not confuse contrasting opinions with errors of fact
- Contact editors only if you believe willful or harmful errors are not being taken seriously

WHAT REPORTERS DISLIKE:

- Unprepared or unknowledgeable pitches
- Pitches delivered too fast or in a convoluted manner
- Pitches delivered on deadline
- PR people who cannot answer basic questions or provide access to the right people
- PR people who whine that the story was not as positive as they had hoped
- PR people who call to follow up on a release without adding anything new
- PR people who call to ask when/if story has appeared
- Unsolicited e-mail attachments
- Overly ornate or poorly designed press materials; including those with tiny typeface

■ ■ ■

CHOOSING THE RIGHT TOOLS TO CONVEY YOUR MESSAGE

By Jay Rubin, President, Jay Rubin & Associates

Marshall McLuhan's catchphrase, "the medium is the message," may be too radical for many public relations professionals to accept. But you would be hard-pressed to find anyone in the business who does not recognize at least some kernels of truth in that statement. PR veterans know from experience that the tools they choose to pitch their stories have a significant impact on the coverage they receive.

So how do you decide which tools are best to convey your message? You usually rely upon a combination of research, experience, and gut feeling. It may also be helpful to consider the same six words so often associated with news content. Here is a set of who, what, when, where, why, and how questions (and some possible answers) worth considering as you shape your pitching strategy.

WHO WARRANTS YOUR PERSONAL ATTENTION?

It is a rare public relations department that has the time, resources, or inclination personally to contact every name on its press lists. Mostly, you will reach out to all your prospects with the same e-mail press release (typically a one-to-two-page document explaining the news value of your message). Or you can buy space for your press release on one of the paid wire services (e.g., Business Wire, PR Newswire) that link up with newsrooms in a wide variety of geographic and subject categories.

You are then able to follow up with those reporters who really count. Pick up the phone. Customize e-mail pitch letters. Send personalized cover notes along with your press release. Offer to set up interviews. Break the news while you break bread with a reporter. Your individual attention sometimes brings extra weight to your message. More importantly, it allows you to tailor your pitch points to the different needs of reporters.

Occasionally, you may consider scrapping the press list and devoting 100 percent of your energy to a single media outlet. If you give an exclusive on a story, you should be confident about significant coverage and that you will not seriously damage your relationships with other key contacts.

Taking the time to build relationships with key reporters—before the urgency of a major news announcement—is standard practice by successful publicists. Familiarity also boosts the odds of favorable coverage in the blogosphere. Pitches to bloggers are more likely to be considered if a publicist is already known in a specific cyber-community, perhaps through comments about previous blog posts.

WHAT WILL INCREASE YOUR RANGE OF COVERAGE?

Publicists use e-mail press releases most often because they can promote virtually any type of news—hard or soft, urgent or evergreen. Reporters favor a standard press release format because it allows significance, timeliness, and other criteria to be quickly evaluated. Web site links are often included to give the media easy access to additional information about your company or client.

If your news is big enough, enhance your coverage opportunities with an e-mail press kit typically including a press release, photos with captions, a quick-reference fact sheet, a biography, and other appropriate background information. Remember to also keep a supply of kits in hard copy. Some press contacts may request a print version, and the kits can subsequently be used as reference materials.

When pitching TV and radio programs, publicists often provide materials that can be integrated into on-air reports. These include B-roll (video and sound that can be edited into a news report), video news releases (self-standing pieces that can be aired as is or edited), or natural sound (audio recorded by a microphone).

Direct links to corporate blogs, podcasts, video clips, and other social media tools increasingly are found in e-mail releases and kits from companies with sufficient budget and staff to pursue these relatively new promotional avenues. Given the fast developing and frequently freewheeling Internet fray, be sure to exercise caution as you expand your reach beyond the parameters of traditional media.

WHEN MUST YOUR MESSAGE BE RECEIVED?

The old days of stuffing press releases into envelopes or being at the mercy of a busy fax machine thankfully are over. Modern media now demand the immediacy of e-mail. However, one fundamental has not changed: the importance of knowing deadlines.

It is not enough to just know the main deadlines for a newscast or a newspaper. These and other outlets may also have e-mail bulletin services or frequently updated Web sites. Get to know every means of distribution the media have to report your story, and exactly when they are likely to do so.

WHERE IS YOUR MESSAGE BEST DELIVERED?

Be ready to take advantage of opportunities beyond e-mail on the computer screen. A press conference; a press breakfast, lunch, or dinner; or an after-hours reception can be ideal ways to reach reporters assembled at a trade show. Industry gatherings are also prime time for company executives to deliver newsy speeches or panel presentations, be interviewed, or just meet and greet reporters who are otherwise hard to reach.

Off the convention circuit, press conferences are on the wane. The same format (scripted remarks by executives, followed by questions from reporters) can now be handled through a telephone conference call with much less expense to the company and much more convenience to all involved.

WHY SHOULD A REPORTER CARE?

Sometimes e-mails, pitch calls, and other routine tactics are not enough to grab attention. That is when a special event, a community service project, an endorsement, or a gimmick can help pique media interest and give you the platform to promote your news.

If you are having trouble attracting national attention, you should also consider pursuing local coverage. National outlets may give you a second look once a media bandwagon starts rolling in various cities. At the same time, do not overlook the importance of hometown news. When your news is limited to certain areas, suburban weeklies may be more accessible and more valuable to you than metropolitan dailies.

To promote important and complex issues not fully appreciated by the media, try scheduling editorial board meetings. These sessions, usually with a small group of journalists from the same publication, allow you and your associates directly to present your case. Op-ed articles can also be terrific vehicles to explain your viewpoint.

How much will it cost?

e-mail is commonplace for more than just utility; it also has a negligible impact on an overall PR budget. The same cannot always be said about disseminating press releases on a paid wire service, commissioning a video news release, or picking up the tab at a fancy trade-show luncheon. Spend wisely and always to promote stories with real news value. Trying to dress up a mundane message is one of the quickest ways to deplete your budget and your credibility.

■ ■ ■

SHIFTING MEDIA TERRAIN HAS RAISED THE STAKES— AND CREATED OPPORTUNITIES—FOR MEDIA RELATIONS

By Tony Plohoros, Principal, 6 Degrees Communications

Nearly every day, we can find more bad news about the traditional media (newspapers, magazines, TV networks): reduced circulations and viewership, plummeting ad revenues, bankruptcies, scaled-back publication schedules, and naturally, layoffs.

Some recent examples of the rapid decline of traditional media include:

- Bankruptcies at Tribune Company, Philadelphia Newspapers, L.L.C. and The Star Tribune (Minneapolis)
- Pay reductions and/or unpaid furloughs at *The New York Times, Boston Globe, Forbes* and Gannett
- The shuttering of *Conde Nast's Portfolio, Vibe, Men's Vogue, Best Life* and a number of other magazines, and of the *Rocky Mountain News*
- The move from weekly to monthly print publication of *US News* and *PRWeek* and from daily printing to an online-only *Seattle Post-Intelligencer* and several smaller newspapers
- Layoffs at the *Wall Street Journal, USA Today, BusinessWeek, Fortune*, ABC News, CBS News, NBC News, and outlets across the country
- A 5 percent decrease in network TV revenues in Q1 2009 vs. Q1 2008
- First half 2009 revenues at *Business, Forbes,* and *Fortune* down 36 percent, 25 percent and 33 percent, respectively

- 2008 was the worst year on record for the U.S. newspaper industry. Total advertising revenues (both print and online) declined 16.6 percent to $37.85 billion, according to the Newspaper Association of America. That's $7.5 billion less than in 2007. Many expect a sharper decline in 2009.

You get the picture. There are fewer journalists and smaller news holes today at traditional media outlets, and we can count on that trend continuing through the likely demise of most printed journalism in the next decade. One might think based on much of the sensational coverage of traditional media's misfortune that its complete extinction is imminent.

That isn't the case, nor is that the entire story. While the traditional media news hole as we know it is most certainly shrinking, there have never been more ways for media relations to effectively reach target audiences. Below, some heartening news about the media, and our ability to place stories:

- There are no space limitations online. While traditional outlets are cutting back their print production and resources, they are plowing more resources into their online properties. Most traditional print journalists are writing more today than they did at the start of this decade because they need to create new online content.
- New online news sources are sprouting up. During the past couple of years, several high-profile and by many accounts successful organizations have been launched, including political news site Politico; nonprofit investigative news organization ProPublica; and Kaiser Health News, an independent health policy and politics organization funded by the Kaiser Family Foundation.
- More recently, Talking Points Memo, another political news Web site, announced in July that it had secured additional investment that will enable it to increase its number of employees from 11 to 20 in the coming months. The site plans to increase staff to 60 in the next few years. The site reported more than 1.6 million unique visitors in June 2009. It started in 2000 as a one-person blog in the aftermath of the 2000 election Florida ballot recount.
- A new nonprofit venture, the *Texas Tribune*, is expected to launch later this year that will focus on Texas government and politics. The *Tribune* will begin with roughly eight journalists and has already received more than $2 million in funding. Other nonprofit sites have already started operations in Chicago, San Diego and St. Louis. Each employs journalists.
- Despite all the buzz on social media and the growing power of blogs, a recent study at Cornell University found that only 3.5 percent of story lines during the last three months of the 2008 presidential election originated in blogs and made their way into traditional media. That means 96.5 percent of stories originated in traditional media.

There are several implications of the shifting media terrain for media relations. First, there are still plenty of opportunities—including many new ones aimed at smaller, more targeted audiences—for us to be successful with proactive efforts. At the same time, we need to be smarter than ever with our planning and research before we pitch. Further, we need to educate our clients about how the value of media placements is changing. Finally, the evolution from print and TV to online makes measuring our efforts not only possible, but relatively simple.

Journalists today are simply under more pressure than they were several years ago. They have to produce more content, and meet deadlines that are now 24/7. They have less time to cultivate sources and build relationships, and most journalists are genuinely concerned for their own futures. Given this backdrop—coupled with the fact that we have every needed tool available to us—it's essential that we're flawless in our pre-pitch preparation. Communicators need to take the time to ensure that we're targeting the right journalist at the right outlet with the right pitch at the right time. This means doing your homework about an outlet, what it will cover (and won't), what might be print or on-air fodder vs. online fare, who's most likely to cover or write the story, what the competition has or hasn't already done and what's going on in the world that might impact your ability to get a story placed.

We also need to account for the possibility that our clients may be among those clinging to their printed pages and TV news shows. As such, they may not understand that a story that only appears online or appears online first can be just as influential and wide-reaching as a story that appears on the front page of *The New York Times* or on NBC *Nightly News*. It's incumbent upon communicators to educate their clients on the increasing value of online content and how print and TV aren't quite as influential as they were in the past. Remember, stories online last forever, and when we share stories, it's all done via links and e-mail.

In fact, several ways in which we can measure the impact of our media relations efforts are the number of sites linking to a story, the number of times a story has been read (or viewed) and the number of comments made (and by whom) about a story. Before the Internet, we didn't have a reliable way of learning how stories traveled and resonated and had to rely on estimated impressions. Thanks to the Internet, we can also track discussions that have been started or behaviors changed due to our media relations efforts. These are the kinds of metrics that can be tied back to driving business objectives.

There has never been a more exciting time to be in media relations. Our ability to reach and influence target audiences and measure the impact of our efforts has never been better. That said, the rapidly changing media landscape requires us to be more on our game than ever before.

■ ■ ■

BEST PRACTICES IN MEDIA RELATIONS

1. *Be quick (but not foolhardy).*

Communication groups should have their own policy—for example, "return 90 percent of press calls within one hour"—based on their resources and the demands of the press reporting on their organizations. But we do not subscribe to the often-stated PR principle to call every reporter back right away. First, it is not always possible. Second, some journalists—those who have not been fair or responsive to your organization—do not deserve a quick response. That we teach others how to treat us is as true in press relations as in anything else. But as a general rule, the earlier you can get back to a reporter the more influence you can have on the story. That is because the reporter, especially one on a breaking story, cannot wait for your call to write the story. He or she will write it whether you return the call or not. Returning a call at the end of the day may permit the insertion of a small quote or no-comment statement into a nearly completed story. But returning a call before the reporter has invested time and energy, and before the reporter has committed to deliver a story of a certain length to his or her editor, often makes it possible to shape the story or even to prevent a false story from appearing.

2. *Know the media.*

Understand the missions of the various print, broadcast, and electronic media. The *Wall Street Journal* is not *The New York Times* and *The New York Times* is not *The Los Angeles Times* or the *Huffington Post*. Research! Know the consumer, professional, and trade media covering your industry. Understand those umbrella terms and use them correctly.

Both coauthors read the *Columbia Journalism Review*, *The American Journalism Review*, and many first-person, behind-the-scenes accounts of life as a reporter. We require the same of our media relations students. Understanding what is important for reporters, the experience of being a reporter, and the pressures reporters face in doing their jobs every day is a critical part of being an effective media relations professional.

3. *Know the reporters.*

Of course you can only know a small number of journalists well. But media directories have brief biographical sketches of journalists, and full bios are available through services such as *Bulldog Reporter* or directly from the journalist. We cannot imagine arranging an interview for a senior executive or official without obtaining a bio of the journalist and without reviewing that journalist's past news reports, features, or editorials. Research! Visit the journalists at the bureau or for lunch. Most spokespeople are not good at this, but doing so is tremendously important. A good time to ask to meet informally with a journalist is a few days after you have been helpful to him or her. It is also effective to call a journalist when he or she first begins covering your organization, and to go to lunch or grab a cup of coffee to get to know each other. Most journalists new to a beat are eager to make such contacts, and generally welcome such approaches. Once they are established it can be much harder to schedule such time with a reporter without having a story to discuss.

4. *Have a plethora of standby statements.*

Most companies know what is likely to become public prematurely. The most enlightened companies have standby statements ready to distribute on such topics well before a reporter calls. The statement should generally be ready for faxing or e-mailing to a reporter. One way to avoid questions on a sensitive subject is to say "we have a standby statement on that; should I e-mail it to you?" Invariably—literally—the answer will be yes, thank you, and goodbye. This avoids the possibility of misspeaking or of being misquoted, and the journalist has the precise words the organization wants to express.

5. *Have a plethora of Qs and As.*

If the spokesperson has days to prepare for a tough interview on a narrow subject and the journalist only has an hour or so, the spokesperson can anticipate every single, reasonable question. If the subject is broad—for example, growth prospects for a particular industry—the challenge becomes greater. But even then, the proposition is irrefutable: The more Qs and As the spokesperson has prepared, the greater the chance of success.

6. *Media coaching.*

Speaking with reporters is different from speaking with other people, because they use your words differently than most people do. In particular, most conversations are private, unstructured, and informal, while interviews are always public, and should be formal and structured. Executives often behave with reporters the same way they behave with everyone else, and often with adverse consequences.

One way to prevent such negative outcomes is to prepare the executive not just on the subject matter to be discussed, but also on the skills necessary to communicate that content most effectively through the news media. The skills for effectiveness in print interviews are in some ways different from those necessary for television, radio, or the Internet.

One advantage of media coaching is that it is often videotaped—even training for print interviews. One reason for the taping is for the executive to see how he or she really comes across. It can be eye-opening, and much more effective than telling the executive how he or she did.

Another advantage of media coaching is that it provides a safe setting to ask the executive difficult questions that would not be as acceptable in a rehearsal at the executive's desk.

Finally, the training provides a safe environment for an executive to fail—far better to fail in rehearsal than on CNN. The training can reveal how weak a particular response to a difficult question may be, and provide an opportunity to improve. It can reveal the gaps in information before the actual interview. Finally, media training can reveal character issues that would be catastrophic in a real interview. We have seen senior executives lie when pressed by a tough media trainer. Like a kid caught with his hand in the candy jar, a person armed with weak information tends to lie. It is far better to expose the lie and the weakness that triggered it in an exercise than with a reporter.

7. *Have B-roll.*

Have plenty of television footage of production, products, and so on. When the deadline or a crisis occurs is not the time to be developing B-roll.

8. *Prepare before and after interview memos.*

When possible, sketch in a preinterview memo the objectives for the interview and other relevant information. The postinterview memo can be a way of preparing colleagues and bosses for the news report and of learning for the future.

9. *Do everything you can to build your organization's reputation.*

The media relations person represents the organization as much as anyone and is in a position of great leverage in this regard.

10. *Do not do anything that puts your organization's reputation at risk.*

11. *Make it interesting.*

Given a choice between "interesting" and "informative," the journalist will choose "interesting" almost every time.

12. *Never speak on background—unless you know what you are doing.*

To most PR people and journalists, the phrase "on background" means that the information can be used, but cannot be attributed to or associated with the spokesperson or organization he or she represents. It is an indispensable part of an ongoing media relations program, and can be helpful in many cases—for example, when you are not sure of something but think the journalist should investigate, or when what you say might seem inappropriate in a news report quoting your organization. Make sure the journalist and you are working from precisely the same definition of terms, and that you explicitly note when you are "on background" and "off."

13. *Never work with a reporter under "embargo"—unless you know what you are doing.*

The rule should be: Do not issue a press release to a world of journalists and mark it "embargoed"—unless you actually want and expect someone to break the embargo. The embargo can be a useful tool, especially when the story is complicated and a journalist would need time to understand it, and when you have a mutually trusting relationship with the journalist. How can a publicly owned company issue a press release on a complicated matter after the New York Stock Exchange closes and expect it to be covered accurately on the evening news or in the morning papers? Make sure that the journalist and you have precisely the same understanding of what the agreement is. Make sure both parties understand exactly when the news can be released.

14. *Never speak "off the record"—never, unless you <u>really</u> know what you are doing.*

The term, at least to many in the media relations business, means that the information will never be reported. Fuhgeddaboudit!

15. *Call every reporter back right away—Fuhgeddaboudit!*

The golden rule taught in public relations courses is that a PR person must return a reporter's call as soon as possible, and in general that is a good rule to follow. The reason, of course, is that the journalist is usually under deadline. But there are exceptions, dictated by common sense.

Again, if a reporter has been unfair to the client or organization you represent, or if the reporter's news media often does a poor job, it does not make any sense to treat that person with the same degree of responsiveness you would the better reporters. Journalists talk, and it often becomes clear to one who feels mistreated by an organization he or she is covering that colleagues in the press do not feel that way. The light can go on. In any case, the PR person has power, as does the organization or client he or she represents, and it can and should be used.

16. *Keep a press log.*

There are two reasons. First, it can be circulated within your organization so that others know what you are doing with the press and so that PR people in the organization are not tripping over each other. Second, it will provide a record so that, in the future, you can reach out to all journalists who, for example, have inquired about a particular product or issue.

17. *Have a "return-call policy."*

It is a good idea to have a policy that says, for example, "we return 90 percent of all press calls within one hour." (Arrange lunch breaks and so forth accordingly.) Setting business objectives is as important in press relations as anywhere else.

18. *Be available nights and weekends.*

It is the deadline, stupid. There is no other way to run press relations. If there is more than one person in the press relations shop, spread the overtime work around. If you are the only one, make sure your superiors know what overtime work is required.

19. *Correct every mistake in the press about your organization.*

There are essentially three remedies: a letter to the editor; a correction notice for publication or broadcast; and a letter or call to the journalist to clarify the matter with him or her but not necessarily for publication or broadcast.

20. *Broadcast, cable and the Internet can get the story out faster and more broadly—sometimes.*

Broadcast can be faster indeed. But often, even today, the print media break the major stories that prove of long-term interest. Getting your story right in just one of the leading newspapers (for example, *The New York Times*, the *Wall Street Journal, Washington*

Post, or one of the major foreign papers) can be worth much more than a press conference, media tour, and an appearance on *Oprah* combined.

21. *If a journalist can cover a fire he can cover anything—not true.*

PR has its myths and so does journalism. Therefore, it becomes important to know the background of the journalist the PR person is working with. In addition to the reporter's bio, sources such as the *Bull Dog Reporter* summarize the kinds of subjects the reporter usually covers.

22. *Get the journalist's agreement, when time permits, for review of quotations, before publication.*

Especially if the matter discussed in the interview is complex, the journalist should agree to give the interviewee the opportunity to review quotes before publication. More journalism schools are adopting this position, and John cannot see the fairness or journalistic good of any other. On complicated stories, John's position is: No review of quotes, no interview.

23. *Journalism support programs.*

A great way of building relationships with the press is to fund programs that support good journalism. Of course this has to be a mutually productive but hands-off relationship. The benefits of a media relationship initiative will sometimes be hard to see, day to day, and some people in the organization might even think the initiative is counterproductive: "If you had not been reaching out to that reporter so often, he wouldn't now be all over us at a time when we don't need the attention."

But over time, the relationship is beneficial in a number of ways. It provides a bridge for two-way interaction independent of any one story. It provides opportunities for executives and others to get to know reporters well, and vice versa. And, above all, it reflects the organization's honest desire for fair journalism.

24. *A media relations person should always be working toward measurable results that support organizational objectives.*

25. *Codify rules of engagement for social media.*

(See next chapter.)

QUALITIES OF A GOOD MEDIA RELATIONS PERSON

The list is brief:

- Good communication instincts (some people are simply not communicative by nature and should not be in media relations)

- Good communication skills. The job interview can reveal much about speaking abilities. To assess writing ability, always give a writing test

- Toughness and an ability to withstand criticism

- Honesty

- Good research skills

- An ability to shine when under intense deadline pressure

- Speed was always important. Today, given the 24/7 news cycle and the importance of social media, it is essential

- Teamwork skills

RESOURCES FOR FURTHER STUDY

Cutlip, Scott M., Center, Allen H. and Broom, Glen M. *Effective Public Relations*, 9th ed. (Upper Saddle River, NJ: Pearson, Prentice Hall, 2006).

Grunig, James E. and Hunt, Todd, *Managing Public Relations* (New York: Harcourt Brace Jovanovich, 1984).

Guth, David W. and Marsh, Charles, *Public Relations: A Values-Driven Approach*, 3rd ed. (Needham Heights, MA: Allyn & Bacon, Inc.).

Hiebert, Ray E. (ed.), *Public Relations Review: A Journal of Research and Comment* (Amsterdam: Elsevier).

Howard, Carole M. and Mathews, Wilma K., *On Deadline, Managing Media Relations*, 3rd ed. (Prospect Heights, IL: Waveland PR Inc., 2000).

Schenkler, Irv and Herrling, Tony, *Guide To Media Relations* (Upper Saddle River, NJ: Pearson, Prentice Hall, 2004).

Schmertz, Herb with Novak, William, *Good-bye to the Low Profile* (Boston: Little, Brown, 1986).

QUESTIONS FOR FURTHER DISCUSSION

1   Should media relations people proactively mention to journalists the reason the organization adheres to a centralized communication policy?

2   Do you think the Grunig-Hunt models of public relations apply today? Which one do you practice? Are you ethically committed to that model?

3   Does the press really have a right to ask anything at all?

4   Is there any reason PR people should not be as zealous about accuracy as the best journalists?

5   When the subject of the interview is technical, is it appropriate to ask the journalist before the interview to agree to clear the quotes before using them? What if the journalist will not agree?

In times of change, learners inherit the earth.

— *Eric Hoffer*

4 SOCIAL MEDIA

By Laurel Hart

■■■

Before the 2008 primary season began, the generally acknowledged frontrunner for the Democratic nomination for President was Senator Hillary Clinton, the junior senator from New York State and spouse of former President Bill Clinton. People had heard of the even-more junior senator from Illinois, Senator Barack Obama, in part because of the rousing speech he gave at the 2004 Democratic Convention. Many viewed his candidacy as the aspiration of an upstart, running before he'd put in his due time at a lower level of the political ladder.

But building on the strength of the candidate himself and the campaign's traditional media outreach, the Obama campaign went on to conduct the most comprehensive, strategic and well-executed use of social media and grassroots organizing in a political campaign to date, and the junior senator from Illinois went on to become the 44th President of the United States.

Whether Democrat or Republican, both sides agreed that the Obama campaign was significantly better than the McCain campaign at harnessing the power of social media to drive support, action, donations, votes, and eventually victory, remapping the way a campaign communicates and interacts with supporters along the way.

The Obama campaign used channels such as social networking sites, blogs, online videos, text messages, photo sharing sites and Twitter to connect supporters with the candidate and, perhaps even more importantly, with each other. The combination of the Obama campaign's platform with this multi-directional action and communication helped propel Obama to the White House.

■■■

WHAT IS SOCIAL MEDIA?

Social media has been called many things: new media (the name used in the first edition of this book), web 2.0,[1] consumer-generated media, user-generated media, the live web.[2] While social media is arguably the most broadly used of these terms, there is no consensus; some use multiple terms interchangeably, and a term is likely to change as the medium changes.

Social media is "often used to describe the collection of software that enables individuals and communities to gather, communicate, share, and in some cases collaborate or play."[3] Charlene Li and Josh Bernoff, in their book *Groundswell: Winning in a World Transformed by Social Technologies*, describe this as a "groundswell," "A social trend in which people use technologies to get the things they need from each other, rather than from traditional institutions like corporations."[4]

Social media has become a fundamental and widespread part of how people and organizations communicate and participate online. Elements of social media have been around at least since the mid-1990s, and the first generally available blog software services were introduced in the late 1990s, with sites like Blogger.com introduced by Pyra Labs in 1999. (It's now owned by Google.) Since the late 1990s, the elements and channels of social media have evolved, and many have become widely adopted.

The Pew Internet & American Life Project (http://www.pewinternet.org/), part of the Pew Research Center and a nonpartisan research organization, researches and reports on "the impact of the Internet on families, communities, work and home, daily life, education, health care, and civic and political life." Their studies (and research by many others) have shown that, regardless of age, geography, gender, education or other demographic segment, social media and web 2.0 technology have become an increasingly important and prevalent part of people's daily lives in the United States—and around the world.

Why Social Media Matters

The world of communication has changed dramatically over the last 30 years, with first computers, then cable news, then widespread Internet adoption, and more recently mobile technology steadily accelerating and shifting the dynamics of public communication. Social media has been a component of that shifting communication landscape since the mid-1990s. Social media is changing the way organizations communicate with people, and the way people communicate and connect with each other, be they employees, customers, partners, competitors, adversaries, advocates, the general public, members of the mainstream media or others.

With social media, anyone can create and distribute content online, easily, quickly, often freely (or cheaply), and with little or no technical know-how. With social media, people can connect with organizations and each other in ways that were limited or not possible before—employees with the mainstream media, customers with employees, the general public with customers, and so on. With social media, many of the traditional barriers—between publics, between bloggers and journalists—have become blurred.

In the seminal book *The Cluetrain Manifesto*, published in 2000 by

Rick Levine, Christopher Locke, Doc Searls and David Weinberger, the authors' first thesis states that "Markets are conversations," and thesis six continues, "The Internet is enabling conversations among human beings that were simply not possible in the era of mass media."[5] In the years since the book's publication, we've seen countless powerful examples of these networked conversations taking place in social media.

Social media is also, in many ways, a continuation of the very best communication principles organizations have long aspired to or practiced. Social media does not replace most other forms of communication; it complements, expands and enriches organizational communication. (Much as the Internet did not replace the telephone.) To be successful, an organization's social media activities must be coordinated with its larger business goals and strategy, as well as with its other communication efforts. But *some* form of social media participation is also becoming necessary for most every organization, whether corporate, nonprofit or governmental. Social media is becoming ingrained in our culture and in the ways that people look to communicate with the organizations that matter to them in their lives.

> Social media is also, in many ways, a continuation of the very best communication principles organizations have long aspired to or practiced.

In addition, some researchers are also beginning to evaluate the dynamic between organizations' participation in social media and their financial performance. In the 2009 "Wetpaint/ Altimeter Group ENGAGEMENTdb Report" evaluating the social media engagement and financial performance of the "world's most valuable brands," the study found that "the most valuable brands in the world are experiencing a direct correlation between top financial performance and deep social media engagement. The relationship is apparent and significant: socially engaged companies are in fact more financially successful."[6] Just as the first chapter of this book maintains that reputation can be measured and managed, and that reputational capital "adds value to the actual worth of the company," we are seeing the first quantifiable indications that "deep" social media engagement is indeed correlated to financial performance. If further research confirms these initial findings, this is a potentially important part of why social media engagement is crucial to a company's reputation management activities.

This chapter is written from the perspective of organizations (mostly corporate, with some nonprofit and governmental applications as well) and provides a broad overview, a glimpse of the many ways that organizations are interacting with social media, and some of the issues and questions social media presents for organizations. There are many good books and online resources that cover these areas in greater depth and breadth, and many are listed throughout and at the end of the chapter. Also, because of the nature of change in social media, some information in this chapter will be out of date essentially as soon as it's put to paper. Our purpose here is to focus less on particular tools, tactics or services, and more on the characteristics, strategies and goals of social media as it relates to organizations' broader business goals and reputation management.

Social Media Characteristics

There are some broad characteristics that define social media:

1. *Authenticity*

People want organizations to communicate as they would in a conversation, in a human, authentic way.

As "markets are conversations," people want organizations to communicate as they would in a conversation, in a human, authentic way. Spin, corporate talk, legalese, b.s. or bluster have never been good principles of communication, but in the era of social media, they have no place at all.

It can be a cultural shift to adopt a more conversational way of communicating. Organizational involvement in social media is also characterized and driven by a desire for more transparency from organizations.

For many organizations, it can be a cultural shift to adopt a more conversational way of communicating. But perhaps even harder is that authenticity also requires a great degree of consistency between communication and action, and across communication channels and organizational functions. For example, if the communication or social media team says one thing while the customer service team is saying or doing something that appears to be completely at odds, it may leave the person on the receiving end feeling that the company is inauthentic. Matching action to communication can help drive the development or sustainment of an authentic organization.

In its study and report, "The Authentic Enterprise," the Arthur W. Page Society summarized this idea by saying, "In a word, authenticity will be the coin of the realm for successful corporations and for those who lead them." This is in part because a company's "actions and reputation, which used to be safe-guarded by a cadre of professionalized functions, are now the responsibility of everyone in the enterprise."[7]

2. *Transparency*

Organizational involvement in social media is also characterized and driven by a desire for more transparency from organizations. The desire for transparency stems not just from the technology but also from some of the business problems of the last 10+ years, from Enron to AIG to Bernie Madoff. Don Tapscott and David Ticoll, in *The Naked Corporation*, define transparency as, *"the accessibility of information to stakeholders of institutions, regarding matters that affect their interests* [emphasis theirs]."[8] "Corporations that are open perform better. Transparency is a new form of power, which pays off when harnessed. Rather than to be feared, transparency is becoming central to business success. Rather than to be unwillingly stripped, smart firms are choosing to be open."[9] At a time when trust in business is at historic lows, transparent communication can be a way to begin to rebuild that trust.[10]

Transparency also relates to the generally public nature of the interactions that take place between organizations and people within social media. In the past, if a customer was dissatisfied with a product, they might write a letter or call the company directly, or tell a few people they knew. Now, those interactions are more likely to take place in the public square of social media for anyone to see, comment on, and spread even further. This also affects people within an organization: in the past, it may have been just the communications, public relations or customer service groups that witnessed those interactions or crises. Now, anyone at an organization can see the events unfold publicly.

One caveat: transparency does not override the kinds of information that organizations have always and must continue to be kept private and confidential (more on this later in this chapter). (Also, note that the book *Tactical Transparency* by Shel Holtz and John C. Havens explores this topic in more depth.[11])

3. *Decentralization of authority*

Social media is characterized by a decentralization of authority and by multi-directional and increasingly two-way conversations. (See Chapter 3, Media Relations, for more on the four academic models of public relations.) Social media enables people to interact with and have the potential to affect each other, an organization, a product, a cause, or government leaders. Instead of top-down, one-directional information dictated by the leaders of corporations, information has more opportunities to move from the bottom up, from the sides and between different groups. However, many still see the two-way symmetric model between organizations and people within social media as an aspirational goal, yet to be fully realized.

> Social media is characterized by a decentralization of authority and by multi-directional and increasingly two-way conversations.

4. *Speed*

Speed is a defining element of social media and a characteristic that presents challenges for organizations in reputation management. The pace at which information is shared and propagated in social media is faster and broader than older forms of communication. In the event of a crisis, this can make it difficult for organizations to catch up, but a fast response can help organizations mitigate the effects of the crisis. On the positive side, speed can work in an organization's favor, as useful, relevant, interesting or novel content is shared amongst networks, amplifying an organization's reach.

> Speed is a defining element of social media and a characteristic that presents challenges for organizations in reputation management.

Part of what drives the increase in speed in social media is the way in which information is networked, categorized (or tagged), and made searchable. The interconnected pieces are easier to spread and share, and easier to find. Our networks online, not just in the social network sense, are part of the acceleration process.

5. *Collaboration*

Finally, collaboration is an inherent part of what defines social media—it is the building of relationships, not just the exchange of information. It is also an important part of how organizations are participating successfully in social media. Limited-time-only campaigns or marketing approaches by organizations have most often had equally limited success. Just as in other forms of communication, how an organization participates in social media depends on the audience and the general business goals but, generally speaking, the ones that have had the most success have

> Collaboration is an inherent part of what defines social media.

approached social media as a collaborative medium that encourages commitment and sustainability.

A Few Social Media Terms

BLOGS

A blog is a Web site with posts typically arranged in reverse chronological order. Blogs can contain text, photographs, embedded video and audio, hyperlinks and other kinds of content. Blogs typically allow comments from readers, and sometimes trackbacks and Twitter mentions. Blog software allows users with little or no technical web knowledge to create their own Web site, often free, quickly and easily. The three most widely used blog software services are Blogger, Wordpress and Typepad.

SOCIAL NETWORKS

Social network sites are "web-based services that allow individuals to (1) construct a public or semi-public profile within a bounded system, (2) articulate a list of other users with whom they share a connection, and (3) view and traverse their list of connections and those made by others within the system."[12] Facebook, MySpace and LinkedIn are currently three of the largest social network sites in the United States, but there are many other social networking sites, some of which are more dominant in other parts of the world.

MICROBLOGGING

Microblogging services allow users to post and read short content. Twitter is one example of a microblogging service, and content, or "tweets" are limited to 140 characters. Part of Twitter's growth is due to the ability to post and read content in a variety of ways, through the Web site, mobile applications, text messages, desktop applications and others. Twitter also incorporates some characteristics of social network sites, and most users have public profiles on Twitter. Other microblogging services include Posterous and Tumblr.

SOCIAL BOOKMARKING

Social bookmarking allows users to store, share, search and organize Web sites, individual web pages and other kinds of content online. The information and bookmarks are not tied to a particular computer or web browser but are accessible either publicly or to a privately designated group of people. Most social bookmarking sites, such as Delicious, are organized around "tags," where saved sites can be searched or viewed by their tag designation, or in reverse chronological order.

RSS

RSS stands for Really Simple Syndication. RSS allows users to subscribe to and "pull" information by feeds. Instead of a user manually checking a Web site to look for new content, the content is pushed from the site to the user. RSS readers such as Google Reader and Bloglines function like an inbox for the web, where new information is highlighted and aggregated in one central place.

PHOTO AND VIDEO SHARING

Photo and video sharing sites like Flickr and YouTube allow people to post, share, tag, search and comment on visual content, and such sites often incorporate social networking elements into the community.

PODCASTS

Podcasts are either audio or video files that can be played or watched online or downloaded to a user's computer or mobile device. Podcasts generally allow people to subscribe so that the content is automatically pushed to the listener or viewer when it's added.

TAGS

Tags are keywords or other identifying labels that help users sort, search and save information on the web.

SEARCH ENGINE OPTIMIZATION

Search Engine Optimization (or SEO) is "the process of improving the volume or quality of traffic to a Web site from search engines via "natural" ("organic" or "algorithmic") search results."[13]

WIKIS

"A wiki is a collection of web pages designed to enable anyone with access to contribute or modify content."[14] Wikis are a way to edit, store, and search information. Wikis can cover any range of content, e.g. broad like Wikipedia, or narrow like wikis specific to a company, individual, particular subject, or project.

For additional definitions of social media terms, see:

- "A-Z of Social Media" on the socialmedia wiki: http://socialmedia.wikispaces. com/A-Z+of+social+media
- "A Social Media Glossary" on The Buzz Bin: http://www.livingstonbuzz. com/2009/02/24/social-media-glossary/

CORPORATE PARTICIPATION IN SOCIAL MEDIA

How a company decides to participate in social media depends largely on its overall business and communication goals, and so each company's approach will be different and should be tailored to its own needs. Social media is just one element of a larger communication picture and needs to fit coherently into the other actions and communication activities of the organization. To build and maintain reputation, the social media activities of a corporation must be in line with its other efforts or there will be a disconnect, with the potential to cause audiences to lose trust in the corporation.

While each company is unique, there are some general categories of how companies are participating in social media.

COMMUNITY-BUILDING

Perhaps the broadest way that companies are participating in social media is in engaging in and building online communities.

Perhaps the broadest way that companies are participating in social media is in engaging in and building online communities. Sun Microsystems, for example, has had a network of over four thousand employees blogging about a range of topics at http://blogs.sun.com/, and the company's CEO, Jonathan Schwartz, was one of the first CEO bloggers and a strong advocate for how blogs and social media could help the company build and participate in online communities. (Note: Oracle is to acquire Sun, with the deal planned to close in 2009.) Countless companies are engaging with existing communities in social media channels like Twitter, Facebook, Flickr and YouTube, and at times are creating their own communities with services like Ning and Yammer.

We often think of Facebook and other social networks as places to interact with our personal contacts, but Facebook can be a powerful community-building tool for corporations, nonprofits, and other types of organizations. Organizations of all stripes are using social networks like Facebook to build, foster, participate in, and grow communities.

CUSTOMER SERVICE

Many companies are using Twitter for customer service to respond to customers' requests for help, problems, or concerns.

For anyone who has spent thirty minutes on hold with a company's customer service phone line, only then to be transferred from one person to the next without anyone able to actually solve the problem, the notion of being able to go more directly to the source to get help probably sounds pretty appealing. Companies like JetBlue (http://twitter.com/jetblue), Comcast (http://twitter.com/comcast-cares), and Zappos.com (http://twitter.com/zappos) are embracing social media as a channel to help customers. Many companies are using Twitter for customer service to respond to customers' requests for help, problems, or concerns. The use of hashtags and user names in Twitter can help organizations identify potential customer service problems as they happen (or in near real time) and potentially staunch problems from spreading and evolving into larger crises.

Others are reaching out via blogs and forums to try to solve customer problems. Customer service is an area where people are hungry for a personal voice and personal expertise, and social media is one tool companies are using to try to change the sometimes broken dynamic of traditional customer service.

MARKET RESEARCH AND PRODUCT DEVELOPMENT

Social media allows companies to go directly to their customers, potential customers, and a general audience to get immediate and direct feedback on its products, services, advertisements or other offerings. Traditional market research—such as focus groups and more quantitative research methodologies such as randomized statistical sampling—still have a place, but social media allows companies to get fast and accessible feedback on things that matter to both the company and the audience.

> Social media allows companies to go directly to their customers, potential customers, and a general audience to get immediate and direct feedback.

A number of companies are using social media to ask customers and the general public to help them shape the future of the company and its products. Starbucks introduced the "MyStarbucksIdea" Web site in March 2008 (http://mystarbucksidea. force.com/), which allows people to submit ideas that other people can then vote on and discuss. Starbucks then posts items that are under consideration for implementation, and updates the site when new initiatives are launched. In the first year, 70,000 ideas were submitted, 94 were "put into action" and 25 were launched.[15] Dell, BestBuy, and other companies also have similar customer collaboration sites.

In addition, social media can be a helpful tool for organizations conducting competitive market research, by evaluating whom their competitors are and what they're doing within the social media space.

(SOCIAL) MEDIA RELATIONS

As mainstream media and social media have blended in the last decade, the line between "old media" and "new media" has become increasingly blurred. Most mainstream media news organizations incorporate social media elements into their online sites and activities, and many blogs, bloggers, and blog networks have the clout and credibility of traditional news organizations. Some stories that once would have originated on mainstream media sites and then spread to the blogosphere are originating in the blogosphere and then picked up by mainstream media. And for stories that originate with the mainstream print media, the majority of the breaking news stories appear first in the online editions before appearing in the print editions.[16]

Companies are also working to build relationships with influential bloggers, much as they have with influential journalists. "Blogger relations" is increasingly part of the media relations mix, and companies are working to find the right balance to participate in and add value to the discussion.

Additionally, corporations are sometimes using social media as a force of media disintermediation, to talk directly with audiences and to tell their own stories in their own words, instead of relying on the mainstream media—or even influential members of social media—to do so.

Social media relations is also transforming the traditional press release and pitching process. In 2006, after a passionate discussion in the blogosphere about the state of the traditional press release, Todd Defren at Shift Communications introduced a template for a "social media release (SMR)."[17] Since it was introduced, companies like Ford Motor Company have incorporated social media releases into their communication mix (http://ford.digitalsnippets.com/), and the International Association of Business Communicators (IABC) is driving adoption standards.[18]

The social media release most often complements, but doesn't replace, the traditional press release. The format is also not right for every topic and should be used strategically. But when it does make sense to use a social media release, it can be a powerful addition to the communication mix. As the name implies, social media press releases incorporate social media elements into the release, such as hyperlinks, multimedia (photos, video, audio, etc.), and comments, and can often be shared or subscribed to via RSS.

The dynamic of how information is pitched to journalists and bloggers is also changing. Peter Shankman created a service called "HARO—Help a Reporter Out" (http://www.helpareporter.com/) in March 2008 that turns the traditional pitching process on its head. Instead of public relations people pitching journalists, Shankman compiles requests from journalists for sources, and those requests are then distributed to a list of potential sources that are subscribers. As of August 2009, HARO had over 30,000 journalists and 80,000 "sources" subscribed, with 3,000 journalist requests a month.[19]

CRISIS MANAGEMENT

> Perhaps the biggest social media crisis mistake that a company can make is to completely dismiss the blogosphere or Twittersphere, and to see the issue as an isolated problem within social media, undeserving of response.

There have been many examples of companies that have felt the sting of social media during a crisis, or where a company's lack of response within social media during a crisis has accelerated or aggravated the problem at hand.[20]

Perhaps the biggest social media crisis mistake that a company can make is to completely dismiss the blogosphere or Twittersphere, and to see the issue as an isolated problem within social media, undeserving of response. Target and Domino's Pizza are just two examples of companies where management at first relegated the problem as one just within social media, and didn't seem at first to understand how crisis dynamics had changed. Both companies saw their problems begin within social media (blogs in the case of Target, and YouTube, Twitter and blogs in the case of Domino's Pizza), but quickly jump to other social media channels and then to the mainstream media, amplifying and prolonging the crisis.[21]

> However, companies that are able to respond quickly to alarms within social media are often able to stop the outcry before it spreads and becomes a crisis.

However, companies that are able to respond quickly to alarms within social media are often able to stop the outcry before it spreads and becomes a crisis (or to shorten the duration of the crisis) by honestly and compassionately addressing people's concerns within the social media space and detailing what they're going to do to fix the problem. In December 2008, a Pepsi advertisement that ran once in one publication in Germany sparked a wider outcry due to the ad's graphic cartoon of a "calorie" using multiple methods to commit suicide. Pepsi social media people responded quickly via Twitter and on blogs with heartfelt compassion and assured people that the ad would not run again. The crisis was contained and over within a relatively short time from when it first began, and the online community acknowledged Pepsi's quick and appropriate handling of the response.[22]

EMPLOYEE ENGAGEMENT

Finally, not all of the ways that companies are participating in social media are with external audiences. Using social media to transform internal communication is a growing and important area of corporate social media adoption.

> Using social media to transform internal communication is a growing and important area of corporate social media adoption.

Best Buy is one example of a company that's used social media on a widespread, internal level. The company created something called Blue Shirt Nation to bring together employees from across the company, including its thousands of stores. Blue Shirt Nation is part internal social network, part internal blogging platform and part wiki. It was built as a ground-up platform, not mandated by a central corporate group, and the platform has seen demonstrable success and widespread adoption since it was introduced in 2006. Blue Shirt Nation has enabled employees to problem-solve, to get to know each other better, to resolve human resource issues and to build an internal community.[23]

Social Media in the Organizational Structure

With many different kinds of organizational involvement in social media, where does social media fit within the organizational structure? Increasingly, social media elements are being incorporated not only by corporate communications and public relations departments, but also by human resources, marketing, information technology (IT), executive management, customer service, sales, and many other areas.

Just as computers are used throughout organizations but typically managed by IT, research is beginning to show that the most common departmental managers of social media are communication and public relations, with some elements managed by marketing. A study partly produced by PRSA, the "2009 Digital Readiness Report: Essential Online Public Relations and Marketing Skills,"[24] found that public relations departments were more likely to manage social media than other departments except in relation to two activities that were more likely to be managed by marketing—e-mail marketing and search engine optimization (SEO).

SOCIAL MEDIA CHALLENGES

Ethical Challenges

> There are significant ethical issues that organizations must be mindful of when participating in social media.

There are significant ethical issues that organizations must be mindful of when participating in social media. Most companies participating in social media communicate ethically, just as most companies participating in other communication channels communicate ethically. Unfortunately, however, there have been numerous cases of organizations, individuals, or agencies violating ethical boundaries of online behavior. For example, Whole Foods CEO John Mackey posted over one thousand messages under a pseudonym on a Yahoo! message board for more than seven years, on topics both trivial (his haircut) and germane (the merger of Whole Foods with a rival and other topics that had the potential to affect the price of Whole Foods stock). His identity was disclosed only through legal proceedings regarding the merger of Whole Foods with Wild Oats.[25] This is one issue that often gets people and companies in trouble online—attempts to obscure identity and affiliation. There used to be an old adage that "On the Internet, nobody knows you're a dog." That simply is not true anymore (if it ever was). Because of the nature of social technologies, true identities can—and will—most often be discovered, with significant damage done at times to that organization's or individual's reputation.

The primary ethical challenge for organizations participating in social media is one of disclosure. In this area, the Word of Mouth Marketing Association (WOMMA) has an illustrative Ethics Code of Conduct,[26] which includes its "Honesty ROI: Honesty of Relationship, Opinion and Identity." The ethics code has been fleshed out since it was first developed, but it began (and still boils down to) saying,

> You say who you're speaking for.
> You say what you believe.
> You never obscure your identity.

- Honesty of Relationship: You say who you're speaking for.
- Honesty of Opinion: You say what you believe.
- Honesty of Identity: You never obscure your identity.

At the time of this writing, the ethics of disclosure is taking on another dynamic as the Federal Trade Commission is evaluating if and how paid sponsorships should be disclosed on blogs and other kinds of social media.[27]

Many organizations have developed their own policies for employees who participate in social media, and the policies most often include ethical considerations.[28]

Legal Challenges

Earlier in this chapter, we talked about how the idea of transparency in social media does not override legal issues and types of content that have always and must remain private and confidential. In *The Corporate Blogging Book*, Debbie Weil notes that legal risks for companies fall into two main areas: "stuff you don't want to reveal (trade secrets, financial information); [and] stuff you can get sued for (copyright, libel, privacy issues)."[29] The same could be said for all of social media, not just blogs.

Highly regulated industries also have particular legal challenges in participating in social media. Some of the challenges include:

> Highly regulated industries have particular legal challenges in participating in social media.

- Publicly listed companies cannot make forward-looking statements, discuss earnings or projections, or disclose certain other kinds of financial information, including material information, unless done through the appropriate (nonselective) channels.
- Pharmaceutical companies have to consider legal and regulatory guidelines and requirements such as adverse-event reporting and off-label marketing.
- Insurance companies are governed by 51 separate regulatory bodies (in all 50 states and Puerto Rico), and cannot market specific products or services on a nationwide basis.
- Alcohol beverage companies must be careful not to market to individuals under the legal drinking age (which is 21 in the United States).

For employees, First Amendment laws most often do not protect free speech as it relates to their employment status, and violating legal guidelines in social media has gotten many people fired. Most employers are "at will" employers, and violating social media or communication legal guidelines can be an offense that can get a person fired without recourse.

At heart, the legal guidelines for social media boil down to areas that all employees should consider in any medium of communication and overlap in places with the ethical guidelines. Don't say things you wouldn't say face to face. Don't talk about confidential, proprietary, or forward-looking information. Be careful with copyrighted and trademarked material. Don't disguise your identity or affiliation. Don't use libelous or defamatory language. Don't reveal private information about your co-workers. In short, think before writing.

Bias

While social media has become broadly ingrained in people's daily lives in the U.S. (and in much of the world), there are issues of bias to consider, and organizations should be mindful of ways that potential bias may creep into their social media activities.

Ethan Zuckerman, of the Berkman Center for Internet and Society at Harvard Law School, in writing about political discourse but in terms that can be extrapolated to corporate participation in social media, described "at least three filters in the voices we hear—access, language and bias."[30] Access to technology and social media is not universal, and access does not automatically correlate to knowing how to use the technology or social media channel. Think of the counter worker at a fast food establishment—how or when would he or she have access (both in terms of time and technology) to social media?

Language is another consideration for organizations with multilingual audiences. An organization might ask itself, "Are certain kinds of communication only happening in English that should also be happening in another language?" Some kinds of social media are starting to incorporate translation ability into the channel itself, but this area is still developing.

Bias might mean only following certain kinds of bloggers or other active social media participants to the exclusion of differing voices. Selective listening risks exclusion of potentially significant people, topics, or issues. For example, it has become fairly common for some people to dismiss MySpace as a social network that no one uses anymore. Yet, the site is number eleven worldwide in terms of numbers of unique visitors in August 2009.[31] It's important to note that just because one social network— or any other social media channel—may be perceived to be more broadly popular, organizations should consider their specific goals and audience when developing a strategy for engagement and not neglect social media channels that may in fact be the right fit for their goals and audience.[32]

Attacks and Campaigns

A major potential reputational issue for an organization is a targeted, coordinated attack or campaign within social media. In the face of such an attack, the key is to determine if the critic's position is based on a deficit, fault, or problem in the company, its leadership or its product(s)—basically, is there a basis in fact in the campaign, and thus, potentially room for improvement.

Perhaps the most famous example of a company that encountered a collective blogosphere outcry over its products and customer service was Dell. In June 2005, new media guru Jeff Jarvis first wrote on his blog, buzzmachine.com, about his problems with the Dell products he owned and with the customer service he'd encountered, with a post called "Dell Lies. Dell Sucks."[33] The technical and customer service problems Jarvis detailed resonated with others. The outcry spread and became known as "Dell Hell." Followed by video of an exploding laptop (and subsequent recall) as well as falling earnings, it seemed that Dell's problems were practically insurmountable. The company also was not participating in the conversation that was happening about them in social media, and their absence in the face of the storm added more fuel to the fire.

Dell slowly worked to regain the trust and support of the public and its customers through a combination of product and customer service adjustments, as well as through communication on its own blogs, outreach to others, and dialogue in social media channels. The company's work paid off, and slightly over two years after the original "Dell Hell" post, Jarvis wrote a column that appeared in *BusinessWeek* titled, "Dell Learns to Listen," in which he said, "In the age of customers empowered by blogs and social media, Dell has leapt from worst to first."[34] But did you catch that timeframe? *Two years.* That's not a short amount of time for a company to be dealing with those kinds of widespread problems and complaints. While Dell has turned around, it took a tremendous amount of sustained work to make it happen.

AIR FORCE BLOG ASSESSMENT RESPONSE DIAGRAM

But what if the online attack is not necessarily based on an underlying problem or fact? The U.S. Air Force has developed a "Blog Response Assessment" that is an excellent starting point for helping to analyze how, if, and when to respond online, and can be useful in evaluating all forms of social media, not just blogs.

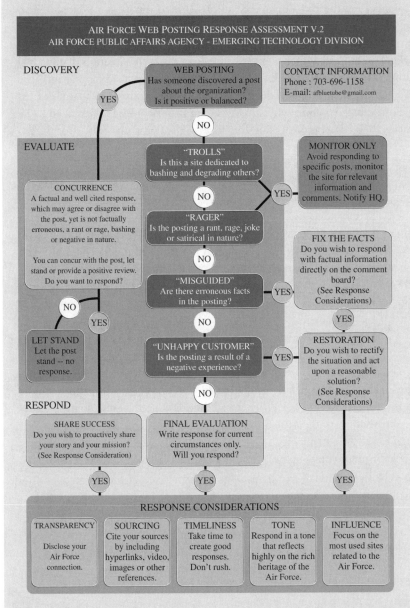

Figure 4.1

FORD MOTOR COMPANY AND THE ECONOMIC CRISIS

The global economic crisis of 2008–9 took few prisoners. Almost every company and industry in the U.S. suffered the effects of the worst economic situation since the Great Depression, and the American auto industry was among the hardest hit. The combination of the economic crisis plus years of flagging product performance, soaring labor costs, slower sales, high gas prices, and other challenges led the Big Three U.S. automakers to the brink of disaster. Two of the three, GM and Chrysler, ended up in bankruptcy despite significant federal government assistance.

The third of the Big Three, Ford Motor Company, was in a different situation than its two major U.S. competitors in the fall of 2008. Even though Ford did not need federal financial assistance, the widespread public perception during the worst of the crisis was that it did. As part of its response, Ford created a comprehensive Web site in November 2008 called "The Ford Story" (http://www.thefordstory.com/). The site detailed the company's plans for the future and how it was going to get there, the current situation, and the progress it had already made.

> The company's social media efforts both during the worst of the crisis and since have extended and expanded the reach of "The Ford Story," as members of Ford's social media team have engaged with audiences on blogs, Twitter, Facebook and other social media channels.

But the Web site was just the beginning. The company's social media efforts both during the worst of the crisis and since have extended and expanded the reach of "The Ford Story," as members of Ford's social media team have engaged with audiences on blogs, Twitter, Facebook and other social media channels. The team members have responded to questions, concerns, accusations, and debate, working tirelessly to tell Ford's side of the story and engage in real dialogue about the state of the company and its products.

Ford's business strategy combined with its social media and traditional media efforts appear to be paying off, and the perception of the company and its products is starting to change. It was the first large car manufacturer to see an increase in sales in 2009.[35] The company also won top quality rankings from the RDA Group in 2009, beating its competitors Toyota and Honda for the first time in a quality ranking.[36] And in the Virtue study of the "Top Social Brands of 2008," Ford came in at number 12, the highest ranking for an auto company.[37]

Through tireless engagement with people across the social media spectrum, Ford's story has started to be not only told, but heard.

■ ■ ■

MAYO CLINIC: ENERGIZING OLD-FASHIONED WORD-OF-MOUTH THROUGH SOCIAL MEDIA

By Lee Aase, Manager, Syndication and Social Media, Mayo Clinic

Using social media is consistent with what has made Mayo Clinic's reputation for more than 100 years. At the turn of the twentieth century it was relatively unusual for patients to survive a hospital stay. They typically succumbed not to their underlying ailment but to an infection resulting from surgery. So when Dr. Will and Dr. Charles Mayo collaborated with the Sisters of St. Francis to pioneer aseptic surgical techniques, which meant that many more patients lived to tell their stories, the surgical survivors were excited to spread the word.

> Using social media is consistent with what has made Mayo Clinic's reputation for more than 100 years.

Even today word of mouth is the most important source of information that makes Mayo Clinic the top choice for diagnosis and treatment of serious diseases. Stories in the news media rank second in influence, and physician recommendation—another kind of word of mouth—is third.

Social media combines the potential worldwide reach of news media stories with the personal touch of a friend's recommendation. With over 90 percent of Mayo Clinic patients reporting that they say "good things" to their friends after a visit, using social media tools to amplify their impressions seemed reasonable.

> Social media combines the potential worldwide reach of news media stories with the personal touch of a friend's recommendation.

But we didn't just immediately jump into blogging, Facebook, YouTube, and Twitter. It was a natural, gradual progression. Mayo Clinic created its "Medical Edge" syndicated weekly TV news resource in 2000 and offered local stations trustworthy health and medical news content. In 2004, we established a similar daily program for radio stations.

Our first "new media" foray involved creating an RSS feed for the radio segments to publish a podcast. And because producing our Medical Edge TV segments typically involved interviewing physicians for 20 minutes or more, while only a few seconds made the broadcast piece, our next step was to make the complete interviews available as audio podcast segments.

Within the next year or so we established a Mayo Clinic Facebook page, YouTube channel, and Twitter account. Part of the goal was to keep others from "squatting" on the name and posing as Mayo Clinic. We saw a "fan" page in Facebook as a way for people to share their stories on our wall, and for their friends to see them. The total out-of-pocket cost for Twitter, Facebook, and YouTube was $0.

Another key low-cost tool that greatly extended our social media presence was a consumer-grade video camera, which lets us shoot, edit and upload to YouTube quickly and easily. We provide the raw video files to journalists for incorporation into their online stories. This video also lets network producers evaluate our subject experts who lack national TV experience, so they can book them for live programs with more confidence.

Low-cost video made blogging realistic for us because we want our blogs to be authentic, not ghost-written, but yet we don't want to take time away from patient care. By shooting interviews with physicians we can take just a few minutes of their time and ask them to explain their studies as they would for a patient in the office.

We have several blogs, and for less than $100 per blog per year we can customize the look and feel, upload audio and video files and map to a subdomain of either mayoclinic.org—our patient site—or mayo.edu—our research/education site. MayoClinic.com, our consumer health information site, also has several blogs.

Sharing Mayo Clinic, which was launched in January 2009, is our flagship blog. It's the place where we feature employees in various roles, but mainly where patients can share their stories. And it provides a glimpse into what makes Mayo Clinic special.

Recommendations: Start by listening and taking advantage of the free or low-cost tools. By keeping your costs low, you will be able to create the breathing room you need to have time to achieve results. If you seek significant financial investments at the beginning, you will be expected to show more immediate traction, and that may be hard to achieve. But if you use the social tools with your existing staff as a way to accomplish your current work more effectively, you will get some wins that will enable you to expand your scope.

■■■

GENERAL BEST PRACTICES

1. *Listen and monitor*

While there's certainly disagreement about some aspects of how organizations should participate in social media, most everyone would agree that the first step for any individual or organization is to listen. Listen to people on blogs, on Twitter, on podcasts, on YouTube. Listen to what people are saying about you, your organization, your product or service, your competitors. Where are they talking? What are they saying? Who are they talking to and with? How do they expect you or the organization to respond or participate?

But, you might say, that's a lot of conversations. There's no way I can follow all of that. It's too much information, coming too quickly, from too many people. First, there are tools and techniques to help manage the flow of information. And second, what are the risks of not listening?

These are just a few of the ways that can help manage the flow of information:

- Create Google Alerts for all relevant search terms for you and/or your organization (its brand, leaders, products and/or services, competitors).

- Set up an RSS reader, such as Google Reader, and subscribe to blogs and other forms of relevant content.
- If you're using Twitter, consider using a desktop or mobile application that allows you to add search into the flow and adds greater flexibility for sorting and following information.
- Explore some of the sites where you can search the realtime web (beyond simply Google), such as Technorati or Social Mention, and then add that search information to your RSS reader.
- As you get more advanced, you may want to consider whether you have a need for a paid social media monitoring service.

As you listen and explore, you'll begin to discover what topics or issues are most important to the people that matter to you. With time and by listening to the community, it will also help you determine the thought leaders and influential members of your network. And with time, you'll begin to see where there are opportunities to join the conversation.

2. *Help your employees help themselves*

Develop a social media policy, and then educate and empower your employees. For sample social media policy guidance, see the policies online for Sun Microsystems, IBM, the U.K. government, and others, as well as Charlene Li's wiki that links to policies from various entities. Organizations take different approaches to social media policies, but many of the guidance and rules that apply to other forms of communication also apply to social media. As Sun says, "Don't Tell Secrets: Common sense at work here; it's perfectly OK to talk about your work and have a dialog with the community, but it's not OK to publish the recipe for one of our secret sauces."[38] Private, confidential, proprietary, and other kinds of information still must be kept within the organization. But employees can also be the best ambassadors for an organization. Organizations don't communicate, human beings do, and employees are an organization's best asset for building and maintaining reputation online.

3. *Participate, don't dictate*

It's important for any organization participating in social media to begin with a focus on their audience, not with a focus on themselves. Social media should not be a new channel for organizations to dump their advertising or other kinds of marketing materials. If all an organization does is use Facebook, Twitter or a blog to promote itself, that organization won't get very far in building relationships and reputational capital in social media.

As an organization or representative of an organization, you want to add value and participate in the community and conversations happening online. Adding value means providing *something* to the people who are having conversations with or about you. What that *something* is depends on who you are and what your business goals are, but it could range from addressing customer service problems (such as JetBlue), or bringing your customers in to help you build a better business or product (such as

Starbucks' "MyIdea" or Best Buy's "IdeaX"). Developing a strategy for social media participation often comes before implementing the actual tools.

4. *Be prepared for the feedback*

So, you're listening and monitoring, you have a social media policy for employees, and you've figured out some ways to add value through social media participation. Now what? Many times, an organization will get through the first few steps of social media engagement, but then won't know what to do or how to handle the feedback that is coming back. You might ask the following kinds of questions:

- How will different departments work together to address feedback?
- Is the organization prepared to respond quickly?
- Is the organization able or willing to incorporate suggestions for improvement?

These are just a few to get started. What else might you ask?

5. *Plan, integrate and measure*

Just like other forms of communication, corporate participation in social media should be strategically planned and integrated with the organization's broader business and communication goals. Remember the kinds of disconnect between actions and communication that we talked about earlier, and how it has the potential to hurt an organization's reputation and perception of authenticity? Planning and coherent integration of social media is really a crucial best practice.

Organizations also need to evaluate and measure social media activities, and make adjustments based on those results. There is a fairly significant amount of disagreement over how to measure social media and what kinds of metrics and tools can accurately and appropriately be used, but most people at this point agree that there *are* some useful ways to measure social media. Katie Delahaye Paine, the "queen of measurement," offers a more in-depth discussion of measurement and metrics on her blogs and in her newsletter (http://kdpaine.blogs.com/), and discusses how "goals drive metrics, metrics drive results." Some kind of evaluation and measurement process is critical, but will need to be tailored to an organization's particular goals.

6. *Embrace opportunity*

Finally, social media can sometimes be scary and intimidating to people and organizations just beginning to participate or looking to expand. The technology and terms can seem foreign. Sometimes people feel like they're late to the party and don't know how to catch up. But there are many different kinds of opportunities within social media, and if you see the possibilities in terms of how it fits within your broader communications and business goals, it just might seem a little less scary. The technology, terms, and particular services will undoubtedly change, but the underlying cultural shifts will likely remain.

RESOURCES FOR FURTHER STUDY

In addition to the resources and books cited throughout the chapter, here are some additional online resources for further study:

Berkman Center for Internet and Society at Harvard University, http://cyber.law.harvard.edu/.

Edelman Trust Barometer, http://www.edelman.com/trust/2009/.

Peter Kim's wiki, "A Master List of Social Media Marketing Examples", http://wiki.beingpeter-kim.com/.

Pew Internet and American Life Project: http://www.pewinternet.org/. "The Project produces reports exploring the impact of the internet on families, communities, work and home, daily life, education, health care, and civic and political life."

Poynter Institute, http://www.poynter.org/.

PROpenMic, a "social network for students, faculty and practitioners", http://www.propen-mic.org/.

Social Media Pack, video series "In Plain English", http://www.commoncraft.com/social-me-dia-pack. An excellent series of videos that explain different elements of social media in easy to understand terms, with simple but compelling images.

Weber Shandwick's report, "Risky Business: Reputations Online", http://www.online-repu-tations.com/findings.html.

More links, tools and resources continually updated on my Delicious page, http://delicious.com/laurelhart.

QUESTIONS FOR FURTHER DISCUSSION

1   How is social media changing the way that companies communicate? What hasn't changed?

2   What are some of the ethical challenges a company may face in social media, and how can a company alleviate those challenges?

3   How are mainstream media and social media interacting with each other, and how do you see that relationship continuing in the future?

4   How is social media affecting public relations?

5   What's different today about social media than when this chapter was written in 2009?

The challenge: To align employees' hands, minds, and hearts with the organization's reputational interests.

5 ORGANIZATIONAL COMMUNICATION

By Jeff Grimshaw and Tanya Mann

- Getting employees aligned is essential to reputation management
- Making smart choices to align employee *behavior* with reputational interests
- Making smart choices to align employee *performance* with reputational interests
- Sidebar: Driving performance through organizational communication, by Maril MacDonald
- Sidebar: The evolution of strategic employee communication at Hallmark: from reporting to strategic communication, by Steve Doyal
- Best practices
- Resources for further study
- Questions for further discussion

■ ■ ■

Some years ago the CEO and COO of one of the most admired companies in the U.S. sat down to make a highly polished video they planned to distribute to all employees. The idea was to convey four values that the leaders said should govern everything that happened in the organization. The four values? Respect, communication, excellence, and integrity. In the video, the CEO was especially emphatic about that last value:

> [We are] a company that deals with everyone with absolute integrity. We play by all the rules, we stand by our word. We mean what we say, we say what we mean. We want people to leave a transaction with [us] thinking that they've been dealt with in the highest possible way as far as integrity and truthfulness, and really doing our business right.

As you might have guessed, the CEO and COO were Ken Lay and Jeff Skilling and the company was Enron. This example underscores the timelessness of the observation that theologian Reinhold Niebuhr made over 70 years ago, when he spoke of the human tendency to express our values "most pretentiously … most convincingly … at the very moment when the decay which leads to death has already begun."

■ ■ ■

Most leaders are not as duplicitous or cynical as Lay and Skilling; nonetheless, far too many look to the organizational communication function merely to help them spit out highly polished products and self-indulgent platitudes. Unfortunately, these products and platitudes are largely irrelevant—or even counter-productive—to the cause of aligning employees' performance and behavior with their employer's long-term reputational interests and competitive advantage. What works? Alignment with reputational interests happens only when leaders treat organizational communication as a tightly integrated and strategic process for engaging employees in open, candid, reality-based dialogue.

Strategic organizational communication: The process of aligning employees' "hands, minds, and hearts" with the organization's reputational interests— as a way to produce competitive advantage.

■ ■ ■

GETTING EMPLOYEES ALIGNED IS ESSENTIAL TO REPUTATION MANAGEMENT

An organization is the sum of its parts. So if, as Doorley and Garcia contend,

> **(behavior and performance) + communication = reputation**

then any serious effort to manage reputation must include a proper focus on aligning the behavior and performance of *the organization's employees*.

> Any serious effort to manage reputation must include a proper focus on aligning the behavior and performance of the organization's employees.

- Aligning employee *behavior*. The goal here is for employees to operate within appropriate boundaries (ethical, legal, regulatory, or otherwise). They are equipped to make sound judgments when they encounter *moments of truth and trade-off* ... situations where short-term results, operational efficiency, or self-interests come into conflict with an organization's stated values and long-term reputational interests.

- Aligning employee *performance*. The goal here is for employees to align their priorities and energies with organizational strategy, deliver branded experiences to customers, invest discretionary effort, and perform their roles in ways that deliver optimum value and results.

Barriers to Alignment

Unfortunately, too many organizations' efforts to drive these two types of alignment are inconsistent, indirect, and ineffective. The Enron story at the beginning of this chapter highlights some of the problems: A product-focused, propagandistic approach to organizational communication delivers gloss—but not much else. Here we'll break down the most challenging barriers to aligning employees' with their organization's reputational interests.

SENIOR LEADERSHIP FAILS TO OWN IT

In many organizations, employees hear compliance, HR, or training as the primary voice of reputation management. As we know, the medium is the message, so those organizations might as well shout, "We're just going through the motions to cover our behinds."

What's needed? As is evident from the best practices we'll highlight later in the chapter, to align and engage employees in support of reputational interests must be a leader-driven and leader-led activity. In the organizations that most effectively promote alignment, the CEO is front and center on the topic.

TACTICAL FOCUS OF EMPLOYEE COMMUNICATION

Historically, leaders in large organizations have looked to the employee communication function to play a primarily tactical role, focused on delivering formal communication *products* "to specs." In this model, the employee communication department is an internal vendor. Communicators provide value and make names for themselves based on their writing, editing, event management, and production skills, as well as their proficiency in the latest communication tools and social media. What gets measured is attention ("How many people visited our news page on the intranet site last week?"), as opposed to actual behavior change ("Are we helping leaders align performance and behavior? And how much?").

What's needed? For senior leadership to effectively "own it," they need the support of highly strategic communicators and trusted advisors to drive employee alignment with the organization's reputational interests. Yes, there need to be tacticians in the mix to support execution. But without the support of strong strategists (who have access to and are trusted by the leaders they support), efforts to drive alignment typically crumble under their own weight.

LACK OF ROLE CLARITY

In a typical organization, the marketing department owns the brand, customer service owns brand delivery, public affairs owns reputation, HR owns employee communication, etc. In this scenario, it should be of no surprise that employees' performance and behavior are aligned inconsistently with the organization's reputational interests, since no one has any clear accountability for creating that alignment.

How big is the problem? A study conducted in 2007 by Brodeur Partners and Watson Wyatt found that across organizations, only half of managers described themselves as very knowledgeable about how their company wanted to project itself in the marketplace and less than half of individual contributors said their company enabled them to take action to deliver the brand and support the organization's reputational interests. What's at stake? The same study demonstrated that the companies that solve the problem and succeed in creating alignment can expect to see increased discretionary effort, retention of top performers, and overall financial performance.

> The companies that solve the problem and succeed in creating alignment can expect to see increased discretionary effort, retention of top performers, and overall financial performance.

What's needed? Alignment and integration, which underscores our earlier point about the importance of ownership at the top of the organization.

NOISE

As the influential social scientist Herbert Simon observed four decades ago, attention is a scarce resource—even if we don't tend to think of it that way. And therefore, he said, "a wealth of information creates a poverty of attention."[1] That "wealth" has exploded in recent years, with Facebook, YouTube, Twitter, blogs, iPhone applications, and thousands of other new information sources competing with leaders for their employees' attention. It's harder than ever to cut through the noise to reach employees in meaningful ways with messages that will help to align behaviors and performance.

Of course, the communication practices in many organizations only compound the problem. Leaders can't expect employees to pick out and pay attention to their genuinely important messages if they've flooded the informational marketplace with cheap imitations. But lots of organizations push out communications to their employees like a Soviet factory—uncoordinated, undisciplined, and without regard to the actual demand or need for what it's producing. This misguided activity often flows from good intentions: "We just did something. And communication is good. Ergo, let's communicate what we just did." In other cases, leaders make supply-side communication choices because it makes them feel good—for example, to show off all the important stuff they're doing—or just because they can (e.g., "We have a cool studio, so let's make some videos.").

> Supply-side communication choices—instead of producing "fully informed employees"—create an environment where employees just ignore most of the information delivered through formal channels while wondering what is really happening.

In any case, uncoordinated, undisciplined, supply-side communication choices—instead of producing "fully informed employees"—create an environment where employees just ignore most of the information delivered through formal channels while wondering what is really happening ... and what things they really ought to align with. This undermines leaders' ability to get their people engaged around efforts to promote the organization's long-term reputational interests.

What's needed? Coordinated, disciplined, demand-driven communication practices. It's impossible for an organization effectively to align its employees' behavior and performance until it has successfully competed for their attention.

Those are some of the challenges to aligning employees' behavior and performance. Now let's focus on some specific best practices for making it happen.

MAKING SMART CHOICES TO ALIGN EMPLOYEE BEHAVIOR WITH REPUTATIONAL INTERESTS

In a famous study[2] conducted at Princeton Theological Seminary, researchers recruited a group of young seminarians and prepared them to give a talk on the Parable of the Good Samaritan. In this parable, a traveler is robbed and beaten by thieves who leave him half dead. A priest comes, sees the beaten traveler, and passes by. And then an assistant priest does the same. Finally a Samaritan arrives on the scene, bandages the man's wounds, and takes care of him at a nearby inn.

After the researchers prepared the seminarians to give a talk on the story and its implications, they sent the students off, one by one, to fulfill their assignment. Some were directed to move very quickly, and told, "You're a few minutes late. They were expecting you a few minutes ago." Members of the second, "medium hurry" group were told, "The assistant is ready. Please go right over." But there was no rush for the members of the third group, who were told, "It will be a few minutes before they need you, but you as might as well head on over."

On the way to their assignment, each seminarian encountered a man on the sidewalk, slumped over, coughing and moaning. Unbeknownst to the seminarians, this man was a confederate—an actor who was part of the experiment.

Of the seminarians instructed to rush to their assignment to talk about the Parable of the Good Samaritan, only 10 percent stopped to help the man. The others walked past him ... or over him. The seminarians in the second group, who'd been told merely to "go right over," fared better: nearly half of them stopped to help the man ... but the other half did not. Meanwhile, a majority of the seminarians in the third group, who weren't in any rush, stopped on their way to speaking about the Good Samaritan to act like one.[3]

What's true of many of the seminarians in this study is also true of many employees in the organizations where we've worked. They know what it means to do the right thing, at least in theory. In fact, like the seminarians, they know it well enough that they can explain it to others. But when they encounter high-pressure "moments of truth and trade-off" where "doing the right thing" and completing an assigned task (or otherwise "getting results" or pursuing other self-interests) seem like mutually exclusive options, they often make the wrong choice. Part of the challenge is that most organizations do a lousy job of preparing their employees for these moments.

> But when they encounter high-pressure "moments of truth and trade-off" where "doing the right thing" and completing an assigned task (or otherwise "getting results" or pursuing other self-interests) seem like mutually exclusive options, they often make the wrong choice. Part of the challenge is that most organizations do a lousy job of preparing their employees for these moments.

Doing what most organizations do—simply communicating a list of values—doesn't cut it. The problem starts at the source: Pronouncements of "Our Values" often emerge from an executive retreat where a facilitator has led the senior team through the ritual of identifying the concepts with which they'd like to imagine themselves associated ("Commitment," "Fun," "Teamwork," etc.). But in moments of truth and trade-off, these lists do little to help employees who need to distill a set of acceptable options and make a wise selection from among the alternatives.

We've identified four best practices in the organizations that are most serious about—and most effective at—aligning employee behavior with reputational interests.

Bright Lines and Well-Defined Boundaries ... Enforced Consistently

Perhaps we were too hard on Ken Lay and Jeff Skilling earlier in the chapter. After all, they really did believe in Enron's four stated values—respect, communication, excellence, and integrity—but only insofar as none of those ever got in the way of making lots and lots and lots of money.

Of course, making money and delivering results is important in any organization. The question is: are there any caveats or constraints? Like Enron, organizations can create an environment where the de facto value is "anything goes ... whatever it takes ... as long as you are delivering results." Or they can communicate what economics Nobel laureate Thomas Schelling calls "bright lines" and "well-defined boundaries."

So that in their pursuit of results and (individual or organizational) self-interests, employees clearly understand "the things you can never, ever do."

To deliver the "out-of-bounds" message with maximum credibility and impact, one can't delegate the responsibility to the HR or compliance departments. The medium is the message, which means employees need to hear it from their leadership.

Vanguard is one of the world's largest investment management companies. And if you are one of firm's 12,500 employees, you know what's out of bounds … the stuff you can never do. You learned it in your first week of work, possibly in a face-to-face setting with the CEO himself. Before he stepped down in 2008, former CEO Jack Brennan (who remains the firm's chairman) frequently showed up at "new crew orientation" to deliver a message.

> "You can make mistakes at Vanguard. But you can never make an ethical mistake, period. You violate our sense of the right thing, and I am personally going to run you over in the parking lot."

"We make mistakes all the time," he'd tell them. "You can make mistakes at Vanguard. But you can never make an *ethical* mistake, period. You violate our sense of the right thing, and I am personally going to run you over in the parking lot. If that makes you uncomfortable, there is a break coming up, and you should leave then. But you can't say you didn't hear it." And then, with their full attention, he recited a list of boundaries. "Violate client confidentiality, and you're out. Accept a gift from a vendor, and you're out. There is no redemption. You send an offensive e-mail, you don't work here anymore."

"Of course," Mr. Brennan acknowledged later, "the 'run you over' bit is hyperbole. And HR hates that I say it. But I do it for a reason. Because it's effective. People get it. I have people saying ten years later, 'I remember you told me that you'd run me over in the parking lot if I ever did anything ethically wrong.'"

Some CEOs might want to be remembered for something else, but one gets the feeling Mr. Brennan is perfectly happy with this kind of legacy. "It's important never to give ground," he said. "And you hate to see somebody's career end because they sent some stupid e-mail. But if we give ground, we create gray areas. There is no gray area."

And therein lies the payoff for employees … and for Vanguard: no gray area means employees waste little time and energy wondering and second-guessing what's really expected, what's really rewarded, and what's really out of bounds. As Brennan explains, "This isn't an easy place to work. But our uncompromising approach on ethical mistakes is part of what makes this an easy place to come to work. Because we are never going to put you in a compromising position." Over the past decade, how many other firms in the finance industry offered the same perk? How many wish they had?

Of course, an organization's out-of-bounds list is credible and instructive only if leaders consistently enforce it, even when the offenders are top performers. Otherwise, all they've given their employees is a "list of stuff you can never do … unless we really don't want to fire you," which is guidance they will find very difficult to interpret and apply. When they make exceptions, the out-of-bounds list loses its value as a practical, reliable tool to help employees make decisions.

Lots of leaders get this in theory, but when the need to act arises, they make excuses why they can't or shouldn't. Not our client Terry Mullen. As president of Lincoln Financial Distributors, a subsidiary of the Lincoln Financial Group, Mr. Mullen knows that keeping boundaries meaningful requires continuous, vigilant reinforcement. A few years ago, at a national sales conference, one of Mullen's top people made an inappropriate, off-color remark at the podium. "So we fired him," Mullen recalls. "He was shocked. He thought, 'I'm the top guy. They can't fire me.' But we did." Shortly after that, another top performer was caught cheating on his expenses. "And he was gone," Mullen says. "If you just say, 'Don't say inappropriate things,' and 'Don't cheat,' but don't do anything about it, no one will listen. The trick is, you have to follow through."

> "If you just say, 'Don't say inappropriate things,' and 'Don't cheat,' but don't do anything about it, no one will listen. The trick is, you have to follow through."

PRACTICAL RULES OF THUMB

A rule of thumb "is a principle with broad application that is … easily learned and easily applied … for making some determination."[4] We've found they can be much more useful than a laundry list of esoteric values to employees who are trying to decide what to do when they don't know what to do.

"OUR VALUES, IN ORDER OF IMPORTANCE"

Our client Nguyen Toan runs the PetroVietnam unit that builds refineries and other technical installations. In recent years they've successfully completed 26 projects, with no failures. Toan says the secret of his success is that he communicates doggedly with his employees about values. "Our top three priorities," he says, "are safety, quality, and productivity."

Of course, building refineries is a dangerous, tricky business, and there is constant tension between these three values. So Mr. Toan also makes the order of importance clear. "We make sure that everyone understands that safety is the most important," he says. And it seems to be working. In the past seven years, Mr. Toan's team has logged nearly ten million man-hours with only one accident—a broken leg. That's an impressive statistic in any industry, let alone in the refinery-building business.

"Then we have quality," Mr. Toan says. "At first, our quality was not very good and after construction, we'd have a lot of repairs and welding to go back and do. We'd spend a lot of time and money doing repairs afterward, delaying schedules. But we started providing incentives for better quality and we're seeing higher quality work emerge. But, back to safety: If someone is hurt in the process, the quality doesn't matter."

"Once we ensure that safety and quality are achieved, we value productivity," Mr. Toan says. "We don't push it too hard, though. Because the faster people work the less safety and less quality there will be."

Life is full of trade-offs. Among the thousands of organizations that have communicated a list of stated values, many could provide more practical value to their employees if they did what Mr. Toan did: List the values in order of importance, equipping employees with a tool that actually helps them evaluate trade-offs from situation-to-situation and make more confident decisions about which alternative represents "the right thing to do."

"AT GOLDMAN SACHS, WE'RE LONG-TERM GREEDY"

Some politicians and pundits cite "greed" as the cause of the financial meltdown that began in 2008. But "greedy" is a subjective term—a disparaging descriptor of someone else's pursuit of his or her own self-interest. Amidst the hand-wringing, one shouldn't forget that self-interest is the basis of capitalism. Gordon Gekko, the Michael Douglas character in the movie Wall Street, was right when he said: "Greed, for lack of a better word, is good. Greed is right, greed works."

Unless it's *short-term* greed. Short-term greed leads smart individuals to do collectively stupid things, which is a large part of what created the financial mess. Through their actions Wall Street CEOs, politicians, and regulators fostered a system that rewarded short-term risk-taking while putting in jeopardy the long-term health of the economy. Short-term greed isn't good and it isn't right and it doesn't work for long because it's not sustainable.

> Our all-time favorite declaration of corporate values. In the 1970s, Gus Levy, then managing partner at Goldman Sachs, was asked what made his firm so special. Levy responded, "we're greedy, but we're long-term greedy." And he meant it. Stories that demonstrated the "long-term greedy" ethos in action became part of the firm's folklore.

Which is why you won't be surprised when we reveal to you our all-time favorite declaration of corporate values. In the 1970s, Gus Levy, then managing partner at Goldman Sachs, was asked what made his firm so special. Levy responded, "we're greedy, but we're *long-term greedy*."[5]

And he meant it. Stories that demonstrated the "long-term greedy" ethos in action became part of the firm's folklore. After the stock market crashed in 1987, Goldman Sachs faced a $100 million loss—at the time 20 percent of the firm's earnings—on an underwriting deal to partially privatize British Petroleum. When some of the underwriters began looking for legal technicalities that would reduce their exposure, Goldman Sachs' managing partner at the time, John Weinburg, pushed back:

> Gentlemen, Goldman Sachs is going to do this [deal]. It is expensive and painful but we are going to do it. Because … those of you who decide not to do it … won't be underwriting a goat house. Not even an outhouse.

When the resulting loss chased other large firms out of the privatization business in Europe, Goldman Sachs picked up the slack and long-term greedy paid off. Similarly, Goldman Sachs left short-term money on the table when they refused to represent any company undertaking a hostile bid for another company. Threatened companies, in turn, took their business to Goldman Sachs,[6] which produced another win for long-term greedy. As the firm grew, this folklore helped employees navigate sticky situations: "We should do the right thing even if it hurts in the short-term, because at Goldman Sachs we're long-term greedy."

And for years, Goldman Sachs avoided the myopia that inflicted most of its competitors. Until it became like everybody else.

In the publicly traded firms on Wall Street (of which Goldman Sachs was one) "you were paid [in recent years] according (more or less) to your profits or fee generation, regardless of the outcome, down the road, of the deals you did or the loans you made or the assets you took on," according to *New Yorker* staff writer Nick Paumgarten. "You had an incentive to generate inflated or ephemeral gains, and, often little incentive not to."[7]

Inevitably, this led to trouble. Goldman Sachs' current CEO, Lloyd Blankfein, has acknowledged that "we participated in the market euphoria and failed to raise a responsible voice" in the lead-up to the financial crisis.[8] The collapse of long-term greedy required the firm to take a $10 billion government bailout. "We believe that re-payment of the government's investment is a strong sign of progress and one measure of the ability to recover from the crisis," Blankfein said in a letter to Congressional leaders. "But real stability can return only if our industry accepts that certain practices were unhealthy and not in the long-term interests of individual institutions and the financial system, as a whole."

In other words, Mr. Blankfein wants to lead a return to "long-term greedy"—and it appears he is backing up his words: In May of 2009, Blankfein instituted new compensation practices. Some highlights:

- To avoid misaligning compensation and performance, the firm will use guaranteed employment contracts only in exceptional circumstances (for example, for new hires) and avoid multi-year guarantees entirely
- The firm commits that cash compensation in a single year will never be so much as to overwhelm the value ascribed to longer term stock incentives that can only be realized through longer term responsible behavior
- The firm will subject equity awards to vesting and other restrictions over an extended period of time. This allows for forfeiture or a "clawback" in the event that an employee's conduct or judgment results in a restatement of the firm's financial statements or other significant harm to the firm's business. The firm can also use the clawback in response to any individual misconduct that results in legal or reputational harm. And equity delivery schedules continue to apply after an individual has left the firm.
- The firm commits to evaluate an employee's outsized gain, just like an outsized loss, in the context of the cumulative record of that individual's risk judgments.

> It would have been far better to have never forgotten Levy's maxim in the first place. According to another well-known saying at Goldman Sachs, "Our assets are our people, capital, and reputation. If any of these is ever diminished, the last is the most difficult to restore."

Of course, it would have been far better to have never forgotten Levy's maxim in the first place. According to another well-known saying at Goldman Sachs, "Our assets are our people, capital, and reputation. If any of these is ever diminished, the last is the most difficult to restore."

REALISTIC, SCENARIO-BASED DISCUSSIONS

When US Airways pilot Chesley "Sully" Sullenberger lost both engines shortly after take-off from La Guardia in January 2009, he stayed cool and made the right call—to ditch the plane in the Hudson River—because he'd trained repeatedly for various crash scenarios. Even if the stakes aren't quite as high in most lines of work, realistic, scenario-based training is a great idea for leaders who want their employees to stay cool and make smart choices in moments of truth and trade-off.

Along with our colleague Barry Mike, we've helped organizations create scenarios based on real-life situations that employees face. Then we help leaders prepare to hold face-to-face discussions with small groups of employees around these scenarios and the right thing to do in the situations described.

In some cases, there are actually "right" answers to the questions and the discussion provides an opportunity to talk about the application of specific compliance-related rules and procedures to actual sticky situations employees face. Here's an example of one such scenario and the associated discussion questions.

> *You and a vendor have developed a great working relationship during the course of a $2.5 million project. The contractor invites you to play golf and have lunch afterward, which you accept. On the way home, you realize you never saw a bill for either the golf or the lunch, which, as best as you can estimate, may have cost about $175.*

- Did you just commit an act of non-compliance?
- Why or why not?
- What is the right thing to do?

Scenario-based discussions like these are a great way to bring the compliance manual to life and take away excuses about "gray areas." Such discussions let employees know unequivocally that the organization's compliance policies aren't like the admonition on the Q-Tip box to avoid inserting the product into the ear canal … a perfunctory message that for practical reasons people routinely ignore.

What's even more interesting are the scenarios that are less about compliance and more about reputational judgment—where there are typically no right or wrong answers from a regulatory or legal standpoint. Mr. Mike notes that clients "are often surprised at how much employees appreciate the opportunity to discuss the practical application of company values to what senior leaders may consider to be relatively mundane but realistic challenges."

Clients "are often surprised at how much employees appreciate the opportunity to discuss the practical application of company values to what senior leaders may consider to be relatively mundane but realistic challenges."

> *Your boss e-mails you and asks you to print out a client document and deliver it to the client within the next hour. While printing the document, you notice many typos, spelling, and format errors. Upon reading the document for consistency, you find that it needs a lot of editing. Your boss has told the client that the document will be delivered within the hour, and the client is counting on it getting there on time. However, in order for you to read through the entire document and make the necessary edits, you will need at least two hours. What do you do?*

After outlining a scenario like this one, the leader then facilitates a group discussion around six questions we prescribe.

1. Which of our values should guide your decisions and actions in this situation?

2. Are there unwritten rules or precedents in our culture that would suggest how to handle this situation, or one like it? If so, are those unwritten rules or precedents consistent with our values?
3. Would you be likely to seek input from others when deciding how to act? If so, whom would you engage? How would you engage them? What would you say?
4. Would our values, and the way we apply them, differentiate us in a situation like this? In other words, would you expect us to handle this situation differently than would a competitor?
5. What positive consequences, if any, would you expect to encounter as a result of making a values-driven decision in this situation?
6. What negative consequences, if any, would you expect to encounter as a result of making a values-driven decision in this situation? How would you manage them?

The discussions are enlightening for leaders and employees. Employees walk away with more practical clarity about what to do when they don't know what to do (and enhanced perceptions of the leader's credibility). And as a result of the opportunity to reinforce expectations, leaders come away with more confidence that employees will make smart decisions when it counts. Additionally, as a result of the opportunity to listen to candid input and discussion about challenges employees encounter, leaders typically come away from these conversations with good ideas about steps they can take to more effectively align employee behavior with long-term reputational interests.

GAP ANALYSIS: WHAT WE SAY VS. WHAT WE DO

Bill Adams and David Spach from Maxcomm, a management-consulting firm, help leaders engage their people in reality-based conversations. They hold face-to-face conversations with small groups of employees around the organization's stated values. For each stated value, the leader guides the discussion around five questions:

1. How well are we currently living this value? (On a 7-point scale, where 1 means "never see it" and 7 means "it's everywhere I look.")
2. What are examples of this value in action?
3. What are examples of violating this value?
4. What's getting in the way of living this value?
5. What's making it easy to live this value?

For leaders willing to listen, the gap analysis exercise provides the opportunity to catch small problems before they become big ones, clarify and amplify expectations, challenge employees' excuses, and identify how the leaders can more effectively align employee behavior with the organization's reputational interests. To a leadership team that cares about aligning words and actions, and has asserted a commitment to, say, "transparency," a comment such as, "I've never been penalized for keeping bad news to myself, but I get targeted every time I try to surface important risks" provides an unpleasant, but important, wake-up call.

> For leaders willing to listen, the gap analysis exercise provides the opportunity to catch small problems before they become big ones, clarify and amplify expectations, challenge employees' excuses, and identify how the leaders can more effectively align employee behavior with the organization's reputational interests.

MAKING SMART CHOICES TO ALIGN EMPLOYEE PERFORMANCE WITH REPUTATIONAL INTERESTS

So far we've focused on aligning employees' *behavior* with the organization's long-term reputational interests. We highlighted best practices for getting them to operate within appropriate boundaries (ethical, legal, regulatory, or otherwise) and make sound judgments when they encounter *moments of truth and trade-off*.

In the rest of this chapter, we'll focus on aligning employees' *performance* with the organization's long-term reputational interests. Here, we'll highlight four best practices for getting employees to align their priorities and energies with organization strategy, deliver branded experiences to customers, invest discretionary effort, and perform their roles in ways that deliver optimum value and results.

COMMUNICATE STRATEGY VIA "COMMANDER'S INTENT"

Commander's Intent (CI) is a concept that originated in the U.S. military. As brothers Chip and Dan Heath describe in their bestseller *Made to Stick*: "CI is a crisp, plain-talk statement that appears at the top of every order, specifying … the end-state of an operation … When people know the desired destination, they're free to improvise, as needed, in arriving there."[9] An advantage of communicating expectations via CI, the Heath brothers explain, is the ability to "align the behavior of soldiers at all levels without requiring play-by-play instructions from their leaders."[10]

> An advantage of communicating expectations via CI, the Heath brothers explain, is the ability to "align the behavior of soldiers at all levels without requiring play-by-play instructions from their leaders."

An effective expression of CI can get everyone focused on and talking about their role in producing strategic outcomes—instead of just tactical activities. "I don't care how many meetings you attend, how many e-mails you answer, how many committees you're on," says ADT senior executive Georgia Eddleman. "I care about what you're doing to get us closer to the targeted end state, whether that's improved quality, increased profit margins, reduced costs, or something else. That's what we're going to talk about, report, evaluate, and compensate. We'll connect it to every single level of the organization in a tangible way, every day."

An effective expression of CI equips employees at all levels with a single criterion against which to evaluate what might otherwise be tough decisions. Herb Kelleher, Southwest Airlines' CEO, understood this well, as reflected in a story he related to political strategists James Carville and Paul Begala:[11]

> "I can teach you the secret to running this airline in thirty seconds. This is it: Southwest is the low-fare airline. Not a low-fare airline. We are *the* low-fare airline. Once you understand that fact, you can make any decision about this company's future as well as I can."

> "Here's an example," Herb said. "Tracy from marketing comes into your office. She says her surveys indicate that the passengers might enjoy

a light entrée on the Houston to Las Vegas flight. All we offer is peanuts, and she thinks a nice chicken Caesar salad would be popular. What do you say?"

Paul stammered. So Herb told him: "You say, 'Tracy, will adding that chicken Caesar salad make us *the* low-fare airline from Houston to Las Vegas? Because if it doesn't help us become the unchallenged low-fare airline, we're not serving any damn chicken salad.'"

How do leaders know an expression of CI will be effective at promoting strategic alignment down and across the organization? The message must be:

- simple enough that everyone can understand it
- broad enough that anyone at any level of your organization can translate it into action
- aligned with everything that *the leaders* are doing. In other words, they can explain how any decision they make or action they take supports the end-state described in the expression of Commander's Intent.

Many efforts to communicate business strategy in large organizations fail to meet these criteria. For example, a large multinational company recently invested significant resources to communicate to its employees the following strategy:

We will …

- Focus investment spending
- Promote a cost-saving culture
- Routinely review our portfolio, making certain that retaining a business is better for our stockholders than divesting it
- Grow our international business
- Tie management compensation to the Company's financial performance

It might be sound business strategy but it's a lousy expression of CI. It's neither simple nor broadly actionable. The vast majority of the organization plays no direct or indirect role in "focusing investment spending," "routinely reviewing our portfolio," or "tying management compensation to performance." And few employees get excited about a strategy they can't do anything to support. The one element of this strategy that everyone in the organization *can* help leaders do is "promote a cost-savings culture." But if all leaders really want is for employees to find new ways to cut costs, why hide it or obfuscate it?

What's the alternative? To retool the message so that it fulfills the three criteria for an effective expression of CI, we advise organizations to focus on a theme like "making smarter choices about how we invest our resources." Everyone in the organization has resources—time and energy, if not human capital and budget—and so everyone can translate it into action. Senior leaders can then position their efforts to focus investment savings, review the portfolio, and revise the compensation system as examples of what they are already doing to act on the strategy (which provides evidence that the strategy is "real" and therefore worthy of being taken seriously).

DRIVING PERFORMANCE THROUGH ORGANIZATIONAL COMMUNICATION

By Maril MacDonald, CEO, Gagen MacDonald

In the world of organizational communication, the only constant is change. In order to stay relevant, communication professionals have to continually question their role and its impact. What are the external forces and dynamics influencing communication? What do leaders need to do to reach employees and other stakeholders in a compelling way in a shifting landscape? What is driving the evolution of the role of internal communication?

Three key forces of change are at the forefront of the evolution: globalization, the digital network revolution, and stakeholder empowerment. The expansion and consolidation of corporations has evolved the operating model from international to multinational to global. In today's global enterprise model, organizations are required to use communication to drive integration and collaboration that foster efficiency and a seamless customer experience around the world. The digital network revolution has accelerated the speed of communication and connection beyond the speed of light. In 2008, Technorati reported tracking 133 million blogs: almost double the number indexed in 2007. An average of 900,000 blogs was created every 24 hours. At that rate, nearly 4.3 million blogs could be in existence by 2014. The implications for communication professionals in the new environment of stakeholder empowerment are great. We can no longer control company messages, segment communication carefully to targeted audiences or preserve distinct expertise in, and control over, the channels of communication.

Against this backdrop of change, employees are demanding that words match actions. They are demanding information that's relevant to their jobs and enables them to deliver what's important to the customer. As noted in the Arthur W. Page Society's report, *The Authentic Enterprise,* in place of the voice of "authority" stakeholders and employees are demanding proof of "authenticity." When asked to rate the honesty and ethical standards of people in different fields in a 2006 Gallup poll, business executives received a confidence rating of 18 percent. The 2009 Edelman Trust Barometer indicated that employee confidence in CEOs as credible spokespeople dropped from 45 percent in 2008 to 35 percent in 2009. These statistics suggest that corporate employee trust and corporate leader credibility are on the line. So, the enterprise must be grounded in a sure sense of what defines it through its mission, values, principles, and beliefs. Those corporate definitions must dictate consistent behavior and actions on the part of leaders. As communicators, we need to position and define the corporation with authenticity, build communication channels that strengthen trust and credibility, and contribute to shifting perceptions by changing corporate realities.

Today's internal communication professionals need to take responsibility to influence and drive employee engagement at a time when employees have raised the bar for authenticity, trust, and credibility to new heights, and employee engagement has taken a front-and-center seat as a key driver of bottom-line results. According to Towers Perin's 2008 Global Workforce Study, 88 percent of all respondents who identified themselves as "highly engaged" believed they could positively influence the quality of company products, 85 percent of these "highly engaged" respondents believed they could positively affect customer satisfaction, with 59 percent believing that they can impact revenue growth. The same study reported that a highly engaged, global workforce improves employee performance by up to 20 percent, reduces turnover by up to 50 percent and increases customer satisfaction ratings by up to 23 percent. A 2007 Watson Wyatt Survey revealed that companies with highly engaged employees experienced 26 percent higher employee productivity, lowered the risk of turnover and resulted in 13 percent higher total returns to shareholders over the last five years. We are spending less time convincing leaders of the bottom-line impact and value of employee engagement; more time is being dedicated to activating collaboration and connectivity across the employee base and coaching leaders to be more engaging by increasing two-way dialogue opportunities and improving leadership communication capabilities.

Given the current reality of the field, what can internal communication professionals do to have the biggest impact in today's changing world? There are six principles of performance communication that provide a roadmap for communication professionals as we foster engagement and drive performance throughout organizations:

1. *Connect to a business result.* Establish communication as an integrated system connected to the business strategy.

- Identify key company initiatives that require strategic communication planning
- Use a cross-functional approach to ensure opportunities and risk are clearly identified and connected with communication strategies
- Develop a "line of sight" connecting employees and their contributions to the organization
- Balance global and local needs
- Develop metrics to create a proactive communication process and connection to performance

2. *Connect heads, hearts, and hands.* Provide clarity, information, and inspiration to engage employees both rationally and emotionally. Employ communication approaches as a powerful, strategic tool to shift stakeholder insights and drive employee engagement, culture change and business results.

- Articulate the vision and business goals to tell a compelling, overarching story
- Explain to employees what you really want them to do
- Provide them with the information to make the right decision
- Help employees understand why they should care

3. *Use communication as a leadership alignment tool.* Execute a systematic way to align leaders around clear, integrated messages that communicate where the company is headed.

- Support leaders in examining the current culture and articulate the desired culture
- Identify obstacles to change and metrics to gauge progress
- Create a shared understanding of metrics and link culture to hard business results
- Create a common language blending the rational and emotional drivers of engagement

4. *Establish strategic communication competencies for leaders, managers, and supervisors.* Use communication competencies to move leaders along the continuum from transactional management to transformational leadership.

- Develop and measure strategic communication behaviors: motivate and inspire; create meaning; articulate a vision; develop trust; influence
- Train leaders at all levels to tell a consistent story and connect to rational and emotional touch points

5. *Analyze information flow.* Provide neutral, objective perspectives on critical informational levers and roadblocks.

- Build dialogue and feedback mechanisms
- Facilitate communication on cross-functional teams and increase involvement
- Identify and measure knowledge-sharing gaps

6. *Move faster than the speed of change.* Understand the cycle of change and identify the opportunities to inspire employees at points when change implementation becomes difficult.

- Prime employees to respond to change in an engaged and focused manner
- Develop an integrated campaign to support each stage of change across multiple audiences
- Communicate critical information as soon as you know it—and keep employees involved and informed through a steady drumbeat of communications

■ ■ ■

HERE TODAY, HERE TOMORROW: THE IMPORTANCE OF STAYING ON MESSAGE (IN WORDS AND ACTIONS)

Employees rarely pay attention to—and invest effort to align with—any new effort or initiative they believe is "flavor of the month" and will soon be forgotten. Unfortunately, that is the default assumption employees in many organizations hold any time leaders introduce something new. "I've learned from experience," employees will sometimes say, "that *this too shall pass.*" Leaders can complain that this is a cynical point of view for their employees to hold—but most of the employees who hold it arrived at it honestly.

So how do organizations show employees that *this time, it's for real*?

It starts with the words leaders use and the consistency with which they use them. "The main thing is to keep the main thing the main thing," as the saying goes. That means all leaders have to use the same message ... and stay on message over time. When Dr. Len Schlesinger, currently President of Babson College, was a C-level executive at Limited Brands, he learned both how important and how hard this is to do. He trained as an academic and likes to play with words.

"Every time I used to talk about issues of strategy and positioning and stuff like that,

I just used a little bit different phrasing," he says. "Because then it was more interesting to me. And I suddenly discovered that every time I used a little bit different phrasing, all of a sudden, people start saying, 'Oh my God, the strategy's changed again.'"

"I spent about a year screwing up the business by using a few different words every 6–8 weeks," Mr. Schlesinger says. "Then I realized: I better just shut up. I better use the same words all the way through." The lesson? "You've got to recognize it's not about just entertaining yourself—unfortunately!"

Schlesinger's experience is common. In fact, through our internal tracking studies in dozens of organizations, we discovered a few years ago a phenomenon we call the *puke point*. It refers to the point in time that leaders become so sick of staying on message (and hearing themselves repeat it) that they "want to be lose their lunch." What's remarkable is that this point in time frequently coincides with an upswing in employee understanding of and engagement around the strategy. In other words, it's important for leaders to stay on message even after they're sick of doing so because that's the critical point in time that employees are just starting to truly "get it."

Keeping "the main thing the main thing" also requires that leaders explicitly connect the dots, making clear how all their decisions and actions—including what they're measuring and rewarding—support whatever it is they want employees to pay attention to and align with. Absent that, leaders tip their hand that whatever they are talking about is likely something in which their interest is ephemeral.

At the most basic level, this is about practicing what you preach. We talked earlier in the chapter about how Jack Brennan at Vanguard communicates boundaries. He also frequently invokes his Commander's Intent, in the form of the firm's mission statement: "We're here to help clients achieve their financial goals by being the highest-value provider." What's most critical, of course, is that he stays on message not just in words but in actions. When we went to his office one day to interview him, he was reviewing his travel schedule. He planned to go to Phoenix for a day, and then return to Philadelphia for a client meeting. Then he planned to immediately turn around and head back to the West Coast for meetings in San Diego, San Francisco, Los Angeles, and Pasadena. And though he didn't point this out to us, we happen to know that he flies coach. So wouldn't it make a lot more sense, we wondered, to move the Philadelphia meeting instead of making two cross-country trips in a very short period of time? Not a chance. "The day I say something and don't act on it, I'm no longer credible," Brennan told us. "The travel is a real pain. But it's the day that worked best for the Philadelphia client. If I am saying they matter and I won't travel hard to do what works for them, then I am not credible."

What Brennan and the communicators who support him recognize is that he is constantly broadcasting messages to the troops, through day-to-day decisions and actions, the things he rewards, what he tells people formally, and what he says informally.

> "Every time I used to talk about issues of strategy and positioning and stuff like that, I just used a little bit different phrasing," he says. "Because then it was more interesting to me. And I suddenly discovered that every time I used a little bit different phrasing, all of a sudden, people start saying, 'Oh my God, the strategy's changed again.'" "I spent about a year screwing up the business by using a few different words every 6-8 weeks."

> Keeping "the main thing the main thing" also requires that leaders explicitly connect the dots, making clear how all their decisions and actions—including what they're measuring and rewarding—support whatever it is they want employees to pay attention to and align with. Absent that, leaders tip their hand that whatever they are talking about is likely something in which their interest is ephemeral.

By sending steady signals on all frequencies, he can count on Vanguard's thousands of employees to tune in to all of his messages.

Another thing that's important for capturing employees' attention and demonstrating the enduring nature of the organization's commitment to something new is to *stop doing other things*. Lots of times employees won't take a new edict seriously when their reality is that "there used to be eight things that are really super important for everybody to get on board with … and now there are nine." Removing some of those items from the "importance pool" to free up energy, attention, and resources signals that you're serious. Here's an example:

Bob Walton recently took the helm of Qualcomm Enterprise Services, a division of Qualcomm that has a proud 18-year history of delivering solutions to the transportation and logistics industry. The company is not as profitable as they were eight years ago. "So I signed up to help develop the business, and to make this division more strategically and financially relevant to Qualcomm as a whole," Mr. Walton says.

In his first six weeks, Walton spent a lot of time with his people explaining his expectations and where he planned to lead the organization. He also told them that he wanted to create an environment in which it was okay to say "no." As Walton says, "We are here to say no to a bunch of things and yes to a few things, and we're really going to knock the ball out of the park on those few things."

It's one thing to say that in a PowerPoint presentation as part of the standard "Hey, I'm the new guy in charge" road show. But Walton moved quickly actually to halt development on a couple of product lines that people thought were sacrosanct. And, he says, "we began pulling out of a couple of countries where continued focus doesn't make sense given our new strategy." This showed that Walton was serious. What's more, it sent the message to the rest of the organization that it was safe for them to take responsibility for saying "no" in order to throw all the system's energy and talent behind the new strategy.

IN TOUGH TIMES, RALLY PEOPLE AROUND A COMMON CAUSE

Severe Acute Respiratory Syndrome—more commonly known as SARS—hit Southeast Asia in 2003, infecting over 8,000 people, killing nearly 800. Very quickly, 80 percent of business travel and tourism to Vietnam evaporated.

Our colleague Binh Nguyen was working at the time at the Duxton Hotel in Ho Chi Minh City. His boss, the hotel manager, faced some tough choices and spent a few days agonizing over what to do. Finally, he brought all of his employees together in the hotel's grand ballroom. "You all know about SARS and what it has done to our business," he said. "And you've seen other hotels in the city cutting jobs by 40 percent." Everyone nodded, prepared for the worst. Then he said, "I also understand that you still have your family to feed. I know what will happen if you don't have a job. So I have an idea." The manager then explained two options: The hotel could cut jobs by 40 percent … or everyone could take a 40 percent pay cut but no one would lose his or her job.

He allowed his employees to ask questions and discuss the options. Then he conducted a vote by secret ballot. Ninety-two percent of employees elected to reduce salaries so that everyone could stay—and fight together (under the leadership of a trusted manager) for their survival.

As one employee recalls, "From that day forward, things changed. Employees came to see each other as brothers and sisters. Before, there was a lot of fighting going on between different departments. But after the vote, everyone recognized that their fellow employees were protecting them and helping them keep their jobs."

That led to more than just camaraderie, however; it produced a sense of ownership and investment. Employees who previously had just "punched the clock," for the first time, started coming up with ideas for how to cut costs. For example, because occupancy was only 20 to 30 percent, one staff member came up with the idea to close down the top floors. They turned off all the lights, shut off the water, and assigned just one person for the upkeep of those floors. They also stopped printing out reports for managers, and used e-mail and other means instead. All together, they saved a billion Vietnamese dong on electricity, water, paper, and other small things. As one employee recalls, "The more we worked together, the more money we saved, and the more our morale grew."

And then something even better happened. When the World Health Organization declared Vietnam SARS-free, tourism started picking up again. Guests poured in, and all of a sudden, every hotel in Ho Chi Minh City was up to full occupancy. For weeks, other hotels didn't have enough staff to meet guest demands and had to turn people away because they couldn't accommodate them. But at the Duxton, they had a full staff and could meet all their guests' needs. Other hotels had to go find new employees and then train them, which took at least three months' time before they were fully up and running again.

> Employees, who previously had just "punched the clock," for the first time, started coming up with ideas for how to cut costs. For example, because occupancy was only 20 to 30 percent, one staff member came up with the idea to close down the top floors. They turned off all the lights, shut off the water, and assigned just one person for the upkeep of those floors. They also stopped printing out reports for managers, and used e-mail and other means instead. All together, they saved a billion Vietnamese dong on electricity, water, paper, and other small things. As one employee recalls, "The more we worked together, the more money we saved, and the more our morale grew."

When those other hotels came to Duxton employees offering them more money to go work elsewhere, not a single Duxton employee left. "Because we had trust," one of them explained to us. "We knew that if SARS or another crisis struck again, the other hotels would throw us into the streets. But we believed that even if we got paid a little less, we'd be safe at the Duxton. So we stayed. We all stayed."

What the manager of the Duxton understood is that in tough times people need a place to channel their fear and uncertainty. He helped them channel it into activity—and in the process—tapped into their discretionary effort by uniting them around a common cause.

Why do meaningful activities lead to discretionary effort? As researcher Kelly Lambert explains, "Our brains are programmed to derive a deep sense of satisfaction and pleasure when our physical effort produces something tangible, visible and—this fact is extremely important—*meaningful in gaining the resources necessary for survival*" [emphasis ours]. She believes it's an evolutionary tool. "Our brains have been hardwired for this type of meaningful action since our ancestors were dressed in pelts," she says.[12]

This explains why it's so important in response to an external crisis to give people a clear and credible call to action around which they can take specific action. It provides both an expectation and a means of reward.

Carlos Nieva, Director of Services for Alcatel-Lucent in Spain, understands:

"Working for a multi-national company, we recognize that they can put their operations anywhere. And so I tell our people, 'Let's give the organization a reason to keep the doors open tomorrow. We have to earn that.'"

Does that scare people? Maybe at first, Nieva says. But it connects people to a purpose. "It gives us a reason on a daily basis to bring all our brain power, all our ideas, all our enthusiasm—to bring everything to the table. Every day is a win—and everybody feels a part of that winning spirit."

He also adds an important reminder: The call to action needs to rally employees in response to an *external* threat. "I tell our people," he says, "that 'The enemy is outside. Never inside. Never inside.'" The greater the perception that there are internal winners and losers, the lower your likelihood of building and sustaining real energy behind your call to action.

Three related suggestions for issuing a successful call to action and rallying employees in tough times:

- *Less is more.* Ed Maibach, a behavioral scientist and Director of the Center for Climate Change Communication, George Mason University, tells us that people are more likely to act to solve a problem if they know they only need to do one thing. Social scientists call this "single action bias." Once you've gotten someone to complete one small task, then you can ask him or her to take on another. It's a great way to build momentum.

  The practical application: When you need to create urgent action and engagement, don't ask everyone to do 20 things. Ask each person or team in the organization to identify one new thing they can do immediately to help solve the problem.

- *Make folk heroes of the first people to get on board.* Nobody wants to be the only person in the organization making a sacrifice or investing discretionary effort. They know that if they're alone the needed change isn't going to happen. So they'd rather resign themselves to failure than to commit their passion to a lost cause. Of course, the problem is: Because everyone feels this way, it can become a self-fulfilling prophecy.

  So what's the solution? One way is to harness the power of social norms. When the right thing to do is ambiguous, people take cues from those around them, according to persuasion expert Robert Cialdini; he calls it "social proof."[13] If you can show that the people who aren't doing the right thing are the outliers, then social proof will push other people to take action.

  That's why it's so important to share success stories and make folk heroes of the people who are doing what's needed. At retailer AutoZone, "Extra Miler" stories describe how someone has gone the extra mile to take care of a customer. Whether it's at a local store or the annual meeting, every Auto Zone get-together begins with one of these stories, which leaders are responsible for pulling from letters or other interactions with customers. The stories might involve, for example, keeping the store open late or driving a part to a customer's home. The practice rewards those who are rallying around the brand (via recognition) while shaping expectations for everyone else.

- *Be more open than ever.* In tough times, leaders often want to retreat from employees and from bad news. That won't work if they want to rally employees, because it's all built on trust.

As we suggested earlier in the chapter, one of the challenges to creating alignment is that organizations are competing for their own employees' attention in an increasingly noisy and crowded information marketplace. And in tough times, what employees value most is information that helps them reduce uncertainty. But tough times are when leaders tend to be most evasive. Too many leaders increase uncertainty and anxiety because of the misguided way they choose to communicate unpleasant topics. The widespread practice of adorning disagreeable information with poetic flourishes (e.g., "It is with deep regret …") helps make the leader feel better but provides no value to the recipient.

> Organizations are competing for their own employees' attention in an increasingly noisy and crowded information marketplace. And in tough times, what employees value most is information that helps them reduce uncertainty. But tough times are when leaders tend to be most evasive.

Instead, leaders should reinforce trust in exactly those moments when trust is most at risk. Dave Watson, CIO/CTO of the healthcare analytics company MedeFinance, has learned that the best thing you can do is give your people "the straight scoop."

He told us a story about working with a staff of engineers. With 400 people in the room, they were exploring some cost cutting ideas, and the staff was appropriately unsettled and unsure about what was happening. One of the engineers working in desktop support asked: "Dave, are you going to outsource us?"

You could hear a pin drop.

Watson answered, "So you don't have to rely on rumors, here's what's happening: We have to take $50 million out of the organization and I am evaluating outsourcing as an option. I would not be performing my responsibilities to the organization if I did not. So yes, we're looking at it. I can't tell you that we made a decision, because we have not. And the best way for us to avoid an outsourcing scenario and remain employed, if that's the outcome that you want, is for us to cost-effectively deliver exceptional service to our clients. Otherwise, they will press for outsourcing."

Watson went on to discuss the opportunities he saw for delivering the service more effectively and more cheaply than a big outsourcing firm. He also laid out in close detail how management would be evaluating their efforts. He told us later that he could feel the tension bleed out of the room. Although there was still uncertainty about the final outcome of their efforts, employees could see a logical process for working out the problem, proving their value to the company, and keeping their jobs. By speaking frankly, Watson had shown them that they had some control over the outcome—over their future—and he had provided them a road map for getting there.

Another best practice in this regard is to communicate probabilities. As introduced by TJ and Sandar Larkin in their seminal work, *Communicating Change*, communicating probabilities means equipping front-line supervisors with the current thinking about what is definitely going to happen, what is probably going to happen, what is truly uncertain, what is probably not going to happen, and what is definitely not going to happen. To many leaders it sounds counter-intuitive to talk about what isn't certain.

But it makes perfect sense from an economic perspective. In the midst of change, people in the organization want to reduce their uncertainty. So if leaders don't provide an alternative, employees will turn to the black market (the rumor mill) for information to fill that need. And when they're no longer paying attention to their organization's leadership, it's difficult to rally them around a call to action.

Here's an example of a probabilities fact sheet that one of our clients recently distributed to all the leaders in the organization. Leaders are, in turn, responsible for diffusing the information to employees. The client updates the fact sheet every few weeks as the situation changes and new information needs emerge.

WHAT CAN EMPLOYEES EXPECT?

As you know, we're undergoing significant change this year. While we don't know everything that's going to happen, if we hold back information until everything is certain, you'll never hear anything. So, based on current information, this is what we expect …

Will happen:
- Our organization will become smaller than it is now
- Fewer local investment projects (due to greater investment in national initiatives)
- Demand for skill sets will change, with greater demand for integration skills
- Skill assessment and development
- We'll implement new practices, processes, and rigor to increase productivity and improve product quality
- We'll recognize and reward top performers
- We'll identify poor performers; they'll improve their performance or find work elsewhere

Probably will happen:
- Further realignment of staff with other functional organizations
- Further leadership and management changes

What's uncertain:
- How much smaller the organization will be than it is now … and when those changes will occur
- Whether we'll need to ask a small number of employees to relocate

Won't happen:
- Large-scale relocation
- Off-shoring or outsourcing of our entire operation

Current as of: October 29, 2008

WHEN IT COMES TO REPUTATION MANAGEMENT THROUGH "DELIVERING THE BRAND," DON'T LET EMPLOYEES PRACTICE ON CUSTOMERS. INSTEAD, REHEARSE THEM BEFORE THE CUSTOMER ENCOUNTER.

Many companies fail to secure their brand investment with the same focus and vigilance with which they secure their tangible assets, such as buildings or equipment. They spend millions to promote a particular essence of the brand, but then neglect to create the conditions of accountability for the employees responsible for delivering a branded experience.

> Many companies fail to secure their brand investment with the same focus and vigilance with which they secure their tangible assets, such as buildings or equipment. They spend millions to promote a particular essence of the brand, but then neglect to create the conditions of accountability for the employees responsible for delivering a branded experience.

In particular, too many companies train their people through activities and exposure to information as opposed to building authentic skills through practice, assimilation, and reinforcement. Many managers falsely assume that someone who went through a class and was "told" how to do something should be competent and confident about delivering a result.

Over some period of time, the employees might become competent, but do a great deal of damage to the brand in the process. The company also risks losing what could have been productive, loyal employees, had they been given the appropriate training and support they needed to be successful.

It makes infinitely more sense to have the individual employee prove that he or she has the skill before getting in front of the customer. To do that, *simulation systems* can dramatically speed the learning and build confidence. That's why management-consulting firm Success Sciences created the Communication Coach Simulation Learning System: to provide employees with the opportunity to complete their learning curve through "live" simulations on a computer rather than on customers and prospects. Communication Coach models exactly what "the voice of your brand" should sound like. Employees then rehearse by doing simulated practice sessions to get more confident, stay sharp, and build "muscle memory." The process takes away excuses about exactly how to handle recurring situations and effectively deliver on the brand promise. They practice on their own, without embarrassment, until they have achieved mastery. Only then they are asked to apply their new skills in actual customer encounters.

THE EVOLUTION OF STRATEGIC EMPLOYEE COMMUNICATION AT HALLMARK: FROM REPORTING TO STRATEGIC COMMUNICATION

By Steve Doyal, Senior Vice President, Public Affairs and Communications, Hallmark

Over the course of our nearly one-hundred-year history, employee communication at Hallmark has evolved into an integrated, highly influential function that links directly with all aspects of the business. Today, the communications group reports directly to the CEO—a position that yields influence, gains insight, and carries responsibility not expected of Hallmark communicators in the past.

COMMUNICATION STAGES

During my thirty-plus-year tenure with Hallmark, the company's communication function has evolved significantly. The stages of evolution could be characterized as reporting, followed by prioritizing, and growing into influence and interpretation:

- **Reporting.** In this stage, those charged with communication responsibilities collected information, wrote it appropriately, and distributed the information as effectively as possible. This was a reactive approach, absent any strategic communication framework.
- **Prioritizing.** In this stage, reporting evolved to include some prioritization of key messages and a degree of context relevant to the audience or business. This, too, was a relatively reactive approach, but signalled a move toward using employee communication as a business enabler.
- **Influencing and interpreting.** In this most recent and current stage, the professional communicators at Hallmark became strategic business partners helping shape business decisions, counselling executives on strategic communication, elevating business literacy, and building employee engagement.

When I started in communications at Hallmark, our group was pretty good at the craft. A premium was placed on employee communication, but it was used to help people in the organization feel like one happy family, rather than address relevant business issues.

As an example, Hallmark has published a daily newsletter every workday for more than fifty years. At its inception *Noon News* shared headlines from news outlets outside the company and information about employees that helped them feel connected to and valued by the organization, such as birthdays and anniversaries.

EVIDENCE OF BUSINESS IMPACT ADDED TO COMMUNICATION ACCOUNTABILITY

Noon News was held relatively captive to the original content design until the communication function began proving the value of better-informed employees who have a more complete understanding of how the business works.

Evolution of the employee communication function occurred as Hallmark leaders witnessed the ability of well-crafted, prioritized communication not only to inform, but also to motivate employees and move the business forward. It was the professional communicators' abilities to sort through a glut of business messages and place them into meaningful order and context that helped clarify the company's direction during the last two decades of the twentieth century. As we built the level of business acumen, employees more clearly understood the actions they could take to support Hallmark's success.

An example of the move toward message prioritization occurred in 1999 when Hallmark was on the verge of announcing a comprehensive change initiative that included completely new alignments within the company and of our more than 20,000 employees. There were new leaders, a new vision, new organization structures—all part of the changes that needed to be communicated. With a model line of 40,000 greeting cards and related products distributed through more than 43,000 retail locations in the United States alone, our company needed to become more consumer-focused and take cost and complexity out of the organization. Hallmarkers needed to understand the case for change and what the changes meant to them. They needed to be convinced of the business rationale behind the decisions. And they needed to be motivated to take personal actions if we were to be successful.

Fortunately, we had a long-established philosophy about handling communication within Hallmark, so we were able to build centralized solutions that supported Hallmark's beliefs and values. That philosophy, generally known at Hallmark as the five Cs of communication, states that communication solutions encompass:

- A conscience that weighs proposed actions against the principles that guide the company
- Cultural integrity that helps the company protect and benefit from our heritage and define our future
- Communication that (1) is calibrated to the particular needs of our institution and audiences, both internal and external, and (2) articulates key messages in ways that reflect the company's culture and mission
- Counsel that is consistent, sound and sensitive to the needs of both management and ownership
- Cost effectiveness achieved either through internal efficiencies and expertise or the wise use of external resources.

The strategy of our 1999 campaign was a multi-phased, multi-disciplined approach to sharing information about what the new organization would look like, how it would better position Hallmark for the future, and what benefits employees should expect from these changes. Large-format, face-to-face meetings were the foundation of the communication. A special print publication provided details about the changes and served as a reference for employees during these pre-Intranet days. Smaller, follow-up meetings were conducted between managers and their work groups, and supported by communication packets of overheads, question-and-answer guides, and other sources of information.

Ongoing measurement of the effectiveness of the changes demonstrated the value of the communication approach from first, a centralized corporate perspective, and second, an employee appreciation of the need for the new structure, the changes, and the various business initiatives essential to a successful change process.

BUSINESS PARTNERS, NOT JUST SUPPORT ORGANIZATION

Today, Hallmark's greatest impact from communication comes in the form of influence and interpretation. Communication is seen as an enabler of business success. We have moved from a centralized function creating one-size-must-fit-all solutions to a hybrid organization that continues to serve Hallmark from a centralized function, but also deploys senior-level communication strategists to sit on every major business area's leadership team. Our communication strategists work as consultants with leadership teams in business areas to facilitate change initiatives.

The centralized corporate communication function continues to serve as the primary source of key business information. Technology plays an ever-increasing role in our delivery system, but the tradition of our daily *Noon News* remains as an acknowledgement of our long tradition of providing employees with timely information.

The result of our current communications structure is exponentially greater influence within the company on the success of the business. With fewer resources, our communications function continues to have a greater impact than at any time in the past.

To accomplish this requires professionals who have broad skills across multiple disciplines, who can think strategically about the business, and can identify the communication implications of business strategy. Our currency is professional expertise, persuasion, honesty, candor, and trust.

In many cases, communication strategists also play a role as managers of people and/or a function. For example, the communication strategist for our greeting card business unit also is our business communications manager, supervising our employee communication and media productions staffs. The communication strategist for our marketing division also has responsibility for national public relations programs and supervises PR program managers. The expectations on individuals in these roles are high, but the professional satisfaction is unequalled.

The success of Hallmark's hybrid approach to employee communications has relied on flexibility, collaboration with internal business partners, and highly skilled and dedicated employees. The model has provided professional development for many people, has elevated the value of communications for Hallmark, and has been a key contributor to rising employee engagement scores as measured by annual organization-wide surveys and frequent location-specific pulse surveys. Those findings allow us to continually refine our programs and better prepare Hallmarkers to contribute to the success of the company in the face of ever-changing business dynamics.

■ ■ ■

BEST PRACTICES IN ORGANIZATIONAL COMMUNICATION

1   Aligning and engaging employees in support of reputational interests must be—can only be—a leader-driven and leader-led activity. Indeed, in the organizations that most effectively promote alignment, the CEO is front-and-center on the topic.

2   For senior leadership to effectively "own it," they need the support of highly strategic communicators and trusted advisors to drive employee alignment with the organization's reputational interests.

3   The various functions that play a role in aligning employees with reputational interests (communication, compliance, HR, marketing, customer service, etc.) actively integrate their alignment efforts.

4   It's impossible for an organization effectively to align its employees' behavior and performance until it has successfully competed for their attention. Cutting through the noise requires disciplined, demand-driven communication practices.

5   To align employee *behavior* with reputational interests …

- Communicate "bright lines and well-defined boundaries" … the things you can never do in pursuit of results or other self-interests … and then enforce those boundaries consistently.
- Communicate practical "rules of thumb" for managing moments of truth and trade-off. These are more useful than a laundry list of esoteric concepts to employees who are trying to decide what to do when they don't know what to do.
- Equip employees for moments of truth and trade-off with leader-led discussions about sticky scenarios that employees actually face.
- Engage employees in dialogue about the gaps between "what we say" and "what we do," amplifying expectations and taking away excuses in the process.

6   To align employee *performance* with reputational interests …

- Communicate strategy via "Commander's Intent" … providing a message with which everyone can align.
- Stay on message (in words and actions).
- In tough times, rally people around a common cause … something they can believe in—in order to reduce uncertainty and unleash discretionary effort.
- Don't let employees practice on customers. Instead, rehearse them before the customer encounter—so they're prepared to deliver a consistent, branded experience at every customer touch-point.

RESOURCES FOR FURTHER STUDY

Conniff, R., *Ape in the Corner Office: Understanding the Workplace Beast in All of Us* (New York: Crown Business, 2005).

Davenport, T., *Thinking for a Living: How to Get Better Performances and Results from Knowledge Workers* (Boston: Harvard Business Press, 2005).

Grimshaw, J. and Baron, G., *Leadership without Excuses: How to Create Accountability and High Performance (Instead of Just Talking About It)* (New York: McGraw-Hill, 2010).

Heath, C. and Heath, D., *Made to Stick: Why Some Ideas Survive and Others Die* (New York: Random House, 2007).

Kersten, E. L., *The Art of Demotivation* (Austin: Despair, Inc., 2005).

Larkin, T. and Larkin, S., *Communicating Change: Winning Employee Support for New Business Goals* (New York: McGraw-Hill, 1994).

Maister, D. H., Green, C. H. and Galford, R. M., *The Trusted Advisor* (New York: The Free Press).

Stack, J., *The Great Game of Business* (New York: Broadway Business, 1994).

Weick, K. E. and Sutcliffe, K. M., *Managing the Unexpected: Resilient Performance in an Age of Uncertainty* (San Francisco: John Wiley & Sons, Inc.).

QUESTIONS FOR FURTHER DISCUSSION

1   Who is ultimately accountable for ensuring employee alignment with an organization's reputational interests? Why?

2   What should professional communicators do when they know there's a sizable gap between "what we say" and "what we do"?

3   What is your reaction to the idea of "long-term greedy?" Why?

4   How integrated are the various efforts inside your organization to align employee behavior and performance with the company's reputational interests? What would it take to improve integration?

5   What are some sticky situations that employees in your organization frequently encounter? How effectively does your organization prepare employees for these moments of truth and trade-off?

6   What's the best way to encourage leaders to give straight answers to employees when uncertainty is high?

7   Does your organization communicate strategy via an expression of Commander's Intent ... so that everyone can align with it? If not, how would you translate the substance of the strategy into an expression of Commander's Intent?

Man is by nature a political animal.

— *Aristotle*

CHAPTER

6 GOVERNMENT RELATIONS

By Ed Ingle

■■■

You Snooze, You Lose

In March 1990, the Energy and Commerce Committee of the U.S. House of Representatives was holding a late-night, closed-door session on proposed clean air legislation. Chairman John Dingell of Michigan—one of the longest-serving members of Congress—presided over the powerful committee.

It was near midnight and the negotiations had bogged down over a key is-sue—how cost-effectively to reduce emissions from power plants to address acid rain pollution in the Northeast. In particular, the discussion focused on how to divvy up the new emission allowances or "credits" among the nation's largest coal-burning utilities, primarily located in the Midwest. The proposed legislation capped emissions by allocating a fixed number of credits to the largest emitting plants. Each credit represented one ton of emissions. The more credits a utility received, the more it could legally pollute. As a result, the credits became a very valuable commodity.

On this particular evening, scores of utility lobbyists and their "hired guns" (i.e., lobbying consultants and lawyers) were huddled outside the closed-door session in the foyer of the Rayburn building. Every hour or so, members and committee staff would emerge from the hearing room only to be swarmed by the lobbyists hoping to make a last-minute case for more "credits" and to hear the latest results of the negotiations.

Bob Schule, former White House legislative aide to President Jimmy Carter and then partner in the Washington lobbying firm, Wexler, Reynolds, Fuller, Harrison and Schule,[1] was on hand with his colleague, Ed Ingle, then a twenty-nine-year-old associate and former program analyst at the Office of Management and Budget in the Reagan White House. Ingle had been with the Wexler firm for less than a year and was getting valuable on-the-job train-ing on the lobbying trade. Schule and Ingle were representing Ohio Edison, a large Midwestern utility.[2] They were joined by Bob McWhorter, senior vice president of Ohio Edison, and Bob Giese, another lobbying consultant to Ohio Edison.

Sometime after midnight, a corporate lobbyist from another large Midwestern utility, who had been sitting on the gray marble floor in the corner of the foyer, slumped over in exhaustion from the long day. His deep sleep caught the at-tention of many of those nearby—when suddenly Giese shouted out, "Quick, grab that guy's credits!" The foyer erupted with laughter and the startled cor-porate lobbyist was jarred from his sleep.

The life-long lesson for Ingle that night on Capitol Hill was this: only those companies who are present and engaged in the policy-making process in Washington will reap the benefits of their efforts. Those not present—or not paying attention—will pay the price of not having a sound corporate government relations function. In other words, "you snooze, you lose."

■ ■ ■

WHAT IS GOVERNMENT RELATIONS?

Few professions can point to the U.S. Constitution as the basis for their existence. Many are surprised to find that the lobbying profession is one of the few. In fact, you need only look as far as the First Amendment to see the eight words that serve as the basis for this vocation:

> Few professions can point to the U.S. Constitution as the basis for their existence.

Congress shall make no law respecting an establishment of religion, or prohibiting the free exercise thereof; or abridging the freedom of speech, or of the press, or the right of the people peaceably to assemble, and to *petition the Government for a redress of grievances*.[3]

> Lobbying: The practice of advocating one's policy position to government officials with the hopes of influencing legislation, regulation, or other government action.

Lobbying can take a variety of forms. Meeting with a member of Congress, a congressional staffer, or an executive branch official to influence public policy is a direct form of lobbying. Phone or written communications (e.g., via letter, e-mail, or fax) to these same decision makers are also regarded as direct lobbying. However, lobbying can also be deployed indirectly. A "grassroots" campaign that encourages constituents of a given congressional district or state to write a letter, send an e-mail, or make a phone call to a member of Congress or Senator can be an effective form of indirect lobbying.

> Government relations: broader term that includes all forms of lobbying and nonlobbying activities that have the ultimate goal of influencing public policy.

For example, providing strategic counsel on political and policy matters to corporate executives is not lobbying, nor is managing the company's political action committee, but both can be important parts of an overall government relations function. Government relations is sometimes referred to as government affairs, and more broadly, public affairs. Regardless of the label, government relations is an important function within a corporation, and lobbying is at the heart of this function.

The lobby of the historic Willard Hotel on Pennsylvania Avenue in Washington, D.C., is thought to be where the term "lobbyist" was first coined in the 1870s during

President Ulysses Grant's administration. After a long day in the Oval Office, President Grant would frequently escape the pressures of the presidency with a brandy and a cigar in the Willard lobby, where he was approached by people seeking his ear on a given issue. Grant called these people "lobbyists."[4] The term subsequently became associated with individuals who seek out legislators in the lobby or hallway outside of a legislative chamber or meeting place.

Lobbyists can work for a corporation, trade association, law firm, lobbying consulting firm, interest group, or other organization. A lobbyist—particularly a corporate lobbyist—is sometimes referred to as a Washington representative or "Washington Rep" in lobbying parlance. Almost every business or political interest is represented by one or more lobbyists in our nation's capital—interests as varied as agriculture, transportation, energy, education, technology, healthcare, women's rights, abortion rights, gun owners, labor, snack food, florists, and pest management.

The first lobbying law was enacted by Congress in 1946, and required the registration of lobbyists, their employers, and their expenses. In 1995, Congress passed the Lobbying Disclosure Act (LDA), which expanded the definition of a lobbyist and greatly tightened reporting requirements. Under the 1995 LDA, lobbyists and/or an organization were required to file semi-annual reports disclosing the specific issues they work on, any interests by foreign agencies or businesses in their lobbying activities, and estimates of their lobbying expenses.

In the wake of the Jack Abramoff lobbying scandal of 2005–6, the lobbying profession came under even greater scrutiny. In 2007, Congress passed the Honest Leadership and Open Government Act (HLOGA), which substantially amended parts of the 1995 LDA. HLOGA further increased reporting requirements of lobbying activities and tightened restrictions on gifts and travel of members of Congress and staff. For example, the frequency of lobbying activity and expense reporting was increased from seminannual to quarterly. And for the first time, HLOGA required registered lobbyists to disclose political contributions on a semiannual basis.[5]

The role of lobbyists was also a popular topic during the 2008 presidential campaign as evidenced by candidates like then-Senator Barack Obama, who promised to limit lobbyists' influence if elected. On his second day in office in January 2009, President Obama signed an Executive Order entitled, "Ethics Commitments by Executive Branch Personnel." The Executive Order placed additional gift and post-service lobbying restrictions on Presidential appointees. Then in March 2009, President Obama also issued a memorandum to federal agencies, laying out restrictions on lobbyist communications related to items funded by the $787 billion economic stimulus legislation (American Recovery and Reinvestment Act) signed into law in February 2009.[6]

Despite the additional scrutiny on federal lobbying in recent years, the lobbying industry in Washington, D.C. is frankly bigger than ever. Total lobbying expenditures in 2009 were $3.5 billion—nearly double the amount reported in 2002 according to the Center for Responsive Politics.

The top 25 corporate lobbying spenders are shown in Table 6.1.

Table 6.1 Top Twenty-Five Corporate Lobbying Spenders (2008)

1	Exxon Mobil Corp.	$29,000,000
2	Pacific Gas & Electric Corp.	$27,250,000
3	Northrop Grumman Corp.	$20,663,252
4	General Electric Co.	$18,660,000
5	Boeing Co.	$16,610,000
6	Lockheed Martin	$15,410,000
7	Koch Industries	$15,130,000
8	AT&T	$15,076,675
9	Southern Company	$13,980,000
10	Altria Group	$13,840,000
11	Verizon Communications Inc.	$13,690,000
12	General Motors Corp.	$13,101,000
13	Chevron USA Inc.	$12,844,000
14	Comcast Corp.	$12,500,000
15	Eli Lilly & Co.	$12,485,000
16	Pfizer Inc.	$12,180,000
17	American Electric Power Co.	$11,238,938
18	BP America	$10,450,000
19	Delta Airlines Inc.	$10,295,213
20	Amgen USA Inc.	$10,150,000
21	American International Group (AIG)	$9,540,000
22	Microsoft Corp.	$8,900,000
23	FedEx Corp.	$8,855,000
24	Monsanto Co.	$8,831,120
25	General Dynamics Corp.	$8,482,439

Source: Congressional Quarterly MoneyLine.com

Case for a Centralized Government Relations Function

> It is critical for an organization to speak with one voice on all government relations matters.

Similar to the case for a centralized media relations function covered in Chapter 3, it is critical for an organization to speak with one voice on all government relations matters.

It is not uncommon for corporate executives to know a number of state and federal policymakers. In fact, these relationships can be quite beneficial to the company and generally should be encouraged. The company's government relations operation should inventory the relationships of its executives and midlevel managers, and seek to nurture them where possible. However, there is the potential for tremendous risk to the company's policy objectives if the communications with these political contacts are not closely monitored and coordinated by a central function.

At any given time, an organization or company may have numerous policy issues before Congress and the executive branch. Some of these issues may fall under the jurisdiction of the same congressional committees or executive branch officials. For instance, a large U.S. company with interests in trade policy may find itself working closely with the House Ways and Means Committee on a trade agreement before Congress. Meanwhile, the company's tax department may have an important tax issue before the same committee. If two parts of a company are talking to the same committee without coordinating through its government relations office, both policy objectives could suffer. Worse, the company risks being perceived by the committee as disorganized and unreliable, which may jeopardize the company's objectives on future policy matters.

Even very savvy and capable corporate executives and managers should not assume that they can navigate the rocky shoals of politics and policy formulation. What may seem a simple phone call, letter, e-mail, or conversation at a social gathering with a government official should not be taken lightly. Government officials may be looking for an endorsement of their idea, legislative proposal, or policy initiative that could contradict other policy objectives of the company or alienate other industry allies.

It is worth noting that some organizations may question the need for a government relations function altogether. But companies like Microsoft have learned that a "Washington presence" is critical to their overall business, and that it pays to engage in the policy and political debate and to have experienced government relations professionals looking out for the company's welfare. Bottom line: a company or organization should integrate government relations into its business plan and ensure that its efforts are coordinated and strategic.

> Companies like Microsoft have learned that a "Washington presence" is critical to their overall business.

ORGANIZING THE GOVERNMENT RELATIONS FUNCTION

Government relations can reside within a number of broader functions within a corporation, including:

- Legal
- Communication or public relations
- Corporate affairs
- A business unit

The location of a government relations function is driven by a number of factors, such as how a company is regulated or potentially regulated by the federal government and the enforcement exposure of a company by regulatory agencies (e.g., Federal Trade Commission, Environmental Protection Agency, Federal Communications Commission, or Food and Drug Administration). Oftentimes, a company that has heavy regulatory or enforcement exposure will locate government relations within the corporate legal department. However, in response to this same regulatory and enforcement exposure—and the likelihood of resulting communication challenges—it also is not uncommon for the government relations function to be located within the communication department.

In some companies, the government relations function falls under the corporate affairs (or public affairs) department. Corporate affairs can serve as a general catchall for a number of functions, including government relations, communication, and community affairs. Government relations can also reside under a particular business unit of a corporation, especially in companies where that business unit may have its own unique exposure to regulatory and/or enforcement activity.

> Regardless where the government relations office resides, it is imperative that there be close coordination with the communication function.

Regardless where the government relations office resides, it is imperative that there be close coordination with the communication function, both proactively on the company's policy objectives, and reactively to unexpected circumstances as they arise.

The configuration of government relations offices within an organization also varies, and is often dictated by the types of issues a company faces, the size of the operation, and the management style of the head of government relations and the needs of his or her superiors. A corporate government relations function typically covers federal, state, and local affairs. Increasingly, larger companies with overseas operations and/or customers are adding international affairs coverage to their government relations functions. Most medium to large companies will have a government affairs office in Washington, D.C., which will house the federal affairs operations, but may also include the state and international affairs functions. (State and international government affairs are covered later in this chapter.) Smaller companies will maintain a government affairs function at their corporate headquarters, which could include as few as one or two people.

A Washington government affairs office for a Fortune 100 company, for example, may include five to ten employees (although a few offices may have as many as twenty to forty employees if the company is heavily regulated or has diverse subsidiaries). The office will usually be led by a vice president, senior vice president, or managing director, who will report to the general counsel or top senior government affairs, communication, or corporate affairs executive back at headquarters. A VP or director of legislative affairs may oversee the office's lobbying activities on the Hill, and a VP or director of regulatory affairs may oversee executive branch lobbying.

Within these offices, you likely will find a combination of political and issue-specific lobbyists. For example, each lobbyist may manage a certain portfolio of issues that he or she will lobby on Capitol Hill and/or in the executive branch. Some offices may divide its lobbying portfolio by the two sides of the Hill and the executive branch; for example, a House lobbyist, a Senate lobbyist, and an executive branch lobbyist. Some may have a lobbyist for each political quadrant on the Hill, for example, a House Republican, House Democrat, Senate Republican, and Senate Democrat.

UNDERSTANDING THE KEY AUDIENCES

For any government relations office in Washington, there are two distinct audiences: Congress and the executive branch. Although they both consist of critical policymakers, these audiences could not be more different in many respects. Congress comprises Senators and House members elected every six or two years, respectively, whose number one goal generally is to get reelected.

> For any government relations office in Washington, there are two distinct audiences: Congress and the executive branch.

The president, the White House, and the political appointees within the cabinet agencies also care about broad public sentiment, reelections (albeit limited to two four-year terms), and the congressional elections which dictate whether a president's party might control the House or Senate. However, they are less moved by the individual voter. As such, the dynamic of how they are lobbied is quite different. For example, one hundred individual voters writing letters to the Department of Health and Human Services about a Medicare provision will not demonstrably change how the HHS secretary will think about that issue. On the other hand, one hundred voters from the district back home writing to a congressman—particularly one who serves on the Ways and Means Health Subcommittee—may indeed have an impact on how that member views the issue and advocates for it in the Congress and with the administration.

Further, political appointees within the executive branch are a mere fraction of the overall federal workforce. While political appointees admittedly occupy the most senior positions within the administration, there are only about 3,000 of them across the federal government among the millions of federal employees. A senior federal career employee is naturally interested in helping the president accomplish his agenda. But a career employee cares less about politics and more about implementing the laws Congress passes via regulation and administering the federal programs under his or her jurisdiction. Lastly, each agency is different, and how you approach a given agency or various officials within an agency should be tailored accordingly.

Capitol Hill is also made up of a wide variety of important audiences. There are one hundred Senators, four hundred thirty-five House Members, and over 15,000 congressional staff—all of whom are associated with various committees, leadership offices, caucuses, and working groups. A successful government relations function will advance its public policy interests by building and nurturing relationships with these key audiences:

- *House and Senate leadership.* It is important to know the members and their staffs who serve in leadership positions in both bodies and on both sides of the aisle. The leadership sets the agenda for each legislative body, and determines which issues get considered and how they ultimately get resolved.

- *House and Senate committees.* Most policy priorities of a company will likely fall under the jurisdiction of a handful of committees. These committees are responsible for holding hearings, drafting legislation, making modifications, reporting legislation out of committee to the full House or Senate, and reconciling the differences in House–Senate conference committees. It is imperative that a company cultivate relationships and build allies with members and staff on these committees—both in the majority and minority.

- *Congressional caucuses.* There is a congressional caucus or working group on a myriad of policy issues, such as: intellectual property, agriculture, property rights, the Internet, Vietnam vets, wine, human rights, oil and gas, biotechnology, adoption, and China. These ad hoc groups are made up of members of Congress who have a personal, professional, or district-related interest in these issues. Members of these groups make great targets for building relationships around issues that are important to your company.

> At the end of the day, the elected officials most inclined to come to a company's aid when it needs help are the members of its home state delegation.

- *Home state Senators and Representatives.* At the end of the day, the elected officials most inclined to come to a company's aid when it needs help are the members of its home state delegation. A company with a big presence in a given state or district has one thing going for it: jobs. If a company does nothing else in Washington, it must make sure it keeps its own home district Congressman and its two senators up to date on issues of importance, and cultivate them as champions for the company.

- *Congressional staff.* The congressional staff who support the five hundred thirty-five House and Senate members are a very important part of the legislative process and should be central to any government relations strategy. This includes the personal staff in each legislator's office, as well as the committee staff. The committee staff (e.g., counsel) and personal issue-specific staff (e.g., legislative assistant) help draft the bills and brief and advise the members. Time and care should be spent in working closely with congressional staff, understanding their value to the process, respecting their relationship and influence with the members, and by all means, not end-running them or blind-siding them along the way.

SIDEBAR: REPUTATION AND INTEGRITY: A PROFILE OF BRYCE HARLOW

One of Washington's most highly regarded corporate lobbyists was Bryce Harlow. During his forty-year career, Bryce Harlow served as a legislative aide to the House Armed Services Committee, senior legislative advisor to presidents Eisenhower and Nixon, and head of the first Washington government affairs office for Procter & Gamble from 1961 to 1978. In the foreword of the biography entitled *Bryce Harlow, Mr. Integrity*, Dr. Henry Kissinger wrote that Harlow "single-handedly created the entire modern advocacy industry."[7]

In June of 1981, about 250 of Bryce Harlow's friends and business colleagues gathered for a dinner in his honor. It was an event to mark not only his exceptional public and private service, but also his special contributions to the profession of corporate representation in Washington. The funds raised from the dinner became seed money for the Bryce Harlow Foundation, which was incorporated in 1982 as a nonprofit organization. The foundation seeks to recognize and inspire gifted leaders, in both public and private sectors, who foster high ethical standards with regard to advocacy, and to "enhance the quality of professional advocacy and increase the understanding of its essential role in the development of sound public policy."

The Bryce Harlow Foundation has continued its annual awards dinners, and the proceeds help fund educational seminars on advocacy and ethics, as well as scholarships for graduate level students interested in pursuing careers in government relations.

Former Vice President Dick Cheney was the keynote speaker at the March 2005 foundation awards dinner in Washington. In his remarks, the vice president commented on the man for whom the dinner was named: "Bryce passed away in 1987, but the foundation has carried on his legacy of service, integrity and patriotism in a way that would no doubt please him." The vice president continued, "Every day in the West Wing, I work in the office that was once Bryce Harlow's office, and he is someone I think of often. For those of you who didn't get to meet Bryce, you should know that he wasn't a famous or a physically imposing man. He used to say that it's easy to keep a low profile when you're only 5 foot 4; but when it came to knowledge about this city and the understanding of the legislative process and personal integrity and wisdom, Bryce Harlow was a man of incredible stature."[8]

Harlow's own words, published by the foundation in 1984 regarding corporate representation in Washington, ring just as true today:

> Corporate representation is sometimes dangerous, often frustrating, and always time-consuming and difficult. It calls for an unceasing effort to educate and motivate current and potential allies—and to discourage and befuddle foes. It requires the coordination of personal visits, telephone calls, and letters from top management; the flexing of political muscle in the home districts of particularly recalcitrant members of Congress; the fine-tuning of press relations and advertising; and, throughout, a dogged determination to prevail. That may sound tedious and vexing and grim. But for the right person, corporate representation can also be fascinating, challenging, immensely satisfying, and—on balance, most of the time—fun.[9]

■ ■ ■

SETTING THE COMPANY'S GOVERNMENT RELATIONS AGENDA

How a company sets its government relations agenda differs from company to company depending on the issues, the corporate structure, and the various personalities involved. Nevertheless, there are common elements for successful agenda setting that should be taken into consideration.

Government affairs agenda setting should not be totally top-down nor should it be only bottom-up. For example, an agenda set solely by the government relations office, without input from senior management and the business units, may be out of step with the company's most important business objectives. Conversely, an agenda set solely by senior management and/or the business units, without input from the government relations office, may not take into consideration the realities of the current public policy and political climate in Washington. As such, a company's government affairs agenda should be the result of a healthy collaboration between the government relations function, senior management, and affected business units.

The government relations office should drive and coordinate the agenda-setting exercise given its understanding of the public policy process. The agenda should be consistent with the overall business and communication objectives of the company and should be updated annually or as changing conditions may dictate. It should take into consideration the business cycle, key lines of business, and related policy and political issues.

> A company's government affairs agenda should be the result of a healthy collaboration between the government relations function, senior management, and affected business units.

The government affairs agenda must also be realistic. Moving an important legislative agenda item from a draft proposal to a bill and on to final enactment can take several years in most cases. It is better to focus attention and limited resources on a realistic number of policy objectives, rather than a long list of items that will never be realized. Once set, it is the charge of the government relations office to implement the agenda. This necessarily involves developing strategy, drafting briefing materials, talking points, and conducting and/or managing the lobbying activities.

SUCCESS AND EXPECTATIONS MANAGEMENT

One of the most difficult tasks of a corporate government relations function is managing expectations within the company. Many times, success in policy and political terms to a senior executive is very different from success to a government relations office.

Politics by its very nature is the practice of the art of compromise. And in compromise, the final result almost always ends up somewhere in the middle. No one side gets everything it wants. So where politics is involved, success is not achieving the perfect, but obtaining a legislative, regulatory, or public policy result that is as close to the company's objectives as possible.

Success from issue to issue may also vary considerably. Success many times is minimizing the damage of harmful legislation that is destined to pass. After the Enron and WorldCom scandals of 2001 and 2002, Congress sought to pass tough corporate governance legislation and nothing short of an act of God was going to stop it. Therefore, success for a company during that debate was minimizing the damage of a regulatory overreach against a political backdrop that was clearly on the side of the public and not corporate interests.

On the other hand, obtaining a provision that expands the federal R&D tax credit to reduce the corporate tax burden for companies that invest heavily in research is undeniable success. But is it still success if the expanded tax credit is only approved for one year, despite the company's support for at least a three-year approval? If you are appropriately managing expectations, you bet it is. The benefits of a tax credit for one year are better than no credit at all, and the company can fight the good fight again next year to seek the tax credit's continuation.

ROLE OF THIRD-PARTY ADVOCACY

Third-party advocacy has become an increasingly important tool for a company's overall government relations strategy. Medium and large companies should not only have a robust government relations operation, but they should also supplement their direct lobbying efforts through the effective use of third-party advocates. Third parties can include trade associations, coalitions, think tanks, and other interest groups which share the company's policy goals.

*   *Trade associations*. Trade associations are formal organizations that generally represent companies from the same industry or "trade." Most companies are members of one or more trade associations that have a presence in Washington, D.C. Trade associations can play a vital role in a lobbying campaign by speaking with one voice on a given issue—representing numerous companies and a large, combined employee base. A company could belong to an association as large and diverse as the National Association of Manufacturers (NAM), while also belonging to more trade-specific associations such as the Business Software Alliance (an association of software companies).

    Trade associations can supplement lobbying activities on an issue that is already being lobbied by individual companies, and they can also effectively serve as the sole lobbying voice in situations where companies may not wish publicly to lobby an issue. Nevertheless, a trade association cannot substitute for a company's own government relations function. On any given policy issue, a company may have unique positions on certain provisions that warrant the

    > A trade association cannot substitute for a company's own government relations function.

need for the company to lobby Congress and the executive branch in its own voice. This is a critical point that bears amplifying. Trade associations are vitally important and play a key role in a company's overall government relations function. However, companies should not rely totally on trade associations in Washington to meet their policy objectives.

- *Coalitions.* Unlike trade associations, coalitions are typically more ad hoc, are established around a certain policy issue, and usually cut across multiple industries. Whereas some coalitions are created under a more formal, long-term arrangement, most coalitions are set up as temporary, informal organizations that exist only for the purpose of achieving specific policy objectives; for example, passage of healthcare reform legislation, corporate tax reform, immigration reform, energy security legislation, and so forth.

  Member companies, and in some cases trade associations, finance coalition efforts. Those companies who pay more typically have more say over the day-to-day direction and priorities of the coalition. The funding may pay for full-time staff and/or outside government affairs consultants to manage the coalition. The coalition allows disparate companies and organizations to come together around a single cause to combine their voices for greater impact with Congress and the executive branch.

- *Think tanks.* Companies seeking to find other voices to support their views on a given policy issue may consider think tanks. A think tank is a collection of academic and government scholars, which may bring a particular political or philosophical bent to its writings and publications; for example, conservative, liberal, libertarian, or somewhere in between. They add credibility and a degree of objectivity to a debate. There are scores of think tanks in Washington. Smaller think tanks may focus on a narrow set of issues, such as defense policy, international affairs, or economic policy. Larger thinks tanks—such as the Brookings Institution, the American Enterprise Institute, and the Center for American Progress—support scholars who cover a wide range of issues. For example, if a particular scholar has written on the issue of energy security, a group of oil companies or its trade association may seek to cosponsor an energy-related symposium with the scholar/think tank to coincide with consideration of energy legislation before Congress.

- *Grassroots advocacy.* One of the most effective tools in a company's government relations toolbox can be the use of third-party "grassroots" advocacy. Grassroots advocacy is an indirect form of lobbying in which constituents of a given congressional district or state are encouraged to write a letter, send an e-mail, or make a phone call to a member of Congress or Senator. "Grasstops" advocacy occurs when influential community leaders (e.g., local or state officials, business owners, and heads of local organizations) are targeted to communicate their feelings on an issue to their respective members of Congress, Senators, or executive branch officials.

> Companies, trade associations, and coalitions are also increasingly turning to new social media tools to augment their grassroots campaigns.

Companies, trade associations, and coalitions are also increasingly turning to new social media tools to augment their grassroots campaigns. For example, many large companies now host their own public policy blogs. Micro-blog sites (e.g., Twitter) and social networking sites (e.g., Facebook) are also being utilized to generate support or opposition to various legislative proposals aimed at influencing the White House and/or Congress. Ironically, the private sector is merely taking a page from President Obama's successful 2008 campaign, which so effectively demonstrated the grassroots power of these new social media tools.

Note that corporate America was not the first to use grassroots advocacy. In fact, it was the extensive use of grassroots activities by various interest groups, such as environmental organizations, senior citizens, small business, and human rights that led companies to recognize grassroots advocacy as not only an effective tool but a necessary one. The sheer numbers of lobbying contacts made possible by a successful grassroots campaign demonstrate to lawmakers that an issue is important to their constituents and worthy of consideration.

ROLE OF THE LOBBYING CONSULTANT

A company's communication department routinely hires outside public relations consultants to supplement its work. Likewise, many companies will enlist external lobbying consultants to enhance its government relations activities and to expand its reach in Washington. In recent years, corporate America has been hiring outside lobbyists at a record clip based on a number of factors. First, companies are increasingly viewing Washington as a more active player in their daily affairs. This is a product of the massive financial bailout and the economic stimulus legislation of 2008 and 2009, and a Democratic White House and Congress eager to address major reform efforts in healthcare, energy, climate change, taxation, and corporate governance.

> Companies are increasingly viewing Washington as a more active player in their daily affairs.

Second, the number of lobbying consultants has increased given the declining cost of entry into the profession as a result of new communications technologies. As recently as 1995, a successful lobbyist needed a downtown office, expensive office equipment and an assistant to type memos, answer the phone, and fax materials. Today, that same lobbyist can thrive with a virtual office via a handheld communications device or "smart phone" to screen calls, receive/send e-mails, post a blog, view attachments, and surf the Internet—whether he or she is in the office, in a restaurant, in the car, or on the steps of the Capitol.

Third, during the same period, U.S. corporations have been under pressure to tighten their own payrolls given the challenging economic climate. It is no wonder that our nation's corporations have turned to a greater use of outside lobbying consultants to help them engage in Washington and take advantage of the opportunities. Since 1998, the top 20 lobbying firms combined (in terms of lobbying fees reported), brought in nearly $3 billion (see Table 6.2).

Who are these outside lobbying consultants? Some are former Senators, House members, and executive branch officials. Others are former congressional staff, White House staff, and agency staff. They may have their own one- or two-person consulting

Table 6.2 Top 20 Lobbying Firms (in terms of fees reported from 1998 to mid-2009)

1	Patton Boggs LLP.	$330,657,000
2	Cassidy & Associates.	$292,955,000
3	Akin Gump Strauss Hauer & Feld LLP.	$271,315,000
4	Van Scoyoc Associates.	$217,603,000
5	Williams & Jensen.	$160,304,000
6	Hogan & Hartson.	$145,604,162
7	Ernst & Young.	$139,387,237
8	Quinn Gillespie & Associates.	$127,363,500
9	PMA Group.	$115,940,578 (firm ceased operations in 2009)
10	Barbour, Griffith & Rogers.	$114,550,000 (now BGR Group)
11	Greenberg Traurig LLP.	$113,148,249
12	Holland & Knight.	$108,109,544
13	PriceWaterhouseCoopers.	$96,004,084
14	Dutko Worldwide.	$93,366,766
15	Alcalde & Fay.	$91,730,660
16	Carmen Group.	$90,130,000
17	Verner, Liipfert.	$88,595,000 (now part of DLA Piper)
18	Clark & Weinstock.	$82,925,000
19	PodestaMatton.	$81,165,000 (now the Podesta Group)
20	Timmons & Co.	$78,001,333 (now part of Prime Policy Group)

Source: Center for Responsive Politics

shops, or they may be part of a larger lobbying firm or law firm. Some law firms have a separate lobbying arm, composed of lawyers and nonlawyers, who handle the government relations work on behalf of clients. Other law firms have partners and associates, who may register as lobbyists and spend part of their time on government relations activities.

Lobbying firms focus exclusively on government relations services, such as: direct lobbying, strategic counseling, coalition building, grassroots activities, and government-related communication. These firms comprise lawyers, nonlawyers, and policy experts, most of whom have worked for Congress or the executive branch, or both.

Lobbying consultants help a company's overall government relations function in several important ways:

> Outside consultants can clearly add depth and breadth to the company's thinking on addressing policy and political challenges.

• *Intelligence gathering.* In Washington, as in Brussels and other capitals, information is power. The quicker you have a piece of information, the sooner you can act upon it, and your likelihood of success increases. Good consultants can greatly extend a company's "eyes and ears" capability to either help thwart bad policy or ferret out opportunities that would have otherwise gone unnoticed.

- *Strategic counsel*. There is frankly no substitute for hands-on experience when it comes to government relations. Outside consultants can clearly add depth and breadth to the company's thinking on addressing policy and political challenges and should be utilized early in a company's strategic process.
- *Direct lobbying*. Outside lobbying consultants can increase a company's "boots on the ground" capability where the tactical lobbying of members and/or staff is needed. Most important, outside consultants will invariably bring with them additional relationships with members of Congress, staff, and executive branch officials which can be leveraged on behalf of the company.
- *Communication*. Some government relations consultants can also effectively supplement a company's communication function in an effort to influence government officials on a given policy issue—both in Washington and in home district media outlets. Consultants can help with message development, drafting press releases, advertorials, op-eds, blogging, social networking, and arranging for media interviews.

A company's government affairs agenda, its priority issues, and the size of its consultant budget will obviously dictate how many outside consultants it may need. It is essential that the company's internal government relations function keep the consultants current on priority issues and engaged regularly—both strategically and tactically. The company should also conduct thorough, annual reviews of its consultants to determine whether the current consultants still map well to the priority issues and are still adding value.

Finally, a company should not only ensure that it follows the letter of the law and the rules that govern lobbying activities, but it should also insist that its outside consultants do the same.

ROLE OF POLITICAL CONTRIBUTIONS

Like it or not, it costs a lot of money to run a House or Senate campaign. Costs are driven by television and radio advertising buys, telemarketing, direct mail, staffing expenses, and political and media consultants. Campaign costs for a U.S. House seat in a contested race can easily exceed $1 million. Costs for running a U.S. Senate campaign can exceed $20 million. Short of major reform in the current political campaign system, these costs will continue to escalate.

Consequently, companies must decide how and whether to participate in the political contribution process. Since federal law prohibits corporate donations to candidates, the only legal option for a company is to establish a political action committee (PAC). Some companies question the need for a PAC, which is money raised through personal, voluntary donations from employees of a company or organization. However, many companies with a Washington presence today either have a PAC or are seriously considering it—particularly in light of the campaign finance law, the Bipartisan Campaign Reform Act (BCRA) of 2002.

BCRA's most notable achievement was ending the prior practice of corporate (and labor organization) contributions or "soft money" going to national party committees, such as the Republican National Committee, the Democratic National Committee, and the party campaign committees for the House and the Senate. Prior to BCRA, organizations and individuals could give large, unlimited soft money donations (e.g., $100,000 or $250,000) to these national party committees as long as the funds were not used to influence federal elections. However, concerns grew as the lines began to blur between the funding of "issue ads" from soft money and the ads' impact on federal political races. Under BCRA, no corporate or labor dollars can be given to these national committees (and individuals must comply with dollar limits). BCRA did preserve "hard money" contributions—personal and PAC donations going to federal candidates—which are subject to strict contribution limits.

A common misperception is that companies with PACs are able to "buy votes" of members of Congress through their donations. When you consider that donations from the largest corporate PACs are limited to $5,000 per election (e.g., primary election or general election), it is hard to believe that a Congressman, whose campaign will likely cost more than $1 million, will change his vote based on a $5,000 donation. And when you consider a Senate campaign that may cost $5 million, $10 million, or even $25 million, a $5,000 donation is clearly not a consequential amount. It is frankly this very reason why Congress and the Federal Election Commission continue to hold PACs out as a meaningful and effective way for individuals, companies, and interest groups to participate in the political process without fear of undue influence.

So if a company cannot expect its PAC to change a member of Congress' vote, then why have one at all? In today's political environment, where the costs of campaigns are so significant, a PAC demonstrates to a Senator or Congressman that the company respects the political process and realizes that it costs money to get reelected. A contribution will not change his or her vote, but it typically will give a company the opportunity to be heard on a priority issue. Most important, a PAC allows a company to support candidates who support its issues and interests.

> A PAC demonstrates to a Senator or Congressman that the company respects the political process.

With that said, a PAC should not substitute for personal political contributions of corporate executives. In addition to supporting the PAC, executives should be willing to show support for key federal and state elected officials, particularly those who represent the district or state where the company is located and/or has significant facilities.

STATE AND INTERNATIONAL GOVERNMENT RELATIONS

This chapter has focused primarily on how a corporation might approach the federal government relations function. Large companies are increasingly deploying state and international government affairs operations as part of their overall government relations activities. Many of the components covered in this chapter are also applicable to state and international government relations. However, it is important to note some unique aspects and the need for coordination across all activities.

State Government Relations

A presence in the state capital of a company's headquarters is an essential part of the overall government affairs function. State governments oversee a number of areas critical to most companies, such as education, transportation, communications, electricity, and tax issues. Local governments also play an important role on many of these issues. As such, corporate state and local government affairs representation is needed to oversee this function. Other professionals also may be situated around the country in state capitals, where the company may have a large employee base and/or a customer base. These representatives are there to monitor legislative activity that may impact the company and lobby state legislators, the governor's office, and agencies.

Relationships developed with state officials can also pay dividends when an official decides to run for federal office. For example, it is common for a city mayor, state legislator, state attorney general, or governor to later run for Congress. As such, coordination between the state and federal teams is important—in terms of relationship building, political giving, and legislative activity that may give rise to federal legislation.

International Government Relations

Many large companies are only now discovering the need for a presence in foreign capitals such as Brussels (EU), Tokyo, and Beijing. The rise in recent years in global competition has brought with it increasing opportunities for U.S. companies and increasing regulatory action by foreign governments. As a result, companies are beginning to hire in-country government affairs professionals, who, like their U.S. counterparts, seek to engage in the policy and political process and build relationships with key officials. Each country and government is unique, requiring a tailored approach. Once again, close coordination between the United States and the international government affairs teams is critical. Policies that start in the U.S. may spread to foreign capitals or vice versa and must be closely monitored. And, in cases where foreign governments are taking U.S. companies to task through regulation and enforcement, U.S. government officials—and the pressures they can potentially bring via communications with their foreign counterparts—may serve to positively impact the outcome of these issues.

> Many large companies are only now discovering the need for a presence in foreign capitals such as Brussels (EU), Tokyo, and Beijing.

AN INTERVIEW WITH KARAN BHATIA, VICE PRESIDENT FOR INTERNATIONAL LAW AND POLICY, GENERAL ELECTRIC COMPANY

As head of GE's international law and policy group and a former international affairs expert with the U.S. Government, Karan Bhatia is regarded as one of the world's top international government relations specialists. In an interview from his Washington, D.C. office, Mr. Bhatia discussed GE's approach to global government relations.

Ingle: What is your role within the company?

Bhatia: I oversee GE's relations with governments outside of the United States. My team works with foreign governments on public policy issues that we consider important to the company's ability to operate effectively around the world. I also oversee our government relations activities with the U.S. Government on international and trade-related matters, including the Departments of State, Commerce and Treasury, the U.S. Trade Representative's office, and the White House's National Security Council.

Ingle: Who do you report to and how is your organization structured?

Bhatia: I report to the company's General Counsel and senior vice president, who reports to the CEO. We have a team of about 30 government relations professionals spread across 13 capitals around the globe, including Washington. We represent the company at the corporate level on cross-cutting international policy issues, such as trade, market access, environment, and technology and innovation. We also coordinate closely with another 20–30 professionals in our businesses' government relations units, who work on business-specific policy matters (e.g., for GE Energy), and with our team of "national executives" (country presidents).

Ingle: Explain GE's approach to international government relations.

Bhatia: We have a very constructive approach to government relations. That is, we seek to build "trusted relationships" with governments around the world—to serve as a resource for policymakers, to help them assess the business consequences of policy change, to share practical experiences from other jurisdictions, and to brainstorm quietly about possible policy innovations. We remain in regular dialogue with policymakers, utilize various advocacy tools such as studies and white papers, and work with third parties, NGOs (non-government organizations), think tanks, and civil society groups as needed. We make it a point to work with governments at all levels—from the senior-most levels to the career ranks—matching them to the appropriate level of GE executive or representative.

Where possible, we try to employ country nationals to help manage our government affairs activities in the various capitals. We do not rely heavily on outside consultants in our international relations work; we feel it is usually more effective to speak directly to foreign government officials.

Ingle:	GE is such a huge global company with over 300,000 employees worldwide. How do you coordinate your activities with other parts of the company?
Bhatia:	It's a challenge. First and foremost, we coordinate very closely with our U.S. government relations colleagues in Washington, D.C., given the natural synergies and shared objectives between our groups. Second, we work closely with GE's numerous business units to make sure our corporate-level and business-level activities are in sync. Third, we work closely with other functional departments within the company such as our corporate communications colleagues—collaborating on public affairs strategies, speeches, Congressional testimony, press statements, etc. In terms of coordination within my own organization, I host a monthly call with each regional government relations team (e.g., Asia or Europe), and I also host a monthly global call with all regional government relations teams.
Ingle:	What are some of your biggest challenges?
Bhatia:	Our constant challenge is to find a way to successfully make the leap to being a truly global company. We cannot escape the fact that we are an American-headquartered company—nor do we want to. We are what we are, and we are proud of that. However, our ultimate goal is to also be seen as a local company in any given country where we do business—a company that is a local employer and invests locally in the community.

American companies have been honing their federal government relations skills in Washington, D.C. for decades, but we are still only in the early stages of international government relations as a profession. And like in the U.S., the role of foreign governments and their impact on how we do business around the world is increasing—so we have our work cut out for us. |

■ ■ ■

ETHICS IN LOBBYING

It takes twenty years to build a reputation and five minutes to ruin it.
— Warren Buffett

■ ■ ■

Adherence to sound ethical principles is vital to the lobbying profession, despite public perception to the contrary. The vast majority of registered lobbyists are decent and principled, and they realize that the fastest way to sink one's career is to cross the ethical line and, in doing so, implicate a government official. Just as the fate of Enron's executives serves as a reminder for all corporate executives as to the importance of strong ethical behavior, Jack Abramoff does the same for lobbyists.

The following is an excerpt from the "Code of Ethics" of the American League of Lobbyists (ALL). Established in 1979 as a nonprofit organization, ALL is the national professional association dedicated exclusively to lobbying. ALL's mission is to enhance the development of professionalism, competence, and high ethical standards for advocates in the public policy arena.

Code of Ethics of the American League of Lobbyists

ARTICLE I—HONESTY AND INTEGRITY

A lobbyist should conduct lobbying activities with honesty and integrity.

ARTICLE II—COMPLIANCE WITH APPLICABLE LAWS, REGULATIONS, AND RULES

A lobbyist should seek to comply fully with all laws, regulations, and rules applicable to the lobbyist.

ARTICLE III—PROFESSIONALISM

A lobbyist should conduct lobbying activities in a fair and professional manner.

ARTICLE IV—CONFLICTS OF INTEREST

A lobbyist should not continue or undertake representations that may create conflicts of interest without the informed consent of the client or potential client involved.

ARTICLE V—DUE DILIGENCE AND BEST EFFORTS

A lobbyist should vigorously and diligently advance and advocate the client's or employer's interests.

ARTICLE VI—COMPENSATION AND ENGAGEMENT TERMS

An independent lobbyist who is retained by a client should have a written agreement with the client regarding the terms and conditions for the lobbyist's services, including the amount of and basis for compensation.

ARTICLE VII—CONFIDENTIALITY

A lobbyist should maintain appropriate confidentiality of client or employer information.

ARTICLE VIII—PUBLIC EDUCATION

A lobbyist should seek to ensure better public understanding and appreciation of the nature, legitimacy, and necessity of lobbying in our democratic governmental process. This includes the First Amendment right to "petition the government for a redress of grievances."

ARTICLE IX—DUTY TO GOVERNMENT INSTITUTIONS

In addition to fulfilling duties and responsibilities to the client or employer, a lobbyist should exhibit proper respect for the governmental institutions before which the lobbyist represents and advocates clients' interests.[10]

BEST PRACTICES

The following are eleven best practices that a corporate government relations professional should seek to employ:

1   Shoot straight. First and foremost, always tell the truth in all of your lobbying communication, oral and written. Nothing sinks your credibility faster than appearing to play fast and loose with the facts.

2   Be consistent. Do not tell one congressional office one thing and another office something else. By all means, you should customize your message to take into account your different audiences (e.g., a member of the Finance Committee versus a member of the Foreign Relations Committee). However, make sure the underlying facts of your advocacy stay consistent. Members and staff—on both sides of the aisle—routinely talk to one another and compare notes.

3   Know your issues. Do your homework before you meet with a government official. Have a clear outline of the key points you want to make, and be prepared to give your thirty-minute pitch in ten minutes if the member or staff starts the meeting late or has to leave the meeting early, which is quite common. Anticipate questions ahead of time, but never shoot from the hip on an answer if you are not sure of the facts. You should not hesitate to say, "I don't know, but I'll get back to you with the answer." Also familiarize yourself with the opposition's arguments and be prepared to address them.

4   Know your audience. As part of doing your homework, you want to know before you lobby a Congressman on an education issue that he was a former teacher (or his spouse is a teacher). Likewise, you want to know before you meet with a Senator on a tax issue that she pushed through a state tax measure (e.g., Internet tax), while in a previous capacity, that conflicts with your company's position.

5   Know your "ask." A government official will want to know why you are meeting with her and what you are "asking" her to do. For example, to a House staff person you might say, "We would like the Congresswoman to consider voting for H.R. 4545 when it comes up for a vote next week in the House." Keep your "asks" to a minimum, and make sure they are realistic. If you have several "asks" of a member or executive branch official, be prepared to prioritize them.

6   Know your environment. Beyond knowing your issue and your audience, you need to be aware of the broader political and policy environment at the time of your meeting. For example, your government relations strategy may call for the introduction of a bill by a friendly member of Congress the last week before the recess. You need to know that the Congressman during that same week might be preoccupied with fighting a base closure commission to keep a military base open in his home district, and your strategy should be modified accordingly.

7   Offer solutions. There is nothing that irritates a government official more than a lobbyist who complains about an issue, but proposes no solution to the problem. Be prepared to offer up an alternative that ideally helps the member accomplish her policy objective, while minimizing or eliminating any detrimental consequences to your company.

8   Listen. Effectively making your pitch is only half of the equation for a successful meeting. The other half is listening effectively. Listen carefully to what the lawmaker or official is saying. For instance, "We will take a look at your issue" is very different than, "I think we can work with you on this issue." Also, listen carefully to their questions and comments and make sure you are being responsive to their exact questions or concerns.

9   Be adaptive. The policy and political environment in Washington is fluid. Conditions can change without notice as a result of unfolding events that might have a direct or indirect effect on your issues. A new presidential initiative on healthcare announced in a State of the Union speech could undercut your own proposal that you had been lobbying on the Hill. In response, you will need to be able to regroup quickly and modify your strategy to reflect these changing conditions.

10   Believe your own rhetoric. Your lobbying strategy must be based on a sound policy argument. The world's greatest political maneuvers and strategies will not carry the day for a policy argument that does not hold water. Government officials will see through a hollow argument, particularly if you do not sound convinced yourself and are not enthusiastic about your message.

11   Play by the rules (and then some). Make it a priority to know the laws, regulations, and rules that affect you as a lobbyist—and live by them. Routinely consult an outside ethics, election law, or political legal counsel. And even if you are meeting the letter of the law, and if something does not feel right, do not do it. Always ask yourself— "would I feel comfortable with my actions being reported on the front page of the *Washington Post*, *The New York Times* or my hometown newspaper?"

> Make it a priority to know the laws, regulations, and rules that affect you as a lobbyist—and live by them.

RESOURCES FOR FURTHER STUDY

Publications

Andres, Gary, *Lobbying Reconsidered: Politics under the Influence* (New York: Prentice Hall, 2008).

Baran, Jan Witold, *The Election Law Primer for Corporations* (Chicago: American Bar Association, 2008).

Luneburg, William V., *The Lobbying Manual: A Complete Guide to Federal Lobbying Law and Practice* (Chicago: American Bar Association, 2009).

Wolpe, Bruce C., *Lobbying Congress: How the System Works*, Congressional Quarterly (1996).

Web sites

The Center for Responsive Politics, http://www.opensecrets.org.Library of Congress Thomas, http://thomas.loc.gov.

The White House, http://www.white house.gov.Wikipedia, http://www.wikipedia.org.

QUESTIONS FOR FURTHER DISCUSSION

1 How significant is it to the practice of lobbying that the First Amendment expressly includes the right "to petition the government for a redress of grievances"?

2 What is the optimal relationship, if any, between the government relations and public relations functions?

3 Given the role of money in political campaigns, how important is it for a company to have a Political Action Committee (PAC) to make contributions to candidates?

4 With lobbying ethics coming under closer and closer scrutiny, how can a company lobby effectively while preserving a reputation for integrity?

5 How important is coalition building in influencing government decision makers?

Good fences do not good neighbors make.
— *Paraphrase of Robert Frost quote*

7 COMMUNITY RELATIONS

■■■

Uniontown, PA, may eventually be transformed from a place where many who drove down Main Street would roll up their windows to what will soon be a showplace, a catalyst for the renewal of Fayette County, among the poorest of Pennsylvania's sixty-seven. At this writing, the town that almost died in the 1950s and 1960s with the coal mines and the birth of the strip malls is receiving a makeover of dramatic proportion: the State Theatre has been renovated and there are now cultural events held there; more than twenty store fronts have been repaired and reopened; three churches have been whitewashed, and the derelicts seem fewer. It is already being frequented by local residents, as well as lawyers, doctors, and other professionals from Pittsburgh, about a 90-minute drive away. Several high-end stores located downtown late in 2005 and more are on their way. Jobs are being created. Local professionals who have lived for years in the suburbs of Uniontown, seldom venturing downtown, now gather with town residents, as they would have in the 1950s.[1]

One man, with the All-American name of Joe Hardy, is a major force. He is the founder of 84 Lumber, the large, national building-supplies company named after the town of Eighty Four, some twenty miles from Uniontown. The company is adding about fifty stores each year, each about ten acres large, from Maryland to Nevada. He is starring in something that many long-term residents see as surreal, more like a movie than reality. And if it were a movie, the producers would somehow have to bring back Jimmy Stewart for the lead.

Mr. Hardy talked extensively about community involvement with John Doorley, coauthor of this book, who grew up in Uniontown, watching it thrive, almost die, and now being reborn. By the time Joe Hardy is finished remodeling Uniontown, he said, he will have spent at least $20 million of his own money. Signs are popping up all over town, with greetings like "God Bless You, Joe," and one resident even proposed that Hardy's visage replace that of General George Marshall of World War II fame, who was born in Uniontown, and who was called by President Harry Truman "the great one of the age." "It's a little embarrassing," Mr. Hardy says.

The story of why Joe Hardy is rebuilding Uniontown (population 12,422), which is the county seat, is clearly an exceptional one in scope and dramatic effect. But it illustrates how and why organizations and their leaders should get involved in the community, for the benefit of both. His six principles of relationship building have made 84 Lumber the country's largest privately held building materials supplier to professional contractors; directed the way he built and runs Nemacolin Woodlands, one of America's best resorts, in the mountains overlooking Uniontown; and made him a very wealthy man. Mr. Hardy said that his principles guide his "philanthropy and community relations, just as they guide my personal and business relationships."[2]

Community Relations: The strategic development of mutually beneficial relationships with targeted communities toward the long-term objective of building reputation and trust.

It seems that few people know how to practice effective community relations as well as Joe Hardy: it is how he built his businesses, and helped a lot of people in the process. And while it can be said that he has a lot of money and can afford to do good things, it can also be said that he knows how to do them well. That is why the authors adopted the Hardy-centric architecture for this chapter.

Reputation = Sum of Constituency Images = Performance and Behaviour + Communication = Sum of Relationships

---

■ ■ ■

HARDY'S RELATIONSHIP-BUILDING PRINCIPLE #1: BE INVOLVED. BE COMMITTED

Joe Hardy:

> *I was born on the other side of the tracks but my mother always told me I was special, like every parent should, really. And she taught me to get involved, to show up. So, over the years, no matter what I was doing in business, I always got involved, in politics and in the community. When it became clear to me a few years ago that the three county commissioners could be of tremendous help in getting things done in Uniontown and Fayette County, I campaigned for and became a commissioner in 2004—the first time I ran for public office, and I was eighty-one. A few years ago, I participated in a policy conference at Carnegie Mellon University and was asked how one makes community programs work. I tried to tell them that it is not so complicated. It is just a matter of making up your mind to do something the community needs, something you have the ability to do, and then doing it as well as possible by working with people you trust.*

In 1954, President Dwight Eisenhower encouraged business leaders to become more involved in politics and government, and that led to the formation of the Public Affairs Council, a Washington, D.C.-based association of corporate government relations and public affairs executives who lobby for various legislative and regulatory initiatives. Beginning in 1980, when he was elected to his first term, President Ronald Reagan made sharp cuts in federal funding for social programs. The initial cuts amounted to over $11 billion and they affected, in the first year, about 57 percent of voluntary agencies. President Reagan urged the business community to make up for the cuts by getting involved, not only with philanthropic contributions but with social service programs. Specifically, he urged businesses to double their contributions and to provide social services previously provided by federal funds.[3]

"Corporate contributions soared," writes Edmund M. Burke in *Corporate Community Relations: The Principle of the Neighbor of Choice*.[4] Burke, the founding director, in 1985, of the Boston College Center for Corporate Community Relations, explains that although corporate gifts to charity rose to $4.4 billion in 1985, they could not compensate for President Reagan's $33 billion cuts. Some argue that the corporate community relations programs that ensued were more productive than the federal give-away programs. In any case, the transition to a more privately funded community support system caused tremendous changes in corporate community relations philosophies, staffing, and funding. At the same time, the pressures on companies to increase their community support initiatives were compounded by rapid increases in the number of applications community service programs made to corporations.

> The transition to a more privately funded community support system caused tremendous changes in corporate community relations philosophies, staffing, and funding.

Companies hired community relations specialists or redeployed staff. According to Burke, similar pressures in other countries in the 1980s resulted in major community relations initiatives by corporations in the United Kingdom, Japan, the Philippines, Australia, and elsewhere.[5]

Neighbor of Choice

The new community relations model—planned involvement that meets the needs of the community and company or organization—was a response to the realization that companies and other organizations situated in a community must obtain what Burke calls a "license to operate."[6] That metaphorical license is more difficult to obtain and retain than the licenses companies actually obtain from government or other regulatory agencies. It is issued based on the written and unwritten set of expectations between the organization and the community. For example, the community will provide certain services, such as roads and other infrastructure, and the organization will work within certain rules, abiding by standards that protect the overall community and its people.

Burke writes that the best way for an organization to obtain and retain a license to operate is to become a "neighbor of choice." Much like companies that try to become an employer of choice or a supplier of choice, companies that want to achieve favored status in the community can establish programs and practices that will tend to make them, over time, neighbors of choice. In other words, the organization will adopt community relations strategies geared toward establishing not just acceptance but real trust.

"The involvement of companies in communities has changed significantly since the 1970s," Burke writes. "It has shifted in response to changing community expectations from checkbook philanthropy to a principle about the way a company should behave in a community. Companies now need to act in ways that build community trust—to become neighbors of choice."[7] (See "Trust" sidebar by James Lukaszewski at end of this chapter.)

HARDY'S RELATIONSHIP-BUILDING PRINCIPLE #2: BUILDING REPUTATION, ONE RELATIONSHIP AT A TIME, IS GOOD BUSINESS

Joe Hardy:

> *I realize that reputation is a popular buzzword today in business, because of the scandals, I guess. But it's strange that companies and other organizations had to be shocked into realizing that everything in life is about relationships. And isn't it true that a person's or an organization's reputation is simply the sum of the relationships that person or organization has built? I am glad that the people of Fayette County are beginning to believe in themselves again, but the main reason for a company to be involved in the community is that it is good business. Don't get me wrong: I am not going to make money off our renovation of Uniontown; I could not sell that to our accountants, because we could not prove there will be adequate financial returns. But helping the people of Fayette County get back on their feet will help everybody (individuals and businesses) over the long term. And besides, heck, if this was Montgomery County (one of Pennsylvania's wealthiest) it wouldn't be any fun.*

"And besides, heck, if this was Montgomery County (one of Pennsylvania's wealthiest) it wouldn't be any fun."

In his seminal text, *Reputation*, Charles Fombrun, emeritus professor of the Stern School of Business at New York University states that:

> The purpose of the typical community relations department is to convey a company's benevolence, corporate citizenship and social responsiveness. Key strategies range from pro bono activities and charitable contributions to relationship building with artistic, educational, and cultural institutions. In this way, companies integrate themselves into their local communities and surround their activities with a positive halo of goodwill.[8]

Three Reputation-Building Strategies

More specifically, Edmund Burke writes that there are three strategies organizations employ to build their reputations in the community into that of a neighbor of choice:

- Build sustainable and ongoing relationships with key individuals, groups, and organizations.
- Institute practices and procedures that anticipate and respond to community expectations, concerns, and issues.
- Focus the community support programs to build relationships, respond to community concerns, and strengthen the community's quality of life.[9]

Those three strategies are responsive to the needs of both the community and the organization. They help build the organization's reputation so that the organization can get along in the community day to day (as neighbors must); also, the strategies build reputational capital that can be drawn upon during the inevitable tough times, such as those accompanying plant accidents or layoffs.

Moreover, a good reputation benefits the company brand in immeasurable ways, including the ability to attract and retain business clients. One of the most popular (and respected) surveys of corporate reputation is *Fortune* magazine's annual Most Admired Companies survey and cover story. Inaugurated in 1984, one of the nine criteria is "social responsibility."

HARDY'S RELATIONSHIP-BUILDING PRINCIPLE #3: CHOOSE THE RIGHT PROJECTS. BE STRATEGIC

Joe Hardy:

> *Nemacolin, which I purchased in 1987 and began renovating in 1988, is now a world-class resort. Guests from all over the world would often want to go down into the valley and visit what they pictured as typical small-town America. Then they would be surprised at how rundown Uniontown was. I realized that much of the problem was physical, with dilapidated buildings and so on, and it became clear to me that I could make a difference in Uniontown by doing what had made me successful: building. I had built a successful business in building materials, and, over the years, I have cultivated many relationships with builders and contractors. I know who the good ones are, the ones I can trust to do a good job. So we renovated one building after another and tore down the ones that couldn't be fixed. I think that companies, like individuals, should contribute to their communities in ways that they are good at. People who have been fortunate usually want to give something back to the community, so they can take those skills that have made their companies successful and, well, use some imagination. Great things can happen.*

"So we renovated one building after another and tore down the ones that couldn't be fixed."

To guide companies and other organizations in planning and implementing their community relations programs, Burke suggests an audit of the community's needs, strengths, and weaknesses, and an assessment of the organization with respect to its community relations plans and programs. Taking those two steps can make the difference between a community relations program that, however well intentioned, fails to meet the needs of the organization and the community, and a program that helps both.[10]

Community Audit

The community audit should be geared toward producing, first, factual information including a quantification, where possible, of the community's needs, along with an examination of the community's own resources. Other companies' community resources should also be identified in order to avoid duplication. Second, the audit should include qualitative information on such things as community attitudes toward the organization as well as the kinds of relationships people in the organization have already established in the community. Third, strategic information should be included in the audit concerning opportunities and threats to the organization in the community. For instance, is there a zoning restriction that could interfere with growth plans, or a pending environmental regulation that sets unrealistic goals? What can the organization do about the threats and opportunities?

Company Assessment

The company assessment is meant to give information that can guide its philanthropic, employee volunteerism, and community partnership programs. This information is just as important as the community audit in determining an organization's ad hoc and long-term community relations strategies and programs.

Identify the Communities

Another important aspect of strategic community relations is identifying the communities important to the organization. They include the fence line and site communities, as well as the employee community, the common-interest community, and the cybercommunity. Of course organizations can only do so much, and must prioritize their community relations efforts, just as they do their business initiatives. But the point of a communities identification effort is to be sure that important communities are not being overlooked, which is to say that the communities that are the most proximal, the largest, or the loudest are not necessarily the most important.

The relationship between an organization and a community will be only as good as the two-way communication. A communication theory called General Systems Theory (see Chapter 1, Sidebar) provides a framework for understanding that no constituency is an island, that communication flows between constituencies, whether it is orchestrated or accidental, and that there is no such thing as not communicating.

The Strategic Use of Corporate Philanthropy

Books have proliferated over recent years advocating the strategic use of corporate philanthropy: the targeted use of corporate philanthropy that takes advantage of the company's strengths and business interests for the benefit of certain social causes and charities. Two philanthropic marketing strategies have been employed with special effectiveness.

The American Express Company coined the term "cause-related marketing" to describe its 1983 program which encouraged use of the American Express credit card by having the company make contributions (one penny for each use of the card and one dollar for each new card issued) to the Statue of Liberty–Ellis Island Foundation.[11]

A second term, "social marketing," describes the adoption by a company of a program that clearly benefits society, while, over the long term, possibly benefiting the company. When First Alert was about to introduce its carbon monoxide detector for the home in 1992, the company learned that only 2 percent of potential customers knew that carbon monoxide leaks in the home could be a problem. The company held up on the introduction of the product and the paid advertising, while the PR people introduced a national (unpaid) carbon monoxide awareness program, consisting of briefings to health and science reporters in print and broadcast. Society benefited, with consumer awareness of the carbon monoxide threat soaring within months to 75 percent, as did the company from a timely, successful introduction of its product.[12]

HARDY'S RELATIONSHIP-BUILDING PRINCIPLE #4: KEEP MOVING AHEAD

Joe Hardy:

> *Once I decided to lead a Uniontown renovation effort, I did all I could to do it right. People have commented on how workers are doing their work in downtown Uniontown in the rain, painting and sandblasting and so forth, as if there is some impossible deadline. Well, in the community, I think, just as in business, once you decide to do something you have to move ahead in a committed, planned fashion. You also have to realize that just about everything you want to do has been done, so why not take advantage of that? So I visited small towns that had been successfully rebuilt. It is good to know if something has been tried before you do it again. If it failed, why did it? If it worked, maybe you can put a twist on it, and do it a little better. I also worked with local politicians and with county and state leaders including Governor Rendell. Eddie and I have a good relationship, and I know he has a tough job. But*

he knows I am serious about Uniontown and Fayette County, and he knows I can be impatient. Uniontown is the county seat and it is important to help bring it back. But there are other towns in the county that need such help and I want the governor to know we are serious. We need his help and I think he trusts in our personal relationship. That can mean a lot moving forward.

> Organizations have to do a better job of requiring loyalty to the organization, the brand, and to the things the organization does well.

Anyone who has worked in a community relations department has seen numerous good and effective projects abandoned, sometimes for good reasons such as budgetary ones, but other times because a new boss wants to institute his or her own programs. Organizations have to do a better job of requiring loyalty to the organization, the brand, and to the things the organization does well. An illustration of a company that has made and adhered to a long-term commitment to a particular, albeit distant, community is the story of Merck and the drug known as Mectizan.

A Developing-World Community

Almost alone in the history of corporate philanthropy in terms of human health benefits bestowed was Merck's decision, announced in 1987, that it would donate its new medicine Mectizan to as many people who needed it for as long as necessary, until river blindness (onchocerciasis) is eliminated as a public health problem. River blindness is endemic primarily to sub-Saharan Africa but also occurs in parts of Mexico, Central and South America, and the Middle East. The active ingredient in Mectizan, called ivermectin, was originally developed as a medicine for veterinary use. After studies indicated its effectiveness against onchocerciasas, a human formulation of the drug—now known as Mectizan—was developed. Seven years of clinical trials then resulted in the approval of Mectizan to treat onchocerciasis.

The disease has ravaged populations in tropical countries for centuries, causing, among other things, blindness. The parasite that causes the disease is spread by blackflies that bite people as often as thousands of times daily. In many African villages, more than half of the adult population would be blind as a result of the disease.

In most cases, treatment with just one oral dose of Mectizan annually will prevent the symptoms and halt the progression of the disease, including blindness, with few, if any, side effects. After much discussion within the company, then-chief executive P. Roy Vagelos, M.D., made an unprecedented decision: the company would give the drug to all who needed it, for as long as needed, for the treatment of onchocerciasis. *The New York Times'* Erik Eckholm wrote in a cover story in the paper's Sunday magazine on January 8, 1989, that: "In this case—the centuries-old torment of river blindness—developments have world health authorities cheering. In what will surely rank as one of the century's great medical triumphs, a dreadful scourge is coming under control."[13] Since then, on top of the costs needed to develop, manufacture, and donate Mectizan, the company has spent millions of dollars to help develop and support the distribution and administration infrastructure. President Jimmy Carter, whose Carter Center in Atlanta, GA, has worked with Merck on the distribution, praised the company lavishly: "I think Merck has set a standard of the highest possible quality. [The Mectizan Donation Program has] been one of the most remarkable and exciting and inspiring partnerships that I have ever witnessed."[14]

Dr. Vagelos knew that Merck, a global company, could not ignore the needs of millions of people in communities oceans away from the company's business center. A physician and renowned researcher, as well as one of America's most successful business leaders, he knew well that the parasite which infects a person's body produces intense itching that is believed to have caused many suicides, terrible skin disfigurement, and, after migrating to the eye, blindness. "The Merck community," he said in 1987, "does not end in New Jersey where we have our headquarters, in Washington or Brussels where we get our new drug approvals, or even in the Western World where we sell most of our medicines. We discover, develop and market important new medicines and, wherever we can make a difference, we must do all that we can."[15]

Together with other initiatives such as spraying to kill the blackflies, Mectizan has made a tremendous contribution. Since the inception of the program and with collaboration from a range of key partners, Merck has donated more than 2.5 billion tablets of Mectizan for river blindness, with nearly 700 million treatments approved since 1987. The program currently reaches more than 80 million people through river blindness programs in Africa, Latin America and the Middle East (Yemen) annually. In fact, in 2008, it was announced that 31 percent of the formerly at-risk population in the Americas is no longer at risk of contracting the disease. Additionally, 300 million treatments for lymphatic filariasis, for which the medicine is also donated, have been approved, with nearly 90 million treatments approved in 2008 alone. But Merck and its partners still have a long way to go, since as many as 120 million people in more than thirty countries are at risk for river blindness.[16]

HARDY'S RELATIONSHIP-BUILDING PRINCIPLE #5: EMBRACE DIVERSITY

Joe Hardy:

> *I know that diversity is also a buzzword today and it can be used in a forced kind of way, as if government regulations and so forth are involved. But I mean it in a very positive way. On the global front, it is good business to embrace diversity. In any case, globalization is here to stay. In the local community, just as is the case internationally, diversity means to me that we can respect people who may look, speak, or think in a different way. People in Western Pennsylvania have certain expressions, such as "youns" (plural of you), but don't let that fool you. They are as smart as anyone. And even though people here have had reason in the past to be discouraged, they can be motivated by opportunity. For example, a large number of our employees at Nemacolin are compensated not just with a salary but with performance-based incentives as well. Many of our employees at Nemacolin Resort are Fayette County residents, and most of them had never worked in a hotel. But we give them great*

"And even though people here have had reason in the past to be discouraged, they can be motivated by opportunity."

*training and they respond by helping us build what is already one of the country's best
resorts, right here in Fayette County. And that means our Nemacolin workers can go
on to any other hotel if they wish—the famous Greenbrier in West Virginia, for instance—because the management there wants our people. That's all good of course for
everyone; even when we lose good people, it all works out is the way I look at it. So
building a hotel or a new 84 Lumber Store is doing something great for a community,
and if we can then go ahead and help people in Uniontown get back on their feet, that
is something extra. It all depends on people, on relationships. My daughter, Maggie
Hardy-Magerko, understands that; she is a very good judge of people, and that is
why she is president of 84 Lumber. I myself phone many friends and acquaintances
each day (sometimes seventy-five, no kidding!) just to wish them a happy birthday,
and these are people from all walks of life. It's all about judging character and building relationships over the years. That's how to get things done. That's a pretty good
way to live one's life, too, I think.*

A CEO can be incredibly important to the planning and implementation of a community relations program. Similarly, the head of any organization, for example the
president of a university, can get involved directly in the community, with impressive,
long-term benefits for the organization and the community. (See Sidebar on Wake
Forest University's program of building relationships with various communities, local and beyond.)

Ambassadors to the Community

The success of any community relations program will in the long run depend on buy-
in and support from people throughout the organization. "People in communities do
not make relationships with companies," Edmund Burke writes, "but with people
in companies and organizations." He identifies CEOs, facilities managers, and employees as all being important in an organization's community relations program. It
is they who know the culture, the unique needs and capabilities of the community in
which they live and work. "Employees are the bulk users of community services and
programs," he continues. "Consequently, employee evaluations of needs and services
in a community constitute valuable information for planning. They are also excellent
sources of information on community attitudes toward the company."[17]

A survey of human resource executives by the Conference Board showed that a
company's reputation was the third most important factor influencing people to become employees of particular organizations. (Only career development opportunities and compensation outranked reputation.) A study by the University of Missouri
showed that a company's corporate social performance is positively related to its reputation and attractiveness as an employer."[18]

WAKE FOREST UNIVERSITY: THE PATH TO BECOMING A NATIONAL UNIVERSITY

By Sandra Boyette, Senior advisor to the president, Wake Forest University

In 1956, Wake Forest College did what few institutions have done in recent history: the school moved from its home of one hundred and twenty-two years, near Raleigh, NC, to a brand-new custom-designed campus in Winston-Salem. The move was initiated by the Z. Smith Reynolds and Mary Reynolds Babcock Foundations, as well as civic leaders in the industrial Piedmont city, located one hundred and twenty miles west of the picturesque town of Wake Forest.

The "new" campus was, in many ways, a reflection of the "old": Old Virginia brick Georgian buildings; fledgling magnolia trees; and a faculty/staff residential community contiguous to the grounds. A few miles from downtown, the campus was somewhat of a town unto itself in its beautiful new environment. Although college employees interacted with the city—joining Rotary clubs, participating in Winston-Salem's rich arts life—financial and industrial executives remained the key civic leaders.

In 1967, the college became a university with a growing reputation for academic excellence; but town and gown had not yet formed any serious bonds.

By 1983 when Wake Forest's trustees selected Dr. Thomas K. Hearn Jr. as the twelfth president, Winston-Salem was headquarters to several *Fortune 500* companies and a number of other corporate giants—RJR Industries, Hanes textiles, Piedmont Airlines, Wachovia Corporation, and AT&T's North Carolina Works among them. The city's economy was thriving. As the former senior vice president for nonmedical affairs at the University of Alabama–Birmingham, Hearn had been active in Birmingham's civic and economic life, and he had great national ambitions for Wake Forest.

With the encouragement of trustees and administrators, Hearn began almost immediately to take Wake Forest into the local community. Early in his tenure, he led the United Way Campaign and established its first Leadership Circle. He founded Leadership Winston-Salem, to train and network local leaders, a step that proved invaluable less than a decade into his tenure. He encouraged Wake Forest faculty and administrators to serve nonprofit organizations in the city. He championed the growth of volunteer programs for Wake Forest students, citing the university's motto—Pro Humanitate—as the imperative.

At the same time, Hearn was taking steps that further elevated Wake Forest's national visibility as a leading academic institution, including a change in the relationship with the Baptist Convention of North Carolina, giving the university's trustees full autonomy. The college and university rankings began to proliferate at that time, too. Wake Forest held its number one spot among regional colleges and universities for several years, until it moved into the national research university category, where it remains in the top 10 percent.

A successful capital campaign—the school's largest ever—more than doubled building space, and applications increased rapidly. The Plan for the Class of 2000, initiated in 1995, created first-year seminars and added forty professors to the college faculty to preserve the advantages of small class size. Wake Forest led the nation in the introduction of technology as a tool of the liberal arts experience when students began receiving IBM ThinkPads, included as a benefit of tuition. From the mid-80s until the conclusion of Hearn's tenure in 2005, nine undergraduates were selected as Rhodes Scholars. Further, the university added a residential program in Vienna, complementing its two longstanding programs in London and Venice, and today, half of Wake Forest's undergraduates study abroad prior to graduation.

By the time Wake Forest hosted its first presidential debate in 1988 (and another in 2000), city leaders were supportive partners in the effort.

But also in the late 1980s, the city's economic fortunes began to turn. Mergers and acquisitions moved corporate headquarters to distant cities. The now-famous leveraged buyout of RJR Industries rattled the confidence of even the most optimistic of the city's movers and shakers. Suddenly, Wake Forest, with its growing medical center and the associated healthcare enterprises, was the city's largest employer. Dr. Hearn became instrumental in leading the fight to reshape Winston-Salem's economy and rebuild its self-image.

Ultimately, he chaired Winston-Salem Business, an organization established to recruit new companies to the area. Later, Hearn became chair of another new organization, Idealliance. Working with this group of corporate and education executives and focusing on biotechnology as the key to economic health, he and others—including Wake Forest's senior vice president for health affairs, Dr. Richard Dean and Winston-Salem State University Chancellor Dr. Harold Martin—committed to the establishment of the Piedmont Triad Research Park. A twenty-five year plan is transforming two hundred acres of the city's industrial topography to a downtown biotech park housing several departments of the Wake Forest School of Medicine and a number of biotech companies, some of which had their beginning in the university's research laboratories.

Concurrently, city leaders—many of whom were alumni of Leadership Winston-Salem, the program founded by Hearn—began an effort to revitalize the downtown area. A blighted area of warehouses and on-again-off-again retail shops has become a burgeoning, attractive arts district. Lofts and condominiums in former office and warehouse space are beginning to attract more residents downtown, with the expectation that eventually, biotech park employees and graduate students living there will keep the area vibrant.

One could argue that Wake Forest's rise in academe gave the university the credibility it needed to become an integral component of the city and region. One could also argue that the move to Winston-Salem opened new opportunity for a larger constituency to support the university's national ambitions. Both arguments have merit. It is certain that good things happened to the university and the city because of a president willing to take on daunting community issues while moving his institution to national academic prominence.

■ ■ ■

Dr. Thomas K. Hearn, Jr. died in August 2008 and is deeply missed by his colleagues at Wake Forest.

HARDY'S RELATIONSHIP-BUILDING PRINCIPLE #6: WHEN THINGS GO WRONG, MAKE THEM RIGHT AS FAST AS YOU CAN

Joe Hardy:

> *Things will sometimes go wrong. It is a fact of life, business, and community relations. Successful people make lots of mistakes. They just know how to admit and fix them fast.*

Wal-Mart has been trying for years to build a store in one of New York City's five boroughs. Each time, small but PR-savvy citizen groups were able to block the behemoth, raising concerns about everything from traffic to alleged exploitive and unsafe workplace practices.

At this writing the company had recently lost a battle to build a store in Queens, and was beginning a new initiative in Staten Island. Immediately, some resident groups mobilized against having a store in that borough, even though many of them admit frequenting Wal-Marts in New Jersey. At this writing, the company was beginning a corporate advertising program to build support among Staten Island residents for a new store.

In founder Sam Walton's day, Wal-Mart was admired as a company that knew how to do everything right, including employee and community relations. How much of the problem now is with the substance of Wal-Mart's policies and actions, versus its communications, is unclear. But what is clear is that the Pushmi-Pullyu Syndrome of a two-headed organization (Chapter 1) applies here. In order for the company to overcome its community relations problems, it will have to behave and communicate in one way—a way that represents a marked improvement over recent times.

COMMUNITY RELATIONSHIPS ARE BASED ON TRUST

By James E. Lukaszewski, The Lukaszewski Group

There are many ongoing challenges to building community trust and ensuring positive relationships with customers, allies, colleagues, government, and employees. It is by far easier to recognize the pattern of those behaviors and attitudes that damage trust, or at least bring credibility into question than to catalog all the activities organizations and companies use or attempt in order to build community relationships. Put in a more interesting way, trust is a fragile but powerful substance like the lignin in trees—it is the glue that holds the fiber of relationships together. Yet, trust is the most fragile and vulnerable agent in any relationship.

The twelve most commonly seen trust-busting behaviors are listed and described below. Avoiding these behaviors or remediating them promptly will help maintain community trust and credibility.

1   **Arrogance:** Taking action without consulting those directly or indirectly affected. Making decisions unilaterally, without important input from key partners. Action without empathy.

2   **Broken promises:** One of the crucial bases of trust is that each party can rely on the commitments of the other, both implied and explicit. When those commitments are broken without prior notification, understanding, explanation, and warning, the first element of the relationship to suffer is trust. Losing the safety of commitment can call into question most other elements of the relationship as well.

3   **Creating fear:** This usually occurs when something you do damages or threatens to damage someone else without their permission, knowledge, or participation. It could be the appearance of decision; it could be the feeling of unreliability in the relationship.

4   **Deception:** Misleading intentionally through omission, commission, negligence, or incompetence in a relationship creates a feeling of separation and distance. It also creates a sense of disappointment because the individual, product, company, or organization failed to recognize that, at the very least, there should be a sense of candor between the parties no matter what the circumstance.

5   **Disparaging opposition:** Any time you hear the phrase, "He's uninformed," or "They're just looking to raise money by their actions," or "It's politically motivated," or "They just don't understand," you immediately suspect that the exact opposite is true, and you're likely to be right. All opponents have friends elsewhere. Some of those friends are your friends as well. Victory is never achieved through disparagement. Disparagement causes suspicion, damages relationships, and creates permanent critics.

6   **Disrespect:** Even adversaries can trust each other to some extent, provided there is a sense of respect. When the reputation of an individual, product, or organization is minimized, trivialized, or humiliated, there is a sense of uneasiness and discomfort that often leads to frustration, anger, and outwardly negative behavior.

7   **Ignoring/avoiding the killer questions:** Too often when preparing for adverse situations the very serious questions—those that can kill reputation and, therefore, destroy trust—are either ignored or sanitized so as to be nearly unrecognizable. The honorable, trustworthy organization or individual prepares for the killer questions first and then determines other information that might be useful and helpful to explain or illustrate.

8   **Telling lies:** Often starting with simple misunderstandings, the truth to one individual or organization can seem untruthful to a competitor or competing interest, simply based on the critic's or competitor's point of reference in relation to a given set of facts and information.

9   **Minimizing danger:** The moment you hear the phrase, "It's just an isolated incident," instinctively you know it's probably just the reverse. The moment you hear the phrase, "It's old news," you instinctively understand that something new and adverse is about to happen, even if it is based on old circumstances. We trust people who appropriately characterize situations.

10   **Negative surprise:** Taking action out of character, out of sequence, out of selfish opportunity, or simply without advance notice to those directly or indirectly affected can seriously damage the relationship of trust and will cause a loss of confidence in the relationship.

11 **Stall, delay:** A great source of frustration is when it is obvious that a situation could be resolved easily and quickly, but is not. Procrastination and denial go hand-in-hand. Keep in mind one of the great axioms of military strategy: timidity, hesitation, and indecision are the basic ingredients of defeat.

12 **Exaggerate your preparation:** One of the most serious mistakes in a relationship is the assumption that one is prepared to manage most adverse situations and that everyone else will understand what you are doing. Trust in relationships is often broken because when adverse situations occur, few step forward, most back away from the organizations most directly affected. No matter how well the situation is dealt with, trust repair and maintenance must be key parts of any preparation and remediation process.

Maintaining a relationship of trust requires constant analysis of the relationship to identify and eliminate negative behaviors, confusion, negative attitudes, and unexpected outcomes.

Copyright © 2005, James E. Lukaszewski. All rights reserved. Reprinted with permission.

■ ■ ■

BEST PRACTICES

Here are some of the things forward-thinking companies and other organizations do to build enduring community relationships.

1   Hardy's six relationship-building principles.

2   Conduct a company assessment and community audit of the most important communities.

3   Learn from others: Celebrating major milestones, whether it is a centennial of service, a decade, or a year, is something that cuts across all industries and organizations. Research what has worked well for others before developing your plan.

4   Do a few things well: There are lots of ideas for special events and programs and the challenge is always deciding what not to do. Focus on a few things rather than many.

5   It is about the customers—not us. Find ways to involve and honor customers. The focus on economic development addressed a pressing community and customer need, while playing to the company's strengths.

6   Strengthen local partnership. Use a centennial, for example, as a reason to educate customers and communities about longstanding company priorities (e.g., philanthropy, volunteerism, service, operational successes). Explore the potential for new community opportunities, particularly where the needs of the customers, the community, and the organization intersect.

7   Recognize and involve employees and retirees. Employees and retirees personify the organization's values through their accomplishments at work, at home, and in their communities. Find ways to say "thank you" for their support and community involvement.

8   Regional and national visibility for a college or university reflect well on its home city. (See Wake Forest Sidebar.) Timely editorials in the local news, commenting on the school's achievements, can only serve to build the town and the relationship, and position the president as a community leader.

9   Local government officials need to be cultivated by universities and not-for-profits, just as prospective donors are. Regular meetings with them to discuss an organization's plans—capital improvements, neighborhood initiatives, large public events—foster trust and can help avoid conflicts.

10   Ensuring that the company's or school's president (Wake Forest Sidebar) leads some purely community activities—a United Way campaign, an arts festival, a leadership training initiative—can exemplify the institution's willingness to "give back" to the community. Despite all the other demands on a president's or CEO's time, early in his or her tenure is a good time for such an activity to set the right tone.

11   Evaluate the number of events at the company, school, or other organization to consider ways that they can be expanded. Publish a regular calendar in the local newspaper as a reminder of the cultural opportunities that the company or school offers to the community. Be certain that the president or CEO when possible welcomes audiences at a number of these events.

12   A company or other organization that is going to spend money on a community relations program or on a particular philanthropic program should set aside a percentage of the funds for communication. It is not just for publicity's sake but rather to ensure that the program will work and endure.

RESOURCES FOR FURTHER STUDY

Burke, Edmund M., *Corporate Community Relations: The Principle of the Neighbor of Choice* (Westport, CT: Praeger, 1999).

Burke, Edmund M., *Managing a Company in an Activist World: The Leadership Challenge of Corporate Citizenship* (Westport, CT: Praeger, 2005).

Center for Corporate Citizenship at Boston College, http://www.bcccc.net.

Grayson, David and Hodges, Adrian, *Everybody's Business: Managing Risks and Opportunities in Today's Global Society* (New York: DK Publishing, 2002).

Merck MECTIZAN® Donation Program, http://www.mectizan.com.

Sagawa, Shirley and Sega, Eli, *Common Interest, Common Good* (Boston: Harvard Business School Press, 2000).

Weeden, Curt, *Corporate Social Investing: The Breakthrough Strategy for Giving and Getting Corporate Contributions* (San Francisco: Berrett-Koehler, 1998).

QUESTIONS FOR FURTHER DISCUSSION

1　Joe Hardy has almost single-handedly been able to rebuild Uniontown, PA. If one man can accomplish that, why can large companies or multicompany organizations not rebuild some of our large, decaying cities?

2　How many companies base their community relations programs on community audits or company assessments? Does yours?

3　Could Wake Forest University have achieved its national reputation for academic excellence without an outreach into communities beyond the traditionally academic ones?

4　Jim Lukaszewski says that, "Maintaining a relationship of trust requires constant analysis …" Elaborate, based on one of your business relationships.

*On Wall Street bulls make money
and bears make money,
but pigs get slaughtered.*

CHAPTER

8 INVESTOR RELATIONS

The authors and Eugene L. Donati

■ ■ ■

In September 2002 a large Japanese company spun off a small molecular diagnostic company, Gen-Probe, based in San Diego, a hotbed of biotechnology. At the time Gen-Probe's stock traded at about $7.00 per share.[1] It would have been easy for newly independent Gen-Probe to focus primarily on its core business, and to wait for Wall Street to discover it. But instead Gen-Probe actively engaged the investment community.

The company spends about thirty days annually—about 12 percent of senior management's time—telling its story to Wall Street. But engagement with Wall Street is not just promotional. Management works very deliberately to keep the Street's expectations in check. The company's philosophy is to "under-promise and over-deliver" on a range of milestones including corporate financial performance and product development timelines.

The way the company engages Wall Street is not particularly esoteric or difficult. But it is intentional. The company's investor relations program employs many traditional tools of the trade, including investor targeting, presentations at brokerage conferences, nondeal road shows, analyst meetings, facility tours, and day-to-day phone contact with the Street.

This work has paid off. A 2004 survey of forty investment analysts by Rivel Research Group gave Gen-Probe an overall corporate reputation score of 5.1 on a six-point scale. This compares to a mid-cap norm of 4.3 in other studies conducted by Rivel. Furthermore, the respondents identified "credible management" as the most important factor in determining whether to buy or sell Gen-Probe stock, and 80 percent agreed that the management team meets this criterion.

The tangible result of Gen-Probe's investor relations focus and positive reputation is telling: this small San Diego firm has become a member of the Standard & Poor's 400 Mid-Cap Index in less than three years. Its stock price has increased more than six-fold, significantly outperforming the broad market and the biotech sector. The firm is covered by a dozen sell-side analysts, and more than 90 percent of the company's shares are held by institutional investors. In all the company has generated more than $2 billion in shareholder value.

■ ■ ■

WHAT IS INVESTOR RELATIONS?

Investor relations (IR) is the subset of public relations and corporate communication that deals with a company's relationship with the investment community. Both current investors (who own a corporation's stocks and bonds) and potential investors (who might be persuaded to own these stocks and bonds) make up the primary audiences for investor relations.

IR is most often employed by companies whose shares are held and traded by the public. Privately owned companies may also use IR in circumstances such as when they have bonds trading on the public markets or when they are owned by a dispersed group of private shareholders.

IR is unique among communication disciplines in that real people make or lose real money every day, based on information, utterances, or omissions from a corporate IR department. Since IR mistakes can cost real people real money, IR is the most heavily regulated of communication disciplines. Laws, government regulations, and stock exchange regulations each dictate how IR is conducted and when. As a result, IR has exacting procedures and deadlines. In the United States, IR practitioners are subject to significant civil and criminal liability if they violate certain principles.

Since IR mistakes can cost real people real money, IR is the most heavily regulated of communication disciplines.

The demands of investors and regulators make investor relations among the most stimulating and academically rigorous of all communication disciplines. IR requires knowledge of communication, finance, law, accounting, and marketing. In general, IR practitioners are well compensated compared to other communication professionals with similar experience and responsibility. IR practitioners may become trusted advisors within corporations and participate at the highest levels of corporate strategy.

In the United States, IR practitioners are subject to significant civil and criminal liability if they violate certain principles.

Corporate leadership has only recently come to acknowledge the strategic importance of IR. From its establishment as a distinct discipline in the 1960s until the mid-1990s, IR was seen as tactical, peripheral to strategic corporate decision-making. Since the mid-1990s, IR has matured into a strategic element of business operation. The reasons are many. For instance, the demand for reliable data about corporations grew as individuals increasingly held stocks, mutual funds, and retirement funds. The Internet erased barriers to information flow, giving Main Street investors access to financial information reserved previously for Wall Street. Further, chief executive officers (CEOs) are now often judged by how well their companies' stock performs. So CEOs are now much more keen on what IR can do. And key to the evolution of IR as a strategic discipline are the several corporate scandals that have compelled more complete, integrated, timely, and thoughtful corporate financial disclosure. Without robust financial disclosure and transparency, a corporation now risks severe damage to its reputation and ability to do business.

IR is viewed as a financial function with an essential overlay of communication practice and theory.

Today, especially in the United States and Canada, IR is viewed as a financial function with an essential overlay of communication practice and theory. It is now common for the head of IR to interact closely with the CEO and make presentations to the board of directors. IR generally takes part in the corporation's strategic processes to a greater degree than corporate communication professionals without IR responsibilities.

THE GOALS AND ROLES OF INVESTOR RELATIONS

The first goal of investor relations is to ensure that a company's securities, that is, its stocks and bonds, are fairly and fully valued in the marketplace. "Fairly and fully valued" means that the price of a company's securities closely reflects both the present value and the potential value of the company. Given that a stock's price is set by the market based on demand for that stock, investor relations involves maintaining demand. IR does this by ensuring investors have access to accurate, timely information about the company so they can appraise the attractiveness of the company's stock relative to other investment opportunities.

> The first goal of investor relations is to ensure that a company's securities, that is, its stocks and bonds, are fairly and fully valued in the marketplace.

IR's second goal is to help fulfill corporations' affirmative disclosure obligations under securities law and government regulation. These are described in detail later in this chapter. Stock exchanges also have their own disclosure requirements, and IR is responsible for helping companies fulfill these disclosure requirements too.

> IR's second goal is to help fulfill corporations' affirmative disclosure obligations under securities law and government regulation.

A third goal of IR is to create competitive advantage. Just as a company tries to create competitive advantage for its products and services in the consumer marketplace, IR works to create competitive advantage for a company's securities in the investment marketplace. To do this, IR uses the same communication tools as other public relations functions and often coordinates closely with those functions, including media relations, internal communications (especially when employees, either directly, or through unions or pension plans, own stock), and sometimes advertising.

> A third goal of IR is to create competitive advantage.

A BRIEF INTRODUCTION TO THE FINANCIAL MARKETS AND INVESTMENT

IR is primarily concerned with communication to the financial markets. Financial markets are physical or virtual places where those who have surplus money (capital) come together with those who need money. In theory, financial markets operate so that capital flows to its most beneficial and lucrative use, defined as where surplus money earns the greatest return relative to risk. In practice, inefficiencies of human actions and communication almost guarantee that capital may not reach its best use. IR supports the goal that capital always reaches its best use by working to eliminate inefficiencies in information and data among market participants and observers.

Those who have surplus money are investors. Financial markets move money from investors to borrowers, in exchange for a promise to repay the money under specified future conditions. A business generally needs money for two purposes: to fund operations or to fund growth opportunities, such as building new factories. When a business needs money, it can turn to several sources. For instance, it can generate cash from internal operations by increasing productivity (and thus earnings) or by closing inefficient operations. A business also can borrow money from a bank. Sometimes a business prefers to ask the general public to become investors and provide the necessary money. A business does this through the financial markets, by issuing bonds ("debt securities"), which in essence are tiny, discrete simultaneous loans from large numbers of investors, or by issuing stocks ("equity securities"), which in essence are tiny, discrete portions of ownership, that is, "shares" of ownership in the company itself, to many investors simultaneously. These bonds or stocks collectively are called "securities" because the supplier of capital (the investor) has secured legal standing and claim on the corporation's assets in certain circumstances.

Debt Securities

Financial news outlets often imply stocks are where the action is, but in the U.S. the debt securities markets are significantly larger, both in dollar terms and in number of issuers. A debt security is a promise. In exchange for borrowing the investors' money (the "principal"), corporations (the "issuers") promise to pay a previously determined return ("interest"), at a stated frequency, for a certain time period. Thus when investors receive debt securities, they gain an income stream for a certain period. Gaining this steady income is why investors invest. Investors in debt securities generally know what their income stream will be, so debt securities are also known as fixed-income securities. When a debt security matures, issuers give back the principal. From the issuer's perspective, the issuer is "renting" the principal.

Debt securities are classified by the time to maturity from its initial offering, that is, the time until the principal has to be paid back. Corporate debt that matures in five years or more from its initial offering is called a "bond," corporate "notes" mature in one to five years, "commercial paper" matures in less than one year. Each of these types of debt has its advantages to a corporation. For instance, commercial paper often funds a corporation's working capital needs to keep operations flowing smoothly.

Equity Securities

Whereas debt securities are essentially loans, equity securities represent actual ownership in a corporation. Equity securities differ from debt in that the money provided by investors is provided permanently to the corporation, that is, the money never has to be paid back. But for this permanent money, investors get a permanent share of ownership in the corporation. Equity securities are commonly referred to as shares, or stocks, for this reason. If the corporation does very well, the investors stand to do very well too. Shareholders gain both from the appreciation in value of a company's stock as set by the stock market and, sometimes, from dividend payments, which are profits paid to shareholders from time to time from excess corporate cash. But shareholders also run substantial risks, too, and are the first to lose their money if a corporation goes bankrupt. Dividends are distributed on a pro rata basis; that is, each share is entitled to an equal portion of the profits. In the U.S., dividends are customarily paid quarterly, in the United Kingdom, semiannually.

Even though shares in themselves are permanent at-risk capital, sometimes investors want out, understandably. The stock exchanges exist, in part, to allow investors to find other investors who are willing to buy their shares of ownership. These transactions often occur on well-established, well-regulated stock exchanges, such as the New York Stock Exchange (NYSE). New York and London are home to the world's leading stock exchanges. Tokyo, Toronto, Frankfurt, Paris, Hong Kong, Singapore, Seoul, Dubai, Sydney, Mumbai, and Shanghai also host important markets. Most stock exchanges today exist only electronically and have no physical location or trading floor. The NASDAQ stock exchange in New York is a notable example. Even the NYSE is rapidly moving away from its trading floor operations. In January 2006, 86 percent of the NYSE's volume occurred on its trading floor. By May 2007, NYSE trading floor volume slipped to just 18 percent, with the remainder done electronically.

What Does "Public Company" Mean?

Some words used in IR have specialized, specific meanings that are non-intuitive and even contrary to usage in everyday English. For example, in the securities markets "public" and "private" carry meanings which derive from the description of whether a company's stock is generally available to any buyer, or whether ownership is restricted to a few. A public company is a business whose stock is available for sale to any member of the general public. A private company is a business whose ownership is restricted by law to present owners and those who may buy its stock by invitation only, directly from the company or from one of its private owners. There is no public market in a private company's stock.

What differences do such distinctions make? By definition, since private companies have no stocks or bonds publicly available for sale, they are not subject to the disclosure obligations required of public companies by law. Privately held companies are not required to disclose their finances, profits, strategies, successes, or failures, and generally they do not. Conversely, public companies are required to make full, timely, and accurate disclosures of information a reasonable observer might believe reflects on the value of that company's securities. Investor relations is the communications skill set that companies use to meet these disclosure requirements and to relay material corporate information to all reasonable public observers so they can make reasonable investment decisions concerning the company.

Why Do Corporations Exist?

The corporation is the dominant form of economic organization in the world today. While forms of government, for instance, may vary widely, the basic structure of the corporation can be found functioning in nearly every corner of the Earth. In part, corporations exist as a way to accommodate the explosive need for capital to invest and grow a business. Other forms of business organization include sole proprietorships and partnerships. Each form has its benefits and drawbacks. But only a corporation allows the raising of large pools of capital from diverse and widely dispersed shareholders, within a legal structure that is permanent. Corporations also can enter into contracts, own property, make use of tax advantages and have established ways of governance that provide certain protections for all involved.

Many corporations first were the brainchild of entrepreneurs, who founded them as a way to profit from a major idea or innovation. From J.P. Morgan, Henry Ford, Andrew Carnegie, and Thomas Edison to today's Bill Gates, Andy Grove, and Steve Jobs, corporations proved a reliable way to take an idea and build an organization around it, to create and distribute wealth for the greater benefit of society.

But as corporations raise capital and expand their ownership structure, the owners become too numerous, or too distant, from the corporation to run its business effectively day to day. Thus owners (shareholders) hire managers as their agents to run the corporation. For this very good reason, ownership becomes separated from management. But this also can cause a significant problem, as owners and managers often have differing outlooks on what goals and risks the corporation should take. For example, owners want to maximize profits, while managers may want to maximize their salaries and perquisites. In fact, this problem caused by the separation of ownership and management—called the "agency problem"—was at the heart of the financial crisis on Wall Street that began in 2007. Managers there were willing to take on incredible risks, because if things went right, managers gained tremendously. But if things went wrong, as they did, it was the shareholders, and in this case ultimately the taxpayers, who bore all the downside risk.

To solve the agency problem, yet keep all the benefits of the corporation form of economic organization, shareholders needed a way to monitor and direct the goals and risks of the corporation, in other words, a way to govern the corporation.

The Role of Shareholders in a Public Company

Shareholder-owners manage a corporation's goals and risk through the system of corporate governance. Under this system, shareholders have two rights: the right to select individuals to represent their interests who in turn direct the CEO and other senior managers on what to do, and the right to have access to a steady, accurate stream of information about the company and its actions. In other words, shareholders elect directors, who assemble as the Board of Directors, whose only duty in the United States is to represent shareholders' interests, in accordance with the law. Directors have a fiduciary duty, or duty of good faith, to serve shareholder interests.

As owners, shareholders are entitled to participate in important corporate decisions. To do this, shareholders are entitled to vote their shares on a one share, one vote basis for the election of directors, under the concept of shareholder democracy. Shareholders vote at meetings which generally take place once per year (annual meetings), but special-purpose meetings can be called any time under procedures set out in the corporation's bylaws. At annual meetings, shareholders decide issues including appointment of the company's independent auditors, election of directors and other issues properly brought before the meeting.

Also as owners, shareholders have the right to access certain information about the company. Some information is available from the company's proxy statement and formal filings with regulators, described below. A key job for IR is providing the rest of the information that current or prospective investors need in order to make informed governance and investment decisions. The concept of the level playing field means that all investors and potential investors must have access to all available pertinent information at the same time. Ensuring that this happens is one of the cornerstones of IR practice. Regardless of how many shares a holder owns, all shareholders and the entire investment market are entitled to equal and simultaneous access to information about the company, which brings up the two key concepts of investor relations and corporate communications: disclosure and materiality.

DISCLOSURE AND MATERIALITY

> The cornerstone of a successful IR practice is the provision simultaneously of all available pertinent information to current and potential investors.

The cornerstone of a successful IR practice is the provision simultaneously of all available pertinent information to current and potential investors. This begs the questions: is all information pertinent? If not, how does one decide whether information is pertinent? And if it is, when and how must that information be disclosed?

Public companies have an affirmative obligation under the law to keep all investors and potential investors informed on matters that they might deem important. First, note the audience: all investors and all potential investors. A fundamental principle of investor relations is that no issuer gives one market participant an informational advantage over others, as noted earlier. Since nearly every person can and does participate in the market (through ownership of mutual funds or retirement accounts, for instance), IR is much broader than a conversation with Wall Street. A variety of initiatives over the last ten years reinforced this mandate for information parity—sometimes in the jargon called a level playing field—aided significantly by the ease, speed, and ubiquity of Internet-based communications. Selective disclosure—telling only some investors important corporate news before other investors—is a violation of U.S. securities law and regulation.

Two related concepts—disclosure and materiality—determine information flow to current and potential investors.

Disclosure is the distribution of information, positive and nega-

> Disclosure is the distribution of information, positive and negative, by a company, voluntarily, or to be in compliance with laws and regulations.

tive, by a company, voluntarily, or to be in compliance with laws and regulations. Disclosure concerns whether and when pertinent information should be released. A series of discrete rules and procedures spells out the scope, content, format, timing, certification, signatories, and other items on communication of this information.

There are two types of disclosure, formal and informal.

Formal disclosure

Formal disclosure requires that specific financial and business information be filed in a highly structured way with government regulators on a regular basis. The Securities and Exchange Commission (SEC), the U.S. government's main market regulator, provides standardized forms for formal disclosure; the three key forms that communication professionals should know are the Form 10-K, the Form 10-Q, and the Form 8-K.

The Form 10-K is a detailed report filed annually on the corporation's ("issuer's") financial results, business, management, and prospects. An outside accounting firm audits the 10-K prior to its release and the SEC then reviews the 10-K in detail.

The Form 10-Q is released by an issuer after the ends of the first, second, and third fiscal quarters and is a scaled-down version of the 10-K. The SEC reviews the 10-Q but the document is not audited by outside firms.

The Form 8-K is a filed by the issuer on an as-needed basis, when the issuer needs to announce certain significant changes in the company, such as new management, change of auditors, or any other critical information the issuer feels the public should know.

Formal disclosure includes two other documents for which there are not SEC forms. These are the proxy materials for the shareholders' annual meeting and the company's annual report to shareholders.

The proxy statement is material made available or distributed to each shareholder in advance of a company's annual meeting, the required yearly gathering of a company's shareholders to review performance and take major decisions through a one share, one vote election. Large corporations may have tens of millions of shares outstanding (and thus tens of millions potential votes) held by tens of thousands of shareholders. Because it is unlikely every shareholder can attend the meeting, a proxy method was developed so all shareholders can vote regardless of whether they attend in person.

A proxy is an authorization to vote a shareholder's securities. Typically, a company's senior managers ask permission to be the substitute elector and shareholders generally grant permission routinely. Thus management often enters the meeting with enough votes in hand to control all decisions; the annual meeting becomes *pro forma*. But increasingly, shareholders are withholding their proxies from management or giving them to dissident shareholders who challenge management on key decisions. Such a situation falls into the category of shareholder activism in which shareholders, as owners of the company, force decisions contrary to those of company management, who are the owners' agents. Recent proxy fights have occurred over issues including limiting executive compensation and directing a company's public policy initiatives in human rights and the environment. Proxy materials must be made available to shareholders thirty days before the scheduled meeting. The SEC reviews and approves all proxy material before distribution.

Finally, formal disclosure includes the annual report to shareholders. Unlike the Form 10-K filed with the SEC, the annual report to shareholders is a "free writing," which does not need preclearance by the SEC. Nonetheless, there is significant legal liability for material omission or misstatement in the annual report. Commonly, corporations use the annual report as a corporate marketing brochure and include the technical financial and operating information in the back; the front becomes a high-quality stylized brochure with essays, pictures, and art. The IR department or the corporate communication department is charged with writing and designing the overall annual report to shareholders. Companies traditionally devote significant time and attention in creating the front part of the annual report. But a growing number of companies are de-emphasizing the hard-copy annual report to shareholders as digital media take primacy.

Informal Disclosure

Informal disclosure involves communication directly to the market that is free form and distributed through a variety of channels. It is not mediated by regulators. Informal disclosure can include press releases, meeting presentations, speeches, tours of manufacturing plants, blogs and so forth. Much, but not all, communication by an IR practitioner is considered to be informal disclosure.

It is vital to note that a corporation is not obligated to distribute any and all information about itself. At one extreme, a voluminous dump of unstructured data from a corporation would be virtually useless for the market. At the other extreme, corporations have a right to keep much proprietary information private. For instance, Coca Cola can keep its beverage formulas secret, no matter how important it is to the company's profits, and thus its stock price. A corporation is obligated to release only pertinent information that is material, and then only under certain circumstances.

It can be said all corporation information is divided into two types: material information and non-material information. The U.S. Supreme Court defined material information:

> A fact will be considered material if there is a "substantial likelihood that a reasonable shareholder would consider it important"[2] in reaching his investment decision—that is, the investor would attach actual significance to the information in making his deliberations.

A corporation has a completely free hand to deal with non-material information as it sees fit. Business-as-usual information such as internal memos, advertisements, day-to-day media relations, and marketing materials are generally not considered material and therefore not subject to restrictions on dissemination. But what "actual signifi-cance" makes information material? Congress, the SEC, and the courts have deliber-ately left this definition vague, allowing each issuer to make this determination based on the situation at hand. Issues of disclosure and materiality are exceptionally nuanced in day-to-day practice. IR and public relations professionals often must seek and defer to the specific advice of their legal counsel.

The Issue of Fraud

The U.S. Supreme Court also has affirmed what is known as the *fraud-on-the-market theory*, which says that misleading statements affect the price of securities in the market as a whole and defraud purchasers or sellers, even if they did not rely directly on the misstatements. Material omissions of information or materially misleading statements distort the price of a company's stock. If performed deliberately, such material omis-sion or misstatement could be considered fraud.

> The significance of fraud-on-the-market theory is that a company's disclosure obligations apply to a much larger universe than its investors.

The significance of fraud-on-the-market theory is that a com-pany's disclosure obligations apply to a much larger universe than its investors, as noted earlier. The company has a duty to the market as a whole and therefore can be sued for improper disclosure even by people who never heard or saw what the company disclosed. In the U.S., a company and its officers, directors, and IR professionals are governed by the anti-fraud provisions of the SEC. In its entirety, SEC Rule 10b-5 reads:

> It shall be unlawful for any person, directly or indirectly, by the use of any means or instrumentality of interstate commerce, or of the-mails, or of any facility of any national exchange,
>
> (a)   To employ any device, scheme, or artifice to defraud,
>
> (b)   To make any untrue statement of a material fact or to omit to state a material fact necessary in order to make the statements made, in light of the circumstances under which they were made, not misleading,
>
> (c)   To engage in any act, practice, or course of business which operates or would operate as a fraud or deceit upon any person, in connec-tion with the purchase or sale of a security.[3]

> In the United States, the SEC has ruled that IR professionals can be subject to civil or criminal liability if they knew or should have known that the information transmitted was materially misleading or a material omission.

The rule does not specify particular content of communication that constitutes fraud. When a person or company commits a material omission or discloses something materially misleading, that action operates as a deceit in the securities market.

In the United States, the SEC has ruled that IR professionals can be subject to civil or criminal liability if they knew or should have known that the information transmitted was materially misleading or a material omission:

Although the [SEC] does not regard public relations firms to be the guarantors of the information they gather for distribution, such firms should not view themselves as mere publicists or communicators of information with no attendant responsibility whatsoever for the content of such information. Indeed, these firms must be aware of their obligation not to disseminate information concerning their clients which they know or have reason to know is materially false or misleading. The obligation is particularly crucial with respect to corporate financial statements, which are one of the primary sources of information available to guide the decisions of investors. In distributing financial information, public relations firms must take special care to ensure that the information which they have received is presented fairly, accurately, and completely. Public relations firms' dissemination of information concerning their clients which they know or should have reason to know is materially false or misleading, in connection with the purchase or sale of securities of such clients, may render them liable for violations of the federal securities laws.[4]

Regulation

To review, disclosure is related to whether and when information must be disclosed and materiality is related to what information must be disclosed. The final question becomes, who is in charge to see this happens?

Securities markets are regulated by an overlapping set of state, provincial, federal, and transnational governmental agencies. In addition, with several exceptions, each stock exchange worldwide has a layer of private regulation pertaining to any security trading on the particular exchange. Such private regulators are termed self-regulatory organizations (SROs) and carry considerable clout in determining standards and methods listing and trading a stock.

The Securities and Exchange Commission (SEC) in Washington, D.C., is the chief governmental regulator in the United States. In Canada, responsibility is held at provincial level with the Ontario Securities Commission taking the lead. The Financial Services Authority (FSA) is the U.K.'s regulator through 2011, when plans call for the Bank of England to assume supervision of banks and other financial institutions. The principal SRO in the United States is the Financial Industry Regulatory Authority (FINRA), which oversees most activities on the NYSE and on NASDAQ.

Over the last two decades technology has enabled capital to move virtually anywhere on the globe instantaneously. Such capabilities led to calls from investors, listed companies, and various national governments for greater regulatory harmonization and creation of a common, precise, legal framework for securities regulation and accounting standards. As it currently stands, a company listing its stock in London, New York, and Tokyo needs to follow three sets of regulations and three sets of accounting standards that are at times contradictory. The current situation adds expense for public companies and is said to cause unnecessary rigidity in global capital flows.

The Financial Accounting Standards Board (FASB) sets accounting standards in the United States. Canada follows rules similar to those set by FASB. Canada and most of the rest of the world follow accounting standards set by the International Accounting Standards Board, based in London. The SEC has set as a goal that all U.S. public companies will move to the global standard, called the International Financial Reporting Standards (IFRS), starting in 2015, with some companies gaining SEC permission to use IFRS earlier.

Recent Disclosure Regulation

Over the last ten years in the United States, a variety of initiatives have gone into effect designed to enhance transparency, level the informational playing field, speed the availability of corporate data, and improve corporate governance.

One key initiative to understand is SEC *Regulation Fair Disclosure*, which became effective in October 2000. Regulation Fair Disclosure (or Reg. FD) generally prohibits disclosure of material information selectively by a corporation to analysts, or others. Prior to Reg. FD, it was common IR practice to hold special closed-door meetings for selected investors and analysts and to limit or forbid general investors' participation in management conference calls, and so forth. Even though stock prices could gyrate wildly during these sessions as the privileged few took advantage of insider status to make a few bucks, the principle was that "sophisticated" information discussed in these venues exceeded that needed by the average market participant. The potential for abuse was obvious.

Under Reg. FD, corporate officers are permitted to conduct closed meetings with certain analysts or investors, but material information may not be disclosed unless it is also made available to the entire market simultaneously through other channels. If new information is blurted out by accident—for instance, by a carelessly speaking CEO—the corporation has an affirmative duty to notify the entire market of that information "promptly." The SEC has interpreted the regulation to mean in no event more than twenty-four hours later or by the beginning of the next day's trading session, whichever comes first.

INFORMATION INTERMEDIARIES: SECURITIES ANALYSTS

When making investment decisions, investors frequently depend on the advice of specialized investment professionals known as analysts. Analysts are experts in specific industries, market sectors, or trends. They are trained in specific academic disciplines, have had intensive financial training, and many are certified as Chartered Financial Analysts or its equivalent.

Securities analysts typically advise investors on issues ranging from asset allocation to promising industry sector opportunities, to recommendations on specific companies. Analysts can cover entire markets, specific geographic regions, entire sectors of the economy, or particular industries or companies. Some cover stocks, some bonds. But analysts all help investors to make informed investment decisions.

Securities analysts can be divided into two classes, depending on the analysts' goals: sell-side analysts and buy-side analysts.

Sell-side analysts are employed by brokerage firms and make recommendations to the firms' customers. They are called "sell-side" analysts because their advice is intended to result in a sale of shares by the brokerage firm to its customers. The research is provided to customers free of charge; the firm is compensated by the commissions it generates from the sale or from profits from the sale of shares the firm may own and sell directly to customers.

The primary work of sell-side analysts is predicting a company's financial performance and therefore the likely profits it will generate. Based on this educated guess, analysts advise investors to buy, hold, or sell their shares. Much quantitative work goes into an analyst's projection of earnings, stock price, and buy/hold/sell recommendations. Analysts work to find any opportunity to better understand companies they cover. They meet with management, call the company's IR professionals, interview customers or suppliers, and review publicly available company information, including those disclosures managed by IR.

Sell-side analysts' work is published in the form of reports on individual companies and industries. It is distributed to clients of their brokerage firms and is sometimes available on the Internet or other sources. Analysts also brief brokers at their firms about their recommendations so brokers can share those recommendations with their customers.

Buy-side analysts also make predictions about stock performance. But they are employed directly by large investors, known as institutional investors, which include mutual funds, insurance companies, trust companies, pension funds, and other organizations. They are called "buy-side" analysts because their firms buy and hold securities for long-term gain. Buy-side analysts make "in house" recommendations only to their own company's portfolio managers. Buy-side analysts review much of the same information and also the recommendations of sell-side analysts before making their own recommendations.

Much disclosure is directed to buy-side and sell-side analysts because they have significant influence over the investment process. Much time of IR and company management is spent working with, meeting with, and attempting to influence analysts positively. Conference calls held after release of material information are intended to give these analysts timely access to company management's perspective on this news and to provide them the opportunity to ask questions. IR professionals also spend considerable time on the phone and in e-mail with analysts answering technical questions, arranging meetings, and otherwise helping analysts understand the company.

INFORMATION INTERMEDIARIES:
THE FINANCIAL MEDIA

Analysts, the markets, investors, and potential investors rely on the financial news media, both traditional and digital, for additional key information about a company or industry. Traditional media has been augmented, and in some ways replaced, by the growing role of digital media. The financial media as a whole has great freedom of action, greater legal protections, and sometime more resources to pursue corporate information than do investors. Journalists frequently are among the first to discern trends and discover change within a corporation or industry, and it is therefore important for investors making investment decisions to pay attention to the press. Given the leading role media plays in investment decision making, investor relations and corporate media relations naturally focus considerable time and energy attempting to inform and generate accurate and positive commentary for a corporation, its management, and its prospects.

Traditional Financial Media

Because of the breaking-news nature of their reporting, wire services play an integral part in the system of corporate disclosure. Key among wire services for financial news are Reuters, Bloomberg News, and Dow Jones Newswires, each of which run various real-time newsfeeds for subscribers, as traditional wire copy, as desktop analytics and as coded feeds into automated trading systems. Each wire service also maintains extensive archives of news and market data for subscribers.

Daily newspapers with global significance in financial news include the *Wall Street Journal*, *The New York Times*, *The Financial Times*, *Les Echos* in French, *Handelsblatt* in German, and the *Nihon Keizai Shimbun* in Japanese. Regional newspapers with heavy financial news content include the *National Post/Financial Post* and the *Globe and Mail*, both of Toronto, the *Australian Financial Review*, *Il Sole 24 Horas* of Milan, Germany's *Frankfurter Allgemeine Zeitung*, the *Asahi Shimbun* of Tokyo, the *South China Morning Post* of Hong Kong, and the *Straits Times* of Singapore. Local newspapers, especially those writing from a company's headquarters city, can be exceptionally influential in financial news.

Three more classes of print publications hold some sway over financial markets and investment, although their influence is waning rapidly. Periodic business and investment magazines such as *Bloomberg Business Week* and *Barron's* still maintain influential readership. Trade publications—for example, *American Banker* in finance, *American Metal Market* for the metals industry, *Variety* and the *Hollywood Reporter* for entertainment, and *Women's Wear Daily* in apparel—specialize in single-industry coverage that can surpass investment insight and expertise in the general media. Finally, newsletters are a powerful but often under-recognized force in investment markets. These highly specialized publications—today often sent as a .pdf file rather than printed-paper—can tout seemingly esoteric investment theories, obscure happenings, or shadowy market prognostications. Some newsletters have a very devoted readership and can move markets and specific stocks with amazing speed.

Broadcast media remains significant for the financial markets. Bloomberg News and Reuters each run audio and video news divisions separate from their wire services. CNBC holds a premier place in United States for cablecast business news and also fields separate cable feeds from Singapore and London. Bloomberg also runs a cable news feed from Hong Kong.

Digital Financial Media

Online newsrooms, digital newsletters, blogs originating from traditional media outlets and personal blogs increasingly drive financial news and stock market activity.

Subscriber-based and no-charge online news services, such as *breakingviews.com* and *The Business Insider* increasingly are gaining readership. News aggregators such as *Yahoo! Finance* and *Google finance* have a large following, especially among smaller investors.

The New York Times' DealBook blog (http://dealbook.blogs.nytimes.com/) and the *Financial Times' FT Alphaville* (http://ftalphaville.ft.com/) each are read globally for market commentary news and insight. Both also offer push editions by e-mail each business morning to subscribers at no charge. The *Wall Street Journal* attempts to compete with its *Deal Journal* blog (http://blogs.wsj.com/deals/?mod=djm_shdealblog), but its main digital work horses are *MarketWatch* (http://www.marketwatch.com/) and its related *Dow Jones Financial News Online* (http://www.efinancialnews.com/). Reuters' entry is *DealZone* (http://blogs.reuters.com/reuters-dealzone/).

Many traditional media outlets also now provide RSS feeds of breaking and posted news stories, which are delivered passively to subscribers' desktops and continually updated.

The rise of digital media also allows for individual experts and pundits to build global readerships at low cost. The *RGE Monitor*, Nassim Taleb's *Fooled by Randomness*, and *Deus Ex Macchiato* are several of the more colorful, influential personal blogs on finance. Expert personal blogs can offer considerable insight into financial market happenings from those inside. The award-winning *Five Blogs Before Lunch* (http://daveibsen.typepad.com/5_blogs_before_lunch/) offers insight on corporate doings and marketing.

TOOLS OF THE TRADE: METHODS OF INVESTOR RELATIONS

IR's informal disclosure function takes up the lion's share of its day-to-day communication work.

IR's informal disclosure function takes up the lion's share of its day-to-day communication work. IR uses many of the same tools and techniques as do other areas within corporate communication.

Press Releases

The press release is a tool common to all communication disciplines. The goal for most press releases is generating media coverage, and releases are written so that journalists can easily incorporate their themes and language into news coverage. IR press releases share this reason, but their primary purpose is to disclose important corporate news, good or bad, to the financial markets. The first audiences are investors, potential investors, and securities analysts. Only secondarily, the IR press release is intended for journalists. IR releases are almost always posted in full on a company's Web site dedicated specifically to IR. These releases generally are distributed before the stock market opens or after it closes, but breaking news releases can be distributed at any time.

Although an IR news release is meant for direct consumption, it seldom is written crisply in simple prose. More typically it is laden with numbers, legal and financial jargon, and boilerplate language. Readers slog through this specialized, sometimes ritualistic, language for a simple reason—money is at stake. IR news releases can and do move securities markets and a company's stock price. IR news releases are subject to the strict laws and regulations governing direct communications with the investment markets and, as a result, are subject to fraud provisions under the law.

IR also uses many other standard corporate marketing and communication methods. These

IR also uses many other standard corporate marketing and communication methods.

include glossy publications, fact books, background documents, executive biographies, photographs, information on products and facilities, and other materials. IR arranges for management speaking opportunities, including at investment conferences. Such conferences are usually industry specific and last several days. Some companies host day or multiday-long meetings for investors and analysts at their corporate facilities, by invitation only. These events enable investors and analysts to experience the company firsthand, tour facilities, see products, and meet a broad range of managers and employees.

Except during mergers, proxy fights, and similar non-routine events, IR rarely does advertising.

Internet and IR

Investor relations uses the Internet extensively. Most, if not all, public companies dedicate IR Web sites that link directly from the main corporate landing page. IR Web sites provide financial information, material news releases, formal government filings, governance information, annual reports, proxy materials, and other required and volunteered disclosure, such as environmental policies and community affairs reports. After the announcement of important news, IR often arranges for investors and others to participate in management-led conference calls via Web casts. Audio or transcripts from these calls can remain on company Web sites as long as their content is relevant.

> Investor relations uses the Internet extensively.

Some companies post PowerPoint presentations from executive addresses to industry conferences. IR also may post a company's governance charters, ethics and corporate responsibility guidelines, analysts' coverage, news coverage, and industry awards. Financial data, tagged in computer eXtensible Business Reporting Language (XBRL), and hyperlinks to external sites such as the Securities and Exchange Commission are common.

Internet discussion forums and dissident investors' Web sites can pose a special challenge to IR. Current best practices suggest monitoring such sites, but not engaging. These sites often deal in unsubstantiated gossip, and IR practitioners are at a disadvantage challenging opponents who can make up things along the way.

IR is also tasked with the important function of stockholder surveillance and market intelligence. Surveillance, a legal and desired activity, is a process that enables a company to know who is buying and selling its stock. It is done by reviewing available public data at exchanges, clearinghouses, and depositories and by other means. Intelligence means monitoring industry competitors' ownership records and financial and stock performance, also via public filings and records. Both tasks are driven by computer technology and IR departments often contract with outside vendors to gather and analyze data for them.

> IR is also tasked with the important function of stockholder surveillance and market intelligence.

Mass Release for Material News

To comply with regulatory requirements for fair disclosure, companies typically follow precise procedures in releasing material news. In order to ensure that all market participants have simultaneous access to news, companies frequently use third-party vendors for the timely distribution of press releases. In the United States, these vendors are the competitors PR Newswire and BusinessWire.

> To comply with regulatory requirements for fair disclosure, companies typically follow precise procedures in releasing material news.

Due to these same regulatory disclosure requirements, social media, blogs, instant messaging, and Twitter are used less frequently in IR than in other public relations specialties. The one-on-one or free-form nature of these channels make record keeping, safe harbor language, and safeguards against selective disclosure difficult. Legal counsel often recommends IR forgo the advantages of most Web 2.0 media for material disclosure, as a result. Once any material information is fully disclosed through the more traditional channels, however, IR then is free to use the full advantage of the Internet channels, and often does. Companies supplement traditional distribution with push e-mails and RSS distribution to proprietary lists of investors, media, and market participants. Annual meetings and CEO speeches are webcast or posted to YouTube. Several companies are experimenting with senior management blogs, although concerns over materiality and time commitment limit these blogs' appeal. Ghostwritten blogs, supposedly by senior managers but actually penned by public relations staff, may damage a company's credibility in IR however.

A spirited debate began in late 2006 when Sun Microsystems CEO Jonathan Schwartz challenged the SEC and its Regulation FD. Schwartz contended that the traditional news release is an anachronism and that posting material information to a corporate landing page, with simultaneous RSS or other push distribution, fulfills the intent of fair disclosure. In 2008, the SEC sought public comment on a proposal to install Schwartz's concept into securities regulations. The SEC also said some companies may qualify immediately for Web-based disclosure, but only under stringent conditions. The proposal was eclipsed by Wall Street's collapse in late 2008 and has yet to be set formally into regulation. However in 2009, both the NYSE and NASDAQ proposed they no longer require a press release as the primary evidence of fair disclosure and will permit other means, as long as the principle of fair disclosure is met.

■ ■ ■

BEST PRACTICES

Reputation Management: Disclosing More than Required by Law

It is important to note the system of corporate disclosure currently in place is a floor, not a ceiling. It is what is required as a necessary fact of doing business as a public company in the United States. But such disclosure is generally not sufficient to establish and maintain long-term investor appetite for company securities. Corporations are permitted to engage in far more disclosure than the minimum requirements, and many do.

For example, there is no requirement that companies speak to individual securities analysts or to groups of analysts. But most companies do. Except for the annual meeting in most states, there is no requirement for companies to meet with or speak directly with their own shareholders. But most companies stay in constant touch with their shareholders and with the analysts who influence them.

In conclusion, companies that disclose more information more frequently than required often establish a competitive advantage for their securities and simultaneously ensure investors are sufficiently comfortable to buy or hold their shares.

Effective management of investor relations can help enhance a company's reputation among its investors and other key constituencies. Among the best practices are:

1	Ground all IR activities in the corporate and financial goals of the company: IR is an integral, not incidental, part of corporate strategy and management.
2	Coordinate closely with the CFO, Media Relations, and, if employees own significant shares, with employee relations.
3	Coordinate closely with the accountants and lawyers on all formal disclosure, especially regulatory filings.
4	Do more than what is required: Make it easy for investors to access information that has been disclosed, including via the company's Web site.

RESOURCES FOR FURTHER STUDY

National Investor Relations Institute

The National Investor Relations Institute (NIRI) is the professional society for investor relations professionals in the United States. It offers a number of publications, seminars, and programs to enhance IR professionals' practice. http://www.niri.org.

Publications

Investor Relations Magazine, http://www.irmag.com.

Berman, Karen and Knight, Joe, *Financial Intelligence: A Manager's Guide to Knowing What the Numbers Really Mean* (Boston: Harvard Business School Press, 2006).

Bowen, William G., *The Board: An Insider's Guide for Directors and Trustees* (New York: W.W. Norton & Co., 2008).

Buffett, Mary and Clark, David, *Warren Buffet and the Interpretation of Financial Statements: The Search for the Company with a Durable Competitive Advantage* (New York: Scribners, 2008).

Levinson, Marc, *Guide to the Financial Markets*, 4th edition (Princeton, NJ: Bloomberg Press, 2006).

Smith, Roy C. and Walter, Ingo, *Governing the Modern Corporation: Capital Markets, Corporate Control, and Economic Performance* (New York: Oxford University Press, 2006).

QUESTIONS FOR FURTHER DISCUSSION

1 Is it more important to be an expert in finance or to be an expert in your company's business (e.g., an engineer in a technology company) to be an effective IR practitioner?

2 What is the optimal relationship between the IR function and the media relations function?

3 Why is an IR person subject to different legal standards (e.g., subject to civil and possibly criminal action if he or she conveys false information) than other communication professionals?

4 How should an IR person balance the desire to position the company as positively as possible with the requirements regarding formal and informal disclosure of material information?

5 When employees own a significant percentage of a company's stock, how should an IR person optimally coordinate with employee communications?

Make sure it plays in Peoria, Paris and Phnom Penh.

CHAPTER

9 GLOBAL CORPORATE COMMUNICATION

By Lynn Appelbaum and Gail S. Belmuth with Katja Schroeder

■ ■ ■

CASE STUDY: SAP BUSINESS SUITE[1]

In an interconnected world, enterprise software has become the invisible force that runs businesses and government organizations worldwide. It helps companies reduce complexity and increase the transparency of their entire operations, including financials, product development, sales, supply chain management, and human resources. With more than 89,000 customers in over 120 countries, SAP is the world's largest business software company. It is best known for providing applications and services that enable end-to-end business processes across a company's functions and entire supply chain.

In 2008, the financial downturn and the rise of new software delivery models like Software as a Service started to challenge SAP's value proposition for its customers. Although it was recognized as a global reputable brand, its core solutions were increasingly perceived to be complex and expensive in the new economic environment. In February 2009, SAP launched SAP® Business Suite 7, a new generation of modular business suites in the global market for its large enterprise customers. SAP Business Suite 7 provides companies with the flexibility to adapt their business and IT needs to market dynamics by offering a modular deployment of the suite's applications. The challenge was to shift the perception of IT buyers in SAP's key global markets that enterprise software suites are slow, complex and costly and introduce today's modular suites that provide a quicker return on investment.

The SAP communications team developed the campaign messages using research from Harvard University and McKinsey that linked competitiveness with the strategic use of information technology (IT). Based on this research, SAP created a message that highlighted the Business Suite's modularity, ease-of-use, and flexibility to its internal and external stakeholder groups, including customers (Chief Information Officers (CIOs), Chief Executive Officers (CEOs), Chief Financial Officers (CFOs), IT Managers and Line of Business Managers), employees, media, bloggers, industry analysts, financial analysts, and academics.

Using a news conference in New York on February 4, 2009, as the global launch pad, SAP rolled out an integrated communications campaign in more than 20 countries, encompassing employee communications, media and social media relations, industry analyst relations, events and marketing activities. A carefully balanced mix of global and local activities started a dialogue about the value of the SAP Business Suite 7 to help companies navigate a changing business environment. The campaign heavily involved user groups, customers, partners, and industry analysts as third-party references to validate the Suite's offering and the overall promise of the global SAP brand to its customer base.

■ **Employees:** Getting employees on board, was one of the key imperatives of the communications campaign. To create internal excitement, SAP placed banners on its corporate portal linking to the Business Suite 7 launch broadcast, hung banners in SAP office buildings worldwide, and distributed a personal video address by SAP Executive Board Member, Business Solutions & Technology, Jim Hagemann Snabe. At the day of the launch, a live broadcast of the news conference via SAP TV was made available to all SAP employees around the world. A recap of the Suite launch was included in the SAP Board Update, the company's internal newsletter.

■ **Media/social media:** On the morning of February 4, SAP Co-CEO Léo Apotheker together with Jim Hagemann Snabe, unveiled the new Suite to 80 influencers in a press conference at the company's New York office. The news event included executive presentations, a customer and partner panel with the participation of Roche, Colgate-Palmolive and IBM, which was moderated by Robert Dye from the Research Board, as well as a product demo for the retail industry. Considering the deadline of business and IT reporters from outside of the U.S., SAP hosted a conference call with 55 Pan-European media shortly before the event and offered Web cast access for international attendees for the entire launch program. The Wall Street Journal broke the news on the new SAP Business Suite 7 with a curtain raiser story on the day of the launch. After the conference, the team hosted more than 80 onsite and phone interviews with 15 SAP spokespeople worldwide. Bloggers and social media were following the launch onsite and via Web cast. The bloggers onsite also had an opportunity to meet with SAP Co-CEO Léo Apotheker. The SAP Business Suite Newsroom provided a series of in-depth resources, including the Business Suite 7 Global Multimedia Release, SAP TV coverage from the New York media event, SAP Business Suite 7 Demo, SAP Business Suite "Fast Facts," Partner and Customer Quote Sheets, Industry Fact Sheets, and a Video segment on SAP Business Suite 7 (http://www.sap.com/about/newsroom/topic-rooms/business-suite/index.epx).

■ **Industry influencers:** Prior to the launch, SAP conducted pre-briefings with select top tier industry analyst firms, i.e. Gartner, AMR, IDC, Forrester, and EAC, to get their input for the messaging and secure references for all media activities and communications materials. The team organized the attendance of key industry influencers at the New York launch event, offering them exclusive access to SAP senior executives after the news event to continue the dialogue.

- **Partners:** In addition to securing partners like IBM as participants and attendees for the launch, SAP started issuing a series of partner announcements to continue the Business Suite roll-out in the weeks following the press event. At the day of the launch, the company hosted a Q&A forum with SAP spokespeople with more than 47 SAP Mentors worldwide, which are high-value members of SAP communities—the SAP Developer Network (SDN), Business Objects (BOBJ) and the Business Process Expert (BPX) community. The SAP Mentors served as evangelists to spread the Suite messages across their business communities, often in the form of Blogs, Tweets, and Word of Mouth.

- **Investors:** To cater to the specific information needs of the financial community, SAP hosted an investor relations roundtable with SAP Executive Board Member Jim Hagemann Snabe following the press conference in New York.

The regional roll-out proceeded with a series of media conferences and participation at industry events, including two virtual news conferences in Latin America (one in Spanish, one in Portuguese, with the attendance of 80 media, on February 4), a press and partner event in India (February 28), a Suite press conference in Japan (February 24), a roundtable at the German IT show CeBIT (March 3–8), and a keynote at the SAP Insider Conference in the U.S. (March 11).

As a result, within four days more than 230 media and blogger articles appeared in more than 20 countries, highlighting strong customer endorsements and positive Suite key messages—modular/easy to digest, simplicity, and cost savings. According to SAP's media measurement method Carma, the Suite launch achieved a powerful favorability rating of 67, making it one of the more positive news items for SAP in the last two years. Nearly 90 percent of all post-launch coverage was favorable, with strong pick-up in the business and trade media.

- More than 80 influencers attended the Suite launch event, including top-tier media and bloggers (*BusinessWeek*, *Economist*, Reuters, Dow Jones, *Financial Times*, FAZ, etc.), industry analysts (Gartner, AMR, IDC, Forrester, EAC), and financial analysts; 55 major European media joined the teleconference. More than 200 media worldwide watched via Web cast.

- Stories appeared in Argentina, Australia, Austria, Brazil, Canada, China, Denmark, France, Germany, India, Italy, Japan, Mexico, Netherlands, Norway, Peru, Portugal, Russia, Spain, Sweden, Switzerland, the United Kingdom, and the United States.

- More than 30,000 people followed the SAP Business Suite launch on Twitter, pushing the story to the top 10 Twitter topics on the day of the launch.
- Over 6,000 SAP employees watched the conference on SAP TV; nearly 4,000 views for the introduction of the Business Suite (internal & external); over 4,000 views of the SAP Business Suite Retail Demo.
- Industry analyst firms, including Gartner, Forrester, AMR, IDC and EAC, who advise IT buyers on purchasing decisions, published positive research notes after the launch and provided references for media materials.

THE GLOBAL IMPERATIVE

Michael Morley, former deputy chairman of Edelman Public Relations Worldwide, notes, "There is not likely to be a phrase you will hear in your career in public relations as often as 'think global, act local.' It is used to encourage international marketers and communicators to adapt their products or messages to be accepted in a variety of local communities around a region or around the world."[2]

> Global corporate communication is the planned, long-term, strategically designed way of managing relationships with publics of other nations. In global corporate communication—as in most corporate communication— news impacts constituents in many locations. Announcements must be coordinated to account for different time zones, languages, and perspectives. And post-announcement follow-up is often more important than the initial announcement.

A global professional communicator needs a broad range of skills beyond the traditional ones. As Robert I. Wakefield, a consultant, author, and researcher specializing in cross-cultural effects on reputation in multinational organizations, noted in the Spring 2000 *Strategist*: "Considering that problems can arise anywhere and instantly become global, professionals are needed who can see the big picture and facilitate interaction between host units and headquarters to avoid these problems. They should be skilled in communication, but also in global economics and politics, mediation, cultural anthropology, and other fields relevant to the global arena."[3]

The Global Village Is Here

Marshall McLuhan's global village is here. Global investments are growing at record levels. In 2007, Americans owned $7.2 trillion of foreign stocks and bonds. Foreigners (excluding China) owned $7.4 trillion of U.S. stocks and bonds, according to the International Monetary Fund.[4]

Several key factors have led to the shift in the global business paradigm. In Fraser Seitel's *The Practice of Public Relations*, former PRSA President Joe Epley identifies three reasons for increased interaction among organizations and global publics:

- The expansion of communications technology has increased the dissemination of information about products, services and lifestyles around the world thus creating global demand.

- The realignment of economic power, caused by the formation of multinational trading blocs, such as the North American Free Trade Agreement (NAFTA), Asia Pacific Economic Conference (APEC), Organization of African Unity (OAU), and the European Economic Community (EEC) [now the European Union or EU].

- People around the world are uniting in pursuit of common goals, such as reducing population growth, protecting the environment, waging the war against terrorism, and fighting disease, particularly AIDS.[5]

In 2005, *New York Times* columnist Thomas Friedman published *The World is Flat*, which examines the implications of business in a globalized world. While globalization itself was already widely practiced by multinational corporations, the book focused on the intense competition that U.S. and European businesses now face from emerging markets. According to Friedman, today's globalization is driven by innovative start-ups from around the world, going beyond outsourcing manufacturing. By 2008, the global financial crisis spotlighted the downside of doing business in a global marketplace causing businesses to focus on the importance of trust and good governance in reputation management to manage their brands. Effective global communication that creates trust, credibility, and authenticity is an imperative for business success in a flat world.[6]

In order to operate effectively in the new international business environment, global communication practitioners need a comprehensive understanding of the many different cultures they will encounter. They must learn not only the local business practices of a host country or an international client, but also the relevant customs and appropriate communication styles. In addition, they will need a thorough knowledge of political, economic, social, and cultural values wherever they are doing business throughout the world. Therefore, in order fully to understand the practice of global corporate communication, one must not only understand the basic principles of public relations and corporate communications, but also draw upon a broad range of global society theories, cultural theories, management theories, and communication theories (see Sidebar). This expansive foundation allows the practitioner to present the most compelling and credible message in a meaningful and relevant manner.

> Global communication practitioners need a comprehensive understanding of the many different cultures they will encounter.

Global reputation management draws upon core communication values and practices honest, informed, timely communication to key audiences, or as Wilcox et al. define it, "the planned and organized effort of a company, institute, or government to establish mutually beneficial relations with publics of other nations."[7] But applying solid research, effective strategic planning, tactical execution, and evaluation assumes a more complex and critical role on a global scale.

The cornerstone for successful communication is to build relationships inside and outside the company that are genuinely mutual and beneficial to both the company and its global constituents.

Trust has become the foundational commodity in effective global branding, even as it is one of a company's most vulnerable assets in a digital age. "Trust is what drives profit margins share price. It is what consumers are looking for and what they share with one another," according to Larry Light, CEO of the Stamford (CT) brand consultancy Arcature.[8] The Edelman 2009 Trust Barometer survey emphasizes that "product quality and company trust and identity are increasingly inseparable ... After direct experience with a company's product, the most important trust issues for stakeholders are its overall reputation, its social and environmental track record, and how it treats its employees."[9]

Establishing trust among global stakeholders can be challenging. The growing global agenda of poverty, human rights, the environment, labor abuses, corruption, consumer issues, and cultural and religious insensitivity place corporate communication among a company's most important assets. As discussed in Chapter 13 on corporate responsibility, human rights are now a business concern.[10]

> Establishing trust among global stakeholders can be challenging.

Today, alongside governments, companies often are viewed as a source or cause of human rights abuse, as well as an international actor with the capacity to promote human rights.[11] Therefore, it is essential that corporate communicators make efforts to build relationships across the broad spectrum of a company's global stakeholders through effective two-way communication.

A Foundation for Global Communication

Global communication practitioners need a comprehensive understanding of the many different cultures they will encounter. As Freitag and Stokes write in their book *Global Public Relations*, "Practitioners who understand and plan for these subtle and not-so-subtle differences among nations and cultures will enjoy the greatest success and satisfaction in the decades ahead."[12]

Establishing trust among global stakeholders can be challenging. In *International Public Relations: A Comparative Analysis*, Hugh M. Culbertson and Ni Chen derive a four-pronged model for global communication incorporating global, cultural, management, and communication theories, relating to PR theory.

- **Global society theories.** Globalization causes turbulence, conflict, competition, and uncertainty. This creates a pressing need for organizations to predict and adapt to changing conditions based on information and research, and to identify, respond to, and resolve conflicts as they arise. Communication professionals can contribute strongly to this process.[13]

- **Cultural theories.** Culture is an important determinant of how communication functions within and between societies. Companies must be open to multicultural influences and take full advantage of their employees' diverse backgrounds and abilities and blend both global and local coordination.

- **Management theories** show a need for cultural sensitivity and for "third culture" practitioners, who transcend boundaries using global media, transnational education, cultural exchanges, and so forth. Effective organizations combine both culture-free and culture-specific values,[14] providing common overall goals at the global level that are then tailored to the local needs of each culture.

- **Communication theories** focus on the increasing influence of global media. People's views of international events are heavily media dependent,[15] since many people have little direct experience of other countries. Activists use the media to publicize their issues and influence policymakers around the world.[16] Communication professionals need to understand and respond to the issues affecting their organization through relationship building and proactive PR.[17]

Each of these findings relates to James Grunig's "Excellence Project," a seminal theoretical PR framework. Grunig states that PR contributes to an organization's success by (1) reducing conflicts and building relationships; (2) supporting management; (3) participating in management's "inner circle"; (4) respecting publics and practicing two-way communication; and (5) respecting diversity.[18]

Gavin Anderson, founder and former chairman of Gavin Anderson & Company, a global corporate communication agency, has identified two competing approaches to international communication—the global versus the multinational.

GLOBAL MODEL

"Global public relations superimposes an overall perspective on a program executed in two or more national markets, recognizing the similarities among audiences while necessarily adapting to regional differences. It connotes a planning attitude as much as geographic reach and flexibility."[19]

MULTINATIONAL MODEL

"International PR practitioners often implement distinctive programs in multiple markets, with each program tailored to meet the often acute distinctions of the individual market."

Anderson argues that the global model is more effective. "Global, as opposed to multinational, businesses demand that programs in distinctive markets be interrelated. While there will always be local differences and need for customization, the programs will probably share more than they differ."[20]

Establishing Credibility and Trust

Credibility and trust is at the core of any global communication program. Effective communication hinges on the ability of a company to communicate in respectful, clear and credible ways to diverse local constituents based on their perceptual context, needs, and interests while supporting the company's global mission and objectives. While a consistent, unified global branding message or identity is essential, a "one size fits all" message risks alienating audiences if the message is misunderstood. A truly effective global brand adapts to local needs while maintaining its essence.

A frequent obstacle to clear communication in large organizations is distrust of central authority, particularly when that authority is far away, in another country, and part of a different culture. It is easy to believe that distant authorities with such different backgrounds and cultures cannot possibly understand local problems and have overriding self interests at heart. While it is difficult to completely eliminate this perception, international communication professionals must strive to minimize it through policies and initiatives encouraging two-way flows of learning, communication and information.

THE GLOBAL CORPORATE COMMUNICATION ROLE

Most global corporate communication practitioners have responsibility for the following functions:

- Employee communication
- Media relations
- Corporate identity and brand management
- Public and community relations
- Crisis communication
- Public affairs/Government relations
- Investor relations
- Annual report and other publications
- Corporate social responsibility/sustainability/philanthropy
- Influencer relations (industry analysts, academia)
- Executive positioning
- Corporate publishing and production including Web site

Most corporate communication functions are chronically understaffed.

- Corporate philanthropy
- Corporate identity or branding
- Web site

In a global context, practitioners must deal with the added aspects of cultural and language diversity, wide geographic reach, time zone differences, local and regional regulation and legislation, and huge disparities in a company's physical plant, IT infrastructure, employment and compensation practices, and budgets from one location to another. This means that many corporate cultures are more like patchwork quilts than unified entities. It is challenging to manage global reputation, image, and brand when a culture is so varied.

STANDARDIZE OR CUSTOMIZE? THAT IS THE QUESTION

One of the greatest challenges is managing a task of such enormous scope with typically modest resources. While communication professionals see the value of their contribution to the bottom line, the function is in fact a cost center, not a profit center.

One of the best ways to promote efficiency in global corporate communication is to standardize as much as possible. This includes the Web site, printed publications, and all signage and corporate identity materials. This saves time and a significant amount of money, and adds an important strategic benefit: reinforcing and strengthening the company's image and brand.

In addressing best practices for global corporate reputation management, effective management of both internal and external audiences is essential to implement a successful strategic plan. We will begin with the internal structure of corporate communication and employee communication, since without excellent internal communication across borders and cultures, it is difficult to execute a consistent and effective global message to external stakeholders. Since every global employee is a potential ambassador for a company's corporate message or brand, excellent internal communication is essential.

The Global Corporate Communication Department

Most corporate communication functions are chronically understaffed. As companies grow, they rarely expand the communication function commensurately. Most organizations promise shareholders that acquisitions will create "synergies"—that is, cost-cutting and layoffs. Few growing companies can afford to ease up on profitability.

An ideal global corporate communication organization would include directors to oversee each of the areas of responsibility listed above, and would also have directors for each of the company's key geographic regions. The reality, however, is often quite different. Many global corporate communication departments consist of a director and a support person. Outside of the largest multinationals, there are rarely dedicated resources at the regional or local level.

Most organizations largely centralize their global communication staff, for several reasons. First, a centralized structure helps ensure that the organization speaks with one voice. In addition, the head of communication needs to be a member of the senior executive team. Communication staffers cannot do their jobs well without being among the first to receive important information. Other staff functions—finance, legal, human resources—tend to be concentrated centrally, though finance and human resources are likely to have larger staffs and regional representation. With limited resources it is often most effective to centralize communication, since each staff member is likely to wear several hats.

Parlez-vous Urdu? Language in Global Companies

The choice of language or languages an organization uses for official communication is key. Even in non-U.S.—or non-U.K.—headquartered companies, English is often considered the official language of business, though a company's primary language may be that of the country where the company is headquartered. Having a single official language makes the preparation of documents easier and faster. A single language also reduces the chance of translation errors.

> One cannot assume that a factory worker in Bangalore, or Buffalo, will be bilingual.

The disadvantage of having a single official language, however, is obvious. One cannot assume that a factory worker in Bangalore, or Buffalo, will be bilingual.[21] It is not just a job function issue. Many senior executives, particularly in the United States, are not fluent in more than one language.

Having an "official company language" rarely means all business is conducted in that language. If the official language is French, for example, but a Chinese salesperson is speaking with a Chinese customer, it would be inappropriate for them to try to communicate in French. However, communication from the corporate center—annual report, press releases, Web site and memos from the CEO—would almost certainly be in French. Many international companies will routinely translate important documents such as annual reports into two or three languages (English, French, and Spanish), depending on their key global markets.

When official documents need to be translated, it is best for the translation to be done in the countries where they will be used. If the documents are intended for the media, they should be translated by someone familiar with local media usage and language. While central translation may be easier to control and cheaper, local translation will save revisions to adapt to local dialects.

Communicating to global external audiences in clear and understandable terms may also be challenging since subtleties of language and expression can be offensive out of their cultural context. Consider the case of a global hotel and gaming company that has as one of its core values a goal to "blow away the customer." When the company planned to announce a development in the Middle East, it removed the core value from its media relations materials as to not offend anyone because the phrase may be taken literally in that part of the world.[22]

THE GLOBAL COMMUNICATION NETWORK

If a company cannot afford a vast global communication staff, there are still ways to provide vital local communication information and counsel as needed. Many companies create global communication networks. These networks include individuals whose functions overlap with corporate communication, such as marketing, human resources, and investor relations. Network members should be heavy users of corporate communication's services. The network can be used as a sounding board, to review drafts or to source local printers and other vendors. Since these people have "regular day jobs," it is important to limit the extent to which their input is solicited. Ideally, the global communication network will be self-selecting, meaning that the individuals in it have expressed interest in serving on such a team.

Working with an international/intercultural communication team provides added challenges to mounting a coordinated communication effort. Some of these barriers include (1) a bias to communicate locally, not globally, about key initiatives; (2) a global team dominated by headquarters perspectives; and (3) a lack of understanding between corporate and local teams. While a global network can provide local market understanding, a corporate communication professional may encounter resistance to corporate directives. Local teams may be skeptical of messages from headquarters and perceive them as out of touch. Homogeneous corporate messages may not reflect the diversity of knowledge, perspectives, and experiences in the field. And when working with daily local pressures from their own country management, there may not be time to contribute to a global collaborative process.

These disparities in culture and possible mistrust of centralized communication make face-to-face meetings among communication practitioners even more important, especially before launching a major campaign. According to Bonin Bough, Director of Digital and Social Media at PepsiCo, "The cost of arranging a face-to-face meeting of your global team before launching a campaign is essential to get everyone's feedback in the planning stage. And if you can't meet in person, then it's essential to video or teleconference. It's a chance to avoid wasteful mistakes before they happen."[23]

INTERNAL COMMUNICATION—WORLDWIDE

The Internet, and increasingly social media, is especially important for global audiences. While global perceptions will vary, the Internet is the one communication mechanism that reaches constituents globally on a 24/7 basis. The Internet is also a significant money saver, eliminating the need to print and mail many items. Fewer companies have printed employee newsletters, and increasingly investors (at least institutional investors) say they would prefer to download annual reports than receive hard copies.

Global corporate communicators need to evaluate when to adapt their Web sites for global audiences. A Web site in only one language can alienate key international stakeholders, especially where the company has local workers. While creating a multilingual site takes time and money, it is important to consider doing so in major markets.

Technology in a Global Setting

Technology is one of the most important tools of effective global communication for both internal and external audiences.

Internally, intranets, extranets, Wikis, collaboration rooms, and e-mails are essential tools that facilitate multidirectional global communication. Colleagues in different countries can collaborate on documents. Shared files, department Web pages, and easy-to-access document drops have removed many technical and physical impediments to knowledge and information sharing (human nature may still present obstacles, however!). Video conferencing has become a meaningful communication and collaboration channel.

Technology, especially the Internet, has radically changed global corporate communication and made it more efficient. Press releases can be distributed globally and instantly shared with social networks. Key documents such as the annual report, executives' bios and quarterly earnings announcements can be archived on a company's Web site for easy download. Even annual shareholder meetings are no longer limited to those near headquarters if the meeting is Web cast.

Posting information and press releases on the Web site on a timely basis is essential. Too often, materials appearing on Web sites are not up to date. Companies can offend or confuse by offering "yesterday's news" on their sites.

> Of course, no amount of communication by telephone, video, or e-mail can replace face-to-face communication.

An extranet, an interactive Web site for members of a global company's PR team, is especially useful to facilitate strategy and tactics "to bring access to a company's assets."[24] In China, for example, where there are more Chinese than Americans online, Web campaigns that include social media and blogs are becoming increasingly important for foreign companies in the mainland.[25]

Senior Management's Role in Global Employee Communication

Employees worldwide are more closely connected both with their peers and with senior management because of global communication technology. Many CEOs e-mail periodic memos to all employees, updating strategic projects or simply sharing thoughts and thereby establishing a relationship, if only virtually, with a broader employee base than in the past.

CEOs may supplement monthly memos to employees with quarterly global conference calls following key announcement, such as quarterly earnings immediately following the company's earnings announcements. Timing is key. A New York-based company, for example, would hold calls at 7:30 a.m. to accommodate employees in as many time zones as possible. Employees who prefer to ask questions anonymously can do so by fax. The chairman and other senior executives can also field questions in their areas of responsibility. The global conference call serves multiple purposes:

- Employees who may rarely meet the chairman and the executive team can hear their voices and get a feel for how they work together.

- Employees learn what is on their colleagues' minds in other countries. During a typical call, a company may receive questions from over ten countries. As most of its employee base does little international travel, this is an effective way to get a sense of the breadth and diversity of the company and to feel part of something larger.

- Anonymous questions ensure that difficult or negative issues being discussed in private or around the coffee machine are addressed publicly. Facing resentment head on—be it about executive compensation, benefits changes, or facility closings—is an invaluable step in allowing an organization to deal with change and move on. Employees are also more likely to trust leaders who tell the truth, however difficult it may be.

- The calls are a high-profile example of senior management's commitment to open, two-way communication with all employees.

- Linking the employee calls with quarterly earnings announcements reminds employees that everything the company does is to help the company grow and increase shareholder value.

Of course, no amount of communication by telephone, video, or e-mail can replace face-to-face communication. Site managers, local HR representatives, and front-line supervisors will always play a critical role in local communication.

For multinational companies, it is important that the CEO and other senior managers make periodic visits to as many affiliates as practical, understanding that too frequent travel can be prohibitively expensive and can take too much time away from day-to-day requirements. A town hall meeting with the CEO is always important, but in cultures that are more hierarchical than the United States, it takes on added weight. In India, it is not unusual for visiting high officials and company heads to be greeted by an elephant (a symbol of good luck) and a military marching band. In many cultures, the exchange of gifts is expected. The global corporate communication professional should learn such customs and brief the senior team in advance to avoid faux pas, embarrassments, or insults.

Because a visit from corporate headquarters can be costly and require extensive advance planning, it is important that the communication professional discourage unnecessary travel to avoid placing an undue burden on colleagues around the world. However, these visits can be very meaningful to employees in the host country. With boards of directors taking a greater interest in corporate governance due to the Sarbanes-Oxley Act, board members often travel with senior management.

Technology's enormous role in facilitating global employee communication is both good news and bad news, since it can make responding to e-mail a full-time job. In any large organization, the opportunity to communicate "too much" grows exponentially. As a result, communication and IT professionals often remind their colleagues to send fewer e-mails, copy fewer people, and remove attachments to avoid clogging up networks and distracting employees from more important matters.

Cascade Communication in Global Organizations

As mentioned earlier, organizational communication research suggests that employees prefer to get the most critical information from their immediate supervisors. This suggests that cascade communication should be an important part of global communication. Indeed, many communication departments and their agencies of record create "communication toolkits" with customizable PowerPoint® presentations and talking points, Q&As, assignments for breakout groups and discussion sessions, and feedback/evaluation forms to rate the effectiveness of the communication.

While managers need tools and information to discuss key issues with their teams, experience shows that effective use of global cascade communication is more difficult to achieve. Here is a vastly simplified example:

Chairman:	Today is an important day in our company's history. We have decided to change our name from "One of the Great Spaghetti and Meatball Factories" to "The World's Best Meatball Factory." Why? Three reasons. First, we recently sold our spaghetti business, and our name should reflect that we're just meatballs now. Second, because we want to claim our spot as the best meatball company, not just one of the best meatball companies. And third, because we want to call attention to our global reach.
Regional manager:	Today is an important day in our company's history. We have decided to change our name from "One of the Great Spaghetti and Meatball Factories" to "The World's Best Meatball Factory." Why? Three reasons. First, we recently sold our spaghetti business, and our name should reflect that we're just meatballs now. Second, because we want to claim our spot as the best meatball company, not just one of the best meatball companies. And third … well, I forgot the third reason.
Country manager:	Today is an important day in our company's history. We have decided to change our name from "One of the Great Spaghetti and Meatball Factories" to "The World's Best Meatball Factory."
Line manager:	Today, our company decided to change its name to "The World's Best Meatball Factory." Is that a stupid name or what?

Limited understanding of the language of a cascade toolkit only compounds the issue, increasing the chances that the manager will misinterpret the news and present it in a different, inaccurate, or negative light. With big news, there is rarely time to translate large quantities of communication materials, so it is important to use cascade communication carefully and discriminatingly in global organizations.

EXTERNAL COMMUNICATION

The Global/Local Issue as a Message Strategy

Since globalization and consolidation are the rule in so many industries, it is a bit of a cliché to say that one's company is the ideal combination of global reach and local understanding. Nevertheless, global companies must address the issue and explain where they aspire to be on the global/local spectrum. Should they tout their scale, scope, and efficiency? Or is the personal touch paramount? Many companies make their position on the issue a key part of their branding, marketing, and advertising strategies. HSBC, for example, calls itself "The world's local bank." The May 2002 press release announcing the launch of an advertising campaign to support the new positioning said:

> Underpinning the advertising is HSBC's philosophy that the world is a rich and diverse place in which cultures and people should be treated with respect. Around the world, the group has built its businesses locally, and HSBC's 31 million customers can be confident that the service they receive has a world of experience behind it. HSBC's advertisements will demonstrate the importance of local knowledge by exploring distinctive national customs and practices. Carrying the strapline 'the world's local bank' the advertising will show that anyone who banks with HSBC can benefit from services and advice from a company with international experience, delivered by people sensitive to the customs and needs of their community.

HSBC's advertising campaign is supported by other corporate communication underscoring the bank's ability to help customers navigate cultural particularities, including messages on the Web site such as: "4 is an unlucky number in Japan. 13 is an unlucky number in the U.K. (the company's headquarters)."

Alternatively, messages can be structured for a geographic region, as illustrated in the Citigroup's 2002 Asian Centennial campaign, the first to include all the Citigroup businesses (see Figure 9.1) and Asian countries under one umbrella. The campaign, created and executed by Citigroup and Ruder Finn, spanned twelve countries in ten different languages. It targeted Asian stakeholders including customers, local government, the community and staff using a regional approach that allowed for tailored local market programs in local languages, while driving regional consistency and cost effectiveness.

In addition to unveiling a special Asian Centennial logo to appear with Citigroup's global branding, they created a book, "Citibank: A Century in Asia," which illustrated their history and achievements along with the region's history. Internally, they worked with each country to tailor major programs, such as a tour of the New York Philharmonic, for local businesses to use during the centennial in their marketing campaigns and drive revenue.[26]

Figure 9.1

Corporate communication executives need to evaluate on a case-by-case basis how best to balance the global or local message.

Global Networking

> International public relations practitioners must have a thorough grounding in the regulatory issues, business practices, and media in their company's important markets.

While the communication function may be centrally controlled, international public relations practitioners must have a thorough grounding in the regulatory issues, business practices, and media in their company's important markets. There are many ways to acquire this knowledge besides using the internal resources of the company.

One way to learn about another culture is to cultivate friendships with public relations colleagues overseas. Public relations associations in different countries are a great resource. Many of these, including the Public Relations Society of America (PRSA), are members of the Global Alliance for Public Relations and Communication Management (http://www.globalpr. org). The International Public Relations Association (IPRA) has members in one hundred countries and provides good networking opportunities. International public relations professionals should also take every opportunity to travel to important markets to visit corporate offices, to meet local public relations resources, and to attend international industry or public relations conferences.

Local institutions, such as the chamber of commerce or the embassy commercial attaché, can be valuable resources for local information and networking. Agencies such as United States Information Technology Office (USITO, http://www.usito. org), a private, nonprofit trade association designed to promote trade and cooperation in the information technology industries of the United States and China, offer members valuable telecommunication updates through their newsletters and the opportunities they offer to network with other multinationals.[27]

Local relationships are not only important for information gathering, they are also key to establishing trust on a local level. Global corporate communication practitioners should strive to use the most credible and respected local sources to represent a business and deliver its message, whether it's a local or headquarters-based company spokesperson, a local government health official, or a celebrated sports or entertainment star.

Membership in international trade associations also provides a platform to meet government officials or potential business partners who can be influential in helping a company. Cultivating good working relationships with local media to understand what's important to them is key. This not only builds better working relations when there's news to communicate, but also allows global practitioners more easily to call on international journalists for inside information on their interests effectively to position news to meet the journalists' agenda.

Regulatory variances between countries can play a significant role in how messages are communicated internationally and can require a working knowledge of global regulations. For example, U.S. regulatory guidelines allow pharmaceutical companies to create messages raising awareness about a medical condition and advising consumers to see their doctors and to ask about a drug by name, while British regulatory guidelines cannot direct the consumer to ask for a drug explicitly by name.[28] Practitioners must be aware of these differences to create appropriate messages that are in compliance with regional guidelines.

Finally, international public relations practitioners must listen to local advice they receive. "In my experience, many of us learn about foreign cultures and hire local consultants to advise us, but then we often don't act on this advice if it differs too much from our own cultural way of doing things, sometimes much to our regret," said Barbara M. Burns, BBA Communications, New York, in her 2001 Atlas Award Lecture on International PR. "The art of bridging cultural differences in communications takes patience, trust of local advisors, and the courage and the wisdom to act in an effective and ethical manner."

Working with Media in Individual Countries

With the proliferation of global media through cable television, satellite, newspapers, and instant dissemination on the Internet, local news, especially bad news, can become global in seconds. Localizing the message is key, and practitioners need a thorough understanding of the local working language and environment to avoid costly gaffes. Working in Malaysia, for example, press releases must be translated into four languages to avoid alienating any segment of the media.[29]

EVOLVING NATIONAL NEWS MEDIA

While media is one of the most powerful tools for reaching global audiences, it is certainly not a magic bullet for wide distribution of a message. In many developing countries, media reaches a relatively small, homogeneous segment of the population because of illiteracy and poverty.[30] In communist or other countries where the media is or recently was government controlled, including China, the former Soviet Union, and certain South American nations, global media play by different rules—often requiring payment via advertising for news coverage.

> Do not underestimate the role that national pride plays in how media respond to and may respond to and report a story.

Do not under-estimate the role that national pride plays in how media respond to and may respond to and report a story. For example, when a multinational company is sponsoring an event, local media will most likely approach it from a local angle—whether it is how a new plant opening will affect local employment or how a new hotel will help the local economy and tourism.

It is essential to understand the local media environment and send messages through the most credible channels. Key considerations include:

- Private or public control of media
- Alignment with political parties
- Alignment with or control by theocracy
- Extent of control over editorial freedom by media owners
- Exercise of controls over editorial freedom
- Journalists' professional standards
- Media's ability to diffuse messages to a wide audience
- Segments of the population receiving either print or electronic media
- Local cultural media practices[31]

Due to differences in media between cultures or geographic areas—and because of the importance of developing relationships with individual journalists covering one's company—it is especially difficult to centralize global media relations. While continuing to use global electronic services to disseminate corporate messages, companies must implement media relations locally. If an organization does not have a local media insider, it is essential to hire either a global communication agency with local expertise in a particular market, or a local boutique agency.

The dramatic changes in China's media illustrate how local, cultural, and political values necessitate a localized approach. With its acceptance into the World Trade Organization in 2001 and its exploding population and economy, China represents one of the greatest growth opportunities for multinational companies.

Mike H. He, PR manager at National Semiconductor Corporation in Santa Clara, California, notes in *Public Relations Tactics*, "The Chinese government still maintains tight control over its major news outlets. [On the other hand,] trade media has experienced an unprecedented degree of freedom, especially in the technology area. Chinese readers are now turning more to trade publications than to government sponsored publications for technology news."[32]

Corporate messages for foreign companies in China must address six areas.

1. Why is the company in China?
2. What is the company's global and local market presence? Who are the competitors?
3. What is the company's investment in China (for R&D, local staff, and local production facilities)?
4. What contributions will the company make to the region or country? (i.e., university donations, training centers, corporate responsibility programs, etc.)
5. How can the company help China/Chinese companies (the company's clients) to be globally competitive?
6. How important is China in the overall business plan?[33]

While differences are apparent, traditional means of reaching media through releases, trade shows, press conferences, by-lined articles, and local spokespersons should be adapted for the local market.

Global Ethics

The blur between editorial and advertising is prevalent in many countries (including our own, in the case of certain publications). Publications frequently will not provide editorial coverage without a commitment to advertising or advertorial placement.

Companies need to establish clear ethical guidelines about their commitment not to pay for editorial material. Such a commitment establishes the credibility of the organization for the long term. The Charter on Media Transparency developed by the International Public Relations Association (IPRA) and available on their Web site (http://www.ipra.org) provides important guidelines. The initiative is supported by the International Press Institute, the International Federation of Journalists, Transparency International, the Global Alliance, and the Institute for Public Relations Research and Education, as well as IPRA.[34]

An additional global media relations challenge is when news crosses international time zones, such as the timing of news releases when a company headquarters is in one time zone, its stock is traded in another, and it is making news in yet a third. While the news should be issued from company headquarters, the timing of the release will need to reflect the target global market where the news has the most import and resonance. Of course, internal communication should be considered at the same time as the media strategy, so employees do not learn about something that might impact them from the press.

Virtual News Rooms

Web sites are an integral tool in managing global media relations. Virtual multimedia news rooms with social media sharing applications are essential in providing timely and archived information on a company, its products and services, and its policy issues. They are a key resource for global journalists to access internal media contacts. Global companies add additional value to their sites by including links to sites about relevant local or regional issues that can help the journalist do their job with greater ease.

> Virtual multimedia news rooms with social media sharing applications are essential in providing timely and archived information.

Global Crisis Communication

During a crisis, an organization usually attempts to handle the media locally. Most crises are local in that they unfortunately often involve injuries or an accident at a facility. Even product quality issues usually, but not always, impact a limited number of shipments to a limited number of stores, cities, or countries. Therefore even if news travels globally through the Internet and other news outlets, an organization should keep perceptions of the issue localized where possible. Responding to a crisis far from its epicenter also sends the unwanted message that those at fault are evading responsibility. Regardless, a global crisis communication plan should be based on the same tried and true principles of any good crisis plan—rapid response, concern for those impacted, accepting responsibility, and taking action.

Time is of the essence in global crisis communication. If handling a crisis from the center means a slower response to local media, the greater the chance that someone else—a competitor, a hostile neighbor, an angry union—will tell the story first which has become especially effective through social media. Since the Internet and social media, such as Twitter, is becoming more pervasive, it is often where people will go first in a crisis. As a result, it is important for global communicators to use the Internet to gain control of messages in a crisis by posting phone numbers to call for information and by updating information regarding the crisis on a regular basis.

> A company CEO is an important global voice that can help maintain trust and brand credibility, especially in a crisis.

A company CEO is an important global voice that can help maintain trust and brand credibility, especially in a crisis. In summer 2008, the stakes were high when Mattel had to recall more than 18.2 million toys, the largest number in company history, because of lead paint and design flaws from a manufacturing plant in China. CEO Bob Eckert took an active role as spokesman, appearing on as many live newscasts as possible. Behind the scenes, Mattel leadership worked with regulators around the world and with retailers to remove toys from the shelves. Internally, the company's senior management and the communications team met seven days a week to ensure all stakeholders were addressed. Eckert said, "My focus was always on, what's the right things to do? All around the world, we apologized to parents. Because parents don't just live in the United States. These were global recall and whenever we had the opportunity, we wanted to apologize to parents and that included parents in China."[35]

Perception often becomes reality, and managing perceptions on a global scale from afar and through different cultural lenses must be done with added planning and care.

Nongovernmental Organizations

Nongovernmental organizations (NGOs), such as Amnesty International, Greenpeace, and Human Rights Watch, are increasingly influential in corporate reputation management. NGO "watchdog" or advocacy groups—numbering nearly 40,000—often serve as consultants to governments and global organizations and have increasing influence in setting global agendas on individual issues. Companies must be increasingly alert and responsive to NGOs' agendas, especially in the areas of human rights, labor issues, the environment, and business practices.

According to Edelman Public Relations Trust Barometer, NGOs are rated among the most trusted global institutions.[36] In many countries, media are increasingly turning to NGOs for their opinions on global issues and they are held as highly credible sources.[37]

In India, for example, Coca-Cola bottling plants require large amounts of water in a region where water can be scarce. The company is highly proactive in working with NGOs, local government, and the communities in which it operates to address environmental and resource issues. Partnering with local entities, Coke has established rainwater harvesting initiatives and shares its water management expertise with local communities to enhance local water collection. In April 2003, Coca-Cola India was honored by the government of Delhi in the State Government Bhagidari (partnership) program for its rainwater harvesting initiatives.[38]

Despite these initiatives, NGOs had a direct impact on the company's local operations. In March 2004, local officials shut down a Coca-Cola bottling plant in southern India over unsubstantiated claims by local residents and activists that it drained local water supplies. Beyond their increasing visibility and credibility in the global arena, Internet technology has enabled activist groups with limited financing to take their message to a global audience. A one-man NGO used a laptop computer, a Web site, and a telephone calling card to build global alliances against Coca-Cola's environmental practices in India.[39]

For its part, Coca-Cola used its Web-based factsheet to publicize its proactive work with the local community, counteracting the anticompany message.[40]

Corporate communication professionals must be vigilant in monitoring NGO agendas through the media and on the Web and must seek common ground effectively to address their concerns. As Coca-Cola did, communication professionals need to use their company Web sites as important proactive tools to advance their policies and agendas and to counteract misinformation.

> Corporate communication professionals must be vigilant in monitoring NGO agendas through the media and on the Web.

Corporate Social Responsibility/Sustainability

Multinational companies increasingly recognize that global reputation is not measured solely by financial performance but also by their contributions to society. Corporate rankings like *BusinessWeek*'s Best Global Brands, The World's Most Reputable Companies (Reputation Institute/Forbes), and *Fortune*'s Most Admired Companies include a company's social performance as part of its ranking criteria. Credibility has become an even more crucial element of global reputation management following the 2008 global economic crisis. Geoff Colvin of *Fortune* stated that "in these turbulent times, a stellar reputation is a powerful asset."[41]

The United Nations 1999 Global Compact advocates that global companies incorporate social responsibility into daily business practices related to human rights, labor standards, environment, and anticorruption and encourages companies and their CEOs to adhere to and promote the compact's principles.[42] Corporate Social Responsibility (CSR) has become an important strategic focus for companies. CSR activities range from philanthropic engagements to socio-economic development and are typically defined by a company's industry and geography.

While becoming more commonplace, the CSR function does not have a clearly defined place in all organizational structures. In 2008 The Boston College Center for Corporate Citizenship conducted a study to determine how companies manage corporate citizenship. Results show that 30 percent place CSR in corporate/public affairs, 16 percent in communication departments, and 12 percent have separate CSR divisions that report directly to executive management or the board. A smaller percent place CSR under human resources, marketing, and legal.[43]

In response to the rising interest in the world's global issues, many companies devote considerable resources to their sustainability strategies. Sustainability was first defined by the United Nations Brundtland Commission in 1987 as a means to "meet the needs of the present without compromising the ability of future generations to meet their own needs."[44] In 1994, John Elkington, founder of AccountAbility, coined the phrase the "triple bottom line" to emphasize that pursuing a sustainability strategy helps companies manage economic, social, and environmental risks and opportunities for increased short- and long-term profitability.[45] Shell framed its message as "People, Planet, Profits" with the help of SustainAbility, to simplify its CSR commitment and the connection that doing good also contributes to the bottom line. Today, roughly half of the Fortune Global 500 share their challenges and progress around human rights, environment, community, and other non-financial issues in their sustainability or CSR reports that are included on corporate Web sites.

The emergence of sustainability has also led to more collaborative partnerships between NGOs, such as the World Wildlife Fund and Greenpeace, and corporations. For example, the Global Reporting Initiative developed the world's de facto standard in sustainability reporting guidelines through a multistakeholder approach.

Institutional investors now acknowledge business opportunities arise from sustainability. Companies acting in a sustainable way are assumed to be stronger in the long run. As a consequence, specialized funds, indices and rating agencies are evolving, including:

- **Dow Jones Sustainability Indexes.** Launched in 1999, the DJSI have become the leading benchmark to track the financial performance of the top 10 percent of companies from 57 industries worldwide.
- **FTSE4Good:** The FTSE4Good Index Series is designed to measure the performance of companies that meet globally recognized corporate responsibility standards, and facilitate investment in those companies. It has become one of the top global indexes along with DJSI.
- **Global Challenges Index:** Drawn from a universe of 900 companies worldwide, this index from the Hannover Stock Exchange and Oekom Research is based on how companies address social and environmental challenges.
- **Global 100—the most sustainable companies:** Corporate Knights and Innovest issue this annual sustainability ranking each year at the World Economic Forum in Davos.

Overall, sustainability has become a board level topic and an integral part of a company's strategy. Top performing companies have established a direct report to a board member who is leading a central sustainability organization. Many companies see greenhouse gas (GHG) and energy management as the most important topic. Some industries, especially Food and Beverage, consider water management important. For example, beverage producer *PepsiCo* believes that reducing water consumption is one area they can make the most difference.[46] Companies with the most advanced sustainability strategies include their network of partners and suppliers in meeting sustainability objectives.

When *Newsweek* released its first Green Rankings[47] on September 21, 2009, rating the 500 largest U.S. companies on the sustainability of their practices, Hewlett-Packard topped the list based on its strong programs to reduce GHG emissions and for being the first major IT company to report GHG emissions associated with its supply chain. It has also made an effort to remove toxic substances from its products.

Building on its corporate commitment to sustainability, coupled with the power of social media, in June 2009, *HP* launched its *"Power to Change"* campaign[48] which encourages users to turn off computers when they are not in use. By early October 2009 more than 23,998 people had downloaded a desktop widget, which tracks the cumulative energy savings. The "Power to Change" campaign is an effective way to help people contribute in reducing energy waste, curbing carbon emissions while saving money.

HEWLETT-PACKARD

Hewlett-Packard's Web site is highly effective in communicating its commitment to sustainability and other global initiatives through its Global Citizenship report.

In 2008 HP created the Global Citizenship Council comprising senior executives, including those responsible for five focal areas—environment, ethics, legal compliance, privacy, and supply chain, as Figure 9.2 illustrates.

The Council's charter is to promote and advance global citizenship strategically across HP. Council members focus on measures that ensure global citizenship is integrated into day-to-day functions. The Council also discusses potential conflicts between global citizenship and business objectives.

The success of global citizenship begins with support from the top. Having the backing of company leadership is essential to raising the visibility, influence and impact of our work at GC. Managing global citizenship effectively across an organization as diverse and far-reaching as HP requires vision, commitment, skill and trust.

Because global citizenship is rooted in HP's company values, it helps guide employees' decisions and their actions. It is a source of motivation and pride, a shared foundation integral to the culture of HP. In 2008, over two-thirds of employees surveyed in our Europe, Middle East and Africa region said global citizenship was "very important" or "extremely important" to them personally.[49]

From a communication perspective, it's important to note that one factor garnering HP its top *Newsweek* ranking is its high Reputation Survey Score, based on a poll of CEO's environmental offices and other green experts. No other company approached HP in its Reputation Survey score ranking. The lesson is that while a corporate commitment to sustainability and CSR is essential in global brand management, the importance of communicating these initiatives to influential leaders and consumers cannot be overemphasized.[50]

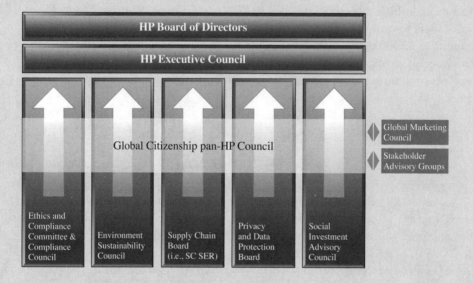

Figure 9.2

■■■

WORKING WITH PUBLIC RELATIONS AGENCIES

Companies, often with limited resources, have several options to communicate in many global markets via public relations agencies.

Global Agency of Record (AOR)

Because the talent and quality of global public relations agencies can vary greatly from location to location, corporate executives should choose carefully when considering bringing on a global agency of record (AOR):

- Look at the agency's regional record of success for other clients in the market(s) and business closest to yours.
- Consider the industry experience of the account managers and their involvement with your account. Some agencies may have a weakness in one practice area.
- Consider selecting different agencies to handle your accounts depending on the product and geographic location.

If the corporate communication professional retains a global AOR, he/she should demand a "bulk purchase" discount. One benefit of an AOR is that the global account team should share information about its client's goals, projects, and issues. The client should not pay for each office to get up to speed. Global AORs may be best suited for a global product launch or for crisis communication, where it is most effective to have a standard set of communication processes globally.

Local PR Agencies

Some companies create their own networks of local PR agencies. There are several reasons for this decision. Some international corporate public relations directors prefer to work with agencies that are specialized in their industry, or have skills to address specific needs in a market.[51] An AOR's local office may not have the best expertise for the situation.

These private networks can include agencies belonging to a global group. It would be rare for a local PR agency to turn down an assignment because their global network has not been assigned as AOR. Sometimes, agencies can be identified and put on standby for situations as they arise, or for special projects. Most agencies will provide assistance on a project basis. In this way, the cost of outside agencies can be kept within budget, but top-level expertise is available when needed.

As noted earlier, whether the corporate communication professional hires an AOR or develops a network of local agencies, building trust between the corporate communication director and his/her department and the local public relations people is essential. Periodic public relations meetings to supplement ongoing communication is one proven method of building these relationships (see Sidebar).

Getting Local Buy-In

The wise international public relations director will spend a great deal of time and effort getting the buy-in of local management. This requires persuading local management that corporate reputation is a valuable asset and that the resources spent on public relations will have a positive impact on the bottom line. These tasks require excellent spoken and written communication, interpersonal skills and a great deal of patience. Earning the support of regional and local managers for the global public relations program is challenging but it pays dividends as management passes the word down the line, easing some of the barriers to international and intercultural communications.

MEASURING THE SUCCESS OF GLOBAL COMMUNICATION

By Barbara M. Burns, President BBA Communications Inc., New York

Periodically measuring the success of global public relations efforts is an essential aspect of any global communication strategy. Major criteria to measure success include:

- Opinion research surveys and evaluation forms
- Focus groups and one-to-one interviews
- Analysis of content on global blogs, chat rooms, tweets and networking sites
- Content analysis of global news clips
- Analysis of speaking engagements
- Newsletter/video distribution

All are useful in determining how a company may continue to improve its success at delivering effective messages and achieving corporate communication goals.

■ ■ ■

HOW TO BALANCE GLOBAL REPUTATION WITH LOCAL MARKET NEEDS: INSIGHTS FROM THE GLOBAL SAP BUSINESS SUITE 7 LAUNCH[52]

By Bonnie Rothenstein, Senior Director, Global Communications, SAP AG

1   *Understand the global influencer ecosystem dynamics*: Identify the key influencers, i.e. media, bloggers, analysts, business influencers and partners, in the early campaign planning stage, map out how these stakeholders influence each other, and which influencers can act as evangelists for the company. SAP, who is servicing the B2B IT market, takes time to understand and bring the key influencers on board who can serve as a third-party reference. For the SAP Business Suite 7 launch, SAP organized a customer and partner panel and briefed industry analysts prior to the launch. This approach helped to provide media and bloggers with the third-party validation they need to include in their reporting.

2   *Consider international market dynamics:* A global company has to consider the news cycle in the regions. SAP scheduled the launch of its new enterprise software suite at a time that allowed key influencers in the U.S. and Europe to attend and meet their publication deadlines. The SAP communications team had colleagues in the key markets on the ground to host media interviews with local spokespeople in their language and with information tailored to their markets.

3   *Align the communications strategy with market needs:* It is the communicator's job to make sure the company messages are relevant for the market. The SAP suite launch took place in the midst of the financial downturn when SAP's customers focused on using IT for cost savings. The messaging used research that proved the value of IT in tough economic times and emphasized the modularity of the Suite. Instead of launching the new Suite in a luxury hotel, the launch event took place in SAP's New York office and had an extensive virtual component that helped keeping a lid on travel and venue costs while reaching SAP's key external stakeholders.

4   *Empower local markets*: Start a dialogue with your communications team colleagues from the local markets early in the campaign planning process to balance the global and local messages. Provide them with global content while empowering them to customize materials to their discretion. They are the local experts and know best how to adapt the campaign to the different cultural aspects in their markets. For the SAP Suite launch, colleagues from the SAP Global Communications team were briefed months before the launch and their feedback was incorporated in the campaign roll-out.

5   *Pursue a participatory approach:* A communications campaign is the starting point of an ongoing dialogue with the entire stakeholder universe. Following the launch event, SAP continued the conversation using local events and briefings, Web based product demos and speaking engagements to visualize the benefits of the SAP Business Suite 7 and listen to the initial feedback from users and prospects.

■ ■ ■

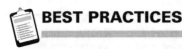

BEST PRACTICES

Effective global corporate communication is a key component of any company's success in today's global marketplace. A good global corporate communication strategy will consider many of the best practices discussed in this chapter, including the following:

■ Global corporate communication staff and resources should be centralized for greatest efficiency and control of message.

■ Certain aspects of the global communication, most notably media relations, must be handled locally.

■ While maintaining the integrity of a global brand is paramount, practitioners must customize messages when necessary to make them understandable and relevant to local markets and audiences.

■ Since resources are limited, an informal global communication network is absolutely critical to ensure communication plans, tactics, and messages will work in different cultures, languages, and countries.

■ The Internet is essential for disseminating information rapidly, simultaneously, and inexpensively and for maintaining the integrity and consistency of a message.

■ Global companies must maintain positive relationships with local leaders and NGOs in the communities where they do business.

■ Corporate social responsibility and other philanthropic programs that address genuine local needs are important investments to enhance global reputation.

RESOURCES FOR FURTHER STUDY

Bartlett, Christopher A. and Sumantra, Ghoshal, *Managing across Borders: The Transnational Solution*, 2nd edition (Boston: Harvard Business School Press, 1998).

Freitag, Alan K.and Stokes, Ashli Quesinberry, *Global Public Relations: Spanning Borders, Spanning Culture* (London and New York: Routledge, 2009).

Friedman, Thomas L., *The World is Flat* (New York: Farrar, Straus & Giroux, 2005).

Gesteland, Richard R. and Seyk, George F., *Marketing across Cultures in Asia: A Practical Guide* (Copenhagen: Copenhagen Business Press, 2002).

"How Do We Fit into the World," *Public Relations Strategist* (Winter 2004).

Howard, Carole M., "Ten Strategies to Avoid Global Gaffes in Media Relations," *Public Relations Strategist* (Fall 2001), pp. 34–7.

Morley, Michael, *How to Manage your Global Reputation: A Guide to the Dynamics of International Public Relations*, 2nd edition (New York: New York University Press, 2002).

Moss, Danny and DeSanto, Barbara, *Public Relations Cases: International Perspectives* (New York: Routledge, 2002).

Sriramesh, Krishnamurthy and Vercic, Dejan, *The Global Public Relations Handbook: Theory, Research, and Practice* (Mahwah, NJ: Lawrence Erlbaum, 2003).

Taylor, Maureen, "Cultural Variance as a Challenge to Global Public Relations: A Case Study of the Coca Cola Scare in Europe," *Public Relations Review*, vol. 26, no. 3 (2000), pp. 277–93.

Taylor, Maureen, "International Public Relations, Opportunities and Challenges for the 21st Century," in Robert L. Heath, *Handbook of Public Relations* (Thousand Oaks, CA: Sage Publications, 2001).

Tilson, Donn James and Alozie, Emmanuel C., *Toward the Common Good: Perspectives in International Public Relations* (New York: Pearson, Allyn Bacon, 2003).

Van Slyke Turk, Judy, with Scanlan, Linda, *International Case Studies in Public Relations* (Gainesville, FL: Institute for Public Relations Education, 2000).

QUESTIONS FOR FURTHER DISCUSSION

1   What does "Think global, act local" really mean?

2   Which is more important for a global company: a consistent look and feel and uniformity of positioning everywhere, or highly customized materials in each country that demonstrate alignment with that country's culture and values?

3   How important is it for a global company to have an "official company language"?

4   How important is state-of-the-art technology in effective global communication?

5   How can a company with far-flung communication staff measure the success of global communication efforts?

"Greater emphasis will be placed on our providing input that produces the most effective decisions—first, what to do; then about what to say and how to say it."

— *Harold Burson*

10 INTEGRATED COMMUNICATION

By Timothy P. McMahon, PhD

A-LO-HA UH-OH!

In summer 2002, I was in Honolulu with Pete Derzis, an ESPN executive. We were about to make the official announcement that ConAgra Foods would become the title sponsor of the Hawai'i Bowl. As the media gathered at an outdoor press conference—with Waikiki Beach and Diamond Head as a back-drop—I took a call from our corporate counsel in Nebraska. The news was not good. Management at Swift & Co., at the time a part of ConAgra and one of the world's largest meat processing companies, was concerned about the possi-ble presence in ground beef of e.coli O157:H7, a potentially deadly pathogen. Food safety, a core value at ConAgra Foods, occupied our daily conversations and was a priority that started at the top with Chairman and CEO Bruce Rohde.

The governor of Hawai'i told reporters that ConAgra Food brands had been a big part of his childhood on the island and "now they are going to become an official part of our holiday celebration." In this moment, with smiling faces on one end and a big problem looming on the other, I took comfort that our communication team was organized and that we had put together a frame-work to deal with such crises. However, the structure was new, as were many of the players who had not yet coalesced as a team. Further, the company's strategy had not fully developed so its actual value in execution was not yet clear to all. We faced two reputation-building moments of truth—one planned and one unplanned. The framework for managing integrated communication was in place. However the team was untested and had not developed the knowledge, depth of relationships, and interdependence needed confidently to manage through a crisis that could affect just about every constituency: employees, customers, consumers, vendors, investors, media, business part-ners, regulators, and special interest groups.

■ ■ ■

This vignette represents the challenge of communicating multiple messages in a com-plex and over-communicated environment. Public relations firm Waggener Edstrom considered this new environment a *communications cataclysm*: an "outbreak of new communication channels [that have] gone from feeding people's hunger for informa-tion and connectedness to overwhelming their ability to absorb information, data and points of connection."[1] Rapidly evolving situations pose adaptive challenges that are complex and unpredictable. This chapter addresses how communications integrates the vital activities of marketing and innovation to better enable a firm to realize its strategic purpose.

The chief marketing officer and the chief communication officer should be joined at the hip, a metaphor for integration that suggests marketing and innovation must permeate all constituencies of the firm and have overlapping relationships. This drives a body of thought and actions called *integrated marketing communication* (IMC).

Integrated marketing communication (IMC) is a customer-centric, data-driven method of communicating with consumers. IMC—the management of all organized communications to build positive relationships with customers and other stakeholders—stresses marketing to the individual by understanding needs, motivations, attitudes and behaviors.[2]

IMC is marketing centered. However, with the increased importance of reputation comes expanded duties for communicators. Top people responsible for the disciplines of communication and marketing see a convergence; on one end is *reputation* and at the other is *brand.* Brand is about "relevancy and differentiation (with respect to the customer) and reputation is about legitimacy (of the organization with respect to a wide range of stakeholder groups)."[3] These functions may report to different people on the inside, but the public makes no distinction. Frederick Reichheld suggested, "loyalty initiates a series of economic effects that cascade through the business system."[4] Ten years of research supported the idea that strong profits and healthy growth stem from a firm's ability to develop customer promoters while reducing customer detractors. This challenge surpasses the focus or ability of the marketing function alone.[5]

Management researcher Charles Fombrun wrote, "Companies develop winning reputations by both creating and projecting a set of skills that their constituents recognize as unique."[6] In marketing parlance, it is called *positioning.* IMC is limited to marketing. What is covered here is *integrated communication* (IC).

Integrated communication (IC), a dynamic communication practice aimed at advancing not just the marketing plan, but the overall operating or business plan of the firm and in so doing aligning *brand* with *reputation.*

IC includes innovation, the organization-wide activity to create *value* for the customer and *profit* for the firm. IC extends beyond marketing to include the entire enterprise and the involvement of each employee with the firm's many publics. This requires a fresh mindset that invites broad participation because to face adaptive challenge it is beneficial to have "every brain in the game."[7]

FOUNDATIONAL CONCEPTS

This chapter is divided into two parts: foundation and tactics. The first part addresses theories that apply to effectively communicating in today's world. The second part discusses tactical issues, cases, and examples of how the theoretical foundation may be implemented to achieve real-world objectives.

For years there has been a tendency to view the communications function as outbound and dependent on reaching the target audience with the right corporate message, rather than two-way and interdependent on creating dialogue and collaboration.

Strategy in the Brave, New World

Echo Research CEO Sandra Mcleod concluded that "successful public relations needs to be as much about listening and being influenced, as influencing and guiding, in order to support organizations in this increasingly technologically connected and fragmented world."[8] For years there has been a tendency to view the communications function as outbound and dependent on reaching the target audience with the right corporate message, rather than two-way and interdependent on creating dialogue and collaboration. This mistaken perspective has held true for both public relations and advertising, though PR practitioners were much quicker to recognize the eroding credibility of traditional unilateral messaging.

The dawning of the democratization of media has radically altered the rules of communication and marketing. PR has emerged as the more effective tool of influence in an over-communicated world. Effective persuasion is predicated on a two-way, symmetrical relationship-building model.[9] In this new model, any attempt to control or cut off information, or demonstrate over-influence will create corresponding resistance. Similarly, entering the conversation with meaningful contributions, balanced by advocacy and inquiry creates trust, collaboration, and leads to the desired outcome for the firm and its many constituents as outlined in the firm's strategic plan.

One of the critical roles of communications is to distribute leadership throughout the organization "because the solutions to our collective challenges must come from many places, with people developing micro-adaptations to all the different micro-environments."[10] This demands a new kind of communication leadership that involves the entire organization in setting direction, obtaining commitment, and facing adaptive challenges that develop along the way.[11] In its landmark study *The Authentic Enterprise*, the Arthur W. Page Society found that the chief communications officer (CCO) must demonstrate leadership in "(1) defining and instilling company values, (2) building and managing multiple stakeholder relationships, (3) enabling the enterprise with "new media" skills and tools, and (4) building and managing trust in all its dimensions.[12] This requires expanding individual and organizational knowledge, vigorously confronting reality, and creating safety to members taking legitimate bold action.

The Role of Marketing: Get and Keep Customers

In his seminal book on marketing, Theodore Levitt explained, "The purpose of a business is to create and keep a customer."[13] Michael Porter pointed to value creation as the condition for customer development and retention: "[V]alue is what buyers are willing to pay, and superior value stems from offering lower prices than competitors for equivalent benefits or providing unique benefits that more than offset a higher price."[14] Management guru Peter Drucker wrote that "any business enterprise has two—and only these two—basic functions: marketing and innovation."[15] These three nuggets provide foundational elements for what must be accomplished to sustain and grow the business enterprise, supported by disciplined communication.

Marketing is a "broad general management responsibility, not just a function delegated to specialists."[16] The primary task of marketing is to identify what is valued and deliver it to the target market that values it the most. For our purposes, *integrated communication* (IC) represents a hook that helps create, capture, and sustain value. When developing a niche or a product, the degree of customization depends on identifying the needs of specific segments of consumers and assessing the firm's ability to meet them. This challenge is best met with multiple constituencies (e.g. employees, customers, suppliers) all having a

> The primary task of marketing is to identify what is valued and deliver it to the target market that values it the most.

Figure 10.1   *Customer review of Philips® BodyGroom Retrieved May 30, 2009 from http://www.youtube.com/watch?v=e7NLyaNO5gc*

say based on a clear understanding of purpose. It may be as simple as gathering product reviews from customers.

Average consumers with video cameras regularly offer their opinions online. Companies don't control this user-generated content (UGC). However, if one considers the digital commons as a tremendous source for consumer input, it is important to join the dialogue, or multilogue.

In the movement from large mass markets to smaller segments, marketers have recognized the importance of the Web as a behavior observation point. Web metrics are often transparent and a traffic count (or number of views) is often affixed to the entry. A consumer shooting his own video review of a product exemplifies how the Web enables anyone to have a say in the position of the brand. While traditional control is lost, the potential for target customer involvement and understanding is heightened.

Web involvement allows marketers to better understand two key positioning questions: (1) Who are the potential customers, and (2) does the product fit their needs? Answers add to traditional demographic, geographic, and lifestyle information. The process is abbreviated as STP: segmentation, targeting, and positioning. If a firm can solve its positioning problem, it can address its marketing mix.

Marketers refer to the Four Ps (product, place, promotion, and price) within the marketing mix. Product involves the package of benefits for customers. Place refers to the channel, or how the product reaches customers. Promotion is about communication and how marketers create buzz. Consumers adopt brands that embody their values. Price is how marketers capture value and is dependent to a large degree on the other three Ps.

> "Like a person, a brand has individual values, physical features, personality, and character. Like a story, a brand has characters, setting, and a plot. Like a friend, a brand offers a personal relationship, one that—in the best-case scenario—evolves as you do."

One of the best characterizations of brand comes from Dave Sutton and Tom Klein: "Like a person, a brand has individual values, physical features, personality, and character. Like a story, a brand has characters, setting, and a plot. Like a friend, a brand offers a personal relationship, one that—in the best-case scenario—evolves as you do."[17]

Customer relationship management (CRM), an area where communications may make an extraordinary contribution, is about developing and managing a long-term relationship between the company and its customers The objective is to sustain loyalty.

Without dialogue with customers about changing needs, the relationship weakens and a firm loses its ability accurately to value until a competitive challenge arises.

In business-to-business (B2B) environments, marketers must understand the quantity and nature of relationships on additional levels. In his revealing book on selling, Neil Rackham wrote: "As the size of the decision grows, more people become involved. Your success may often depend not just on how well *you* sell, but on how well the people in the account sell to each other"[18] Cohesive corporate communication promotes understanding among employees as to exactly how the company adds value. Corporate social presence, discussed later, aligns meaning between employees and customers, a significant measure of brand strength.[19]

The Role of Communication: Move People to Desired Action

Much of what has been discussed recognizes that organizational success depends on the will of people, their adaptability, and their ability effectively to deal with reality. Pre-eminent PR researcher James Grunig explained that "with the two-way symmetrical model [of public relations] practitioners use research and dialogue to bring about symbiotic changes in ideas, attitudes, and behaviors of both the organization and publics."[20] In this model, advocacy is balanced with inquiry to form skills of honest investigation.[21] This is facilitated through dialogue and honest communication. In the practice of integrated communication, *values* must first be understood and will guide decision-making.

In a two-way world, where a *mommy blogger* dispatching 140-character Twitter-rants can call into question a firm's marketing efforts, it is not enough to have a vision. What is important is to be adaptive and engaged. Leaders must understand that a plan is based on today's best guess and may be disrupted. Without organizational self-awareness and shared values, members up and down the organization will struggle for a coherent and sincere response.

THE SOCIAL NETWORK MULTILOGUE

We call it social media, but what is occurring in the new digital environment is actually social networking. PR agency executive Mark Hass characterized it as *multilogue*. "Because of digital media and their social network offspring, we are living in a multilogue world in which the conversation is three dimensional. While companies talk to stakeholders and consumers, consumers talk to one another and to stakeholders, etc." In this sense, communicators have now been forced to yield control of their messages to publics once considered compliant *receivers*. What follows are a couple of lessons about how the multilogue has affected the work of communicators.

When the Ford Motor Company constructed its launch plan for its Fiesta, a model that had enjoyed success in Europe and South America, it "tapped 100 top bloggers and gave them a Fiesta for six months. The catch: once a month, they are required to upload a video on YouTube about the car, and they are encouraged to talk—no holds bared—about the Fiesta on their blogs, Facebook and Twitter."[22] Ford's social media head Scott Monty emphasized the bloggers are free to say what they want, a critical rule to be observed in the social media space.

How firms act, react, and interact forges perception of the brand as acting responsibly with its public's best interests at heart. Being open to honest dialogue demonstrates a sincere effort to get to the best outcome for all involved. This is walking the talk, a critical authenticity test for brands.

> Being open to honest dialogue demonstrates a sincere effort to get to the best outcome for all involved. This is walking the talk, a critical authenticity test for brands.

A firm may seek understanding and support from its constituencies as Domino's did in April 2009 (see Figure 10.2). Within 48 hours of a posting on YouTube, there were a million downloads of a gross-out video shot by two disgruntled Domino's kitchen workers. Reportedly, social scanning by Consumerist.com correctly identified the Domino's in Conover, NC, as the location where the video originated. Domino's President Patrick Boyle responded on YouTube with a thoughtfully constructed message that demonstrated Domino's sincere concern and plan of action. Though a little slow to react—and in this environment that may be measured in hours—Domino's got good marks for its response.

Today's technology allows the average person to take center stage. PR icon Richard Edelman reported in 2006 that, for the first time in the firm's global monitoring, the "most credible source of information about a company is now 'a person like me,' which has risen dramatically to surpass doctors and academic experts."[23] Ensuing editions of the Edelman Trust Barometer confirm this shift. This erosion stems from a steady stream of evidence of people repeatedly being betrayed by the men and women who hold power. Traditional authority is a certain casualty of the social network multilogue; communicators must know how this is changing their role. It is in this sense that the public defines the brand.

Figure 10.2

How to lead in the new model

"Too many people in authority work to make those under them dependent on them. The more dependent the followers, the more indispensable the authority figure feels."[24] The challenge in an over-communicated and fragmented world is to distribute leadership so employees are ready, willing, and able to go beyond their job descriptions. The challenge is to move from dependence to interdependence. The CEO and CCO must provide the questions, not the answers. This is a radical departure for many who believe leaders lead and followers follow.

> The challenge in an over-communicated and fragmented world is to distribute leadership so employees are ready, willing, and able to go beyond their job descriptions. The challenge is to move from dependence to interdependence.

In this context, leadership needs to move to "an influence relationship among leaders and followers who intend real changes that reflect their mutual purposes."[25] CCOs will do well to establish an organizational arrangement that is honest, engaging, and empowering. Abraham Zaleznik concluded that management control is overrated and breeds a sense of being manipulated, while leadership sacrifices the appearance of order for authentic employee engagement. Effective leadership today is broad-based and truly empowers members of the firm to take bold, legitimate action on behalf of the firm.[26]

The expanded role of measurement

The haunting phrase, "trust, but verify" is increasingly embedded in a communicator's solemn responsibility to a firm. The stakes are simply too high to guess on message accuracy, its desired effect, or its return on investment (ROI). It is imperative that CCOs devise a reliable and accessible set of measures. That begins with understand what is to be measured.

Outputs, outtakes, and *outcomes* are three measures that must be properly evaluated. Outputs measure the ability to disseminate a message. Outtakes measure how a message is received and understood. Outcomes measure the behavioral change that results from communication. Third-party providers are available to help in each area. Accurate measure here permits communicators to isolate communication problems. The ultimate measurement answers the question: will your constituents (customers, employees, investors, etc.) enthusiastically recommend the firm to others.

The IC Hook® Model

The metaphor of a hook is not new and has been associated with a lure to catch fish, something to hang things on, or a means to get attention, like a repeated musical refrain. The IC Hook® (see Figure 10.3) illustrates the parallel roles of communications and marketing. It is a framework to organize and manage the work of *integrated communications*. The four quadrants of the chart serve as a roadmap describing the activities that make IC powerful, measurable, and valued.

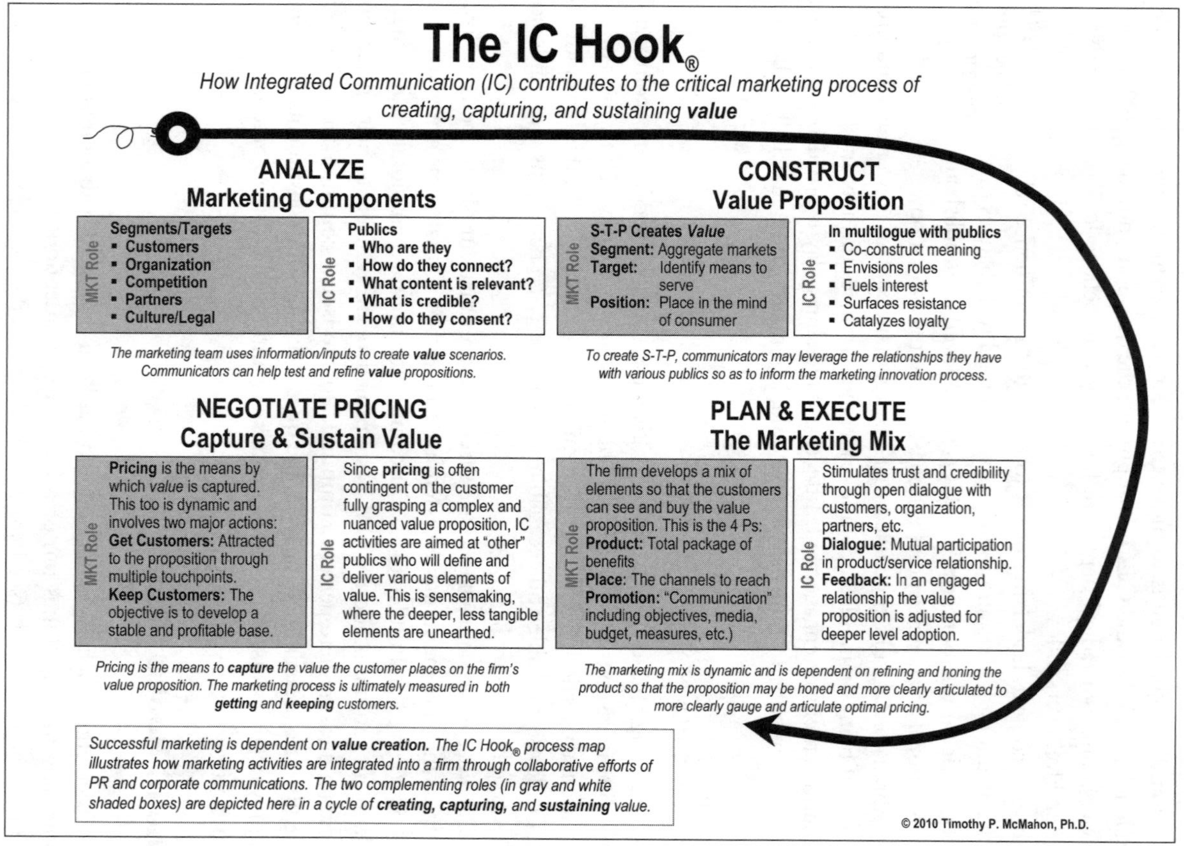

The IC Hook®

How Integrated Communication (IC) contributes to the critical marketing process of creating, capturing, and sustaining value

ANALYZE
Marketing Components

MKT Role

Segments/Targets
- Customers
- Organization
- Competition
- Partners
- Culture/Legal

IC Role

Publics
- Who are they
- How do they connect?
- What content is relevant?
- What is credible?
- How do they consent?

The marketing team uses information/inputs to create value scenarios. Communicators can help test and refine value propositions.

CONSTRUCT
Value Proposition

MKT Role

S-T-P Creates Value
- Segment: Aggregate markets
- Target: Identify means to serve
- Position: Place in the mind of consumer

IC Role

In multilogue with publics
- Co-construct meaning
- Envisions roles
- Fuels interest
- Surfaces resistance
- Catalyzes loyalty

To create S-T-P, communicators may leverage the relationships they have with various publics so as to inform the marketing innovation process.

NEGOTIATE PRICING
Capture & Sustain Value

MKT Role

Pricing is the means by which value is captured. This too is dynamic and involves two major actions: **Get Customers:** Attracted to the proposition through multiple touchpoints. **Keep Customers:** The objective is to develop a stable and profitable base.

IC Role

Since pricing is often contingent on the customer fully grasping a complex and nuanced value proposition, IC activities are aimed at "other" publics who will define and deliver various elements of value. This is sensemaking, where the deeper, less tangible elements are unearthed.

Pricing is the means to capture the value the customer places on the firm's value proposition. The marketing process is ultimately measured in both getting and keeping customers.

PLAN & EXECUTE
The Marketing Mix

MKT Role

The firm develops a mix of elements so that the customers can see and buy the value proposition. This is the 4 Ps; **Product:** Total package of benefits **Place:** The channels to reach **Promotion:** "Communication" including objectives, media, budget, measures, etc.)

IC Role

Stimulates trust and credibility through open dialogue with customers, organization, partners, etc. **Dialogue:** Mutual participation in product/service relationship. **Feedback:** In an engaged relationship the value proposition is adjusted for deeper level adoption.

The marketing mix is dynamic and is dependent on refining and honing the product so that the proposition may be honed and more clearly articulated to more clearly gauge and articulate optimal pricing.

Successful marketing is dependent on value creation. The IC Hook® process map illustrates how marketing activities are integrated into a firm through collaborative efforts of PR and corporate communications. The two complementing roles (in gray and white shaded boxes) are depicted here in a cycle of creating, capturing, and sustaining value.

© 2010 Timothy P. McMahon, Ph.D.

Figure 10.3

TACTICAL TOOLS

Communication Toolbox

Here are some of the tools communication professionals commonly use in integrated communication to achieve an objective, create meaning, counter resistance, or simply move closer to a desired outcome.

Effective Persuasion

Organizational behavior professor Jay Conger pointed to four essential steps in effective persuasion: (1) establish credibility; (2) frame your goals in a way that identifies common ground with your audience (positioning); (3) reinforce your position by using vivid language and compelling evidence; and (4) connect emotionally with your audience.[27] Conger noted research suggesting that most managers strongly overestimate their credibility. In the workplace, credibility grows out of expertise and relationships. Expertise is shown by repeatedly demonstrating competence. Relationships develop when people see others as trustworthy and having their best interests at heart.

> In the workplace, credibility grows out of expertise and relationships.

Meaning = Empowerment

Language is the sum and substance of meaning making within a group. "The individual mind (thought, experience) does not thus originate meaning, create language, or discover the nature of the world."[28] People use language to relate to each other in a given environment and to define their reality.

In this manner, communication is about mining shared meaning, and it leads to the most elusive commodity in organizations: empowerment. Quinn and Spreitzer discovered two forms of empowerment: organic and mechanistic. They found the organic is "less predictable but more likely to create conditions where members have integrated their own values with larger values shared by the organization."[29] Mechanistic is top-down and tends to be delegated, specific, and more dependent on compliance. This form, while effective in certain circumstances, did not engage employees as wholly. The researchers remarked that one group they studied "feared empowerment would create 'loose cannons,' a fear more imagined than empirically observed." When the people of a firm are connected through values, they can be organizational advocates as powerful as cannons.

Metaphors

Lakoff and Johnson explained that a metaphor creates coherence allowing people to understand something by relating it to what they know.[30] Amid a controversy regarding contributions, Richard Nixon demonstrated a keen understanding of how metaphor can be used to recoup credibility. While running for vice president on the ticket with Dwight Eisenhower, he referred to his wife as wearing a Republican cloth coat, to rustle a positive conservative notion held by his audience. No furs or leather for this second lady to be! TV cameras showed Pat Nixon wearing the coat on TV, but the candidate created the metaphor by calling it out verbally. His speech proved that even uncharismatic speakers can use powerful words to shape perception. The speech generated an enormous amount of pro-Nixon mail, and he and Eisenhower went on to victory.

Framing

"People respond to the meanings they have for words and events rather than to the words and events themselves."[31] Framing is the tool used to create appeal in the minds of the audience. It uses words that are most important to gaining approval on issues. Targeting is crucial to successful framing—just as Nixon reached out to Republicans with his cloth coat message.

Bridging gaps

Nirmalya Kumar brought this time-tested concept into sharp focus when he wrote: "Three mutually reinforcing changes are enabling faster and more coherent coordination of customer value creating activities within organizations."[32] Organizations are moving from functions to processes, from hierarchies to teams, and from transactions to partnerships. These changes stem from the need to better serve customers in a world where an abundance of choices and channels has overheated the environment.

> Effective integrated communication drives the process, creating meaning and understanding for all employees.

The challenge in creating value in today's marketplace is not simply about creating a product or service. It also requires the ability to deliver it on demand through coordinated teams of multitalented employees who organize around the customer. Effective integrated communication drives the process, creating meaning and understanding for all employees.

Storytelling

Stories help people understand how beliefs translate to behaviors. One such story repeated frequently at Southwest Airlines is about a flight attendant popping out of the overhead luggage bin. At Southwest, this story has become a symbol of company spirit. Wall space there displays company history, values, and culture. It is not uncommon for a newcomer to be shown a wall display that reflects one of the company values. Culture is a powerful thing built upon effective communication.

Corporate branding

"The first step to having a cohesive brand is to have a cohesive company."[33] Brand concept begins with an easy-to-understand promise. The popular bug killer, Raid®, for example, uses "Kills bugs dead" as its advertising slogan. A product brand, with its features, functions, and benefits, is usually easier to promote than a corporate brand. That's especially the case when a corporation is a holding company that owns many brands. Corporate identity begins with a clear understanding of corporate values.

Does Virgin® mean records? Maybe it once did when the name stood over the door of a single record store—but not today. The firm's iconic Times Square store closed in 2009, but Richard Branson created an organization that marches to the beat of a different drummer with a set of values different from its competitors and this intangible is what endures. One of the distinct values of Virgin is "irreverence." It gives Virgin brand leverage because a significant number of customers identify with the unconventional image Virgin brings to businesses including airline and train travel, cell phones and credit cards. Virgin's Web site expresses its character. Would you expect to see the phrase "Boredom Sucks" on the Verizon® Web site? Not likely. But it fits quite naturally with Virgin cell phones.

The Virgin brand (see Figure 10.4) appeals to both customers and employees in a fresh way, with alignment externally and internally. When meaningful and recognizable values are in place, brands can add value through ethereal benefits that often bring a deeper level of commitment. This level of brand equity is difficult for competitors to replicate.

Figure 10.4   Virgin territory: the Web site of Richard Branson's company

VISION, VALUES, AND PURPOSE

> A vision provides reference points for decision-making, and it motivates individuals to be a part of something greater than they could accomplish alone.

A vision provides reference points for decision-making, and it motivates individuals to be a part of something greater than they could accomplish alone. More than ever, the vision is clarified from the bottom up, and when that happens it is truly empowering. It can set an organization apart from all others—the desired outcome of integrated communication.

Several years ago, a salesperson for ConAgra Foods visited a very large retail buyer who complained that his customers needed a complete dinner that was inexpensive, easy-to-make and gave the impression of something special for the family. The sales rep took the challenge back to the culinary team who came up with a hot casserole prepared in the time it took to change out of work clothes and set the table. Because the product was baked, a house would be filled with a fresh-from-the-oven aroma, a user-valued benefit. Banquet Homestyle Bakes (see Figure 10.5) became a smash hit generating hundreds of millions of dollars in its first year, and it redefined the home meal solutions category. When the company and its customers share the vision, value-creation soon follows.

NEW CORPORATE PRESENCE

A new corporate presence has emerged as organizations bring their identities to life through corporate social responsibility and corporate social engagement.

Marketing communications executive Carol Cone pioneered a discipline of communications called Cause Branding®, also known as cause-related marketing. It helps companies and nonprofits integrate values and social issues into brand equity and organizational identity (see http://www.coneinc.com/Pages/cause_brand.html).

Cone seized on two findings in her study of ConAgra Foods' social responsibility issues. First, employees were highly concerned about leveraging their expertise

Figure 10.5

in sourcing, producing, and distributing food to benefit society. Second, a U.S. Department of Agriculture statistic pointed to 12 million American kids who go hungry each year. Studies show that hunger is a root cause for many of the problems young people face today, from concentrating in school to conduct after school. ConAgra Foods launched Feeding Children Better, a multi-year commitment to help eliminate childhood hunger in America. This demonstrated corporate marketing in action—bridging the gap between customer need and organizational capability.

Southwest Airlines' break-the-rules business model generates enormous value because management encourages employees to act on its vision. Printed below is the Mission Statement of Southwest Airlines.

The Mission of Southwest Airlines

The mission of Southwest Airlines is dedication to the highest quality of Customer Service delivered with a sense of warmth, friendliness, individual pride, and Company Spirit.

To Our Employees

We are committed to provide our Employees a stable work environment with equal opportunity for learning and personal growth. Creativity and innovation are encouraged for improving the effectiveness of Southwest Airlines. Above all, Employees will be provided the same concern, respect, and caring attitude within the organization that they are expected to share externally with every Southwest Customer.

Southwest Airlines' newsletter, *LUV Lines*, sparks dialogue about company news and information. In their book about the company, Kevin and Jackie Freiberg wrote that "this dialogue almost always results in a better understanding of the implications of the information and its relevance to what people do."[34] When a front-line employee has a firm grasp of the issues, it has a seemingly magical effect on customer satisfaction because that so rarely happens elsewhere.

Responsibility also spurs corporate social presence. GMR Marketing, a pioneer in creating corporate and brand presence, uses the tagline, "The way to live marketing!" According to its Web site, "Live Marketing is the engagement and stimulation of the senses in a uniquely personal brand experience." A cold Pepsi at a summer concert or the aroma and sizzle of a Johnsonville bratwurst at a state fair are among the experiences GMR captures for its clients. GMR created a series of lifestyle, value-oriented connections to bring ConAgra Foods to life. This led Joe Gibbs, three-time Super Bowl winning coach and two-time NASCAR Cup champion team owner, to represent ConAgra Foods' many brands at a Walmart meeting. Gibbs embodied the values of the company: honest, competitive, family oriented, and committed to winning. In addition, the red and white #20 NASCAR Bush Series car carried the ConAgra Foods logo on its hood and displayed 30 company brands on various other parts of the car. A die cast scale model was created and distributed to customers, employees, and suppliers. Walmart employees and customers also were put in touch with the Joe Gibbs Racing Team at events across the country and by personal customer visits by Coach Gibbs.

Once called sponsorships, these connections extend beyond just famous names. *Activation* is the term used to describe the way a sponsorship becomes Live Marketing. For example, ConAgra Foods built a mobile kitchen pulled by a big rig that criss-crossed the country with samples of many ConAgra Foods products. Big Hungry, as the truck was called, even made a special trip to lower Manhattan in 2001 to serve Thanksgiving meals—butterball turkeys and all the trimmings—to 9/11 rescue and recovery workers. This event was put together by hundreds of employee volunteers throughout the company who wanted to pay tribute to the thousands of firefighters, police, and rescue workers at Ground Zero. Traditional advertising also is often tied into these marketing efforts, including the messages below that appeared in the *Wall Street Journal*.

Figure 10.6

SUMMING IT ALL UP: BEST PRACTICES

The best approach to best practices is to develop measurement standards that help track and evaluate activities. Here are two checklists, which appeared on the Institute for Public Relations Web site.

The first is from a presentation titled "How Do Companies Measure Success?" by Donna Coletti:[35]

1	Think like a business manager, with a communications hat.
2	Prioritize PR activities against company objectives.
3	Develop programs with the objective of helping the company reach its objectives (always have a target outcome by stakeholder).
4	Think of editors as a channel to the final stakeholder.
5	Develop PR metrics which correlate to company objectives/goals.
6	Develop programs which encompass the entire competitive landscape and how competitors will react.

This second is from a presentation titled "Best Practices in Public Relations Research" by the venerable PR scholar Don Stacks:[36]

1	Conduct background/secondary research to establish *benchmarks*
2	Establish *achievable goals*.
3	Ask *appropriate research questions*.
4	State *measurable objectives*.
5	Employ the *appropriate methodologies*.
6	Understand the need for *programmatic research*.
7	Have the *budgets/resources* necessary.

THE BIG SHARE: INTEGRATED COMMUNICATION STRATEGY IN AN ERA OF SOCIAL MEDIA

By Mark Hass, President of Edelman, China and former Partner of MH Group Communications, New York social media strategy firm based in New York; previously CEO of MS&L Worldwide

Social media and the dynamics they create have permanently changed contemporary communications and led integrated marketing campaigns into a new, more creative and potentially more effective direction.

Social networks, such as Twitter and Facebook, have cast a contextual cloud over communications that is forcing marketers to cede significant control of their brands and messages to the growing ranks of engaged consumers. Their influence on reputation and purchasing decisions often outweighs the effect of expensive marketing campaigns.

Public conversations about issues or brands have assumed a three-dimensional quality. It is difficult, if not impossible, to control or precisely predict where these conversations will lead. Communication strategies once built to control messages must now be assembled on a flexible foundation based on partnership and what is known as the Big Share.

Learning to share has been a tough lesson for many companies. Business pages and blogs are filled with stories of how companies have stumbled because they either ignored this new reality or plunged into social networks with clumsy marketing efforts that relied on old, control-based techniques.

Cincinnati-based P&G has been a leader in shaping effective programs that use social networks to forge a new type of relationship with customers. The company's former CEO, A. G. Lafley, was an early advocate of these relationships, and he has aligned the company's huge marketing operation behind the concept.

For example, Protecting Futures, a 2009 winner of the industry's prestigious Cannes Gold Lion, artfully connected P&G's FemCare line of feminine hygiene products to a global community of women concerned about the fate of young women in Africa. It used control techniques such as advertising, media relations, and Web outreach, but also allowed its customers within social networks to drive the direction of the program and make it their own.

The Obama presidential campaign found similar success in an issues-based, rather than product-based, environment. It also won a Cannes award, as best integrated campaign, because it so effectively adapted traditional advertising to the reality of the Big Share. The campaign successfully integrated the new techniques into a holistic marketing effort led as much by Obama supporters within social networks as by the campaign itself.

Protecting Futures and the Obama campaign offer several important lessons for marketers looking to create their own social media strategies:

1. Don't focus communications on a product's price or features. Instead, determine the core values of a brand and link them to those of your customers. A values-based campaign that is connected to the real world creates a platform to share and will aggregate customers faster and keep them longer. It is especially appealing to the legion of young consumers, 18–25 years old, who rely on those networks for information and networking.
2. Engage consistently and transparently with customers and share the task of defining a product. Nothing is more valued by social network participants than regular and honest involvement.
3. Be a convener within a social network, rather than a leader. Share, don't control. Listen more often than talk.
4. Make your messages simple. Core messages are flexible bits and pieces that members of a social network will craft into creative, rich content. That content (video, music, photos, blogs, Wikipedia entries, Twitter tweets) makes a brand entertaining and engaging, and will reshape it in unexpected and beneficial ways. Offering up these pieces of multimedia content in an accessible way is a new challenge for marketing and communications departments, which have long been geared to pumping out fully assembled creative.

It's important to note that the knowledge to be gleaned from recent case studies has a short half-life. In today's world, flexibility and constant innovation are required.

As social networks become larger and more complex, best practices will be invented by those, often upstarts, dedicated to speed, change and innovation.

The final and lasting lesson about social networks is that the Big Share presents big opportunities for companies willing to engage and a big threat for those remaining on the sidelines.

■■■

RESOURCES FOR FURTHER STUDY

The following Web sites are great resources for this subject matter:

Journal of Integrated Marketing Communication, http://jimc.medill.northwestern.edu.

American Marketing Association, http://www.marketingpower.com.

Arthur W. Page Society, http://www.awpagesociety.com.

International Association of Business Communicators, http://www.iabc.com.

Public Relations Society of America, http://www.prsa.org.

Institute for Public Relations, http://www.instituteforpr.com.

The following books are excellent reading in this area:

Bossidy, L. and Charan, R., *Confronting Reality* (New York: Crown Books, 2004).

Fombrun, C., *Reputation: Realizing Value from the Corporate Image* (Boston: Harvard Business School Press, 1996).

Heifetz, R., Grashow, A., and Linsky, M., *The Practices of Adaptive Leadership* (Boston: Harvard University Business Press, 2009).

Kumar, N., *Marketing as Strategy* (Boston: Harvard Business Press, 2004).

Moser, M., *United We Brand* (Boston: Harvard Business School Press, 2003).

Schultz, D., and Schultz, H., *IMC: The Next Generation* (Boston: McGraw-Hill, 2003).

Scott, D.M., *The New Rules of Marketing and PR* (Hoboken, NJ: Wiley & Sons, 2009).

Silk, A.J., *What is Marketing?* (Boston: Harvard Business School Press, 2006).

Welch, J., and Welch, S., *Winning* (New York: HarperCollins, 2005).

QUESTIONS FOR FURTHER DISCUSSION

1   *Integrated Marketing Communication* (IMC) focuses on selling the product and building customer relationships through marketing and public relations, whereas *integrated communication* (IC) places greater emphasis on the growing importance of an organization's relationships that create its identity, image, and reputation. The argument is that brand is about differentiation and reputation is about legitimacy. What is the importance of this distinction?

2   What is the importance of a strong, well-aligned organizational identity and life to the vitality of the firm's identity, image, and reputation; and to the execution of its corporate strategy?

3   What role does the expanding influence of social media have on the effectiveness and role of integrated communication?

4   Why does the concept of a "multilogue" make more sense than that of a "dialogue" in the current landscape of communication?

5   Does a firm need to "break the rules" of top-down communication to engage its multiple constituents effectively?

6   Can you think of an example of where cause marketing failed to engage its constituents? If so, what caused the disconnection?

7   How does the idea of two-way communication challenge the principle that corporate communications is about articulating a firm's corporate strategy?

Plan for what is difficult when it is most easy,
  do what is great while it is small.
The most difficult things in the world must be done
  while they are still easy,
the greatest things in the world must be done
  while they are still small.
  – *Lao Tzu (604–581 B.C.), The Tao-te Ching, or The Way and Its Power*

CHAPTER

11 ISSUES MANAGEMENT

■ ■ ■

When Merck began its AIDS research in 1986, pharmaceutical companies had been savaged by activists, patient advocates, the research community, the government, and the news media for failing to do enough research and for pricing their drugs too high. Demonstrations were held at several company headquarters. There was violence.

Merck Public Affairs began meeting with AIDS activists and patient advocates in late 1990, at which time the company had begun to make progress with its research, but was nowhere near introducing a drug to market. The pharmaceutical industry had never before faced such a powerful consumer group as people with HIV, and in the decade following the first cases of AIDS in 1980, the industry had not reacted well. Business people and scientists were not used to dealing with sensitive issues like those surrounding sexual practices and illicit drug use, or with people who were often angry and aggressive. The activists' primary concern was both the availability and affordability of potentially life-saving medicines.

In those early days, Albert Angel, Linda Distlerath, and John Doorley in Merck Public Affairs believed strongly that Merck had every reason to be forthright and proactive with the activist community as the company battled to develop effective medicines that could be made widely availably. An issues management strategy of engagement, consisting of aggressive internal and external initiatives, was adopted. For example, hundreds of employees and company researchers in the U.S. and abroad were trained to understand and meet with the activist community. Activists were invited to speak at several Merck sites, and they routinely toured the research facilities and met with the researchers. In a six-year period (1990–96), Public Affairs held over 100 meetings to listen to activist needs and relay Merck's plans and policy positions. The company made several changes in policies and research protocols based on activist input.

By late 1994, after having tested thousands of compounds that failed because of safety issues or viral resistance, it looked like one compound, later known as Crixivan, might make it to market. But the chemistry was extraordinarily complex and the production process was difficult.

In January 1995, several leading activists let the company know that they did not believe that Merck could not produce enough Crixivan to expand clinical (human) trials and provide a compassionate (pre-marketing) use program. To manage this issue, Merck Public Affairs recommended that activists bring their own chemist consultant to Merck to discuss the complex chemistry of Crixivan. Public Affairs assured the community—and its chemist—that it could decide for itself. Understandably, Merck lawyers were not happy, but after confidentiality agreements were signed, the meeting took place at the company's Rahway, New Jersey research facility in January 1995. Activist Tom Blount, upon hearing his own consultant praise what Merck had achieved, began to cry and walked from the room. He knew there would be no quick solutions.

John Doorley followed Tom into the hallway, and Tom apologized for having been so skeptical about the company's efforts to date. This was not the first or last time that Merck's relationship with AIDS activists—which ABC-TV's *Nightline* news program later called "remarkable"—would be tested. But the relationship proved strong and successful in terms of permitting the research effort to proceed unimpeded, in a scientifically valid way.

When Crixivan reached the market in March 1996, Martin Delaney, founding director of Project Inform, one of the most respected activist organizations, wrote to the company saying its behavior "demonstrates that Merck is responsive to the public and holding true to the traditions of its founders. In my 11 years of AIDS activism, neither I nor my cohorts have ever been motivated to write another letter like this. Our congratulations to all of your team."[1]

■ ■ ■

ISSUES MANAGEMENT OVERVIEW

Issues management is a corporate process that helps organizations identify challenges in the business environment—both internal and external—before they become crises and mobilizes corporate resources to help protect the company from the harm to reputation, operations, and financial condition that the issue may provoke. Issues management is a subset of risk management, but the risks it deals with are public visibility and reputational harm.

> Issues management is a corporate process that helps organizations identify challenges in the business environment before they become crises.

Enlightened companies have formal issues management processes, at both the enterprise-wide level and in individual business units or geographically defined operations. Sometimes the corporate communication department runs the function, but often the function is run from the legal, quality assurance, government relations, or risk management departments. Wherever issues management may reside in an organization, typically it is an interdisciplinary function involving multiple corporate perspectives and several communication functions.

Establishing the Issues Management Function

A formal issues management function involves establishing a multidisciplinary issues management team consisting of all major business areas.

Every company's issues management structure should align with its business operations, marketplace realities, and leadership styles. But as a general principle, the most effective issues management structures have several elements in common. They adapt these elements to their unique circumstances and needs.

Figure 11.1 shows a diagram of a typical issues management structure.

> Every company's issues management structure should align with its business operations, marketplace realities, and leadership styles. But as a general principle, the most effective issues management structures have several elements in common. They adapt these elements to their unique circumstances and needs.

1. *Governance*

There needs to be some senior body to whom the standing issues management team reports. That governance structure is responsible for review and approval of major recommendations and plans; identification and assignment of

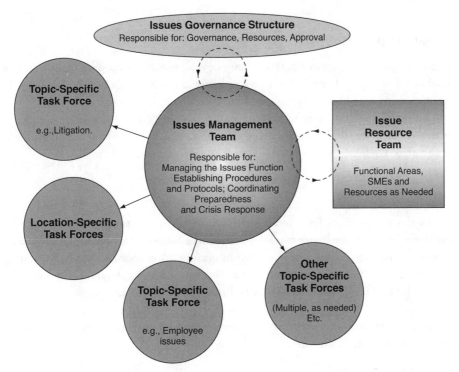

Figure 11.1   Typical issues management structure

resources to manage issues; and supervision of the work of the issues management team.

2. *Issues management team*

This is a standing group of people who represent core functional areas across the organization (e.g., legal, manufacturing, human resources, public relations, marketing/advertising, sales, security, administration, information technology, etc.). It meets on a set schedule, and also whenever a pressing or breaking issue warrants. The duties of the issues management team include:

- Establishing procedures for consistent assessment of issues, planning for managing the issues, and communicating about events or decisions regarding those issues.
- Serving as eyes and ears within the company and among stakeholders outside the company.
- Developing an issues agenda and working through that agenda in a systematic fashion.
- Naming individual issue champions to have authority to develop plans and documents on particular issues, which are then to be reviewed by the entire team. Each issue champion heads a topic-specific task force (see below).
- Serving as a central clearinghouse for any issue that may threaten the company's reputation.
- Managing the approval process for communications about any particular issue.

3. *Topic-specific task forces*

These are groups of employees tasked with developing understanding of a particular issue or set of issues. The task forces are typically led by a member of the issues management team who has been designated the issue champion for that task force.

The task forces can be assigned based on geography, on functional area, on kind of threat (e.g., litigation), or on any other criteria that the issues management team determines. Each task force reports to the issues management team.

4. *Issues resource team*

Serves as a group of predesignated experts in particular functional areas who can be harnessed by either the issues management team or by the topic-specific task forces as needed. This may include lawyers, communicators, IT professionals, administrative personnel, or members of particular business units. It is not a standing structure, but rather a group of individuals who may be brought into particular issues as needed.

Initial tasks for the issues management team include identifying issues that matter to the company. Typical issues are:

- Possible legislative activity impacting the company, its competitors, its products, its pricing, or its marketplace.

- Regulatory events and business climate changes. For example, between 2001 and 2005 there were significant changes in the regulatory climate in the United States for the public accounting, investment banking, pharmaceuticals, and insurance industries.

- Changes in social trends that make previously accepted practices unacceptable. After nationally televised U.S. Senate hearings on the 1991 nomination of Clarence Thomas to the U.S. Supreme Court made the issue of sexual harassment highly visible, workplace standards for many companies were revised.

- Competitors' activities, both positive and negative. For example, in 2004 Marsh Inc., an insurance brokerage, mutual fund, and consulting organization, suffered a series of setbacks in the wake of investigations by New York State Attorney General Elliot Spitzer. This called into question the integrity and soundness of many other insurance companies, and the insurance industry as a whole was cast in a negative light.

- Lawsuits, including class action lawsuits where a large number of people claim to have been harmed by a company's products or business practices.

- Product quality and safety issues, especially issues that require the recall of defective products or put customers' lives, health, safety, or financial condition at risk.

- Internal problems, such as the need to re-state earnings or change accounting treatment of previously disclosed earnings.

- Activities by groups with specific agendas, such as the AIDS advocacy organization mentioned above.

Prioritizing Issues

Once an issue is identified, it is important to understand how significant it is and what corporate resources will be needed to manage the issue effectively.

The two critical factors in assessing the importance of an issue are: likelihood—how likely is it that this issue will play out to the company's disadvantage; and magnitude—if it does play out to our disadvantage, how significant could the harm be?

Any given issue can be measured on a magnitude/probability matrix (see Figure 11.2). The farther up and to the right on the chart, the more compelling the issue. The upper right contains issues with high magnitude and high likelihood; the upper left, issues with high likelihood and low magnitude; the lower right, low likelihood and high magnitude, and the lower left for issues where both magnitude and likelihood are low.

Single issues can be plotted on this matrix, which functions as a tool to allocate resources and management attention to a given issue. High likelihood/high magnitude issues would get primary attention. Various scenarios of how issues might play out can also be plotted on the matrix to help give a sense of the relative resources required to manage an issue in dynamic circumstances. Multiple issues, here represented with individual letters, can be plotted to help the issues management team prioritize its work based on the relative magnitude/probability of each issue (see Figure 11.3).

If an issues management team considered a range of issues plotted on the graph, it would focus on the two issues in the upper right portion, issues g and d. Second,

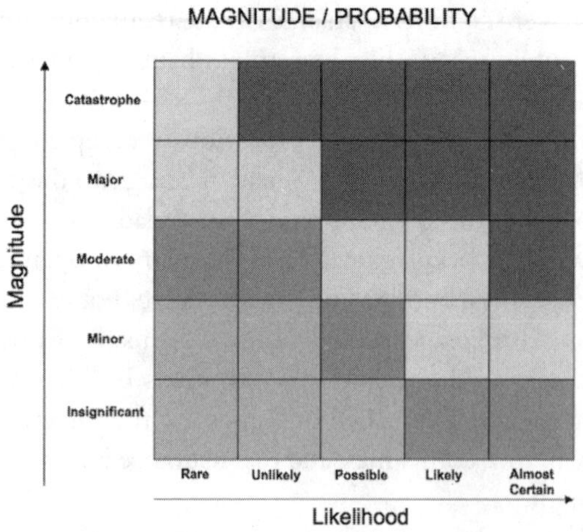

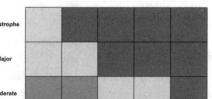

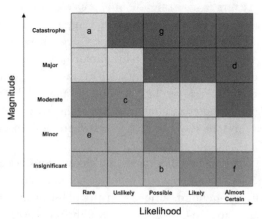

Figure 11.2

it would appraise the single issue with low likelihood but high magnitude, a, and the two issues with moderate magnitude/probability or high probability but low magnitude, c and f. The two issues where both magnitude and probability are low, e and b, would be put on a watch list and periodically reviewed.

For each issue identified, the issues management team would next develop a plan to analyze it, allocate resources to influence events to lessen its impact, and engage stakeholders in support.

Figure 11.3

Issues Management Planning Process

In general terms, the planning process for issue management is similar to the public relations process described by Hunt and Grunig and others.[2]

Typical steps are as follows:

Formula for Issues Management Success
Research/Risk Assessment + Planning + Action + Communication + Evaluation = Crisis Avoidance

---

THREE FIRST STEPS

- Establish a mechanism (e.g., regularly scheduled meetings, ongoing research, periodic discussion with key stakeholders) to identify potential issues/crises before they occur.
- Prepare background documents and analysis. The longer the document, the more important the executive summary.
- Empower the communications team to advocate with lawyers, business heads, and company members who might not see the connections between discrete issues and the business interests of the enterprise.

DEVELOP AN ACTION PLAN

- Develop an issues management and communication plan with objectives, strategies, tactics, messages, budgets, timelines and an evaluation mechanism.

ENLIST OR ADAPT THE CURRENT COMMUNICATION PROGRAM

- Aggressively manage the communication program.

EVALUATE AND REVIEW

- Periodically assess results.

DEVELOPING AN ISSUES MANAGEMENT PLAN

The starting point of an issues management plan is an analysis that identifies both the problem to be solved and the organization's ability to provide meaningful impact on the issue. Effective analysis attempts to develop understanding of the external environment and

> The starting point of an issues management plan is an analysis that identifies both the problem to be solved and the organization's ability to provide meaningful impact on the issue.

the company's internal state, as well as ways the company might adapt operations, practices, procedures, or structure. In other words, the analysis is intended to develop both situational awareness and self-awareness.

All too often companies focus on understanding and trying to manage external issues without acknowledging the internal realities of the company. Issues management then becomes ineffective because the company is constrained throughout the process by internal obstacles such as lack of buy-in or sufficient resources. Over 2,000 years ago the Chinese philosopher-warrior Sun Tzu identified the need for both situational awareness and self-awareness in navigating through perilous times. He wrote:

> If you know others and know yourself, you will not be imperiled in a hundred battles; if you do not know others but know yourself, you win one and you lose one; if you do not know others and do not know yourself, you will be imperiled in every single battle.[3]

This chapter describes an approach to issues management planning that has been field-tested by dozens of companies and organizations from Fortune-25-size financial firms and small not-for-profit advocacy groups; by publicly traded companies and private concerns; and by U.S. corporations and companies based abroad. It has been applied to issues that threatened a company's survival, and to minor bumps that merely caused embarrassment; to issues that were planned for and expected well in advance, and to those that arose suddenly and became public quickly. The planning process allowed these companies to respond effectively, quickly, and definitively and to protect their reputations, operations, and financial conditions.

The plan should consist of two key sections:

The analysis names the problem and how it is likely to affect the organization and stakeholders who matter to the organization.

- An analysis identifies the issue, event, or potential crisis and assesses the scope and likelihood of operational or reputational damage. The analysis section names the problem and elucidates how it is likely to affect the organization and stakeholders who matter to the organization.

The plan prescribes the steps to take to protect the company from operational harm and protect or restore the company's reputation.

- The plan prescribes the steps to take to protect the company from operational harm and protect or restore the company's reputation. Bear in mind that drafting the plan—the proposed solution—without a clear understanding of the problem can be highly counterproductive. It is possible to craft at least an outline of an analysis quickly. An analysis can catalyze an entire management team into a common understanding of the problem and of the ramifications if the issue remains unaddressed.

The issues management analysis and plan may be written in complete sentences or paragraphs, in bullet points, in presentation slide format, or in any other medium that works for the company in question. The style of the written document is less important than the quality of the thinking and the level of engagement by management in the issues raised in the plan.

Introducing the Issues Management Analysis and Planning Template

The *Issues Management Analysis and Planning Template* provides a structured way to think about solutions to a problem. It provides an ordered, outlined overview of a basic, viable, and strategic issue-management approach. It is a predictable, goal-oriented process which clarifies actions and messages in support of business goals.

ISSUE ANALYSIS

Threat assessment
- Magnitude
- Likelihood
- Define affected stakeholder groups
- Research additional information

ISSUE MANAGEMENT PLAN

- Business decisions/actions
- Business objectives
- Issue management strategies
- Actions to take (tactics)
- Staffing
- Logistics
- Budget
- Communications plan
  - Communication objectives
  - Communication strategies
  - Target audience(s)
  - External
  - Internal
  - Tactics
  - Targeted messages
  - Documents
  - Logistics
  - Success criteria

What the Elements of the Issues Management Analysis and Planning Template Mean

ISSUE ANALYSIS

Issue analysis is descriptive: It answers the question "what?" It addresses what happened, and what could happen if the issue is not handled properly. It helps to establish both self-awareness and situational awareness.

This establishes the context in which an issue is to be understood and the challenges it presents. It leads management toward an issue management plan and communication plan calibrated to the magnitude and likelihood of the event or threat. The analysis is intended to provide management, internal and external staff, and other company employees with a common understanding of the nature of the threat and the possible consequences. The subsequent action plan should be crafted to neutralize damage resulting from the threat identified in the analysis.

The key elements of the analysis are:

Threat Assessment

The analysis begins by naming the problem: It presents a clear description of the threat and the various ways it could play out. There are many kinds of threat:

- A negative event within the company, such as termination of key employees, discovery of malfeasance, abrupt departure of key leaders, filing a lawsuit, or the verdict in a lawsuit.
- A negative event outside the company but directed at it, such as litigation, a competitor's triumph, or legislative or regulatory activity.
- A routine business process or decision that risks being misunderstood or will be the subject of opposition.
- An accepted business practice that becomes controversial because the political, social, or business environment has changed.
- An event or change in the business environment that affects the company's competitiveness, financial stability, or operations. These could include natural disasters, new legislation, acts of terrorism, or similar issues not directed at the company but from which the company suffers collateral damage.

In addition to naming the threat, the analysis should address why the threat is something to be managed:

- What is the likely impact on the company, its stakeholders, and its operational and financial health?
- What is the likelihood that the issue, left unmanaged, will cause harm?
- What is the likelihood the company can minimize or prevent that harm?
- What is the likelihood the company will make matters worse?

SAMPLE THREAT ASSESSMENT: AN EMBEZZLEMENT

The threat assessment should assess the specific business processes, business relationships, and elements of the business environment that might be affected. For example, a company discovering employee embezzlement might identify the following as areas of concern:

> The threat assessment should assess the specific business processes, business relationships, and elements of the business environment that might be affected.

- Reasons existing control structures did not detect the embezzlement earlier
- Facilitation by or participation of other employees
- Vulnerability of other areas (financial reporting, physical property theft, accuracy of pre-employment data, etc.)
- History of similar events
- Advisability of involving law enforcement
- The need to dismiss the employee; and what to say internally upon the employee's dismissal
- Desirability of investigating via internal or external legal and accounting resources
- Likelihood of news of the embezzlement leaking
- Advisability of proactive disclosure of discovery and steps taken to identify scope and prevent recurrence
- Materiality of the dollar amount and the need to disclose into the financial markets
- Connections between the embezzlement and seemingly unrelated problems that might become public in the same timeframe
- The probability that competitors, adversaries, activists, regulators, or others may use the event to agitate against or embarrass the company

■ ■ ■

In addition to the business processes, relationships, and environmental challenges, the threat assessment should also identify the likely visibility that the threat represents, either left to itself or if mishandled, including visibility in the news media and likely public comment by investors, adversaries, regulators, legislators, ratings agencies, securities analysts, employees, and others.

To the degree that the issue is caused or may be inflamed by an adversary, the threat assessment should also anticipate the adversary's likely plan of attack and next moves.

Alternative Scenarios

It may also be useful for the threat assessment to include a number of possible scenarios, particularly when the threat is outside the control of the company. For example, if a regulatory investigation is underway, there may be several scenarios including:

- The investigation concludes that there was no malfeasance on the part of the company or its officers.
- The investigation concludes that there was malfeasance on the part of a single or limited number of employees of the company.
- The investigation concludes that malfeasance was widespread and endemic within the company.

Similarly, in the case of a pending verdict in litigation, the scenarios could include:

- The company has a major victory.
- The company has a major defeat.
- An ambiguous verdict that finds for us in some elements of the case, but against us in others.
- The company settles on favorable terms that are publicly disclosable.
- The company settles on confidential terms.

For each scenario, there would be a corresponding list of considerations, including an assessment of the likely response to each outcome among those who matter to the company, and the company's and adversary's likely next steps (appeal, settlement discussion, initiation of new litigation, etc.).

Magnitude analysis

The magnitude analysis assesses the relative magnitude of the threat's impact on the company's reputation and operations. If the threat could play out according to several scenarios, the reputational and operational impact of each scenario should be assessed. This assessment involves the same process as was described above, in the discussion of prioritizing various issues.

Likelihood analysis

The likelihood analysis assesses the relative certainty or probability that any particular event will take place and will cause operational or reputational damage. As with the magnitude analysis, the likelihood analysis should take account of different scenarios.

The likelihood/magnitude matrix described earlier in this chapter should be used to plot the relative impact of an issue or set of scenarios.

Affected stakeholders

The stakeholder analysis creates an inventory of the stakeholder groups likely to be most affected by the issue and their likely attitudinal or behavioral predispositions. These could include internal groups such as employees, specific internal functions or departments, or affiliated groups who function as internal resources, such as contractors, agents, brokers, or an independent sales force; or external groups such as regulators, customers, investors, allies, or adversaries.

For each stakeholder group named, the analysis should assess the likely attitudinal or behavioral outcome of the event, under each likely scenario.

WHAT ADDITIONAL INFORMATION IS REQUIRED?

The analysis should also identify additional specific information that needs to be obtained in order either to fully assess the threat or to begin the planning process. It also identifies the internal and external resource persons who need to be consulted or involved in the planning process.

THE ISSUE MANAGEMENT PLAN

Once the issue or event has been analyzed, the issue management plan can be constructed. Whereas the issue analysis was descriptive, the issue management plan is prescriptive: it prescribes a course of action to deal with the situation as presented in the analysis.

> Whereas the issue analysis was descriptive, the issue management plan is prescriptive: it prescribes a course of action to deal with the situation as presented in the analysis.

Not all of the following categories may apply in every case. However, each category should be considered for each issue, event, or crisis, and the decision not to include one or more categories in any particular written plan should be made based on the issue in question.

At the very least, every plan should include business objectives, issue management strategies, actions to take, communication objectives, communication strategies, messages, and tactics.

Business Decisions and Actions

Business objectives
Business objectives describe outcomes: what will be or what ought to be if the company's management of the issue is effective.

> Business objectives describe outcomes: what will be or what ought to be if the company's management of the issue is effective.

The business objectives are the goals that the actions and communications will accomplish. They are formulated as desired outcomes: the resulting status or change in the business environment that action and communication is intended to create.

For example, business goals could include:

- Maintain market share despite a product recall or pricing pressures
- Prevent regulators from taking action against the company in the wake of discovering problems
- Prevent proposed legislation from restricting a company's ability to operate in its marketplace profitably
- Sustain productivity during a management shakeup
- Protect the company's independence in an environment of consolidation
- Preserve the ability to raise capital in the wake of a financial scandal
- Avoid involuntary bankruptcy

Issue Management Strategies

The issue management strategies describe how the business objectives will be achieved. They delineate the conceptual frameworks which a company will use to organize its energies and deploy its resources to influence the business environment and protect the company's operations and reputation, and to remedy any damage. They further describe ways the problems identified in the analysis will be fixed.

Strategies are not actions to take. Rather, strategies describe how you will organize tactics.

It is easy to confuse the two, and the difference between strategies and actions to take (tactics) is described in greater detail below. In general terms, though, strategies will be the constant processes to be employed using many changing tactics.

Actions to take (tactics)

Actions to take describes the specific business decisions that need to be made. These are the tactics to implement in response to or in anticipation of the issue unfolding. The actions could be changes to an operating process, convening of a team of people designated to handle the company's response to the issue, articulation of steps to take to reach various stakeholder groups, or any other concrete step.

For the plan to work well, the actions to take should each put into operation at least one of the issue management strategies. An action that does not derive from one of the strategies is likely to be counterproductive in at least three ways: first, it may not help solve the problem and could even make it worse; second, it expends resources that could otherwise be directed to solving the problem; third, the misguided action makes management mistakenly believe that it is taking effective steps to solve the problem.

The *Actions to take* section could also include a menu of possible actions to be considered under various scenarios, as well as timelines of events known or expected to take place in the future, or targets for certain company-initiated activities to take place. The timetable may also prescribe regularly scheduled meetings or conference calls for the core team, its advisors, and management to review progress and facilitate decision-making.

Secure area

> Depending on the scope and duration of an issue, a company may consider establishing a secure room or suite of rooms to serve as a location for the issue management team to work.

Depending on the scope and duration of an issue, a company may consider establishing a secure room or suite of rooms (known informally as a "war room" or "operations center") to serve as a location for the issue management team to work. Such a facility usually has restricted access and robust technological capability including phone lines, conference call capability, secure computers, printers, fax, and copiers, plus cable television, presentation slide projection capability, and a shredder. Much of the work product generated by the team can be produced in the room, and meetings of the core team can take place there, which will reduce distraction and curiosity in normal operating areas of the company and diminish the flow of rumors.

The difference between issue management strategies and tactics (actions to take)

It is easy but counterproductive to confuse strategies and tactics. The two must be kept clear and distinct. The tactics serve the strategies, which in turn serve the business objectives.

Issue management strategies describe in conceptual terms how the objectives will be accomplished. They describe how the tactics will be organized.

The strategies are unlikely to change as the issue unfolds. But the actions to take—the tactics—are likely to change. Multiple actions can support a single strategy. And as the circumstances evolve, some actions may be discontinued and others begun, all in the service of a single strategy.

> It is easy but counterproductive to confuse strategies and tactics. The two must be kept clear and distinct. The tactics serve the strategies, which in turn serve the business objectives.

For example, a *strategy* could be: identify the scope and severity of an embezzlement. For that single strategy there could be a number of actions to consider. These could include:

- Retain a forensic accountant to review the books and determine whether other funds were stolen, as well as how the embezzlement took place
- Retain an outside law firm to conduct a thorough investigation
- Review whether there were any other instances of dishonesty by the employee, including expense reports, prior employment and educational data, vendor relationships, and the like
- Cooperate with law enforcement authorities investigating the criminal elements of the embezzlement

These actions are not mutually exclusive; all or part could be conducted simultaneously or in sequence. New tactics may arise as the issue unfolds, as the company learns more about the embezzlement, and as the stakeholders who matter to the company react to the crisis and to the company's initial responses.

All proposed tactics should be compared to the strategies to determine whether each possible tactic serves an existing strategy. No tactic should be embraced unless it demonstrably supports at least one strategy. And the totality of tactics need to demonstrably support the totality of the strategies. If there is a strategy that is not supported by at least one tactic, the tactics list is not sufficiently developed.

If it becomes difficult to differentiate between strategies and tactics, a simple rule of thumb could help: *Strategies are conceptual, tactics are tangible.* You can assign a precise cost or date for the tactics, whereas the strategies transcend such tangible precision. In the embezzlement example above, the strategy is to identify the scope and severity of an embezzlement. However tempting, it is difficult to assign a particular cost or date to that strategy. The tactics, on the other hand, are more concrete. The first tactic is to retain a forensic accountant to review the books. This is tangible. You can point to a particular accountant to be hired for a particular fee to deliver a report on a particular date. The other tactics are similarly concrete, and each could be quantified if necessary.

> Strategies are conceptual, tactics are tangible.

Staffing

The issue management plan should designate the team or teams who will work on the issue day-to-day. Most plans identify a core team that is accountable for results. That team is often empowered to prepare the plan for management review and approval, and to implement the plan once approved.

Some plans identify both the core team and a governing group of managers to whom the core team will report and who can facilitate the allocation of resources quickly.

The plan should also identify other resources, both internal and external, that the team can draw upon or who may be asked to join the core team. These can include legal counsel, accounting or investment banking counsel, crisis communication counsel, operations, security, human resources, and other functional experts who can contribute based on the company's needs and the specifics of the crisis.

> Part of organizing the core team is developing a complete and up-to-date working group list of all the people involved in managing the issue.

Part of organizing the core team is developing a complete and up-to-date working group list of all the people involved in managing the issue. This should include names, titles, assistants' names, and all relevant addresses, phone, mobile phone, e-mail, pager, and other contact information.

The staffing section of the plan may also describe the frequency of core team or management team meetings, conference calls, and other contact, as well as an expedited process for review and approval of documents.

Logistics

The logistics section of the plan, which is optional, identifies the operational details that need to be addressed for the plan to work. The logistics section covers everything from who will be responsible for what work product, to the number of desks, printers, photocopiers, phone lines, etc. that will be required for the secure "war room," to ensuring access to the building after hours, to making certain that teams working late are fed and have transportation home at night or a place to sleep.

The logistics section of the plan can range from a single piece of paper to a large three-ring binder to a computerized database. This helps the core team or its leaders understand how to operationalize the tactics they recommend and the day-to-day procedures of the crisis team.

Budget

The budget section is also optional, and addresses the costs of managing the issue, including the retention of outside experts, out-of-pocket expenses, and remediation of the underlying crisis, including possible costs of litigation, medical care, reconstruction of facilities, etc.

Very often cost is the least important consideration in an issue. But it is useful to have some accountability and predictability in cost; at the very least to have a mechanism to assure that resources are properly allocated and to understand the consequences of assigning additional resources to an issue. But in general terms, crisis responses are not driven by a budget, and certainly should not be held up while a budget is being developed and approved.

Communication planning

Because most issues are or could become public, and because much damage to a company's operations and reputation is based on public reaction and criticism of the company, each issue management plan should include a communication section.

> Most issues are or could become public, and much damage to a company's operations and reputation is based on public reaction and criticism.

The communication section is intended to support the business strategies and actions to take. It should be written following the establishment of the business strategies and specification of the actions to take. Because speed is a factor in managing breaking issues, it may not be necessary to wait until the logistics and budget sections are completed before beginning communication planning.

Communication objectives

Communication objectives answer the "conceptual what" questions. What will be the end result of our communications efforts, effectively implemented? Objectives describe desired outcomes, not the processes by which these outcomes will be accomplished.

> Objectives describe desired outcomes, not the processes by which these outcomes will be accomplished.

Whereas business objectives describe the desired change in the business environment, communication objectives describe the attitudes, emotions, or behaviors to be exhibited by your stakeholders as result of your communications program. Communication objectives could include:

> Communication objectives describe the attitudes, emotions, or behaviors to be exhibited by your stakeholders.

- Changes in knowledge, awareness, understanding, support, or feelings
- Steps we expect our audiences to take, such as approving a course of action, supporting a point of view, or trying a new product
- Neutralizing or minimizing the impact of negative visibility on audiences' thinking.

For example, if a business objective is to maintain the company's stock price, the communication objective may be to maintain investor confidence in the company's management team and prospects for future success.

Communication strategies

Communication strategies are ways in which the communication goals will be achieved. Communication strategies answer the "conceptual how" questions. In broad overview, how will the communication objectives be accomplished? Communication strategies describe where, when, and under what circumstances stakeholders will be engaged.

As with business strategies and actions to take, it is common to confuse communication strategies, which answer "conceptual how" questions, with communication tactics, which answer "operational how" questions. The difference between business strategies, communication strategies, and communication tactics is critical.

The communication strategies provide conceptual frameworks for accomplishing the communication objectives. They provide the broad game plan for all communications activities. For example:

- A business objective could be: Maintain the company's stock price.
- A communication objective to support the business objective may be: Maintain investor confidence in the company's management team and prospects for future success.
- A communication strategy to support that communication objective may be: Keep analysts and investors aware of progress being made to solve problems.
- Among the many communication tactics to support that communication strategy could be:
  - Send an e-mail to all analysts with an update
  - Hold a conference call with analysts and investors
  - Post regular updates on the Web site
  - Be prepared to field inquiries from analysts and investors
  - Conduct an interview with a financial newspaper that is read by investors.

Audiences

The audiences section lists the stakeholder groups to whom the communications will be directed. While not every communications plan needs an audience section, it provides a reality check in the form of an inventory of the groups who matter and to whom communications will be directed.

> The tactics section ought to include at least one mechanism for reaching each audience, either directly or indirectly.

The audience inventory, in turn, informs the balance of the plan. In general, the tactics section ought to include at least one mechanism for reaching each audience, either directly or indirectly.

It is common for audiences to be prioritized in a number of ways. A typical prioritization order is:

- Internal: Board of Directors, all employees, departmental, regional, or specific-level employees; senior management, etc.
- External: Current shareholders; the market as a whole; governments, academics, activists, etc.

It's also common to differentiate *ultimate audiences*, those you ultimately want to reach and who matter directly to the success of the organization, and indirect or influencer audiences, who are not necessarily your constituents but through whom you reach your constituents. Examples include:

- Ultimate audiences: Employees, shareholders, regulators, the general public
- Influencer audiences: Media, analysts, academics, consumer advocates, etc.

Ultimate audience/influencer audience

A stakeholder group that in some circumstances is an ultimate audience may in other circumstances be an influencer audience. For example, if we are seeking initial analyst coverage of our stock, analysts are an ultimate audience. However, if we wish to persuade shareholders to accept a point of view, we may consider the analyst to be an intermediary audience, to whom we communicate in order for the analyst to then communicate our message to shareholders.

The list of audiences in the plan may or may not be identical to the list of affected stakeholders in the analysis portion of the template. The difference is the following: for purposes of analysis it is useful to identify those stakeholder groups that are affected by the issue in question. However, not every affected stakeholder group would necessarily be an audience of communication. Similarly, some audiences (e.g., the media) may not be an affected stakeholder group, but may be instrumental in reaching an affected stakeholder group (such as customers) to whom direct communication may not be attempted.

Messages

Messages are the critical thoughts we wish the stakeholders to internalize; the core themes we wish to reinforce in all communications.

The word "message" has many possible meanings, but for the purposes of developing an issue management plan, it should be understood to mean what you want those stakeholders who matter to the company to think, feel, know, or do—and what you need to say in order for those groups to think, feel, know, and do those things. As a general rule, the messages can be determined by focusing on the communication objectives: the desired attitudinal, emotional, or behavioral outcomes among ultimate audiences.

> Messages are the critical thoughts we wish the stakeholders to internalize; the core themes we wish to reinforce in all communications.

One way to determine the messages is to undertake the following process:

1. Assume your ultimate audiences. What do you want them to know, think, or feel about either the company or the issue in question? What is the strongest credible thing you can say that, if believed, will cause them to know, think, or feel this way? This becomes your first message.
2. Assume that your audience has fully internalized the first message. What is the second thing you want them to know, think, or feel about either the company or the issue in question? This becomes your second message.
3. Assume that your audience has fully internalized the first two messages. What is the third thing you want them to know, think, or feel about either the company or the issue in question? This becomes your third message. As a general principle, three messages are the maximum you can expect any audience to internalize.

These three sentences become the three topic sentences that drive all substantive communication about the issue. Just as tactics may change but strategies usually will not, the factual support to a particular message may change as the crisis unfolds, but the message usually will not. And different support statements may be used with different audiences, or with the same audience at different times, while the message remains unchanged.

Using core messages

The three core messages stand by themselves, and should be included in each communication the company makes. These three messages become the quote in the press release; they become the topic sentence in employee meetings; they become the outline of presentations to the investment community; they become the three themes in letters to regulators or to customers; they serve as hyperlinks on the company's Web site, driving a visitor deeper into the supporting detail of each. The three messages need to be repeated every time the company communicates, requiring a very high tolerance for repetition.

The ability consistently to articulate the top three things a company wants its stakeholders to know is a critical attribute of leadership, and essential to effective management of issues. General Electric's CEO Jeff Immelt has said, "Every leader needs to clearly explain the top three things the organization is doing. If you can't, you're not leading well."[4]

It is only at this point in the planning process that attention should turn to the tactics. Paradoxically, most companies reflexively default to tactics as a first resort: "We need to hold a press conference …" or "We need to send out a press release …" This is the rookie's mistake in issue management and crisis avoidance. It is impulsive, thoughtless activity, and it is often both self-indulgent and self-destructive. But once the plan is in place, a framework for using the tactics effectively can be established, and the implementation of the plan can be accomplished in a flexible, effective, and cost-effective way.

> Paradoxically, most companies reflexively default to tactics as a first resort. It is often both self-indulgent and self-destructive.

Communication tactics

Communication tactics are the specific communication techniques that will be employed to convey the messages to the ultimate audiences. The tactics part of the plan is a substantive inventory of the communications activities to be undertaken. It is what will actually be done to send the messages. As a result, it tends to get the most attention.

Because communication tactics involve what people actually do, they may tend to drive the communication planning process. It is easy for people to focus on interesting tactics ("let's hold a press conference," "let's do a CD-ROM") regardless of the purpose or if sufficient resources are available for effective execution.

Choice of tactics should be driven by two general considerations, each of which requires a degree of discipline.

> Communication tactics should be driven by the communication strategies.

- First, communication tactics should be driven by the communication strategies: The tactics should not be determined until after there is a clear articulation of the analysis, the business objectives and strategies, and the communication objectives and strategies. There should be at least one strategy that demonstrably accomplishes each objective. And each tactic should demonstrably support at least one strategy.

- Second, tactics should be doable. Napoleon once remarked, "Amateurs worry about tactics, professionals worry about logistics." What is sustainable should govern tactics. The plan should not, for example, include labor-intensive tactics unless it also addresses staffing and other resources. And it shouldn't promote "gee-whiz" technologies unless it also addresses how those technologies will be obtained and delivered.

| Tactics should be doable.

There should be specific communication tactics listed to support each strategy (and, as appropriate, each stakeholder group).

Communication tactics are deliverable items. They may include:

- Employee memoranda or e-mails
- Press releases
- Web site postings
- Press conferences
- Op-ed articles in newspapers
- Advertisements
- Investment community conference calls

Because each tactic is subordinate to a specific strategy to achieve a known objective, it is easy to discard tactics that aren't working and replace them with new tactics that are more likely to work.

One virtue of the systematic planning process that this template represents is that it allows for prompt mid-course correction without losing sight of objectives. If the objectives, strategies, audiences, and messages are clear, it is easy to adapt the plan to assure it is accomplishing its purpose.

Documents

The documents section of the plan is optional. It is intended to serve as an inventory of specific pieces of writing necessary to execute the communication tactics.

The document section identifies each individual communication required to implement the tactics. Since each piece of communication needs to be drafted, and since all need to be consistent and mutually reinforcing, this section constitutes a work list of documents to be produced before tactics can be executed.

These documents will include:

- Press releases
- Media Q&A
- Employee e-mails
- Employee Q&A
- Call center scripts
- Call center Q&A

Note three different Q&A documents are called out above. Since each is a Q&A format, a document inventory makes it clear that a separate Q&A is needed for three separate stakeholder groups. The three Q&As will provide different emphases and different levels of detail, but all three will be consistent with and mutually supportive of each other.

Communication logistics

The communication logistics section identifies the resources and tools necessary to implement strategies and execute tactics. Like the documents section, it is optional. Like the documents section, it serves as a kind of reality check against tactics. It may include timeline of preparation and execution of tactics. It may also include the resources necessary to prepare the tactics for execution, or the individuals tasked to draft documents, seek approvals, or perform other tasks.

 ## BEST PRACTICES

■	Focus on the goal, not just on the processes
■	Get management buy-in
■	Name an accountable leader
■	Involve all relevant business functions
■	Set tangible communication objectives and measure success against them.
■	Follow the plan, focusing on the goal; adapt the tactics to changes in the environment, but keep the emphasis on the goal

RESOURCES FOR FURTHER STUDY

Issue Action Publications

Issue Action Publications, affiliated with the Issues Management Council, publishes a range of resources for those with issue management responsibility. It publishes two monthly newsletters:

*   Corporate Public Issues and Their Management
*   The Issues Barometer

It also publishes a range of issue management books. It can be found at http://www. issueactionpublications.com.

Issues Management Council

Issues Management Council is a professional membership organization for people whose job includes issue management. It offers conferences, publications, and other resources. It can be found at http://www.issuemanagement.org/.

QUESTIONS FOR FURTHER DISCUSSION

1   Why is it so important to get management buy-in for an issue management process?

2   What is the optimal relationship between the issue management process and media relations and employee communications?

3   How can an effective plan make issues management more effective?

4   What is the difference between ultimate audiences and intermediate audiences?

5   Why is message discipline so important in issues management?

Our greatest glory is not in never falling,
but in rising every time we fall.

– *Confucius*

C H A P T E R

12 CRISIS COMMUNICATION

■ ■ ■

It was a Monday morning in the spring of 1990, and Helio Fred Garcia, head of public relations for the global investment bank CS First Boston, had just taken a call from a business reporter for *The New York Times*. The reporter, with whom Fred had worked for several years, said that he had it from an impeccable source within First Boston that a young stock trader had just committed suicide because he was being investigated for insider trading. The reporter said he was calling for a statement, but that he didn't need confirmation; the story would surely run in *The New York Times* the next day. Fred said, "I'll look into it and get right back to you."

If the story was true, it would be bad news for the company. Insider trading was the corporate scandal of the era, and the recent movie *Wall Street*, with insider trading as the plot line, had elevated the once-obscure crime to the level of popular culture. An insider-trading scandal at First Boston would set off alarm bells. The company's reputation would suffer, its operations would be disrupted by distraction, personnel changes, customer unrest or defections, and possibly even by arrests.

If the story was false, a typical corporate response—for example, "as a matter of policy we don't comment on personnel matters or investigations"—would not have prevented the story from appearing. It would have appeared, with Fred's "no comment" statement in the second or third paragraph.

A *New York Times* story about a suicide provoked by an insider trading investigation would be believed by most people who read it. Other media —both print and broadcast—would follow the story, and a proverbial journalistic feeding frenzy would ensure that the firm would be in the headlines for days, if not weeks. And just as in the case of a true story, the firm could expect reputational harm as well as operational and financial disruptions.

One thing was clear: First Boston had to get ahead of the story so that if true, the firm would proactively announce it, and if false, *The Times* might be persuaded not to run it or to downplay it.

On the firm's sixth floor trading room, the head of trading was sitting by himself in a glass-enclosed conference room, rather than at his usual open desk on the trading floor. He seemed surprised when Fred arrived and asked him about the young trader. "How did you hear about this so fast? Well, it's a tragic situation. Yes, he did commit suicide. He has been with us for about a year, and was a very good trader. Friday he went to his family's home in Chicago. I just got off the phone with his father, who said that the young man took his own life over the weekend, after what the father described as 'an emotional family encounter.' I'm just now breaking the news to his colleagues on the trading floor."

Fred asked, "Was he under investigation for insider trading?" The head of trading said unequivocally that he was not. Fred asked why *The Times* would think he was. The head of trading pondered a moment, and offered, "The only thing I can imagine is that on Friday his trading desk was the subject of a routine compliance department audit. Maybe someone heard about the audit, and assumed that the suicide and the audit were related. But the audit was routine. There's no suggestion of any impropriety. And the suicide seems to have been prompted by whatever happened at home, not here."

Fred had most of what he needed, but had to ask one more question. "Was the young man, his department, or the firm under investigation for insider trading or anything else?" The reply was unequivocal. "No. As far as we know everything is fine."

Although the tragic event apparently had nothing to do with company behavior or performance, the routine ways of speaking with the media would not be persuasive. Such routine communication would predictably result in severe reputational, operational, and financial harm. Fortunately, Fred had standing permission from his bosses to use his judgment when dealing with reporters. By the time he got back to his desk, his plan was clear. He called the reporter, and said, "For the record, First Boston does not comment on either personnel matters or investigations. I can offer more information, but it would have to be on background, meaning you can use what I tell you but you cannot attribute it to me or to any official at the firm." The reporter agreed to that ground rule. Fred corroborated the young man's employment and suicide, as well as the discussion with the father. Fred said, "I have no idea what the emotional family encounter was about, and I leave it to your sense of decency whether to call the father and ask about it. I can tell you that he was not under investigation for anything, nor suspected of any improper activity. I can further tell you that on Friday the compliance department conducted a routine audit of the desk on which he worked. So let me ask you, before you damage the memory of this young man and cause his family unnecessary pain, and before you put the firm's reputation at risk, please go back to your source and confirm whether what you heard was an accurate account of what happened, or a rumor or speculation about two unrelated events."

A half-hour later the reporter called back. He said, "I have looked into this further, and now believe that the suicide was unrelated to the person's duties at your firm. So this is a personal tragedy, not a business event, and doesn't rise to the level of a story in *The New York Times*."

■ ■ ■

This chapter covers:

This chapter lays out some of the disciplines of crisis communication, crisis management, and effective crisis response.

INTRODUCTION

Fortune magazine's cover on October 1, 2007 featured a single sentence pulled from an expansive interview with American Express Chief Executive Officer Ken Chenault: "We have to remember that reputations are won or lost in a crisis."

> "We have to remember that reputations are won or lost in a crisis."

The second half of that sentence isn't surprising: reputations clearly are won or lost in a crisis. Mr. Chenault's insight, which *Fortune*'s editors recognized as worthy of a cover, was the first part: "We have to remember." Indeed, it is precisely in a crisis that leaders are most likely to forget that they will be judged not on the nature of the crisis they face, but on their response to it.

One of the core roles of the corporate communication function is to help organizations and their leaders make decisions and communicate clearly when something goes wrong.

Every organization, at some point, will be on the receiving end of an event that risks reputational damage. And the epidemic of crises following the Enron/Arthur Andersen/WorldCom scandals of 2001–5, and crises at Bear Stearns/Lehman Brothers/Citigroup/Merrill Lynch/Bank of America in 2008–9, showed that a sterling track record, a respected management team, political connections, and financial clout are not sufficient to protect an organization from major reputational, operational, or financial harm. Indeed, some of the companies noted above—former pillars of their industries—no longer exist.

> Every organization, at some point, will be on the receiving end of an event that risks reputational damage.

Effective crisis response—including both in what a company does and what it says—provides companies with a competitive advantage and can even enhance reputation. In particular, companies that handle crises well tend to protect those things they hold most dear, including

> Effective crisis response— including both in what a company does and what it says—provides companies with a competitive advantage and can even enhance reputation.

- Stock price
- Operations
- Employee morale and productivity
- Business relationships
- Demand for their products
- Support of public policymakers
- Strategic focus.

Ineffective crisis response can cause significant harm to a company's operations, reputation, and competitive position, and can even put an enterprise's existence in jeopardy. And because time is one's enemy in a crisis, the sooner a company recognizes that business as usual does not apply the sooner it is likely to mobilize its resources to respond effectively in a crisis.

> Time is one's enemy in a crisis.

Here is just one tangible example of competitive advantage and disadvantage based on handling crises well or poorly.

Two Oxford University researchers demonstrated the extent to which effective and ineffective crisis response affects a company's enterprise value. Rory F. Knight and Deborah J. Pretty studied the stock price performance of prominent publicly traded corporations that had suffered significant crises. They calculated each company's stock price performance attributable to the crisis—stripping out market movements and other factors unrelated to the crisis that might have affected the stock price, and calculating what they called the "cumulative abnormal returns" for each company.[1]

Knight and Pretty (see Figure 12.1) found that companies that mishandled crises saw their stock price (calculated as cumulative abnormal returns) plummet an average of 10 percent in the first weeks after a crisis, and continue to slide for a year, ending the year after the crisis an average of 7 percent below their pre-crisis prices.

Companies with effective crisis response, on the other hand, saw their stock fall an average (cumulative abnormal returns) of just 5 percent in the weeks following a crisis, about half the initial decline of companies that mishandled the crisis. More significant, companies with effective crisis response saw their stock price recover quickly, and remain above their pre-crisis price thereafter, closing an average of 7 percent above their pre-crisis price one year after the crisis.

> The tangible difference between effective and ineffective crisis response was, on average, 22 percent of a company's market capitalization.

In other words, the tangible difference between effective and ineffective crisis response was, on average, 22 percent of a company's market capitalization. Knight and Pretty assess the reasons for this disparity, and conclude that the most significant factors are not the scope of financial damage or reduction in cash flows caused by the crisis. Rather, the most important determinant of a company's ability to recover and increase its market capitalization after a crisis is the management team's response. Knight and Pretty conclude that positive stock performance

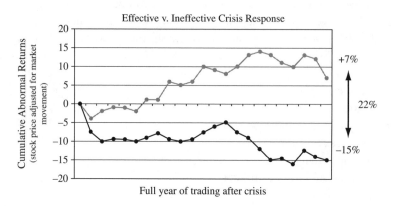

Figure 12.1

springs from what catastrophes reveal about management skills not hith-
erto reflected in value. A re-evaluation of management by the stock market is likely to result in a re-assessment of the firm's future cash flows in
terms of both magnitude and confidence. This in turn will have potentially large implications for shareholder value. Management is placed in
the spotlight and has an opportunity to demonstrate its skill or otherwise
in an extreme situation.[2]

Whether a company survives a crisis with its reputation, operations,
and financial condition intact is determined less by the severity of
the crisis—the underlying event—than by the timeliness and quality of its response to the crisis. Institutions that suffer the same very
severe crisis can experience dramatically different outcomes based
on the timeliness and quality of their respective responses.

> Whether a company survives a crisis with its reputation, operations, and financial condition intact is determined less by the severity of the crisis—the underlying event—than by the timeliness and quality of its response to the crisis.

And the single largest contributor to reputational and other harm
in the aftermath of a crisis is perception of indifference, especially
when there are victims. Companies, governments, and leaders are
forgiven when bad things happen. But they won't be forgiven if
they're seen not to care that bad things have happened. This is a lesson that many leaders and PR professionals fail to understand or to
act on in the initial early phases of a crisis.

> The single largest contributor to reputational and other harm in the aftermath of a crisis is perception of indifference.

Take, for example, one paragon of ineffective crisis response:
Exxon's March 1989 spill of crude oil in Alaska's Prince William
Sound. In prior years dozens of ships had hit rocks and spilled crude
oil into pristine waters. But there is only one oil ship—the *Exxon
Valdez*—and one company that people remember years later. Moreover, people remember the Exxon spill not because the oil was any dirtier than any other oil spilled
by any other ship; not because Prince William Sound was any more pristine than any
other body of water into which oil spilled. Rather, people remember the Exxon Valdez
because in the weeks immediately following the spill Exxon was perceived to be indifferent to the damage the spill caused. Fifteen years after the spill a federal appeals court
upheld a lower court judgment of $4.5 billion against the company (in addition to the
more than $3 billion it had previously paid for cleanup and related costs). The Court
said its purpose in upholding the award was to achieve "retribution and justice." *The
New York Times* opined that such a judgment and such a purpose were entirely appropriate, given Exxon's indifference in the initial phase of the spill.[3] (Another appeals
court later reduced the size of the judgment.)

It is the perception of indifference, not the severity of the problem that is a common denominator in many of the well-known crises of the early 2000s—from the
priest sexual abuse scandal in the Roman Catholic Church to the early phases of the
Ford Explorer/Firestone Tire recall to scandals involving market timing in mutual
funds.

The perception of indifference also proved to be a defining element of the presidency of George W. Bush. Until August, 2005, President Bush maintained steady
public support. He had been seen to rise to the occasion after the attacks on the World
Trade Center and Pentagon on 9/11/2001. Although the war in Iraq was unpopular,

President Bush maintained public support at about 50 percent. But in the days immediately after the flooding of New Orleans caused by Hurricane Katrina, he seemed disengaged, uninformed, and unconcerned about the plight of New Orleans citizens. On day 3 after the flood Federal Emergency Management Agency (FEMA) chief Michael Brown appeared on *CNN* and admitted that the government had been unaware of thousands of people stranded in the New Orleans convention center without food and water for days—a fact that had been widely reported on television—until told about the situation in an interview. Two days later the President, invoking the FEMA chief's nickname, told him on television, "Brownie, you're doing a heck of a job …"

Two weeks after the flood, as the federal response was just getting into full swing, *Time* magazine's Web site published a cartoon of a man standing waist-deep in water, holding a sign that implored, "Leadership Please."[4] The next day FEMA chief Brown resigned. That week President Bush's approval ratings fell to then-record lows.[5]

Wounded by the Katrina experience, the President suffered his first major legislative setback, when his own base objected to his U.S. Supreme Court nominee, Harriet Miers. The President ultimately withdrew the nomination. His ratings continued to fall; six months after Katrina President Bush's approval rating was in the low 30s. His ratings never recovered. His party lost the mid-term congressional elections in 2006. And by the time he left office he had the lowest approval ratings of any president in recent memory.

A Crisis Is a Crisis Because …

A crisis isn't necessarily a catastrophic event, but rather an event that, left to usual business processes and velocities, causes significant reputational, operational, or financial harm. The suicide example that opened this chapter is such an event: left to usual business processes, velocities, and ways of speaking, the harm to the company could have been significant.

But how does a professional communicator know whether his or her company faces a crisis? The question is important because in a crisis timing is critical: Actions that could effectively prevent any harm to a company's reputation on day 1 may be completely ineffective on days 2, 5, or 10.

When a company is in a crisis or approaching one, business as usual needs to be suspended, especially the sometimes ponderous ways decisions get made in complex organizations. Knowing whether such a suspension is necessary is often the first and most difficult decision. The risk for companies and other complex organizations is in failing to recognize that business as usual must cease.

It is all too easy for companies to recognize too late that they're in a crisis, because often the organization itself doesn't recognize it until people outside the organization are already feeling the effects. There is a natural tendency to assume that a crisis is by definition a catastrophe; that a crisis exists only when damage

A crisis isn't necessarily a catastrophic event, but rather an event that, left to usual business processes and velocities, causes significant reputational, operational, or financial harm.

Actions that could effectively prevent any harm to a company's reputation on day 1 may be completely ineffective on days 2, 5, or 10.

When a company is in a crisis, business as usual needs to be suspended.

has already been done or only when the event in question is potentially catastrophic. That's much too narrow a view. Many crises are not catastrophes, but small-scale interruptions in routine business that, if ignored or handled poorly, can easily escalate to cause significant operational or reputational harm.

The American sociologist Tamotsu Shibutani defines a crisis as

> any situation in which the previously established social machinery breaks down, a point at which some kind of readjustment is required ... A crisis is a crisis precisely because [people] cannot act effectively together. When previously accepted norms prove inadequate guides for conduct, a situation becomes problematic, and some kind of emergency action is required. Since activity is temporarily blocked, a sense of frustration arises; if the crisis persists, tension mounts, and an increasing sense of urgency for doing something develops.[6]

So companies need to be prepared in two ways for crises: they need to understand what constitutes a crisis in the first place; and they need an early warning system that helps them understand when business as usual has ceased to exist—or is likely to cease to exist—and that therefore business-as-usual practices need to be suspended. The corporate communication function is often an important part of that early warning system.

> Companies need to be prepared in two ways for crises: they need to understand what constitutes a crisis in the first place; and they need an early warning system.

One way to think about crises is suggested by Steven Fink in his book *Crisis Management: Planning for the Inevitable*. Fink describes a crisis as a "turning point," not necessarily a negative event or bad thing. "It is merely characterized by a certain degree of risk and uncertainty."[7] Fink refers to crises as "prodromal," or as precursors or predictors of something yet to come:

> From a practical, business-oriented point of view, a crisis (a turning point) is *any prodromal situation that runs the risk of*:
>
> A. Escalating in intensity.
> B. Falling under close media or government scrutiny.
> C. Interfering with the normal operations of business.
> D. Jeopardizing the positive public image presently enjoyed by a company or its officers.
> E. Damaging a company's bottom line in any way.[8]

Fink points out that as a turning point the crisis could go either way:

> If any or all of these developments occur, the turning point most likely will take a turn for the worse ... Therefore, there is every reason to assume that if a situation runs the risk of escalating in intensity, that same situation—caught and dealt with in time—may not escalate. Instead, it may very conveniently dissipate, be resolved.[9]

Fink's approach to crises anticipates both catastrophic events and also routine dealings that are suddenly the subject of attention. It finds merit in early intervention and affirmative management of business processes as well as the communications about the event.

Our own definition of a crisis integrates much of what Fink and others have suggested:

> A crisis is a non-routine event that risks undesired visibility that in turn threatens significant reputational damage.

This "non-routine event" may be the result of a normal business practice that suddenly becomes controversial, or it may be an attack from outside the organization. The crisis consists not in the fact that the event is non-routine, but in the possible consequence of the event: visibility that could threaten damage to the organization's reputation.

A crisis is a non-routine event that risks undesired visibility that in turn threatens significant reputational damage.

If It Smells and Feels like a Crisis ...

One quick way to determine whether something that just happened or is about to happen is likely to become a crisis is to convert the descriptions of crises summarized above into questions.

For example, to use Fink's definition, ask:

- Is this situation a precursor that risks escalating in intensity?
- Does it risk coming under close scrutiny?
- Will it interfere with normal business operations?
- Will it jeopardize our public image or bottom line?

If the answer to one or more of these is yes, a crisis exists.

To use our own definition, ask:

- Is this a non-routine event?
- Does it risk undesired visibility?
- Would that undesired visibility in turn threaten reputational damage?

If not, then a company probably does not need to do anything out of the ordinary. But if the answer is yes, the company needs to recognize that the situation is anything but business as usual, and that the company needs to behave and communicate in different ways.

One virtue of these definitions of crisis is that they focus on outcomes: on the effect that the crisis may have on the stakeholders who matter to a company, and how the company can maintain the trust and confidence of those stakeholders as the event plays out.

One problem, of course, is the word "crisis." The very word can cause alarm and even panic. But the original meanings of the word are not nearly as dire. The original Greek word from which our "crisis" is derived, Κρισισ (*krisis*), originally meant decision, choice, event to be decided, sudden change for better or worse, turning point, and the power of judgment. So a crisis, originally, was a deci-

The Greek word from which our "crisis" is derived originally meant decision.

sion that would determine whether a course of events would unfold one way or another, for better or worse—very similar to Fink's view of crisis as turning point.

In Chinese, the character that translates into the English word crisis is *wei ji*, a combination of two ideograms: 危机. *Wei* means danger or fear. *Ji* means opportunity or desire. So the shorthand meaning of *wei ji* is danger plus opportunity. There is some dispute as to whether the two ideograms mean "danger plus opportunity," "dangerous opportunity," or "opportunity for danger." But whatever the syntax or grammar, the thoughts suggest something less clear-cut than a catastrophe.

> In Chinese, the character that translates into the English word crisis means danger plus opportunity.

QUICK CHOICES AND THE LEAST BAD OUTCOME

Sometimes organizations and their leaders are presented with situations where all the possible outcomes are bad. The challenge then is to choose the path with the least bad outcome, and to execute actions and communications effectively.

Take US Airways flight 1549, which made an emergency landing in the Hudson River on January 15, 2009. Captain Chesley B. Sullenberger, III, a former US Air Force fighter pilot, a pilot union safety official, and a sometime plane crash investigator with the National Transportation Safety Board (NTSB), exhibited exceptional leadership skills when his Airbus 320 aircraft hit a flock of geese when taking off from New York's LaGuardia airport that afternoon.

The geese took out both of his plane's engines at approximately 3,200 feet as the plane was making a left turn over the borough of the Bronx. With no power in his engines, Captain Sullenberger had a choice to make, and very little time to make it.

- He could try to get back to LaGuardia, flying in a loop back to one of its runways. Downside: If he missed the runway, he'd crash into a highly populated urban setting, in a plane filled with jet fuel. The possibility of massive fatalities onboard and on the ground was high.
- He could cross the Hudson River and try to land at Teterboro, a general aviation airport just across the George Washington Bridge in New Jersey, which he told air traffic controllers he could see. Downside: If he missed the runway, he'd come down in a heavily populated residential area.
- Or he could attempt a controlled water landing in the Hudson River.

He chose the latter, recognizing that a water landing, even in freezing temperatures, was a better (or less bad) option than the risk of fire, explosion, and loss of further life on the ground. While calm, he quickly—almost instinctively—made the tough call.

Using his plane as a glider, he passed the George Washington Bridge at about 900 feet. He brought the plane down in a classic landing position, with the nose just above the tail, allowing the plane, in the words of one witness, to skim across the water like a flat pebble.

Captain Sullenberger not only made the right call on strategy—which choice to make—he also was able to execute the decision effectively, gliding his plane to a landing that didn't result in the aircraft coming apart, or sinking, or flipping over.

The 81-ton plane settled into the river, intact and afloat. The Hudson at the time was filled with ferries, small boats, and the usual Coast Guard, New York Police Department, and New York Fire Department watercraft. Within minutes the plane was surrounded by rescuers on boats, in helicopters, and in the case of NYPD rescue divers, in the water.

The 5-person flight crew kept the passengers calm and led an orderly evacuation. All 150 passengers, including a 9-month-old baby, got out. One had two broken legs; others had impact injuries. And some had to be treated for hypothermia. The air temperature was about 30; the water temperature close to freezing. But all the passengers, and all five crew, survived. New York State Governor David Paterson called the event "A miracle on the Hudson."

According to reports from the passengers and New York City Mayor Michael Bloomberg, Captain Sullenberger then walked through the plane twice to assure that there was no one left. One witness said that the back of the plane was filled with water to neck-height. Captain Sullenberger was the last to climb into a raft. The last passenger to leave the plane told the news media that in the raft he gave the captain a hug and called him "our hero."

The next day, US Airways stock rose 15 percent, on a day when the market as a whole rose only a half of one percent.

■ ■ ■

TIMELINESS OF RESPONSE: THE NEED FOR SPEED

> The first determinant of success in protecting reputation in a crisis is the speed with which an organization reacts.

The first determinant of success in protecting reputation in a crisis is the speed with which an organization reacts.

> There is a first-mover advantage in crisis response: whoever defines the crisis, the organization's motives, and its actions first, tends to win.

As in other areas of business, there is a first-mover advantage in crisis response: whoever defines the crisis, the organization's motives, and its actions first, tends to win. Silence on the part of a company is seen as indifference or guilt, and allows critics, adversaries, the media, and the blogosphere to control the communication agenda. And after nearly a decade of highly regarded companies proving unworthy of the benefit of the doubt, stakeholders are increasingly withholding the benefit of the doubt when companies are silent in a crisis. Further, stakeholders tend to interpret even routine operational setbacks as integrity lapses. As a result, silence on the part of companies tends to cause an overreaction among stakeholders, in financial markets, and in the workplace.

When a crisis looms, the usual business processes and decision velocities need to be suspended and decisions need to be made in ways that reassure key stakeholders that a company and its leaders (1) understand that there's a problem; (2) take it seriously; and (3) are taking steps to address the problem. But many leaders recognize too late that business-as-usual practices have to be suspended.

Crises require special handling. Most routine corporate events can be handled by normal communications methods through traditional channels following usual procedures. But when a company determines that it faces a crisis it is important to recognize that routine decision-making processes, routine communications, and routine timeframes can be counterproductive.

In particular, time is an enemy in a crisis. The sooner a company is seen as taking the event seriously, acting responsibly, and communicating clearly, the more likely it is that the company will emerge with its reputation and operations intact. Former *Wall Street Journal* reporter Ronald Alsop, in his book *The 18 Immutable Laws of Corporate Reputation*, states that:

> Crises aren't like fine wines; they don't improve with age. A communications void is highly dangerous during a time of crisis. Silence gives critics time to gain the upper hand and reinforces the public's suspicion that a company must be guilty. Without information from the company, rumors and misinformation can proliferate fast.[10]

The Golden Hour of Crisis Response

Crisis communicators speak of the "Golden Hour" of crisis response: the early phases when the opportunity to influence the outcome is the greatest. The Golden Hour is a metaphor from emergency medicine, first coined by Dr. R. Adams Cowley, a veteran of the U.S. Army Medical Corps, who discovered that wounded soldiers who were brought to a field hospital within an hour of suffering their wounds had a very high likelihood of survival. Soldiers with the same wounds brought in just a half-hour later had a significantly lower probability of survival. The difference was literally a matter of life and death. Dr. Cowley applied this lesson to civilian emergency medicine, and coined the term "Golden Hour" in 1961.[11] It is now an accepted standard in trauma care in dealing with, for instance, heart attacks. The Golden Hour refers not to a precise duration but rather to the observation that incremental delays have a greater than incremental impact on the likelihood of success.

This has translated into a relatively well-established principle in dealing with the news media: fielding an inquiry from a newspaper reporter at 10 a.m. and responding definitively by 11 a.m. can allow one to prevent a story from being published, or significantly to shape what the story will look like (as we saw in the *New York Times* inquiry about a suicide that opens this chapter). But waiting until 5:30 to respond to a 10 a.m. inquiry significantly diminishes the likelihood that a story can be shaped: by then the story has already been written and edited, and at best a company can insert a paragraph refuting the central accusation. But the accusation and all the commentary based on it will be in the story.

A similar principle applies beyond the media, where incremental delays can result in greater than incremental setbacks with other critical stakeholders, from employees to investors to customers. And in a world of 24-hour news and instantaneous social media, and where seemingly disparate stakeholder groups are linked electronically, a setback with one stakeholder group can quickly cascade to setbacks with others. This is especially the case when the crisis is being fed by an adversary who can embarrass the organization. Whether the adversary is a lawyer bringing suit, a union organizer, a community activist, or an ambitious regulator, the adversary often counts on organizations taking excessive time to respond. This makes the adversary's job much easier, allowing the adversary to begin a cascade of negative news among many stakeholders before the company can develop a sufficient response, at which point it may be too late for the company.

A good example of effective crisis response was given by McDonald's Corporation when its 60-year-old Chairman and Chief Executive Officer, James Cantalupo, died of a heart attack on the morning of April 19, 2004 while attending McDonald's Worldwide Owner/Operator Convention in Orlando, Florida. Mr. Cantalupo had been instrumental in reconfiguring McDonald's menu away from the seemingly unhealthy focus on fats and super-sized portions to more healthy alternatives such as salads and grilled chicken.

At 8:07 a.m. that morning (East Coast time) the company issued a press release announcing his death. When the stock market opened at 9:30 a.m. the stock traded down on heavy volume. There was a significant risk that attention would be drawn to the irony of Mr. Cantalupo's suffering a fatal heart attack while spearheading the move away from McDonald's fat-rich menu. Indeed, some early news accounts made just that point.

But at 10:42 a.m., just over two and a half hours after announcing Mr. Cantalupo's death, and just 72 minutes after the stock market opened, McDonald's announced that Charlie Bell, President and Chief Operating Officer, would be the new CEO, and Andrew J. McKenna, the Board's presiding director, would be the non-executive Chairman of the Board. The analysts focused on McDonald's' future rather than its tragedy, the media coverage was factual and forward-looking, and the stock quickly recovered.

The next morning's *Wall Street Journal* praised McDonald's ability to make and announce its decision quickly:

> The swift decision gave immediate reassurance to employees, franchisees, and investors that the fast-food giant had a knowledgeable leader in place who can provide continuity and carry out the company's strategies. It may also shift any spotlight away from McDonald's high-cholesterol, fat-rich foods and prove a savvy public relations move.[12]

The *Wall Street Journal* noted that such quick action is uncharacteristic of large companies. It quoted Jay Lorch, a Harvard Business School professor: "The speed with which they moved is exactly what you would expect to happen, but few companies are as prepared as McDonald's appears to have been for this calamity."[13]

McDonald's had a clear succession plan in place. Its directors moved quickly to implement the plan and announce the new CEO. If they had delayed, the company would have been subject to continued stock volatility as well as speculation about its future and its strategy of emphasizing more healthy choices in its restaurants, and would even have risked late-night comics pointing out the irony of the manner of Mr. Cantalupo's death. Worse, its worldwide franchisees, gathered at the convention where Mr. Cantalupo had died, would have seen a leaderless organization. McDonald's prompt actions and announcements prevented the turmoil that a delayed appointment and announcement would have caused, and allowed the company and its stakeholders to focus on the future.

Another company that learned the value of the Golden Hour is Boeing Co. From 2002 to 2004 Boeing was involved in a series of scandals involving the recruitment of Pentagon officials for senior positions in the company while these officials were still overseeing Boeing and other defense contractors for the government. Eventually, Boeing's Chief Executive Officer, Phil Condit, was forced to leave the company. He was replaced by retired vice chairman Harry Stonecipher, who promptly instituted a revised *Code of Conduct*. The new single-page *Code* includes the following sentence: "Employees will not engage in conduct or activity that may raise questions as to the company's honesty, impartiality, reputation, or otherwise cause embarrassment to the company."[14] It also requires that employees promptly report any unethical conduct.

Ironically, soon after implementing the *Code*, Mr. Stonecipher conducted a romantic affair with a female subordinate. A fellow employee, following the *Code*'s requirements, reported his suspicions to the company's Board, which promptly investigated. Mr. Stonecipher was immediately fired for violating his own code. In a single news cycle the company announced the CEO's departure, and he was gone. The company was able to get on with life with minimal distraction and harm to its reputation.

Paradoxically, both McDonald's and Boeing's quick responses took place in the absence of CEO input; the decisions were directed by their boards.

Why are McDonald's and Boeing's responses so uncommon, and the Exxon/New Orleans kinds of response so prevalent? One big reason is the tendency of CEOs and others in positions of authority to assume that they can manage their companies in bad times the same way they do in good times. But many leaders misjudge their own ability to control the course of events, and wait too long before suspending business as usual. Indeed, Alsop describes all-too-typical corporate behavior:

> Many leaders misjudge their own ability to control the course of events, and wait too long before suspending business as usual.

> Too often companies become complacent. They begin to feel almost invincible. Their financial performance is strong, and they fall into the trap of believing they have little to worry about. Then they're blindsided by a crisis and don't have a response plan in place. Flailing around and looking helpless aren't inspiring to your stakeholders.[15]

> Flailing around and looking helpless aren't inspiring to your stakeholders.

One of the critical roles for corporate communication professionals is to help their organizations understand how core stakeholders are likely to perceive a company's silence or inaction in the wake of a crisis. As the keepers of corporate reputation—and in many cases also keepers of a corporation's conscience—corporate communication professionals need to be on guard to the common institutional barriers to taking crises seriously.

This need for speed is not intended to suggest that a company should communicate reflexively or without careful thought. But it is an argument for establishing a quick response capability with preauthorization to suspend business as usual in order to be able to respond quickly in the aftermath of a non-routine event that risks undesired visibility.

> Perfect is the enemy of the good-enough.

In many ways, the perfect is the enemy of the good-enough: companies often want to be certain of every fact, to dot every I and cross every T, before making any statement. This abundance of caution can be a healthy impulse in normal times. But in the earliest phases of a crisis, something less than perfect, so long as it is accurate, is better than silence. Sometimes just an acknowledgement that the company is aware of a problem, is studying it, and will take appropriate action is sufficient.

> Sometimes just an acknowledgement that the company is aware of a problem, is studying it, and will take appropriate action is sufficient.

One quick test of when to respond in a crisis is to ask these questions:

- Are others speaking about us now, shaping the perception among those who matter to us? Will they be soon?
- Will those who matter to us expect us to do or say something now? Will silence be seen as indifference to the harm caused, as arrogance, or as guilt?
- If we wait, will we lose the ability to determine the outcome compared to acting or communicating now?
- What is the minimum amount we can say now that shows we are taking this problem seriously? That we are not indifferent to the harm caused?

TEN AVOIDABLE MIS-STEPS

There are ten predictable, avoidable behaviors that organizations typically engage in when a crisis breaks that get in the way of effective and rapid response. The behaviors have two negative effects. First, they make the crisis worse; second, they distract attention from solving the underlying problem, while lulling management into a false sense that the crisis is being dealt with.

The ten mis-steps are:

1. Ignore the problem: Management seems unaware and is surprised by a crisis that others saw coming, or that they themselves were warned about but chose not to take seriously.
2. Deny the severity of the problem: Management takes only minimal steps to address a problem, or downplays its significance, resulting in an inadequate response.

3. Compartmentalize the problem or solution: Management mistakenly assumes that others will appreciate its own functional division of labor, and defines the crisis or its solution as specific to a department, division, geographic region, or other compartment, while the stakeholders who matter most view the problem as an enterprise-wide crisis and expect an enterprise-wide response.

4. Tell misleading half-truths: Management tries to misdirect attention by speaking literally true statements with the intention of misleading, which challenge adversaries or whistle-blowers to uncover the full story.

5. Lie: Management tells a deliberate untruth with the intention of deceiving.

6. Tell only part of the story; let the story dribble out: Management reveals only the smallest amount of bad news it feels compelled to on any given day, but repeats the cycle on subsequent days, leading to multiple bad news cycles. The operative principle of telling bad news is to bundle bad news into as few news cycles as possible, preferably just one.

7. Assign blame: Rather than taking meaningful steps to solve the problem, management tries to redirect attention away from itself and to someone else.

8. Over-confess: Managements unaccustomed to criticism often implode publicly and turn public statements into private therapeutic sessions in which they unburden themselves of pent-up frustrations.

9. Panic and paralysis: Work grinds to a halt as management and employees focus exclusively on the fear or the thrill of the crisis, and companies suffer operational or financial harm from reduced productivity.

10. Shoot the messenger: Management creates a culture of punishing those who bring problems to their attention, resulting in problems being buried and compounded.[16]

Corporate communication professionals need to be on guard against these behaviors, and find ways to overcome them quickly.

■ ■ ■

CONTROL THE COMMUNICATION AGENDA

Speed is one ingredient of effective communication; robust content and effective distribution of the messages are others. One of the goals of crisis communication is to influence the way key stakeholders think and feel, and what those stakeholders know and do. To do so requires controlling the communication agenda, and not allowing the media, adversaries, or the rumor mill define a company's situation.

So crisis communication needs to be grounded in the desired outcome: the end state in the audiences with whom you're communicating.

Content needs to be crafted sufficiently to influence the audience's frames of reference. And the channels through which communication takes place needs to be sufficient to reach audiences effectively.

Once you have determined the goals of communicating and the core messages, the process of communicating is relatively straightforward. Once you've decided what you want to say and to whom, the rule for doing so is the following:

- Tell it all
- Tell it fast
- Tell 'em what you're doing about it
- Tell 'em when it's over
- Get back to work

Tell it all

This admonition should not be confused with an instruction to bare the corporate soul and confess every sin and weakness you know of.

"Tell it all" means bundle everything that will inevitably be known into the smallest number of news cycles possible. Rather than letting bad news drip out over time, take all the pain all at once.

Further, "Tell it all" should not be confused with saying more than you know, are legally permitted to say, or find it prudent to say. For example, if the crisis is still unfolding, tell only what you know, but all of what you know. If the extent of damage hasn't been determined, don't speculate; say that the extent of damage hasn't been determined. If you have a contractual obligation to keep certain information confidential, don't break the contract. If you know the names of people killed or injured, but the next of kin haven't been notified, don't disclose the names. But in each case you will be advantaged by saying what you *do* know and the reasons you are not disclosing; e.g., "The extent of damage is still being investigated by the fire marshal, and we'll let you know as soon as the investigation is concluded;" or "The identities of those killed are known, but we will not release the names until next of kin have been notified."

Tell it fast

It is common for companies to want to delay disclosure of bad news until the last possible moment. The risk, of course, is that others will be talking about the problems before the company does, and that the negative news can take on a life of its own.

"Tell it fast" says that to the degree possible, it is better to be the one who brings the news to the public's attention, rather than reacting to someone else's account of the news. Even when the company isn't the first to disclose, "Tell it fast" suggests that speed of communications throughout a crisis is critical: it keeps the company in the driver's seat and prevents the story from getting out of hand. And to the degree that you are susceptible to rumors—which, in a crisis, is often—"Tell it fast" allows you to control or eliminate damaging rumors.

The manner in which one communicates quickly should be based on the specifics of the particular crisis. It could include a press release; it could be an employee meeting or memo; it could be an interview with a reporter. Or it could be all or none of these. But whatever the specific communication vehicle (or combination of several), the tactical goal is to speak completely and quickly so as to take the high ground and control the communications agenda.

TELL 'EM WHAT YOU'RE DOING ABOUT IT

It is important, as early in the communication process as possible, to outline the reme-dial steps that are underway to resolve the underlying issues in the crisis. If such steps haven't yet been determined, it is sufficient to outline the processes being put in place; e.g., "We have launched an investigation, which we expect to be completed soon, to discover the cause of the problem and to identify solutions."

Many companies (and many lawyers) are reluctant to talk about steps the company is taking because there's so much uncertainty in the early phases of a crisis. They need to overcome this reticence, and to know that the public will expect to be told not only what happened, but what's being done about it.

TELL 'EM WHEN IT'S OVER

Similarly, many companies are reluctant to open old wounds when a crisis is resolved. This instinct, while understandable, is counterproductive. There will always be some people whose last interaction with the company was in the context of a crisis. If the crisis is past, and the company has recovered, it needs to update those who matter (and the databases) to let the world know that the crisis has been solved.

GET BACK TO WORK

Once the crisis team has been assembled and communication is being handled, don't let the crisis distract attention from the important work of running the company. Too many people want to be crisis managers. The tasks should be clearly assigned; people not directly involved in the crisis communication should be directed to return to prior duties.

Even those who are needed in some element of crisis communication, such as senior executives, eventually need to stop communicating and get back to work. This includes the CEO, who has many other claims on his or her time than an exclusive focus on the crisis.

CHECKLIST FOR CRISIS RESPONSE PREPAREDNESS

Are you prepared for a crisis facing your organization? Here's a checklist to help you under-stand your level of preparedness:

1. Have a clear sense of what constitutes a crisis, and know how to mobilize energy and re-sources quickly.
2. Develop an early warning mechanism/rapid response capability.
3. Designate a senior executive as responsible for crisis preparedness and response.

4. Make this executive accountable and provide sufficient resources to conduct a thorough analysis of vulnerabilities, crisis response strategies, and crisis implementation.

5. Pre-authorize this executive to take initial response steps without going through usual corporate approval processes.

6. Test the system with wargames, table top exercises, and other processes that challenge leaders to make tough decisions and act quickly.

7. Remember that the best plan won't help if executives don't know what to do.

8. Recognize when business as usual needs to be suspended. A quick test:
   - Are others speaking about you now, shaping the perception about you among your key stakeholders? Will they be soon?
   - Are the stakeholders who matter expecting you to take prompt action or to communicate with them now?
   - Will silence be seen as indifference to the harm the crisis is causing?
   - Will delay in taking prompt action provide an opening for your adversaries or others to define your involvement negatively?

9. Control the agenda: Don't let the media, adversaries, or the rumor mill define your situation.

10. Keep in mind the Golden Hour of crisis response: incremental delays cause greater-than-incremental harm to reputation.

11. Develop messages and tactics with a goal in mind: how do you want your key stakeholders to think and feel, and what do you want them to know and do?

12. In a crisis, assure both self-awareness and situational awareness:

13. Coordinate all functions of the crisis response with frequent meetings/conference calls.

14. Correct mistakes early.

15. Understand what your stakeholders, adversaries, the media, and others are saying about you.

16. Keep your focus on the goal: influencing stakeholders. Decisions become clear when you keep stakeholders in mind.

■ ■ ■

DEALING WITH RUMORS

A challenge facing nearly every organization in a crisis is the circulation of rumors that, unaddressed, can cause significant reputational harm, sometimes even more damage than the crisis event itself. (The suicide example that began this chapter is an example of such a rumor.)

> Rumors are particularly damaging because they often seem nebulous.

Rumors are particularly damaging because they often seem nebulous. It is hard to figure out where a rumor started, how it is building momentum, and where it might end. And people tend to pass rumors along, whether or not they actually believe them.

Sometimes rumors are deliberately planted by people who are out to hurt a company or to profit from its distress, such as Wall Street short-sellers, disgruntled former employees, community activists, competitors, and people suing a company.

Once started, rumors can spread among employees, customers, suppliers, lenders, investors, and regulators. Rumors can feed other rumors, and rumors from several different sources can be combined in the retelling from one person to another. And when rumors hit the newspapers, television news programs, radio or the Internet they get formalized and are then seen to be an accurate rendering of reality. Worse, people who may have been skeptical of the original rumor, on seeing or hearing the same thing in the newspapers or on television, often conclude that the news account proves the accuracy of the rumor.

Rumors can also become self-fulfilling. For example, a bank that is completely sound can quickly get into trouble if rumors circulate that it is in financial distress. Depositors can cause a run; customers can avoid dealing with the bank, and eventually it will find itself in financial distress.

And if the rumor is about some kind of malfeasance or inappropriate activity, it commands a high level of credibility. As noted in the best-selling book *A Civil Action* by Jonathan Harr, "It is the nature of disputes that a forceful accusation by an injured party often has more rhetorical power than a denial."[17]

The sociologist Tomatsu Shibutani notes that rumors arise from uncertainty, from the absence of context and concrete information by which those affected by a crisis may understand its significance. Whenever an information vacuum exists, rumors will arise to fill the void. Shibutani elaborates:

> Rumors arise from uncertainty.

> The discrepancy between information needed to come to terms with a changing environment and what is provided by formal ... channels constitutes the critical condition of rumor construction. Demand for news may arise in an effort to cope with an unexpected event or in sustained collective tension, when [people] are mobilized to act but have no clear-cut goals ... When activity is interrupted for want of adequate information, frustrated [people] must piece together some kind of definition, and rumor is the collective transaction through which they try to fill this gap. Far from being pathological, rumor is part and parcel of the efforts of [people] to come to terms with the exigencies of life.[18]

Rumors often ameliorate anxiety, uncertainty, and fear, especially when people feel that a crisis directly affects them. This is commonly the case in employee populations when rumors about layoffs, cutbacks, restructuring, hiring freezes, benefit reductions, or other changes arise. Rumors allow employees to express collective frustration and validate each other's fears. Rumors can also be subversive, providing an alternative communication channel and establishing an unofficial culture.

Because crises are by nature characterized by uncertainty, rumors are a fact of life in crises. The good news is that preventive and remedial actions are possible, allowing professional communicators to minimize the damage from rumors, or even to stop them in their tracks (as happened in the suicide example that opened this chapter).

> One of the important roles corporate communication professionals fill is to be an early-warning and rapid-response mechanism for rumor control.

One of the important roles corporate communication professionals fill is to be an early-warning and rapid-response mechanism for rumor control. But being effective in preventing or controlling rumors requires an understanding of the psychological and sociological factors that drive people to listen to, pass along, and believe rumors. More importantly, being effective requires companies to act in counter-instinctive ways: to make and communicate decisions faster than they may be accustomed to making them, and to be more forthcoming with information than they otherwise would be.

> Paradoxically, telling more and telling it faster has the effect of eliminating a rumor.

Paradoxically, telling more and telling it faster has the effect of eliminating a rumor. Most executives are uncomfortable with the notion that they must affirmatively disclose information in order to stop the flow of information. It is a paradoxical situation, but the results will pay off.

Fighting forest fires is a good analogy. Sometimes it is impossible to fight a forest fire using direct methods such as building a firebreak—a cleared area around the area that is in flames in order to stop a fire from spreading. Firefighters may then engage in a practice called "backburning," where they set a fire to remove fuel (for example, brush) between the spreading edge of a wildfire and the control line established by the fire commanders on the scene.[19]

Just as it is paradoxical to start a fire to put out a fire, so too is communicating to shut down communication. But as with fighting a forest fire, it works, and sometimes it is the only thing that works. The backburn removes the fuel that would feed a fire, just as timely and robust communication removes the fuel—uncertainty and fear—that feeds a rumor. But like a backburn, the communication must be done at the right time and in the right way. Therefore, effective rumor control requires a high degree of both courage and discipline to recognize that counter-instinctive actions in the short term have a predictable, though paradoxical, long-term benefit of preventing rumors from proliferating.

The Morphing of Rumors: How They Change over Time

One of the defining elements of rumors is that they are not static. As a rumor passes from person to person, it tends to change in predictable ways, through a process that social psychologists call leveling, sharpening, and assimilation.

In the 1940s two Harvard University psychologists, Gordon W. Allport and Leo Postman, conducted experiments on how the content of rumors changes as the rumor passes from person to person. They concluded that as a rumor travels, it tends to grow shorter, more concise, and more easily grasped and told:

In subsequent versions, more and more original details are *leveled* out, fewer words are used, and fewer items are mentioned ...

As leveling of details proceeds, the remaining details are necessarily *sharpened*. Sharpening refers to the selective perception, retention, and reporting of a few details from the originally larger context. Although sharpening, like leveling, occurs in every series of reproductions, the same items are not always emphasized. Much depends on the constitution of the group in which the tale is transmitted. Those items will be selected for sharpening which are of particular interest to the reporter ...

Assimilation ... has to do with the powerful attractive force exerted upon the rumor by habits, interests, and sentiments existing in the reader's mind ... Items become sharpened or leveled to fit the leading motif of the story, and they become consistent with this motif in such a way as to make the resultant story more coherent.[20]

Allport and Postman emphasize that while leveling, sharpening, and assimilation are independent mechanisms, they function simultaneously. The result is that a story becomes more coherent, more interesting, and therefore more believable with each retelling. But as in a game of "telephone," later participants in the chain are likely to experience the rumor differently than earlier participants. Indeed, Allport and Postman's conclusions were based, in part, on their own experiments on the "telephone" phenomenon.

But unlike the game of "telephone," rumors do more than simply level, sharpen, and assimilate the stories contained in them. Participants in rumor transmission have an investment both in the content of the rumor and in the status that transmitting the rumor conveys. In particular, some people see retelling a rumor as a status-enhancing activity. Sociologists refer to this as a process of exchange, where information is a commodity with value, and the sender derives status from being seen to be "in the know." The French sociologist Jean-Nöel Kapferer explains:

By taking others into his confidence and sharing a secret with them, the transmitter's personal importance is magnified. He comes across as the holder of precious knowledge, a sort of front-runner scout—creating a favorable impression in the minds of those he informs.[21]

The sender therefore has an interest not merely in passing the information along, but also in persuading the receiver to believe and act on the rumor. But often in order to achieve desired status the transmitter needs to enhance the details even more than the leveling and sharpening that Allport and Postman found.

And as a rumor changes with each telling, there is a reason for each transmitter to modify, or assimilate, the details of the rumor in ways that increase his or her status. Indeed, rumors cannot continue without exaggeration. This is a process known as snowballing, where the rumor's importance seems to grow with each telling. According to Kapferer,

Exaggeration is common when it comes to rumors. It is not some kind of pathological or aberrant phenomenon, but rather a logical consequence of communication. Rumors can be viewed as a process of commodity exchange. In the rumor process, once information is shared among too many people, its value seriously diminishes, and the rumor thus stops short. The end of the rumor does not mean disbelief: it means silence.

Snowballing is the only way for a rumor to last. It is a necessary condition of rumor persistence. Indeed, identical repetition kills the news value of all information. Were a rumor repeated word for word, without any modification whatsoever, throughout its diffusion process, its death would be thereby accelerated. If everyone's friends have already heard it, or everyone imagines that they have, nobody would then dare speak of it again: for there would be a high risk of receiving no reward, or worse, of receiving negative reinforcement.

On the contrary, the permanent addition of new details, the systematic inflation of figures (at the outset, one dead man; then five; then one hundred, etc.), amplification and exaggeration are value-boosting devices. They make possible the continuation of communication within a group. Snowballing is not some innate or odd trait that rumors have: a rumor, i.e., a contagious process of information exchange, would not last long without this value-added process.[22]

It is regrettably common for management teams in a crisis simply to dismiss the rumor mill's significance, or to insist that employees get back to work and pay no attention to rumors. This is counterproductive. It is precisely when people are feeling vulnerable that they seek reassurance. And if management does not take their concerns seriously, people will find reassurance from those around them.

The result of inattention to the emotional needs of external stakeholders can be reduced demand for a company's products, decline in stock price, negative media coverage, and increased regulatory scrutiny. Inattention to the emotional needs of employees can include significant distraction, reduced productivity, and—through leveling, sharpening, assimilating, and snowballing—the transmission of ever-more damaging, distracting, and counterproductive rumors. Being a closed environment, employee populations tend to be rumor-incubators, especially when management tends to withhold important information. Such internal rumor processes are sometimes seen by employees to be the only credible sources of information about the company, in contrast to what employees consider to be propaganda from official sources.

Preventing Rumors

Rumors arise and are believed when official information is lacking or is not believed. Rumors can be avoided—along with their attendant negative consequences—if companies recognize the need to provide sufficient clarifying detail and information as early as possible in the life of a disruptive event. Kapferer makes this point dramatically:

"They constitute an informational black market."[23] And the way to prevent a black market is to create a robust legitimate market: in the case of rumors, by diminishing the demand for information, and diminishing its value, by increasing its supply.

So what is a rumor? In *The Psychology of Rumor* Allport and Postman define it as follows:

> A rumor, as we shall use the term, is a specific (or topical) proposition for belief, passed along from person to person, usually by word of mouth, without secure standards of evidence being present.
>
> The implication in any rumor is always that some truth is being communicated. This implication holds even though the teller prefaces his tidbit with the warning, "it is only a rumor, but I heard …"[24]

The most important element of this definition is that a rumor exists in the absence of secure standards of evidence, but is taken by the recipient to be true. But in the presence of secure standards of evidence a rumor will not arise. Allport and Postman elaborate:

> Rumor thrives only in the absence of "secure standards of evidence." This criterion marks off rumor from news, distinguishes "old wives' tales" from science, and separates gullibility from knowledge. True, we cannot always decide easily when it is that secure standards of evidence are present. For this reason we cannot always tell whether we are listening to fact or fantasy.[25]

Allport and Postman give a compelling, if now somewhat out of date, example of how a rumor can be prevented by providing verifiable factual information before rumors have a chance to start:

> Rumors thrive on the lack of news. The almost total absence of fear-inspired rumors in Britain during the darkest days of the blitz was due to the people's conviction that the government was giving full and accurate news of the destruction and that they, therefore, knew the worst. When people are sure they know the worst, they are unlikely to darken the picture further by inventing unnecessary bogies to explain their anxieties to themselves.[26]

This latter concept—that when people are convinced they know the worst they are unlikely to darken the picture further in order to justify their own anxieties to themselves—can be of critical importance in situations that affect people over time. When people—whether as employees facing corporate downsizing or whose company is for sale, or investors in a corporation under investigation—do not believe they know the worst, they look for the slightest scrap of information to validate their fears. But when employees know what will

> When people are convinced they know the worst they are unlikely to darken the picture further in order to justify their own anxieties to themselves.

happen next, what the worst case is likely to be, or that the worst is in fact over, they are less likely to be driven by rumors or look for hidden meanings.

In short, ambiguity provokes anxiety, and anxiety prompts rumors. Conversely, absence of ambiguity reduces anxiety, and in turn diminishes the strength of rumors. Allport and Postman observe: *"Unguided by objective evidence, most people will make their prediction in accordance with their subjective preference."*[27] And in the presence of objective evidence, it is possible for people to move beyond their subjective preference, even their subjective fears.

For crisis communicators, the challenge is to help clients and employers summon the courage to disclose what is necessary to provide objective evidence that helps people move beyond their subjective preferences. The good news is that Allport and Postman provide a way to do so.

Controlling Rumors — Mathematically

Fortunately, rumors tend to follow predictable patterns, and intervention in specific ways can help an organization overcome, or even kill, a rumor.

The breakthrough work on rumors—including how to kill false rumors—was conducted during World War II by Allport and Postman. Much of their work was classified, but after the war it was published, first in *Public Opinion Quarterly* in 1946, and then in their 1947 book, *The Psychology of Rumor*. One of their most significant contributions to the study of rumors was a mathematical formula that described the way a rumor works. The formula further suggests ways to control or eliminate a rumor.

The two factors that influence a rumor are (1) its importance to the listener and (2) its ambiguity. In order to control a rumor, one must either diminish the level of importance one assigns to the rumor if true, or eliminate the ambiguity around the factual basis of the rumor, or both. Eliminating ambiguity is particularly important if the rumor is in fact completely false. But even where the rumor has some mixture of truth and fiction, eliminating ambiguity about the fiction can help control the rumor and ground it in reality. Once an unambiguous reality is established, it may be possible to reduce the level of importance of the content of the rumor, thereby diminishing its transmission to others.

Take, for example, the suicide story that began this chapter. Through a process of leveling, sharpening, assimilation, and snowballing, the *New York Times* reporter had presented Fred with a rumor: that a trader had committed suicide because he was being investigated for insider trading. Simply denying the rumor would not have been persuasive to the reporter. But Fred was able to provide an unambiguous alternative explanation: that there had been a routine compliance audit of the trader's department, and that the trader's father had described the suicide as following an "emotional family encounter." Both those pieces of specific detail reduced ambiguity about the cause of the suicide. And because the link between job performance and the suicide was effectively broken, the importance of the rumor declined significantly.

Allport and Postman summarize these two factors of importance and ambiguity:

> Rumor travels when events have importance in the lives of individuals,
> and when the news received about them is either lacking or subjectively

ambiguous. The ambiguity may arise from the fact that the news is not clearly reported, or from the fact that conflicting versions of the news have reached the individual, or from his incapacity to comprehend the news he receives.[28]

The ambiguity can further arise when a company's credibility is weak, when the company sends mixed messages, and when people have become conditioned to distrust what the company says. In such cases, even when the company is telling the truth, people are disinclined to believe it. Allport and Postman observe, "Most important of all ... rumor will race when individuals distrust the news that reaches them."[29]

Allport and Postman elaborate how the two factors of importance and ambiguity work together, and note that there is a mathematical relationship:

THE BASIC LAW OF RUMOR

The two essential conditions of importance and ambiguity seem to be related to rumor transmission in a roughly quantitative manner. A formula for the intensity of rumor might be written as follows:

$$R \sim i \times a$$

In words this formula means that the amount of rumor in circulation will vary with the importance of the subject to the individuals concerned (i) *times* the ambiguity of the evidence pertaining to the topic at issue (a). The relation between importance and ambiguity is not additive but multiplicative, for if either importance or ambiguity is *zero*, there is *no* rumor. Ambiguity alone does not sustain rumor. Nor does importance.[30]

Because the relationship between importance and ambiguity is multiplicative, an incremental decline in either can result in a greater than incremental decline in the scope of the rumor.

Here are some ways to think about the model quantitatively. The elements of the Allport and Postman Model of Rumor Dynamics are:

- $R \sim i \times a$, where:
- R is the rumor: its reach, intensity, duration, and the degree that people will rely upon it;
- i is the *importance* of the rumor to the hearer or reader, if true;
- and a is the level of *ambiguity* or uncertainty surrounding the rumor.

In other words, the reach, intensity, duration, and reliance on a rumor is roughly equivalent to the importance one attaches to the rumor if true, multiplied by ambiguity surrounding the rumor, especially surrounding its denial. Note that simply denying a rumor does not eliminate ambiguity; it may even increase it. Rather, eliminating ambiguity requires giving an affirmative factual demonstration that gives people a basis for not relying on the rumor; in Allport and Postman's words, providing objective evidence sufficient to overcome people's subjective preference.

Here's how the math works. Assume a scale of 0 to 10, 0 being non-existent and 10 being certainty. If both importance and ambiguity are high, say 10, the scope of the rumor will be quite strong:

$$R \sim i \times a$$
$$R \sim 10 \times 10$$
$$R \sim 100$$

In other words, when both the importance and ambiguity are at their highest, ten, the scope of the rumor will be at its highest, 100. But reduce just one of the factors and the scope of the rumor declines considerably. Assume that importance remains high, 10, but that ambiguity can be reduced to 3. Apply the model as follows:

$$R \sim i \times a$$
$$R \sim 10 \times 3$$
$$R \sim 30$$

The scope of the rumor has declined from 100 to 30, or by more than two-thirds. Reduce both factors and the decline is even more dramatic. Say both are 3:

$$R \sim i \times a$$
$$R \sim 3 \times 3$$
$$R \sim 9$$

Because anything multiplied by 0 equals 0, if either ambiguity or importance is reduced to zero the rumor disappears.

The scope of the rumor has reduced from 100 when importance and ambiguity were at 10, to just 9 when each is reduced to 3.

Because anything multiplied by 0 equals 0, if either ambiguity or importance is reduced to 0 the rumor disappears. Assume that importance is still 10, but ambiguity is completely eliminated, at 0:

$$R \sim i \times a$$
$$R \sim 10 \times 0$$
$$R \sim 0$$
The scope of the rumor is zero, and the rumor disappears.

In practical terms, this formula lets a professional communicator and a management team do several powerful things. Knowing that importance and ambiguity drive a rumor, a company can be far more efficient in identifying what it needs to do and say than if it wasn't so aware. Second, knowing the formula gives clients and bosses confidence that they can influence the interpretation of events. The formula empowers management to focus communications in ways that can have impact on how the company is being perceived. Best of all, the formula can disarm negative information, killing a rumor and preventing further damage.

Dynamics of the News Cycle in Controlling a Rumor

When applying the $R \sim i \times a$ formula, one critical element of success is how early one can influence the two factors that drive rumors: importance and ambiguity. Corporate managements, however, have little appreciation for the need to pre-empt rumors, or for the seemingly arbitrary and somewhat confusing deadlines under which journalists work. The Allport and Postman model empowers crisis communicators and companies to disclose more sooner, thereby controlling the rumor and decreasing the likelihood of a negative story.

THE RULE OF 45 MINUTES, 6 HOURS, 3 DAYS, AND TWO WEEKS ...

But it is possible to persuade management to make decisions and to communicate quickly. There are specific points in a news cycle where it is possible to kill a negative story or control a partially accurate story. Miss one of these points and you will suffer reputational damage. Worse, the distance between the points, the intensity of the crisis and the potential for reputational harm, grow in almost an exponential fashion as bad news spreads.

And while these points result from careful observation of how the news cycles and the rumor formula interact, the same orders of magnitude apply beyond the media, when progressively larger groups of people, over time, become invested in a rumor.

The First 45 Minutes

Give or take, you have maximum influence on the outcome of a story in the first moments after the rumor arises. During this time, only a small number of people, and possibly only one reporter, know about a rumor or are working on a story. If you follow the $R \sim i \times a$ formula to convince a reporter not to pursue a story in those first 45 minutes or so, the chances are high that the story will disappear. If, on the other hand, you are unable to respond to the reporter within that 45-minute timeframe, a number of powerful and negative things happen. First, the original reporter is likely to be working the phones trying to confirm the rumor, retelling it to sources who themselves can pass it along to other reporters. Second, given the proliferation of all-news television, radio, and the Internet, the chances are high that the story will break quickly. Third, in the retelling of the rumor from the first reporter to other sources and other reporters, the substance of the rumor will change. As the rumor becomes known in slightly different forms by many different people, it will become harder to find a definitive demonstration that unambiguously puts the rumor to rest.

Once the story breaks, many more reporters and bloggers become aware of and pursue it. It becomes much more difficult to control the story, if only because you now do not know precisely which reporters and bloggers have heard the rumor. Controlling the rumor now becomes less a function of persuasion—a private intervention with a single reporter—than of a public statement to influence your ultimate stakeholders. Because the original rumor has become a matter of public record, refuting it may require going public with the media and all your stakeholders, including direct communication with employees, customers, and regulators, among others.

6 Hours

Once a story crosses a wire service, is broadcast on television or radio, or becomes the subject of social networking/social media, it is, at least for the moment, out of your control. It may still be possible eventually to control the rumor and even to kill the story. But now it will be much more difficult. And it takes much longer. As a general rule, once a story is broadcast or spreading in the blogosphere you can expect to have at least six hours of negative coverage.

During these six hours, more and more reporters and blogs are coming to the story, and the story is being rebroadcast on competing media outlets. More and more people become aware of the rumor, and it grows exponentially. If a story appeared on one all-news cable television, the odds are high that it will appear on others and on the regular network or local TV news stations that night, and in drive-time radio. Your customers, employees, suppliers, competitors, regulators, and local community are made aware of the rumor and can begin to act on it, to your reputational and business disadvantage.

If, during this part of the cycle, you succeed in following the $R \sim i \times a$ formula in your public statements, the chances are high that the rumor can be controlled and the story will fade away. But by then the reputational damage may have been done.

If you are unable to control the story during this phase of the cycle, however, expect several days of negative news. And all the while, the processes of leveling, sharpening, assimilation, and snowballing are morphing the rumor into something far less manageable. And as more and more people learn about the rumor and become invested in it, it becomes harder and harder to reach them with the demonstration that puts the rumor to bed.

3 Days

Once a story hits the daily newspapers, you can expect it to be alive for several days. During the day the story appears there is likely to be television and radio commentary about the story, as well as gossip among your customers, employees, and competitors, with all the attendant distortion. The day following publication, newspapers that missed the story on day one are likely to pick it up as their own day 1 story. Even newspapers that carried the story on day 1 can carry a second-day story of reaction to the first story. And those who come late will themselves carry their own second-day stories on day 3.

During this period it is still possible to invoke the $R \sim i \times a$ formula successfully. But by this time you will have suffered several days of reputational damage and will have seen a much wider range of people exposed to the negative rumor, and many more versions of the rumor that may be inconsistent with each other. It becomes much harder to refute.

If you cannot control the story during these three days, expect at least two weeks of negative coverage.

2 Weeks

After the daily newspapers have had their run, there is still a further news cycle that includes weekly and semi-monthly magazines, industry trade publications, weekend newspaper wrap-up sections, and the Sunday morning talk shows. If a story has been alive for three days in the daily press it is unlikely to escape some notice from the weeklies and semi-monthlies. During this period you can still invoke the $R \sim i \times a$ formula to kill the rumor and prevent its further spread. But by then you will have suffered several weeks of negative coverage and reputational harm. And, as noted above, Kapferer points out that snowballing is the only way for a rumor to last. It is a necessary condition of rumor persistence. Identical repetition kills the news value of all information.

So for rumors to remain alive they need constantly to grow in strength and importance. The rumor in the second week of its life may bear no relationship to the rumor as it existed in the first 45 minutes, when only a few people knew about it and when the processes of exaggeration hadn't begun.

If, however, you are unable to control the story in this timeframe, expect continuous coverage, coverage of Clinton-Lewinsky or O. J. Simpson proportions. A company is unlikely to recover quickly from this kind of scrutiny.

All of this suggests that it is a fundamental mistake for corporations to make decisions about crisis communications on their own routine timelines. They need to recognize that however arbitrary and at times irrational news media deadlines may seem, companies can control their own destinies better if they can kill rumors as early in a news cycle as possible.

Successfully employing both the $R \sim i \times a$ formula and the "Rule of 45 minutes, 6 hours, 3 days, and two weeks ..." can help prevent reputational damage and keep the company focused on its own agenda. Failure to recognize the power of these two formulas puts the company at the mercy of the rumor mill, gossip mongers, and the irrational-seeming dynamics of the news media.

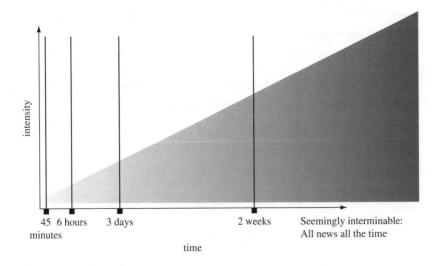

Figure 12.2   *(Illustration by Lisa Wagner)*

BEST PRACTICES

Effective crisis communication requires both discipline and flexibility, and a keen focus on the desired outcome of communication. Among the best practices are:

1   Know when to suspend business as usual: have a clear sense of what constitutes a crisis, and how to mobilize energy and resources quickly.

2   Get pre-authorization to use judgment quickly when dealing with incoming media inquiries.

3   Keep in mind the Golden Hour of crisis response: incremental delays cause greater-than-incremental harm to reputation.

4   Control the agenda: don't let the media, adversaries, or the rumor mill define your situation.

5   Develop messages and plan tactics with a goal in mind: how do you want your key stakeholders to think and feel, and what do you want them to know and do?

        When you've determined this, follow this process:

- Tell it all
- Tell it fast
- Tell 'em what you're doing about it
- Tell 'em when it's over
- Get back to work

6   Be attentive to rumors, and work to eliminate them as quickly as possible. Follow the formula for diminishing or eliminating rumors: $R \sim i \times a$.

7   Note that there are particular points in the cycle of bad news where you can take control of your destiny. The most powerful point is the first:

- 45 minutes
- 6 hours
- 3 days
- Two weeks

RESOURCES FOR FURTHER STUDY

- Logos Institute for Crisis Management & Executive Leadership: A research, publishing, and executive education organization run by coauthor Helio Fred Garcia, the Logos Institute provides a range of publications, some free of charge, that provide insight, analysis, and tools for managing and communicating about crises. See http://www.logosinstitute.net.
- The Lukaszewski Group: Run by premier crisis management advisor James E. Lukaszewski, the Lukaszewski Group provides:
  - Strategic guidance for senior management during crises and recovery
  - Hands-on management of critical crisis problems
  - Management leadership development during crises
  - Counsel on prevention, readiness, response, and recovery.
    See http://www.e911.com.
- Crisis Manager newsletter is a free electronic newsletter on current crisis topics published by crisis management advisor Richard Bernstein. See http://www.bernsteincrisismanagement.com/newsletter.html.

QUESTIONS FOR FURTHER DISCUSSION

1   If a crisis requires accelerating the decision-making processes, how can a communicator get management's attention early enough to suspend business as usual?

2   Why do incremental delays in managing and communicating in a crisis have a greater-than-incremental impact on the result?

3   How do rumors affect employee morale and customer demand for a company's products or services in a crisis?

4   What is the optimal role of corporate communication professionals in a crisis?

5   If a crisis is a turning point, how can a company act promptly enough to prevent the turning point moment from turning negative?

You cannot escape the responsibility of tomorrow by evading it today.

— *Abraham Lincoln*

CHAPTER

13 CORPORATE RESPONSIBILITY

By Anthony P. Ewing

■■■

NIKE'S JOURNEY

Nike, by 1996, had built a $5 billion sporting goods business and its "swoosh" logo embodied the celebrity-fuelled American sports culture worldwide. But the global brand that symbolized performance and excellence to millions would soon acquire some truly frightening attributes—greed, exploitation and indifference to human suffering.

Warning signs had appeared as early as 1992, with a *Harper's* magazine story criticizing Nike labor practices in Indonesia. However, the storm of anti-Nike publicity and activism which would inflict lasting damage on the company's reputation did not gather fully until 1995, when concerns over globalization and sweatshops converged, capturing the attention of activists, consumers, and policymakers. Between April and August 1995, the CBS television news magazine *Eye to Eye* ran a segment portraying Pakistani children as young as six stitching Adidas and Reebok soccer balls; U.S.-based labor activists publicized the plight of workers fired for organizing a union in a Salvadoran apparel factory supplying Gap and Eddie Bauer; and state officials freed enslaved immigrants from an El Monte, California, garment sweatshop.

It did not take long for Nike's business practices to become the focus of intense scrutiny. By 1996, media coverage of working conditions in Asian factories had turned Nike into the corporate poster child for the inequities of the global economy. The allegations were serious and attention grabbing. Indonesian factory workers making Nike sneakers were paid less than the local minimum wage and required to work excessive overtime. Pakistani children were stitching Nike soccer balls. Factory managers in Vietnam subjected workers to physical, verbal, and sexual abuse and exposed workers to toxic chemicals.

Negative press coverage prompted a broad range of constituencies important to Nike to question the company's motives and business practices. Columnists pointed out the enormous disparities between the price of celebrity-endorsed sneakers sold in the United States and the wages earned by the Indonesian women who made them. Activists accused Nike of ruthlessly exploiting workers and the environment in the company's global pursuit of profit at any cost. Students organized campus protests and boycotts of

Nike products, demanding that Nike disclose the location of its subcontracted factories worldwide. Government officials in North America and Europe introduced measures to ban imports of apparel and sporting goods made with child labor. Socially responsible investment funds, using the same strategies they had applied a decade earlier to encourage corporate divestment from Apartheid South Africa, began to screen their investment portfolios for labor and environmental policies, and submit shareholder resolutions urging companies to adopt codes of conduct for their suppliers. Meanwhile, the plaintiffs' bar in the United States began testing novel legal strategies to hold companies accountable in U.S. courts for the abusive treatment of workers in foreign markets.

Nike's initial response to the rising tide of criticism was instinctively defensive. At first, Nike spokespeople denied responsibility for the conduct of the company's suppliers and sought to discredit critics. The following is an excerpt from a Nike press release, responding to an allegation that Nike Air Jordan shoes were made in Indonesia for 14 cents an hour:

> One has to question the credibility of an individual whose organization is largely financed by labor unions opposed to free trade with developing nations. It's also too bad that Kathie Lee Gifford has found it necessary to avoid the media spotlight by pushing Michael Jordan into it.[1]

Nike's high-profile founder and chairman, Philip Knight, responded angrily to criticism of Nike's business practices through letters, press statements, speeches, and other public communications, arguing that Nike's presence in developing markets contributes to higher standards of living and that the company does its best to ensure that labor abuses do not occur. In the midst of growing pressure from universities to ensure minimum labor standards in the production of university-licensed apparel, and heated anti-Nike rhetoric on college campuses, Nike cancelled a contract with the University of Michigan in a dispute over applicable codes of conduct. Knight went so far as to withdraw a personal donation to his alma mater, the University of Oregon, publicly linking his decision to the University's criticism of Nike's labor practices.

But under steady pressure from stakeholders to take meaningful steps to address labor practices in its supply chain, Nike's approach began to change. By necessity and through much trial and error, Nike has become a corporate responsibility leader.

Nike's efforts to restore its reputation and demonstrate responsible practices parallel the emergence of corporate responsibility as a corporate discipline. Nike has implemented almost every innovation in the field. In 1992, the company adopted a code of conduct and set minimum labor standards for its suppliers. Since then, Nike has acknowledged responsibility for social and environmental conditions in its supply chain and changed the way it sources certain products to improve environmental performance and reduce the risk of labor violations. Executives have engaged in the public debate over globalization and in conversations with the company's critics. Nike joined governmental and industry-wide efforts to eliminate sweatshops and participates actively in multi-stakeholder partnerships to develop factory standard setting and monitoring mechanisms, and to support programs for workers and communities. Nike created the position of vice president for corporate responsibility to lead the company's efforts and signal the issue's importance. The company launched internal monitoring of its supply chain, expanded its compliance to include external third-party monitoring, and made its audit results public. Nike signed on to international corporate responsibility initiatives like the United Nations Global Compact and references international human rights, labor and environmental standards in its own standards. Nike began issuing a Corporate Responsibility Report on its social and environmental performance in 2001 and has become an advocate for common standards and reporting guidelines. In its most recent Corporate Responsibility Report, Nike sets quantifiable environmental and social performance targets that seek to connect corporate responsibility efforts with the company's return on investment.

> Corporate responsibility must evolve from being seen as an unwanted cost to being recognized as an intrinsic part of a healthy business model, an investment that creates competitive advantage and helps a company achieve profitable, sustainable growth.[2]

Communication has played a key role in every step of Nike's journey through the complicated terrain of corporate responsibility. At first, Nike did a poor job communicating corporate responsibility. In 1997, a *Wall Street Journal* article questioned whether Nike's public relations efforts on employment practices had done any good at all. By 1998, in a speech to the National Press Club, Nike CEO and Chairman Philip Knight was acknowledging the company's responsibility for the business practices of Asian manufacturers and announcing unilateral initiatives to adopt United States air-quality standards for foreign factories, raise the minimum working age to 18 for all footwear manufacturing workers, and permit the external monitoring of Nike suppliers. Nike's response to stakeholder pressure shifted from merely asserting, to actively demonstrating corporate responsibility.

The cultural change at Nike since then has been dramatic, a point the company readily acknowledges:

> From our early years up to the 1990s, the stakeholders we thought most about were athletes and consumers. In the 1990s, we ignored an emerging group of stakeholders. We learned a hard lesson ... Non-governmental organizations, trade unions and others have opened our eyes to new issues and viewpoints, and have enabled us to draw on their experience and expertise. This does not mean

that we will always agree with our stakeholders, but we know from experience that constructive engagement is usually the approach that brings about the best insight to the challenges we all have an interest in addressing.[3]

■ ■ ■

[S]ocial accountability is just another management art that corporations are going to have to learn. In the long run, the corporation that does the best job of managing its operations will also do the best job of adapting to social needs.

— Harold Burson[4]

■ ■ ■

Leading companies know that corporate responsibility matters.

Leading companies know that corporate responsibility matters. Meeting the non-financial expectations of stakeholders helps a company to manage risk, protect its reputation, attract and retain employees, grow its markets and improve its financial performance for shareholders.

Demonstrating corporate responsibility is a key challenge for business leaders, and effective communication is a central element of every successful corporate responsibility program.

Demonstrating corporate responsibility is a key challenge for business leaders, and effective communication is a central element of every successful corporate responsibility program. Most companies have not had the benefit of spending years at the center of the corporate responsibility debate, like Nike, learning what works and what does not.

This chapter is intended to provide an overview and practical guidance to business leaders, managers, and others who seek to better understand corporate responsibility and the challenges of communicating it.

CORPORATE RESPONSIBILITY

Definition

Corporate responsibility means meeting the expectations of stakeholders; it goes beyond philanthropy and legal compliance.

The first challenge is defining corporate responsibility. Companies use "corporate responsibility," "corporate social responsibility," "corporate citizenship," "business ethics," and "sustainability" interchangeably to describe corporate initiatives ranging from philanthropy, to legal compliance, to social and environmental programs.

According to economic theory, the sole responsibility of business is to maximize profits. As long as companies obey the law, there are no requirements or duties beyond the financial imperatives of the corporation. Any corporate activity that elevates societal interests above the interests of shareholders is an inappropriate use of corporate resources. In this orthodox view of the world, there is a strict separation of governmental and corporate responsibilities. An economist might argue that Nike has no responsibility for the activities of its independently owned suppliers and Nike's efforts to improve working conditions in its supply chain constitute mismanagement.

Few companies take such a narrow view. The definition of the role of business in society has evolved from a focus exclusively on shareholder returns, to the acknowledgment by business of a much broader group of corporate stakeholders and range of responsibilities.[5]

For some observers, corporate responsibility means companies simply follow the rules. Corporate responsibility comprises the ethics programs, codes of conduct, and compliance efforts necessary to meet legal and regulatory requirements.

> Compliance is just the starting point for any discussion of corporate responsibility.

But compliance is just the starting point for any discussion of corporate responsibility. When apparel companies were accused of running sweatshops in the early 1990s, a common corporate response was to deny any legal responsibility for factories the companies did not own. Legal precision did nothing to improve conditions for workers, however, and stakeholders were not satisfied. Corporate stakeholders expect legal compliance; increasingly they demand voluntary standard setting beyond the legal minimum. Smart companies realized that irrespective of legal liability, their credibility was tied to acknowledging responsibility for working conditions in their supply chain and setting standards that exceeded legal minimums. When U.S. companies manufacture products in developing countries, advocates and customers expect the companies to adhere to U.S. levels of health and safety and environmental protection in their foreign factories, even if local standards are lower or unenforced.

Many corporate responsibility initiatives go beyond compliance to set minimum standards for business conduct, and for social and environmental performance within a company's "sphere of influence," even in the absence of legal requirements or enforcement.

Increasingly, business leaders understand that corporate responsibility also goes beyond philanthropy, such as charitable giving. While corporate philanthropy is expected, charity alone no longer meets stakeholders' expectations for corporate responsibility.[6]

General Electric (GE) has adopted a comprehensive corporate responsibility definition for its own operations by combining the traditional financial notion with compliance and a broader concept of ethical decision-making: "Good corporate citizenship comprises strong economic performance over time, rigorous legal and accounting compliance, and going beyond compliance when there are opportunities to create benefit for society and the long-term health of the enterprise."[7]

For the purposes of this chapter, corporate responsibility encompasses corporate efforts to meet the non-financial expectations of stakeholders.[8] Under this definition, corporate responsibility goes beyond philanthropy and legal compliance. Stakeholders include investors, employees, business partners, suppliers, customers, governments, regulators, international organizations, non-governmental organizations (NGOs), and the communities where businesses operate. Most of the examples in this chapter are of companies seeking to set minimum social and environmental standards for their operations or in their supply chain.

The Business Case

Companies face growing pressure to act responsibly.

Business practices are a particular focus of scrutiny. The globalization of business and communication means that the activities of companies in foreign markets are no longer invisible to stakeholders at home. Stakeholders routinely call attention to the broader social impact of corporate activities on the communities and societies where they operate.

Human rights are now a business concern. Alongside govern-
> Human rights are now a business concern.

ments, companies are viewed as a source of human rights abuse, as well as international actors with the capacity to promote human rights.[9] Over the last fifteen years, human rights advocates and the media have shined a spotlight on human rights conditions in a wide range of transnational industries including oil and mining; the manufacturing of apparel, carpets, footwear, sporting goods, and toys; agriculture on farms that produce coffee, tea, cocoa, and bananas for global markets; and the pharmaceutical and technology sectors. The abuses at issue include child and forced labor, discrimination, dangerous and unhealthy conditions for workers and communities, and complicity in human rights abuses committed by governments.

Environmental performance is the most prominent focus of corporate responsibility efforts. Following the 1989 Exxon Valdez oil spill in Alaska, environmental groups and institutional investors came together to promote principles for corporate environmental conduct.[10] Since then, environmental sustainability has become an element of corporate strategy. In response to sustained pressure from stakeholders, companies are setting policies on climate change, natural resource management, and environmental stewardship. Sustainability advocates promote "triple bottom line" reporting that accounts for a company's economic, social, and environmental performance.[11]

Corporate governance, financial reporting, and corporate compliance continue to be central concerns of stakeholders, fuelled by corporate scandals and the financial crisis. Companies operating in the United States have adopted corporate ethics and compliance programs in response to regulations such as the U.S. Sentencing Guidelines, the Foreign Corrupt Practices Act, stock exchange regulations, and the Sarbanes-Oxley Act.

For many years, companies have used corporate philanthropy to burnish corporate reputation, improve corporate relationships and support good works. Today, stakeholders look to the private sector to go beyond traditional corporate giving to align philanthropy with business strategy and use the considerable resources and expertise of business to tackle social problems.[12] Calls for pharmaceutical companies to provide universal access to life-saving drugs are just one example.

Pressure for greater corporate responsibility comes from many sources. It can take the form of socially responsible investment funds and customer preferences for responsible brands (market-based pressure), government regulation of business activity or civil litigation against companies (legal pressure), and advocacy campaigns and media coverage targeting corporations (public pressure).

Companies have responded to increased scrutiny of business practices, calls for greater corporate accountability, and the expanding definition of corporate responsibilities in many different ways, ranging from hostility and inaction to acknowledgement, engagement, and the transformation of business strategy. For some companies, corporate responsibility efforts are simply a means to meet minimum requirements or silence critics. Companies that take corporate responsibility seriously, however, define corporate responsibility broadly and make the business case for their efforts.

> Companies that take corporate responsibility seriously define corporate responsibility broadly and make the business case for their efforts.

> Social responsibility is a matter of hardheaded business logic. It's about performance and profits, and attracting the best people to work for you … To work effectively we need trust and the confidence of the society in which we are operating.
> – John Browne, Chief Executive, BP[13]

> To me, opportunities to do business and do good are not mutually exclusive, nor are they less valuable for having a positive business impact. This marriage of business opportunity with global need can create a model that our Company and others will see as an opportunity to deliver more than financial performance and have a far-reaching impact.
> – Jeffrey R. Immelt, chairman and CEO, GE[14]

The business case for adopting responsible corporate practices includes:

- Managing and mitigating risk
- Protecting and enhancing reputation, brand equity and trust
- Attracting, motivating, and retaining talent
- Improving operational and cost-efficiency
- Ensuring a license to operate
- Developing new business opportunities
- Creating a more secure and prosperous operating environment[15]

Effective corporate responsibility improves the bottom line by managing risk. Market-based pressure poses the risk of lower sales and a higher cost of capital. Legal pressure presents the risk of liability and less operating flexibility. Public pressure puts at risk a company's most valuable intangible assets—corporate reputation and brand equity. All of these risks ultimately affect company financials.

Public trust in institutions and corporations has never been lower.[16] With corporate reserves of "reputational capital" depleted, meeting stakeholder expectations of corporate responsibility becomes for many companies the critical business objective that allows the company to stay in business, remain independent, or preserve market share.

In the best cases, corporate responsibility creates competitive advantage. By adopting sustainable water management practices, Central American coffee suppliers make themselves more attractive to coffee buyers like Starbucks, whose stakeholders demand minimum environmental standards. By partnering with human rights groups to set standards for Internet companies seeking to protect the freedom of expression and privacy of their users, Google can respond to Chinese government Internet censorship in a way that balances human rights concerns and business objectives.

High-profile brands like Nike, Starbucks, and Google have been thrust into corporate responsibility leadership and have led efforts to set standards for social and environmental performance. Pressure often spreads from leaders to an entire industry sector. Starbucks was the first major coffee company to offer Fair Trade Certified coffee, but since then the largest coffee retailers—companies including Sara Lee and Proctor & Gamble—have followed suit.[17] The experience of the first industries targeted by human rights, labor and environmental activists—the apparel, sporting goods, extractive, and agricultural industries—has shaped second-generation corporate responsibility strategies in healthcare, financial services, and information technology.

COMMUNICATING CORPORATE RESPONSIBILITY

Executives place a high priority on corporate responsibility and expect its importance to grow.[18] As the global financial crisis has reduced public trust in companies to historic lows, the ability to demonstrate meaningful corporate responsibility has become a critical requirement of executive leadership.

> Corporations may be tempted to communicate instead of improving performance; to report only what is legally required; or to say nothing at all.

Communicating corporate responsibility presents companies with a unique set of challenges. Corporations may be tempted to communicate instead of improving performance; to report only what is legally required; or to say nothing at all. But corporate responsibility communications will fail if the company ignores corporate critics or asserts responsibility without action to back it up.

Effective corporate responsibility communications are accurate, credible, and transparent. Companies that excel understand their diverse audiences and available tools; and seek to adopt best practices for communicating corporate responsibility. The most powerful communications make meeting stakeholder expectations part of corporate strategy and a condition of business success.

Audiences

Corporate responsibility audiences include every traditional stakeholder—customers, employees, and investors—and extend to include the media, investment analysts, regulators, policymakers, international organizations and the vast array of nongovernmental groups active on these issues.[19] Leading companies take into account the expectations of all key audiences and make sure that stakeholders understand their efforts.

Choosing language carefully is particularly important. Corporate responsibility topics may be unfamiliar both to the audience and to the spokespeople. An abstract concept like human rights, for example, can be difficult to explain in corporate settings, but employees and other corporate audiences will easily understand the importance of adequate working conditions, non-discriminatory treatment, and protections against abusive treatment.

Tools

Communicating corporate responsibility employs all of the traditional corporate communication tactics, as well as unique corporate responsibility tools, such as codes of conduct, monitoring and certification initiatives, training and education programs, and due diligence.

Codes of conduct

A code of conduct is often a company's first step. The past fifteen years have witnessed an explosion of voluntary codes.

A code of conduct communicates minimum standards for employees, suppliers, or business partners. Codes also convey messages to corporate stakeholders generally. Royal Dutch/Shell's 1997 revision of its Statement of General Business Principles was a first step toward restoring Shell's reputation among stakeholders after the public criticism surrounding Shell's conduct in Nigeria. The changes made by Shell, particularly acknowledging the company's responsibility to "express support for fundamental human rights in line with the legitimate role of business," signaled an important corporate policy change and implicitly acknowledged that Shell had been wrong to insist that the company had no role to play in advocating human rights to the governments where Shell operates. The about-face was so abrupt that the *New York Times* editorial page, which two years earlier had excoriated Shell for its failure to intervene, applauded Shell's new statement of principles in an editorial titled, "Citizen Shell."[20]

The content of a code communicates a company's priorities and can help define the limits of a company's responsibility. A code also provides an opportunity to reference widely accepted standards. More and more companies, for example, reference the Universal Declaration of Human Rights as the common standard for corporate human rights programs.[21]

While codes are a useful tool, they create an expectation of a compliance program and can become targets for criticism if companies fail to live up to the standards they set.

Monitoring and certification

Setting standards creates an expectation of further communications that demonstrate compliance. Companies participating in the UN Global Compact, for example, must communicate annually with stakeholders about progress implementing the Global

Compact principles. Companies seek to ensure code compliance by monitoring performance through audits, surveys, inspections, and other means.

A challenge for companies is how to handle monitoring results. Companies are justifiably reluctant to make public the results of internal monitoring of social and environmental performance. It goes against corporate culture and practice to publicize any internal processes, let alone internal processes that reveal poor corporate performance. While many companies keep code monitoring results confidential, a number of companies have begun to share this information with external parties, report instances of noncompliance, or summarize findings in public reports. Chiquita Brands, for example, invited independent observers to participate in the company's internal assessment of its code of conduct and the company's compliance with the multi-stakeholder workplace code, Social Accountability 8000, at its banana farms in Latin America. The Fair Labor Association (FLA), a multi-stakeholder initiative to improve working conditions in apparel production, summarizes the findings of independent monitoring visits to factories producing apparel for participating apparel brands. The FLA publishes tracking charts of individual factories that detail noncompliance findings and remediation efforts by participating companies. Compliance programs with the highest levels of transparency make all monitoring results public.[22]

Independent certification is another way to communicate code compliance. Under the apparel industry Worldwide Responsible Accredited Production program, for example, an independent board certifies factory compliance with published standards without disclosing the results of independent monitoring visits. The certification itself, if issued from a credible source, communicates adherence to minimum standards. Similarly, the FLA accredits the workplace compliance programs of participating companies.

TRAINING AND EDUCATION

The newest initiatives focus less on standards enforcement and more on education and training to improve corporate responsibility performance. Many of the first companies to adopt codes and monitoring are now shifting from a policing to a partnership approach to code compliance. Efforts like the Fair Labor Association (FLA) 3.0 seek to identify key performance indicators that address the root causes of code violations, and then partner with suppliers to build their capacity to achieve sustainable social and environmental compliance. In factories where excessive working-hour violations are common, for example, the FLA has sought to educate factory management that less frequent overtime results in higher quality, fewer accidents, and less employee turnover.[23]

DUE DILIGENCE

The most effective corporate responsibility efforts anticipate and prevent issues before they become stakeholder concerns. Due diligence—information-gathering, research, stakeholder outreach, and impact assessments designed to identify and mitigate risk—has become a key feature of effective corporate responsibility programs. Robust due diligence earns credibility among stakeholders.

Anticipating stakeholder concerns over corporate interaction with government security forces in Indonesia, BP commissioned an independent human rights impact assessment of its planned Tangguh LNG natural gas pipeline project. The impact assessment highlighted stakeholder human rights concerns and made specific recommendations for engaging local communities, ensuring that BP respected human rights, and providing for project security. By demonstrating effective due diligence and acting upon the recommendations, BP was able to manage the corporate responsibility risk of a potentially controversial investment.

NON-FINANCIAL REPORTING

By all indications, non-financial reporting is on a trajectory to becoming standard business practice in the early 21st century.[24]

To communicate corporate responsibility results to diverse stakeholders, and in some cases to meet regulatory requirements, companies are reporting publicly on non-financial performance.[25] So-called "triple bottom line" reporting adds social and environmental performance to traditional financial reports. Non-financial reporting "is now the norm, not the exception, among the world's largest companies."[26] Nearly 80 percent of the world's 250 largest companies are publishing non-financial reports.

The strongest corporate responsibility reports communicate accurate information that is complete, relevant, and measurable. Complete information provides a full picture of a company's actions and performance. When addressing efforts to enforce minimum labor standards, for example, it is insufficient for a brand that subcontracts most of its manufacturing to communicate only efforts to enforce standards in its own facilities. Relevance in corporate responsibility communications is analogous to materiality in financial reporting. If a reasonable stakeholder would consider certain information to be relevant, companies should seek to disclose it. The fact that a pharmaceutical company prices life-saving drugs below cost in developing countries is relevant for investors concerned about the role of the private sector providing access to medicines. Finally, companies should provide information that is measurable. The objective is to go beyond mere compliance to demonstrate corporate action. Investors and other stakeholders want to be able to compare corporate responsibility efforts over time and establish a basis for measuring future performance. While metrics for corporate environmental performance are well developed, quantifying social performance, such as human rights conditions, is still an emerging discipline.

Effective corporate responsibility reports:

- Prioritize issues
- Place a company's efforts in the context of business objectives and strategy
- Reference best practices and widely accepted standards
- Provide sufficient detail for stakeholders to make their own assessment of performance
- Serve as a basis to measure future performance
- Acknowledge obstacles and challenges, such as issues for which a single company's efforts are insufficient

Corporate responsibility reports demonstrate actions taken, serve as the basis for third-party assurance, and are a means to share results and best practices. Some reports feature a management discussion of corporate responsibility issues, along the lines of the management discussion and analysis required in corporate financial reports. Companies have strengthened their reporting by asking independent experts publicly to critique their reports. Chiquita, Gap, Nike, and Ford have included statements from independent experts in their non-financial reporting. Feedback from stakeholder groups can be a valuable resource for companies seeking better to understand the issues, information, and metrics of greatest interest for external stakeholders.

Efforts are underway to standardize non-financial reporting. The Global Reporting Initiative (GRI), launched in 1997, is a multi-stakeholder process that provides a voluntary reporting framework for economic, environmental, and social issues.[27] The GRI Guidelines help companies to present a balanced picture of their corporate responsibility performance, promote comparability of corporate responsibility reports, serve as an instrument to facilitate stakeholder engagement, encourage incremental reporting, and seek to establish performance indicators for key issues. Hundreds of companies, including Ford, GE, Nike, Shell, and Starbucks, use the GRI Guidelines as the basis for their corporate responsibility reporting.

While companies often begin corporate responsibility reporting as a way to communicate with external stakeholders, many companies find that the process itself—gathering information from across the organization, identifying the issues that matter to stakeholders, and developing targets and ways to measure results—proves to be most valuable as a means to drive corporate responsibility strategy internally throughout the company.

BEST PRACTICES

Companies that communicate corporate responsibility effectively tend to follow seven rules.

1. Demonstrate responsibility; do not assert it
2. Get the facts
3. Engage critics
4. Earn credibility
5. Define the company's "sphere of influence"
6. Connect corporate responsibility to business strategy
7. Be transparent

1 Demonstrate Responsibility; Do Not Assert It

As in all corporate disciplines, actions speak louder than words when communicating corporate responsibility. Managers must resist the temptation to demonstrate corporate responsibility via press release. Corporate communications face a high threshold to meet stakeholder expectations, especially when audiences are highly skeptical. So-called "greenwashing"— presenting an environmentally responsible public image that is unfounded or intentionally misleading[28]— has become sufficiently widespread that stakeholders have formed groups devoted to exposing the worst corporate offenders. Many audiences assume that corporate statements, if they are not misleading or outright false, will be self-serving and provide only a limited perspective. Few companies can reasonably expect external audiences to take their statements at face value.

Corporate communications and marketing should support, not drive, corporate responsibility programs. The most effective communications are actions that address the expectations of stakeholders. Enforcing minimum labor standards in your supply chain is more effective than issuing a statement to explain why the company was unaware that its main supplier fired employees for attempting to organize or that a subcontractor routinely administered pregnancy tests to prospective employees.

Attempting to "spin" issues of corporate responsibility is even worse. In the 1990s, the U.S. energy company Unocal faced intense criticism over its pipeline project in Burma from activists who alleged that the company was complicit in human rights abuses committed by the military to clear the pipeline route. In a 1996 internal e-mail to a Unocal spokesperson, a company executive advised a colleague how to evade difficult questions: "By saying we influenced the army not to move a village, you introduce the concept that they would do such a thing; whereas, by saying that no villages have been moved, you skirt the issue of whether it could happen or not."[29] Communication that misleads never meets stakeholders' expectations. In fact, Unocal knew of Burma's poor human rights record before the company invested. Companies that view corporate responsibility as simply a public relations issue, or that fail to take any meaningful action to improve performance or address deficiencies, unnecessarily increase their legal, regulatory, and reputational exposure. In 2005, facing various lawsuits and engaged in merger discussions with ChevronTexaco, Unocal ultimately settled the lawsuits and agreed to compensate the Burmese villagers who had sued the company for complicity in forced labor and other human rights abuses.

Assertions of corporate responsibility without the appropriate due diligence, policies, and procedures in place to back them up will do more harm than good. Critical stakeholders will quickly point out any inconsistencies between word and deed. Whenever a company talks about corporate responsibility, the communication should be based on corporate action. The first act is usually some form of due diligence.

2 Get the Facts

Responsibility begins with accurate information. Companies often find themselves in crisis mode when they first address corporate responsibility. Facing accusations of irresponsible practices—sweatshop working conditions, complicity with human rights violations, poor environmental practices—companies must first provide accurate information.

Without a clear understanding of conditions on the ground, companies cannot respond to critics or improve corporate responsibility performance. Sporting goods manufacturers were caught flat-footed in 1995 when media accounts portrayed thousands of children stitching soccer balls in Pakistan. Nike, Reebok, and other companies had codes of conduct that prohibited child labor, but had failed to conduct due diligence or implement the standards beyond their principal Pakistani suppliers. When challenged, the industry could not say confidently that its supply chain was free of child labor. In fact, children were stitching soccer balls at home in an extensive subcontracting network.

The critical first step for the sporting goods industry to demonstrate corporate responsibility was commissioning local experts to survey the role of child workers in soccer ball production. Contrary to the most sensational media accounts, the survey found that the worst forms of child labor were not prevalent and the number of young children affected was smaller than originally reported. Sporting goods brands, once they understood the reality on the ground, convinced their suppliers to eliminate home stitching and monitor the age of workers.

Accurate information not only informs smart business decisions, it minimizes the legal and regulatory risks associated with public communications. Nike, for example, got into legal trouble when critics challenged the company's public statements on working conditions in foreign factories (see "Legal Considerations" below). Appropriate due diligence should have shaped both corporate action and communication.

Allegations of corporate irresponsibility often prompt calls for government regulation of corporate conduct. Companies that provide policymakers with reliable information and demonstrate that they are taking an issue seriously can reduce pressure for regulation. When U.S. chocolate manufacturer Hershey Foods was confronted with news accounts of child trafficking and slave labor on West African cocoa farms, the company's initial response was one of bewilderment: "[N]o one … had ever heard of this. Your instinct is that Hershey should have known. But the fact is we didn't know."[30] Shortly thereafter, under threat of U.S. legislation that would ban cocoa imports from West Africa, chocolate companies and the global cocoa industry mobilized around the issue, and commissioned independent research to assess working conditions. They averted legislative or regulatory action by committing to a voluntary, industry-wide program to eliminate the worst forms of child labour from cocoa production.

Accurate information is just as important for advocates who seek to improve corporate performance. A common set of facts provides a basis for engagement and collaboration among stakeholders. In 2001, after Mexican police intervened in an apparel factory labor dispute, factory customers Nike and Reebok worked with independent factory monitoring and labor rights organizations to establish common findings on factory conditions, worker sentiments, and applicable law. Agreement on the origins of the dispute allowed the apparel companies and their various stakeholders to work with factory management to reinstate illegally fired workers and protect the right to organize. The collaborative effort based on common facts resulted in the first independent union in the Mexican maquiladora sector and met the expectations of key corporate stakeholders.

3 Engage Critics

The catalyst for a company to address corporate responsibility, more often than not, is public criticism. The first instinct of corporate managers accused of corporate irresponsibility is to defend the organization by ignoring or attacking its critics. Both tactics are likely to backfire.

In December 1995, *The New York Times* ran an editorial arguing that the world's largest oil company, Royal Dutch/Shell, had failed to shoulder its responsibility to intervene with the military government of Nigeria on behalf of the activist Ken Saro-Wiwa.[31] In 1994, Shell had called in Nigerian government security forces to protect its facilities from violent attacks and quell unrest in the area of its oilfields. Saro-Wiwa, a prominent political opponent of the Nigerian dictatorship and of Shell's operations in Nigeria, was arrested by government security forces for allegedly inciting a riot and sentenced to hang in a trial widely criticized as corrupt and politically motivated. Initially, after Saro-Wiwa was found guilty, Shell argued that it was "not for a commercial organization to interfere with the legal processes of a sovereign state." After a storm of public criticism following Saro-Wiwa's execution, however, Shell changed its policy on human rights engagement, asserting its right and responsibility to make its position known on any matter which affects the company, its employees, customers, shareholders, or community.[32] Learning from its experience as the focus of intense criticism, Shell now regularly engages critics, participates in multi-stakeholder initiatives like the Voluntary Standards on Security and Human Rights and the UN Global Compact, and actively monitors human rights risks wherever the company operates.

Shell's competitor BP faced a similar issue in Colombia. Human Rights Watch accused BP of complicity with Colombian security forces that had a record of human rights abuse.[33] Rather than adopt an exclusively defensive posture, BP entered into dialogue with critics and, along with Shell, other energy companies, and human rights advocates, joined a process convened by the U.S. and British governments to develop the Voluntary Standards on Security and Human Rights.[34] BP has made engaging critics a key element of its business strategy as the lead partner in a consortium building a natural gas pipeline from Georgia to Turkey. The pipeline project generated initial opposition from human rights and environmental groups. When Amnesty International released a report critical of BP and the human rights impact of the pipeline,[35] BP engaged Amnesty in dialogue, and sought to address some of the human rights concerns by incorporating international human rights standards in the legal agreements governing the project. According to one BP executive, the dialogue was valuable: "Our work with Amnesty International was an eye-opener; they viewed things in a way we never would have."[36] Engaging its main critic and taking stakeholder concerns seriously earned the company credibility.

Most companies, however, are exceedingly cautious and reluctant to engage critics. In 2003, the Coca Cola Company received a letter from Human Rights Watch expressing concern over hazardous child labor in the production of sugarcane in El Salvador, sugar that is purchased to make Coke.[37] In a series of communications with Human Rights Watch, Coca Cola sought to distance itself from the issue of working conditions in the sugarcane fields by asserting its responsibility only for conditions at its direct supplier, the large processing mill covered by Coca Cola's Guiding Principles for Suppliers. While Coca Cola deserves credit for a certain level of engagement, the company's response is reminiscent of Nike's initial response to allegations of child labor and Shell's original position on raising issues with host governments. By adopting a legalistic approach and distancing itself from controversy rather than engaging critics and exploring possible remedies, Coca Cola may have missed an opportunity to manage a supply chain risk to its reputation, gather accurate information, and promote human rights in the communities where it both sources and sells its product.

A company may not agree with or ultimately adopt the recommendations of a human rights organization or labor union, but engaging that external stakeholder in honest dialogue can earn credibility and demonstrate a corporate commitment to addressing the issues at stake. Engaging reasonable critics can also provide valuable information and expertise, and set the stage for collaboration or partnership.

4 Earn Credibility

Communicating corporate responsibility places a high premium on credibility. Due diligence and engaging critics earns credibility. Companies also earn credibility by submitting to third-party assessments, adopting widely accepted standards, acknowledging obstacles, and partnering with stakeholders.

The most powerful corporate responsibility communication comes from third parties. The opinions of credible experts and independent stakeholders almost always carry greater weight than corporate assertions, especially in an atmosphere of deep mistrust of corporate motives. Independent third-party monitoring was one of the first expectations of stakeholders when companies began to adopt voluntary codes of conduct. A single statement of support from a respected former critic can do more for a company's reputation than years of corporate communication.

Adopting widely accepted external standards earns credibility. Voluntary corporate standard-setting is often criticized as a self-serving tactic designed to head off stricter government regulation. Companies can counter this argument by adopting standards for corporate conduct that are widely accepted by stakeholders. A survey of leading multi-stakeholder and business codes of conduct reveals an emerging core of global standards for business.[38] On human rights issues, for example, the private sector has found it useful in many instances to reference international legal standards, such as the Universal Declaration of Human Rights; and voluntary standards such as the OECD Guidelines for Multinationals and the UN Global Compact.[39]

Acknowledging problems earns credibility. Reasonable stakeholders put corporate responsibility efforts in perspective. There is a limit to corporate influence; a single company cannot solve systemic problems affecting social and environmental conditions wherever they operate. When a company cannot meet the non-financial expectations of stakeholders, it should explain why. Failing to acknowledge problems and limitations is more likely to damage credibility than addressing stakeholder concerns directly.

Many corporate responsibility reports are notable for the candor with which they acknowledge failures and address obstacles to improved performance. In 2003, Gap Inc. issued its first Social Responsibility Report. In addition to describing the company's internal and third-party factory monitoring process, the report detailed the regional distribution and frequency of specific violations of Gap's Code of Vendor Conduct. While Gap's reporting prompted media coverage of the poor factory conditions it revealed,[40] Gap's candor earned the company credibility among stakeholders:

> We think this goes far beyond the public relations fluff that other companies put out a lot of the time. By making some very candid admissions, they are taking an important first step toward cleaning up the problems.
> – Bob Jeffcott, Maquila Solidarity Network

Partnering with stakeholders earns credibility. Nike has worked to restore its credibility among stakeholders by partnering with competitors, labor, government and experts to improve working conditions in foreign factories. Stakeholder engagement—group consultations, stakeholder interviews, facilitated workshops, one-on-one meetings, advisory committees—allows a company to identify issues of concern, tap needed expertise, build relationships, and communicate corporate responsibility performance in a highly targeted fashion. Stakeholder dialogue is gaining prominence as an effective means to rebuild corporate reputation.[41]

Voluntary "multi-stakeholder" programs bring together diverse actors to tackle common problems on the corporate responsibility agenda. These partnerships allow companies to share information, resources, and responsibilities. Sector-specific initiatives like the Fair Labor Association draw strength and credibility from the participation of diverse stakeholders.[42]

5 Define the Company's "Sphere of Influence"

No company can, or should, assume responsibility for all the issues of concern to its stakeholders. Leading companies evaluate and prioritize the corporate responsibility issues they face and allocate corporate responsibility resources accordingly.

Corporate responsibility programs are an opportunity for a company to define its responsibilities consistent with the firm's "sphere of influence." The influence a company has over social and environmental conditions varies depending on the company's industry, operations, geography, relationships, and products. An apparel brand sourcing products from independently owned factories may have little influence over local government human rights policies, whereas an oil company that represents substantial direct foreign investment in that same country may have a great deal of influence over government policies and therefore a much higher degree of responsibility. Working conditions for a company's own employees are at the center of the company's "sphere of influence," as are the environmental impacts of a company's own facilities.

Beyond the workplace, a company's sphere of influence may extend to its suppliers, the communities where it operates, the government or even its customers or those who use its products. A company's sphere of influence is also a function of the conditions at issue. Agricultural and heavy manufacturing companies have environmental impacts that technology companies do not. Arms manufacturers and tobacco companies produce products that raise stakeholder concerns about their end use. Drug companies face issues of access to healthcare and the role of the private sector addressing global health threats such as HIV/AIDS.

Companies can fall into the trap of accepting too much responsibility when other entities—local governments, for example—must act to achieve lasting improvements. Freedom of association in China illustrates the limits of corporate influence. Many companies operating in China, such as Nike, Mattel, and Gap, have codes of conduct for employees and suppliers that acknowledge the fundamental right of free association. But no such right is protected in China, where independent organizations are illegal and the government restricts most forms of association. Companies have experimented with parallel means of achieving authentic worker representation in Chinese factories, but true freedom of association can only exist when the government acts to ensure it. Freedom of association is a human rights expectation of stakeholders that companies can influence within their own operations, but not necessarily beyond the factory walls.

A clear definition of a company's sphere of influence, consistent with a company's business, can go a long way toward meeting the non-financial expectations of stakeholders. Nike, for example, in its corporate responsibility report, now characterizes the company's influence over factory working conditions in relation to six stakeholder groups (government, industry, civil society, consumers, factory management, and Nike itself): "Key to our working toward systemic change as the definition of success is recognizing where Nike has direct control over change as opposed to the ability only to influence change."[43]

The multi-stakeholder Global Network Initiative calls on its member companies to "prioritize circumstances where it has the greatest influence and/or where the risk to freedom of expression and privacy is at its greatest."[44] The way a company defines its sphere of influence will determine the appropriate scope for its corporate responsibility program.

Conversely, companies that seek to define their influence and responsibilities too narrowly risk a stakeholder backlash. Unocal's attempts to reframe fundamental human rights issues as beyond corporate control of the energy company, for example, at best confused stakeholders, and at worst were perceived to be so offensive that they energized corporate critics. After allegations of mistreatment by food suppliers and poor wages for migrant workers in the United States, Taco Bell originally tried to avoid responsibility, asserting, "We don't believe it's our place to get involved in another company's labor dispute." But the company changed its position when it faced protests at its restaurant locations and a consumer boycott. Taco Bell has tried to improve labor conditions for migrant workers in the United States by enforcing new labor standards for its food suppliers. As one commentator put it, "It seemed increasingly unwise for the nation's leading purveyor of Mexican food to be publicly linked with the exploitation of poor Mexicans."[45] Consumers and other stakeholders easily understood Taco Bell's potential influence over key suppliers. The company's failure to acknowledge its own influence damaged its credibility.

6 Connect Corporate Responsibility to Business Strategy

Stakeholders expect corporate responsibility to be an integral part of business strategy. Investors who value information on social and environmental performance want companies to explain what the company is doing to incorporate sustainable practices in the company's long-term strategy. Customers, employees, and partners look for signals that initiatives reflect an ongoing organizational commitment rather than an *ad hoc* response to an isolated issue. The most effective communications demonstrate how a company's corporate responsibility efforts advance key business objectives.

Corporate responsibility efforts are most effective when they are integrated, well-understood and rewarded at all levels of an organization, from the boardroom to the factory floor. Every business function in an organization should be able to state the business case for corporate responsibility. As with all corporate strategy, corporate responsibility initiatives carry the greatest weight when sponsored by the company's CEO and senior executives. But unlike traditional business disciplines such as marketing and investor relations, there

> Every business function in an organization should be able to state the business case for corporate responsibility.

is no well-defined way to conduct corporate responsibility throughout a company. Functional responsibility for corporate responsibility initiatives can be found in legal departments, operations, sourcing, government relations, investor relations, and corporate communications.

Leading companies adopt initiatives that align business and corporate responsibility objectives. According to Michael Porter, "Companies need to move away from defensive actions into a proactive integration of social initiatives into business competitive strategy."[46]

Global executives cite educational systems and talent constraints as critical issues for the future success of many companies. In 2008, the investment bank Goldman Sachs partnered with universities and development organizations to launch 10,000 Women, an effort to promote entrepreneurship and management education for women in the Middle East, Asia, and Africa. Goldman committed $100 million dollars over five years to the program, its largest charitable donation ever.[47] But the corporate responsibility effort goes beyond traditional philanthropy. The initiative has the potential not only to benefit women in developing countries, but also to grow both the talent pool and the economies where Goldman hopes to do business. According to Nancy Birdsall, President of the Center for Global Development, "Women's entrepreneurial capital has gone untapped for far too long in the developing world. Building women's human capital will have a multiplier effect: not just filling existing needs for scarce business skills, but creating new demands, new jobs, new wealth." The program also provides mentoring and networking opportunities for Goldman employees. 10,000 Women is designed explicitly to connect corporate responsibility and business strategy.

7 Be Transparent

Transparency is the most important of all the best practices for communicating corporate responsibility. Since the very first corporate responsibility efforts, stakeholders have sought more transparency from companies, and expectations of greater transparency continue to grow.

Transparency—communicating accurate information that is complete, relevant and measurable (see "Non-financial Reporting," above)— allows stakeholders to make their own assessments of corporate performance. As a rule of thumb, more information is better than less. High levels of transparency earn greater credibility with stakeholders and critics, create incentives for continuous improvement, and encourage the adoption of best practices.

Of course, there are drawbacks to communication. Companies that embrace full disclosure risk becoming the target of critics. No compliance program can eliminate all violations, and it only takes one media exposé to damage corporate reputation. The risk is substantial for a company that has never disclosed before or a company that has been the focus of intense attention. Many companies make public only what is required by law. But often, that is a short-sighted strategy.

In the apparel industry, for example, mounting pressure to eliminate sweatshops created a need for transparency that eventually outweighed corporate concerns over proprietary information and public criticism. At first, apparel brands relied on their own codes of conduct and monitoring. Stakeholders, however, expected greater assurance about apparel supply chains. For years, companies resisted calls by advocates for full disclosure of factory locations. A number of well-known brands joined multi-stakeholder programs with varying levels of independent monitoring and public disclosure of monitoring results. Despite its experience as a target of criticism, in April 2005, Nike announced that it would disclose every contract factory worldwide where its products are made, reversing the company's longstanding position against factory disclosure. Nike determined that the benefits of full disclosure outweighed the risks of publicizing individual violations. By unilaterally disclosing all of its contract factory locations and supporting industry-wide approaches to improve working conditions in apparel factories, Nike also used its corporate responsibility strategy to level the playing field among well-known apparel brands and competitors. Six months after Nike, Levi Strauss followed Nike's lead by disclosing the locations of its own suppliers. Nike's principal rival, Adidas, ultimately disclosed factory locations in 2008.

The trend is toward greater transparency. Industries more recently under the corporate responsibility spotlight, such as Internet and communications companies, have built robust public reporting requirements into their corporate responsibility programs. Companies must overcome any cultural bias against public disclosure and seek levels of transparency sufficient to establish facts, demonstrate corporate responsibility performance and earn credibility among stakeholders.

Legal Considerations

Corporate communication was at the center of an important legal case that shapes current thinking about what a U.S. company can and cannot say publicly about its corporate responsibility efforts.

In 1998, Nike was sued for unfair business practices under California law. The plaintiff argued that Nike's advertising and public statements about working conditions in its supply chain presented a deceptive image of the company, and that Nike falsely claimed to protect workers through its code of conduct. The communications cited in the lawsuit included corporate advertising, press releases and publications; the CEO's letters to university presidents, athletic directors, and *The New York Times*; and the CEO's remarks at Nike's annual meeting of shareholders. In these communications, Nike responded to criticisms of the working conditions in its foreign supplier factories and made assertions about labor standards and Nike's compliance efforts.

The legal question at the heart of the case, *Kasky v. Nike,*[48] was whether Nike's public statements about its labor practices and about working conditions in factories making its products should be considered commercial speech, like advertising, which the government can regulate for false or misleading statements; or free speech, which enjoys a higher level of protection under the United States Constitution. Nike argued that its statements made in response to public criticism and on a public issue deserved protection as free speech. In a 4–3 decision, the California Supreme Court found that Nike's statements were commercial in nature and intended to induce consumers to buy its products. After the U.S. Supreme Court chose not to decide the company's appeal of the California decision, Nike settled the case. As part of the settlement, Nike agreed to pay $1.5 million to the Fair Labor Association. The underlying facts of the case—whether Nike's statements were indeed false and misleading—never reached a jury.

Initially, *Kasky* had a chilling effect on the communication of corporate responsibility efforts in the United States. Companies began to reconsider their public statements about working conditions and corporate compliance efforts, particularly communications made in California. After *Kasky* was filed, Nike suspended its reporting and declined invitations to speak on corporate responsibility issues in public fora in California.

Most companies active on corporate responsibility issues, however, including Nike, have concluded that the benefits of communicating outweigh the risks of litigation or of not communicating at all. *Kasky* reinforced the need for due diligence. Companies are more careful to ensure the accuracy of what they say, but they continue to communicate. Within a year of the *Kasky* settlement, Gap, Inc., a California-based apparel brand, issued a corporate responsibility report widely considered to be groundbreaking in its detail and scope.

> The benefits of communicating outweigh the risks of litigation or of not communicating at all.

Kasky highlights the need for standardized corporate responsibility reporting. Non-financial reporting suffers from the absence of universal, or even widely-accepted, standards; no consensus on relevant indicators; and underdeveloped metrics. Defining common reporting standards and how they will be enforced will be near the top of the agenda for the next generation of executives responsible for communicating corporate responsibility.

RESOURCES FOR FURTHER STUDY

Further Reading

Elkington, John, *Cannibals with Forks: The Triple Bottom Line of 21st Century Business* (Oxford: Capstone, 1997).

Ewing, Anthony P., "Maturing Multi-Stakeholder Programs: Lessons for Corporate Responsibility Advisors," *CSR Journal*, January (2009).

Ewing, Anthony P., "Understanding the Global Compact Human Rights Principles" and "Implementing the Global Compact Human Rights Principles," in *United Nations Global Compact and the Office of the High Commissioner for Human Rights, Embedding Human Rights into Business Practice* (2004), available at http://www.unglobalcompact.org.

Harvard Business Review on Corporate Responsibility (2003).

McIntosh, Malcolm, Waddock, Sandra and Kell, Georg (eds.), *Learning to Talk: Corporate Citizenship and the Development of the Global Compact* (Sheffield: Greenleaf, 2004).

Porter, Michael E. and Kramer, Mark R., "Strategy & Society: The Link Between Competitive Advantage and Corporate Social Responsibility," *Harvard Business Review*, December (2006).

Ruggie, John, *Protect, Respect and Remedy: A Framework for Business and Human Rights*, Report of the Special Representative of the Secretary-General on the issue of human rights and transnational corporations and other business enterprises, UN document A/HRC/8/5, 7 April 2008.

Schrage, Elliot J. and Ewing, Anthony P., "The Cocoa Industry and Child Labor," *The Journal of Corporate Citizenship*, vol. 18, Summer (2005).

Spar, Debora L. and La Mure, Lane T., "The Power of Activism: Assessing the Impact of NGOs on Global Business," *California Management Review*, April 1, 2003.

Sullivan, Rory (ed.), *Business and Human Rights: Dilemmas and Solutions* (Sheffield: Greenleaf, 2003).

World Bank, *Strengthening Implementation of Corporate Social Responsibility in Global Supply Chains* (October 2003).

Web Sites

10,000 Women, http://www.10000women.org

BSR (Business for Social Responsibility), http://www.bsr.org

Business & Human Rights Resource Centre, http://www.business-humanrights.org

Ceres, http://www.ceres.org

Ethical Corporation, http://www.ethicalcorp.com

Fair Labor Association, http://www.fairlabor.org

Global Network Initiative, http://www.globalnetworkinitiative.org

Global Reporting Initiative, http://www.globalreporting.org

International Business Leaders Forum, http://www.iblf.org

Social Accountability International, http://www.sa-intl.org

United Nations Global Compact, http://www.unglobalcompact.org

Worldwide Responsible Accredited Production, http://www.wrapapparel.org

Noteworthy Corporate Responsibility Reports

Chiquita Brands, http://www.chiquita.com/CorporateCommitment/CRReports.aspx
Fair Labor Association, http://www.fairlabor.org/what_we_do_public_reporting_b3.html
Ford Motor Company, http://www.ford.com/en/company/about/sustainability/default.htm
Gap, http://www.gapinc.com/public/SocialResponsibility/sr_report.shtml
General Electric Company, http://www.ge.com/en/citizenship/
International Center for Corporate Accountability (Mattel and Freeport McMorRan reports),
        http://www.icca-corporateaccountability.org
Nestle, http://www.nestle.com/SharedValueCSR/Overview.htm
Nike, http://www.nikebiz.com/responsibility/
Novo Nordisk, http://www.novonordisk.com/sustainability/reports/reports.asp
Pfizer, http://www.pfizer.com/responsibility/
Shell,   http://www.shell.com/home/content/responsible_energy/sustainability_reports/dir_
        shell_sustainability_reports.html
Starbucks, http://www.starbucks.com/sharedplanet/customGR.aspx

QUESTIONS FOR FURTHER DISCUSSION

1   How has the meaning of corporate responsibility evolved over time?

2   What is the relationship between corporate responsibility and corporate communication?

3   Why is transparency important to stakeholders?

4   How can corporate responsibility be integrated throughout a company's operations?

5   How can corporate responsibility create competitive advantage?

Talk low, talk slow, and don't talk too much.

– *John Wayne*

14 PUBLIC RELATIONS CONSULTING

By Louis Capozzi, retired CEO, MS&L

■ ■ ■

Our public relations firm, MS&L, had been working with Jules Prast, the Vice President of Corporate Communication at Philips, for several years when we met in a bar in Berlin, circa 2000. MS&L was handling most of the Dutch electronics giant's product PR, while two other firms took on their technology and corporate work.

We'd been asked by the client to create a collaborative spirit between our public relations firms—to avoid making passes at each others' assignments, to look for opportunities to cooperate, and to participate together in the overall planning and strategic direction of the Philips communication effort.

MS&L, the biggest of the three firms and the one with the largest book of Philips business, worked hard to create the collaborative relationship with the other firms. It wasn't hard for us—collaboration and collegiality were already hallmarks of our firm's corporate culture.

That night, though, after the second beer, Jules leaned across the table and offered us the opportunity to pitch for the entire global account.

I nearly spilled my beer, so flabbergasted that I went on instinct and politely refused. "How can you ask us to collaborate with the other firms on the one hand, and then quietly sneak behind their backs to steal their business," I said.

We talked about it for a while, and in the end we told Jules that when he had decided to fire the other firms—and he had told them about it—then we would be happy to pitch for their assignments.

Months went by. Another meeting, in another bar—this one in New York City— and Jules gave us the news that the other two firms had been dismissed. We agreed on a plan for the pitch, and several weeks later we met in London and were awarded the global account.

Reflecting back on that experience, Jules told me, "I offered you the business on a silver plate and you turned it down. The way you handled that showed style and character, and deserved my respect."

We had built MS&L around a culture of collaboration, collegiality, and mutual respect. By staying true to that culture, we ended up winning what would become the agency's largest global account for many years.

■ ■ ■

OVERVIEW: THE PUBLIC RELATIONS CONSULTING BUSINESS

This chapter covers the business of public relations consulting. That's as opposed to the "profession" of public relations, which covers everyone who works in public relations—from corporate communicators to those in associations and non-profits, to government communication staff.

Public relations consultants work in firms that offer communication advice and services to clients—for a fee. Consultants must balance the interests of clients, employees and the firm's owners. This "triple squeeze" creates unique challenges for managers and adds an extra dimension of reward—and stress—to what is already a challenging profession.

> Public relations consulting: the business of providing advice and counsel, as well as communication services, to clients for a fee.

> Public relations consultants work in firms that offer communication advice and services to clients—for a fee.

Clients want great work and service, at a reasonable price. Employees want new challenges and opportunities, as well as a chance to advance in status and pay. Owners want growth and a fair return on their investment. It sounds simple, yet these three dynamic factors are in constant tension. To provide great work and service, you need to hire more and better people—and pay them more. That drives down profits for the owners. To boost the profits, you need to get higher productivity out of your existing staff. That means longer work hours and lower wages for the staff. That's where the tension exists.

Managing the "triple squeeze" poses substantial challenges. But with the right perspective and the right skills, great results can be achieved.

This chapter attempts to bring the experience of working in a public relations consulting firm—often called "the agency business"—to life.

THE HISTORY OF PUBLIC RELATIONS CONSULTING FIRMS

Public relations consulting began as an industry in the early 1900s. And at the beginning it was an industry dominated by individual counselors—larger than life figures who helped shape the reputations of entire industries and became legends in the field.

The Pioneers

An ex-newspaperman named Ivy Lee created one of the first consulting firms in 1904. His clients included the Pennsylvania Railroad, Standard Oil, and Guggenheim. He's credited with inventing the press release at a time when he had to convince clients that they had an obligation to inform reporters about events before they learned about them elsewhere.

Lee is often called the "father" of modern public relations consulting, an honorific he often shares with Edward Bernays. Nephew to Sigmund Freud, Bernays was the first to offer clients influence on public opinion. He coined the term "public relations counsel" and taught the first course on the subject at the University of New York (now New York University) in 1923. In that same year, Bernays wrote *Crystallizing Public Opinion*, a book counselors would find instructive and prescient today.

An associate of Bernays, Carl Byoir, founded the first large-scale public relations consulting business in 1930. It became one of the most recognized firms in the business, and was eventually taken over in 1980 by Hill & Knowlton, then the largest firm in the industry. Byoir created the March of Dimes for President Roosevelt, but the roots of his firm were deeply embedded in work for large industrial clients.

Another pioneer, John W. Hill, who started Hill & Knowlton in 1927 after an 18-year career as a journalist, shared that focus on industry. It would become the world's largest public relations firm by the mid-1960s, and it remains a leader in the field today. Founded in Cleveland, Ohio, the firm built its business on work for the American Iron and Steel Institute. Hill moved the firm's headquarters to Manhattan in 1934, and began the growth of New York City as a major center for the public relations consulting business.

Another pioneer with beginnings in business-to-business communication, Harold Burson, began his firm as a one-man-band in 1947. In 1952 he met an advertising man named Bill Marsteller whose client, Rockwell Manufacturing Company, was looking for a PR firm. They won the account together, and then merged their businesses. Burson-Marsteller became one of the world's largest and most respected public relations consulting firms, a reputation it still enjoys today. Harold, aged 89 at this writing, still comes to the office every day and is considered the "dean" of public relations consulting.

The Modern Landscape

Today's public relations industry would be unrecognizable to the pioneers of the business. In 1968, the first year records were kept by the O'Dwyers Newsletter, the largest firm in the world was Hill & Knowlton with $6.5 million in fee income. The largest firms today are global giants, each exceeding $500 million in fee income with employees numbering in the thousands. They are big businesses and, mostly, part of even bigger communication conglomerates.

Beginning in the 1960s, most large PR firms were being bought by advertising agencies. While the ad agencies reported to brand managers or marketing directors, the PR firms were counseling the CEO. The ad agencies saw public relations as a way to move up the ladder, and to broaden their offering to clients.

By the 1980s consolidation in the advertising industry began. As a result, a new force emerged in the communication industry—the publicly traded communication holding company. And within those holding companies most of the largest global public relations networks now reside.

The first of the holding companies was Interpublic. Founded in 1960 with advertising giant McCann Erickson as its base, the company bought literally hundreds of advertising, public relations, and marketing communication firms. Today, two of the largest and most successful PR firms live within Interpublic—Weber Shandwick (arguably the largest firm in the world) and Golin Harris, which also ranks in the top tier of the industry.

The largest of the holding companies today, Omnicom, was founded in 1986 when DDB Needham merged with BBDO in a deal the industry dubbed "the Big Bang." Omnicom went on to acquire another large ad agency, TBWA Worldwide. It now owns three large, powerful public relations firms—Ketchum, Fleishman Hillard, and Porter Novelli.

Another holding company giant emerged in 1985 when Martin Sorrell bought a shell company called Wire and Plastic Products on the London Stock Exchange, and began acquiring communication firms. He bought J. Walter Thompson advertising, which owned Hill & Knowlton public relations. Later, acquisitions of Ogilvy (with Ogilvy PR), Y&R (with Burson-Marsteller and Cone & Wolfe), and Grey Advertising (with GCI) gave WPP an enormous public relations portfolio.

The newest of the holding company giants, Publicis, began as a French advertising agency and grew through a series of dramatic acquisitions, including Saachi & Saachi advertising, and another holding company called Bcom3. The Bcom3 acquisition brought American advertising giant Leo Burnett into the Publicis Group, and also top-ten PR firm Manning Selvage & Lee, now MS&L.

In this holding company environment, public relations firms have thrived. The industry has enjoyed fantastic growth, and the PR operations now represent significant portions of the group's revenues and profits.

> Budgets for a single client often exceed the size of even the largest firms a few decades ago.

Today, the world's largest public relations firms manage networks of dozens of offices across the globe. Budgets for a single client often exceed the size of even the largest firms a few decades ago. The size, scope, and influence of public relations consultants has grown to put the industry on the same level as any other communication discipline, and in many cases at the top of the business.

Specialty Firms

While the huge global networks dominate the industry today, a large number of high-quality specialty firms have also developed, in both industry segments and audience sensitivities.

Financial communication consultants, such as Sard Verbinnen, Citigate, Brunswick, Kekst, and Financial Dynamics, specialize in advising clients on mergers, acquisitions, and other financial matters. Such transactions require intense, focused efforts at high levels. When faced with such a situation, many clients turn to these specialists to work with the lawyers and investment bankers on the communication aspects of the transaction. Their depth of expertise, and their ability to dedicate staff to an intense, but short-lived assignment, make them effective partners on financial deals.

In recent years large-scale healthcare consultancies that specialize in the marketing of prescription drugs have also emerged. Firms like Chandler Chicco, Noonan/Russo, and Spectrum Science help clients navigate the difficult waters of drug communication in this highly regulated sector.

Technology specialty firms grew up in the "Dot-Com" era that began in the 1980s, and several have survived the bursting of that bubble in the late 1990s. Waggener Edstrom, Text 100, Broedeur, and others offer specific technical expertise, insights and relationships that help technology clients communicate effectively. A large trade press, an acutely interested business press, and an increasingly wired public need to be factored into technology communication programs, both online and in traditional media.

The public affairs arena has spawned specialty firms offering clients specialized skills, unique experience, and personal contacts to help them deal effectively with the government. Firms like APCO, Quinn Gillespie, Glover Park, and Penn Shoen often employ former government officials to assist their clients. Often Republicans and Democrats will team up to be able to offer the broadest possible representation in Washington. Jack Quinn, for example, was President Clinton's White House Counsel, while his partner, Ed Gillespie, was the Republican National Chairman.

There are a wide range of other specialty firms as well, including food and nutrition, fashion, travel, entertainment, etc. There are also firms that specialize in audience segments, like children or moms or elders. You can find a firm for nearly every niche, from strawberries to skateboarding.

> You can find a firm for nearly every niche, from strawberries to skateboarding.

Small to Mid-Sized Firms

Finally, there exists a vast network of small to mid-sized public relations consultancies—literally thousands of independent consultants and firms ranging in size from a few people in a small local market to dozens operating on a national or even sometimes a global basis.

Trade Associations

As the public relations industry grew, the need emerged for trade associations that represent firms' mutual interests. Today, such organizations exist in most countries, and regional or global coordinating bodies have also been formed.

In the U.S., the Council of Public Relations Firms (CPRF) was formed in 1998, and now represents more than 100 PR consulting firms across the country, including most of the industry giants. It represents the premier global, mid-size, regional, and specialty agencies across every discipline and practice area. The Council's mission is "to advance the business of public relations firms by building the market and firms' value as strategic business partners." Activities include advocacy, setting industry standards, management programs, and events that convene the leadership of the industry.

The CPRF publishes a wide range of useful information, from a code of professional conduct to information helping clients select and manage their agencies. Their Web site is http://www.prfirms.org.

Associations similar to the Council exist in most countries of the world. Some of the largest are the PRCA in the U.K., Assorel in Italy, and GPRA in Germany. These individual country associations come together under the umbrella of a global organization called ICCO, the International Communications Consultancy Organisation.

ICCO acts as an "association of associations." It convenes the leaders of nearly 30 national associations in Europe, the Americas, and Asia to share information, perspectives, and ideas. The ICCO board includes a representative from each member country, and builds relationships among firm leaders around the world. It publishes an annual "World Report" on the state of the industry, has developed a global standard of practice called the Stockholm Charter, and shares information on member organizations at http://www.iccopr.com.

Agency Structure and Areas of Practice

How clients use consulting firms

Firms can offer an external view, and often have experience in areas not covered by the in-house communication staff.

Many clients ask their firms for advice and counsel on the activities of the organization and its communication. Firms can offer an external view, and often have experience in areas not covered by the in-house communication staff. Additionally, the input of external advisors often carries weight internally, especially when other staff functions—such as the lawyers—bring in their own "experts" to advise management.

Firms often provide creative idea development as well. Even in the largest internal departments, the same few people are usually charged with developing new ideas and angles for promoting the interests of the organization. Because consulting firms are larger collections of people, and because people can be brought in who do not regularly work on that particular client, new perspectives can be brought to bear and fresh ideas emerge.

Many clients use consulting firms to manage specific programs that are well contained and can be delegated to the firm with a minimum of staff oversight. Examples might be a sponsored event, or a product marketing program. Large multinational organizations in particular rely on firms with global networks to manage broad global campaigns.

Finally, clients employ consulting firms to get work done efficiently. In any internal department, there will be small teams assigned to specific jobs. Even the largest departments, like the one I ran at Aetna in the 1980s (with nearly 200 staff) might only have two or three people on any one specific area of practice. As a result, the internal department has a limited ability to delegate work to the lowest possible level. As a result, senior people might often find themselves dealing with matters that could be much more efficiently performed by lower level employees. Public relations consulting firms are designed to offer this kind of efficiency to clients.

How consulting firms organize

Most firms use a "pyramid" structure to offer clients all of the advice and services they require. The largest number of employees are at the bottom of the "pyramid"—assistant account executives (AAEs). These are the firm's lowest-level employees. Many are right out of school, perhaps having done an internship as part of their education.

AAEs do the most routine jobs for clients, putting together contact lists, monitoring the media, writing reports and, yes, stuffing envelopes! Since they have the lowest salaries, their services can be offered to clients at the lowest rates.

As the seniority of the employees increases, from AAE to account executive, up to supervisor, VP or senior VP, the number of employees in that group decreases, and the salaries, and concomitant billing rates go up.

> As the seniority of the employees increases, from AAE to account executive, up to supervisor, VP or senior VP, the number of employees in that group decreases, and the salaries, and concomitant billing rates go up.

In addition to this "pyramid" structure, larger, full-service agencies generally organize by practice area. Typical structures would include corporate and financial, healthcare, consumer marketing and technology practices. These practices would be organized in the firm's key offices, and also globally.

Finally, many larger firms organize around clients. Global account teams, organized in support of a multinational client, might often be as large as a practice area, and in many cases be larger than any one of the firm's offices. Global account directors manage these teams, as well as the global and headquarters client relationship.

FINANCIAL MANAGEMENT

Public relations consultancies are both professional service providers and businesses. A successful consultancy must manage both the quality of its work and the financial performance of its business in order to be successful.

> Two financial skills are critical for the agency manager – budgeting and firm profitability.

Two financial skills are critical for the agency manager—budgeting and firm profitability.

Budgeting

Budgeting client assignments correctly ensures the firm will be properly compensated for its work. Most firms use estimates of hours or man-days required to provide clients with budgets for their assignments. Tightly constructed, explicit budgets protect the interests of both the firm and its clients. Poorly prepared budgets cause financial and relationship issues.

Budgeting two ways improves accuracy and helps check for omissions. One way to budget involves making a list of all the tasks involved in a project, and deciding the level of staffing required (how many people and at what level for how many hours) to accomplish each task. As a cross-check, a second budgeting method can be employed—simply estimating how many people will work on the assignment, and for how long, Both budgets must include detailed estimates for the "out of pocket" expenses—all the things that must be purchased to accomplish the task.

Agency Financial Metrics

Most consulting firms estimate annual revenues at the beginning of the year, then adjust their expectations quarterly based on actual experience.

Revenue budgets include confirmed contracts with clients, estimated income from existing clients who have not yet signed contracts (discounted by their likelihood for success), and an estimate of new business income for the year (based on past experience).

Expenses are generally managed as a percentage of income. Most firms target their total compensation ratio (salaries and benefits) at between 50 and 53 percent of income. General and administrative expenses should be between 20 and 22 percent, and occupancy costs (rent) should be held under 7.5 percent. With the ratios at this level, the firm should be able to make a 15–20 percent pre-tax profit.

Good Financial Management

> An adage in the consulting business is that you win clients with ideas, and you lose them over money.

No one likes to be surprised by a budget that's out of line. An adage in the consulting business is that you win clients with ideas, and you lose them over money. Good financial management means "no surprises."

Use monitoring systems to avoid budget surprises. Communicate often with clients. Money may not be easy to discuss, but it's very important to preserving a positive relationship. Know your client's preferences with regard to billing. Do they have monthly cutoff dates for processing bills? Do they require detailed activity reports with invoices?

The firm's owners don't like surprises either. Monitor your financial performance closely. Report changes as they are emerging, and communicate the steps you are taking to adjust for those changes.

In the end, financial success equals firm success. It's a business, and the metric for business is revenue growth and profitability. By monitoring and managing your financial performance, you can concentrate on what's really important—the quality of your work and the satisfaction of your employees and clients.

MANAGING CONSULTANTS AND CONSULTANCIES

> The old adage, "the inventory goes down in the elevator every night" applies.

Public relations firms are only as good as the people they can attract and retain in their businesses. The old adage, "the inventory goes down in the elevator every night" applies.

Managing a consultancy presents unique challenges. Firms attract and reward entrepreneurs. "Star power" attracts business. But at the same time teamwork is the key to success. No individual can be as strong as the firm overall—best teams win.

On top of that, work in a consultancy can be extremely stressful. Pressure-packed workloads, looming client deadlines, and management financial pressure combine to create a difficult work environment.

The key to success is a truly collaborative culture—a culture that puts the firm first, that promotes a spirit of teamwork, saying we're stronger together than we are as individuals. Add to that an honest, open dialog and a climate of trust and mutual respect and you've got the ingredients for a successful consulting firm.

Dr. W. Edwards Deming's theory of management works perfectly in a consulting firm environment. His philosophy of "joy of work" and intrinsic rewards sets the stage for creating a successful corporate culture in a consulting firm (see Sidebar.)

> The key to success is a truly collaborative culture—a culture that puts the firm first, that promotes a spirit of teamwork, saying we're stronger together than we are as individuals.

THE DEMING SYSTEM OF PROFOUND KNOWLEDGE

Professor Howard Gitlow is Executive Director of the University of Miami Institute for the Study of Quality in Manufacturing and Service. He is one of the world's leading authorities on Dr. W. Edwards Deming's theory of management. Dr. Deming is well known for his work on a management theory that has become the foundation for many successful companies today.

According to Dr. Gitlow, Deming's theory of management, called the *System of Profound Knowledge*, promotes "joy in work" and will "unleash the power of human resource contained in intrinsic motivation. Intrinsic motivation is the motivation an individual experiences from the sheer joy of an endeavor."

Dr. Gitlow describes Deming's theory of management as based on four paradigms:

1   People are most effectively motivated and inspired by a mix of intrinsic and extrinsic rewards. Intrinsic motivation comes from the sheer joy of performing an act, and releases human energy that can be focused into improvement and innovation of a system.

2   Manage using both a process and results orientation, not only a results orientation. Management's job is to improve and innovate the processes that create results, not just to demand results.

3   Management's function is to optimize the entire system so that everyone wins, not to maximize only his or her component of the system. Managers must understand that individuals, organizations, and systems of organizations are interdependent.

4   Cooperation works better than competition. In a cooperative environment, everybody wins. Customers win products and services they can brag about. The firm wins returns for investors and secure jobs for employees. Suppliers win long-term customers for their products. The community wins an excellent corporate citizen.

According to Deming, says Dr. Gitlow, leaders who practice these four paradigms can increase quality and simultaneously decrease costs. Waste and re-work is reduced. Staff attrition and litigation decrease, and customer loyalty increases. The key is to practice *continuous improvement* and think of a business as a system, not as bits and pieces.

■ ■ ■

CLIENT SERVICE: A CREATIVE COLLABORATION

Building and maintaining positive partnerships with clients may be the most important skill a consultant possesses. Fortunately, some data exist on the drivers of client satisfaction.

Tom Harris, founding partner of Golin Harris, a leading consulting firm, conducted a study of the key drivers of client satisfaction. The following chart shows the top elements on the list. (The higher the percentage, the more important the factor is to the clients.) As you can see, relationship elements score as high or higher than technical skills to drive client satisfaction. In fact, "chemistry" was the highest-ranked element in defining a satisfied client.

> Building and maintaining positive partnerships with clients may be the most important skill a consultant possesses.

> "Chemistry" was the highest-ranked element in defining a satisfied client.

Harris Survey

Key Client Satisfaction Drivers

Technical Elements

Overall quality of work	70%
Meets deadlines, keeps promises	66%
Creativity	50%
Quality of writing	49%
Thorough attention to detail	58%

Relationship Elements

Chemistry	74%
Client service	73%
Quality of my account team	73%
Quality of management	69%
Stability of staff	54%

The following precepts can serve as a guide for success in managing client relationships :

1. *Listen before talking and acting:* Good listening skills are a key to good consulting skills. As one anonymous pundit is often quoted, "Before you shoot off your mouth, make sure your brain is fully loaded."

2. *Know your client's company and industry:* Read everything you can about the client's industry, and master their jargon. Study the mysteries of the client's organization, and discern how and where public relations fits into the puzzle.

3. *Be passionately supportive of the client's product or service:* Clients want their consultants to love them. Never underestimate the client's enthusiasm for their product. Passion sets apart the great consultants. And don't ever serve Coke at a Pepsi meeting.

4. *Manage expectations, deliver on promises:* Clients want their consultants to slay dragons, drink the blood of the bad guys, and bring them stars beyond their reach. Be careful about what you promise. And be compulsive about delivering once you do.

5. *Be available, respond quickly, and meet deadlines:* When clients ring the doorbell, answer quickly. Information, public opinion and the media move at light-speed pace. Consultants must be speedy, on time, and on target.

6. *Lead the relationship:* Anticipate events that will affect your client. Develop new ideas. Remember why the client hired you in the first place, and live up to that standard every day.

7. *Be true to your client:* Stay true to the strategy you and your client have agreed on, and use the methods and processes you have defined together in advance.

8. *Make quality your cornerstone:* Produce impeccable work in every way. Sloppy writing or typing means sloppy thinking. And evaluate results together, using methods you've agreed on in advance as well.

9. *Communicate often:* With both your team and your client. Use phone calls, personal visits, and e-mails to keep a constant dialog intact with your client. Monitor activity of the company, competitors, and the industry and send news along to the client when you find it. Also, be sure to keep your team in the loop on all of your interactions with the client.

10. *Bill accurately, clearly, and promptly:* Remember, money is the root of all evil. It's the consultant's job to make it easy for clients pay the bill. Be sure there's no disconnect between their view of the budget and yours. And remember, clients don't share your sense of urgency about payment.

11. *Watch your language:* Our words define us. Avoid statements that demean your advice—phrases like "we came up with this idea." Consultants don't "come up" with ideas, they think and plan strategically, and make thoughtful recommendations. They "build" or "engineer" ideas and solutions.

Even with the greatest care and commitment to success, sometimes client relationships go awry. You know your client is unhappy when:

- They don't return your calls
- There is tension in the air
- Conversations feel strained
- Sarcasm creeps into their dialog

Done well, client service is a joy. Done badly, it's a nightmare.

Bad client relationships are no fun. And they're not good for business either. Watch for the warning signs. Be over-sensitive to displeasure. Draw them out—and show genuine interest in solving the problem. Look for an acceptable solution, and ask for their feedback. Done well, client service is a joy. Done badly, it's a nightmare.

WHAT CLIENTS EXPECT FROM THEIR CONSULTANTS

By T. A. Fassburg, Vice President, Corporate Communication for Philips Electronics North America, a unit of Royal Philips Electronics of the Netherlands

My employer, a global corporation, had just completed the acquisition of a major film studio in California. My boss at the time tasked me with writing the annual report that explained the corporate strategy for the acquisition and our aspiration for its future. But he insisted that a visit to the studio was essential to learn the secret of profitable film making before beginning serious writing. Off I went to Los Angeles, notebook in hand, ready to learn the wisdom of Hollywood. In interviews with scores of our movie executives, everyone pointed me to an elderly gentleman by the name of Joseph Schwartz, who, they claimed, was a sage. An appointment with him was finally maneuvered, and I found him in a small, cramped, paper-strewn office in the basement of the movie company headquarters.

"I understand you have the secret to successful movie making in Hollywood," I offered, "I'd really like to understand it." "It's easy," Joe countered. "I can explain it in three words: Make … more … hits!"

What clients expect from their consultants can be explained even more succinctly—in fact, in one word: *results*.

No matter how close and collegial the relationship, it won't last if the results of a program aren't delivered as promised.

But it's how the results are delivered that distinguishes a great consultancy from a merely good one. And great results are delivered through four attributes: leadership, wise counsel, surprising creativity, and common business sense.

WHAT DEFINES LEADERSHIP?

Whenever briefing a new agency, I always tell them, "Please lead me; please don't make me lead you." That means the agency should know as much about my business as I do. Unrealistic? Maybe. But it points to the need for an agency to know its client's industry, products, competitors, and allies. That way, an explanation won't be necessary for every action the company takes, or more significantly, to locate where the opportunity areas lie. It takes work for an agency to get up to speed quickly, but it's well worth the investment on both parts.

Leadership presumes a high level of professional expertise.

A great consultancy is a master of its tools. It constantly educates its employees about the latest public relations techniques and trends. I had never heard of "blogs" until my agency, at the time, told me how important they were to building brand perception and their usefulness with stakeholder outreach. By educating me, of course, the consultancy profited with a multiyear Internet program that had beneficial results for both of us.

Leadership also elevates client service to a fine art.

Sometimes the alchemy between client and agency can spin gold. In my case, it only happened once, but the client service director seemed to anticipate my every move. He called to update me on happenings in my global account before I could pick up the telephone to call him. He delivered program recommendations based on his knowledge of my business prior to my asking for them. He made changes in account personnel in advance of requests from me or my colleagues because he was so close to our business he knew which of his people were producing and which were not. It was magic.

The second attribute to expect from a consultancy is *wise counsel*. You would think that a consultancy's advice is their stock in trade, but it's harder to get than you think. Some agencies will soften the truth to protect the relationship. Tell the client what he should know, not what he wants to hear. They may not like hearing the truth, but they are far better served when they do.

Going hand-in-hand with speaking the truth is the adage, "under-promise and over-deliver."

Case in point: one of our agencies recommended that we undertake a wide-ranging research project that probed consumer attitudes about technology, our healthcare system and how people felt about their lives, in general. They promised that we would receive "an *avalanche* of publicity" about the research and our bravery for initiating it.

No one wrote a word about it. Not one.

We didn't fault the consultancy for recommending the program. We had reviewed it and agreed with it. Where the agency did take the blame was for not testing the program with journalists beforehand to get a sense of its newsworthiness, and especially for setting our expectations in the stratosphere.

The third attribute which is key for a consultancy is *surprising creativity*. Offer the client something new, different, creative, challenging … something that changes the rules of the game. But warn them of the consequences of this creativity so they can make an informed decision.

A great example of this is the work Philips' agency performed when we introduced a new men's electric razor, which was designed to trim hair below the neck … and below the waist. At the heart of their recommendation was a cross-promotion with a nationally syndicated radio talk show impresario, a man known for outrageous behavior and controversy. He was also known as the single most popular radio talk show host with our target demographic—young men under the age of 25.

After hours of negotiating ground rules with the radio program, debating among ourselves, and preparing for the worst outcome scenario, we decided to move ahead with the show.

It was a blockbuster success.

The agency's program generated a tsunami of coverage, but more importantly, the product flew off our retailers' shelves.

That's surprising creativity.

The final element is *common business sense*. Commercial clients and consultancies are in business for the same reason: to make money. So it's critical that consultants treat the business like a business. That means documenting decisions, preparing and tracking budgets, and issuing timely and accurate invoices.

Inaccurate, late invoicing can sink the best of relationships.

Here's a true story: bumping into a colleague at a holiday party a couple of years ago, I complimented him on what I thought was one of the best public relations campaigns I had ever seen. The creative was compelling and ignited a media frenzy. His company executives were profiled on television and were in demand on the speaker circuit. By all measures, it was a great success. But when I asked him about the agency that executed the program for him, he told me that he fired them.

Astonished, I asked, "Why?"

He responded, "Because their invoices were so late and so incorrect, it took six months for our auditors to sort it out, and by that time, we had depleted the new year's budget. They were a great shop, but we'll never be able to use them again."

So, that's my view on what clients expect from their consultancies: great results delivered with leadership, wise counsel, creativity, and a business-like approach to the business. Easy to say, but challenging to achieve.

■ ■ ■

PITCHING AND WINNING NEW BUSINESS

Great client service helps you retain and grow your current clients. But every consultancy needs a robust new business initiative to attract *new* clients to the firm as well.

Differentiating your firm in new business, and standing out from the pack as a result, is one of the greatest challenges facing public relations consultants. The solution lies in a well-organized, well-planned, well-rehearsed and well-presented approach.

> Differentiating your firm in new business, and standing out from the pack as a result, is one of the greatest challenges facing public relations consultants.

Organizing the Pitch

Right from the beginning, you need a plan. How will you get off to a winning start? How can you engage the client in a dialog, rather than a monolog? How will we bring our ideas to life? A solid plan will answer all of these questions.

First, pick the team. Think about the levels of people needed and the specific expertise the client requires. Bring the team together to develop the pitch plan, and get them working right away on gathering background materials. Solicit their questions and ideas on how to shape the proposal.

Next, analyze the client. Use your networking and research skills to find out what you can about both the organization and the individuals involved. Learn about the issues, the corporate culture, their past and other agency relationships, and the personalities of the people you'll meet with. Dig to discover who you're competing with; this can provide you with clues on how to differentiate yourself.

Rank the make-or-break factors. What's going to win this pitch, or lose it? Is it experience, chemistry, or the enthusiasm of the team? Does your firm's size and resources make a difference? Are they looking for a consultant who really knows their business? Will a blockbuster creative idea tip the situation in your favor, or will they decide on price?

Presenting to Win

Consultants put an enormous amount of effort into a new business presentation, often investing the full estimated profits of the account for the first year. They pore over secondary data, conduct original research, and analyze the competition. The best strategic minds in the firm work to gain insights that will help the potential client succeed. Creative teams develop ideas that sizzle.

But all of that effort can go to naught without a well-planned and well-executed presentation. Here are ten ways consultants create successful presentations.

1. *Plan carefully:*

Analyze the audience you'll be talking with. Who is the decision maker? Who will be your team leader? How will you present—standing, sitting, from the front of the room? What visuals will support your recommendations? And what are your audio/visual needs?

Where will you present? At the client's offices or your own? Be sure to check out the room in advance. Know the lighting, the layout, and the A/V system. Check for distractions like open curtains, a messy service area, or leftover office supplies from the last users of the room, and clean it up.

How many people will sit at the table? Are there the right number of chairs? What will the seating arrangement be? Should you prepare name placards for all the participants? God is in the details on these logistics, and they can be critical.

2. *Listen first, then talk:*

Find a way to engage the audience in a dialog. Begin by asking them to introduce themselves, and to tell you a little about their jobs. Ask them what they hope to see or learn from the presentation. Confirm the schedule—how long do they have to meet with you?

3. *Home in on their key needs:*

Don't sell the client a drill, when what he really needs is a hole. Be sure you spend the bulk of your time on the client's key issues. Avoid distractions or "side trips."

4. *Don't let the presentation do all the work:*

Avoid the trap of endless PowerPoint slides with lists of bullets. Yes, they keep you on track and remind you what to say next, but they're boring and visually dead. At the same time, watch out for too many PowerPoint gimmicks. Fly-ins, 3-D images, tricky fonts are tempting, but be careful not to make the presentation into a circus show. Remember, you are a consultant imparting important advice. An entertaining presentation is helpful; a silly one detracts from your gravitas.

5. *Be careful with criticism:*

Consultants often make a classic mistake, effectively telling the prospective client "You have big problems, but we can save you." It's important to tell clients what they need to hear, not necessarily what they want to hear. But remember, they are not your client yet, and you should be very careful with the way you talk with them about problems or negative issues. It might be a good idea to ask the client to explain a negative situation, allowing them to give their view before you characterize the situation yourself.

6. *Rehearse, rehearse, rehearse:*

When your team is ready and the presentation's complete, do a dry run, working out everyone's role and walking through the pieces of the presentation. Next, do a formal rehearsal. It's often helpful to invite a senior consultant who has not been involved in the program to act as a "pitch doctor," listening to the rehearsal and offering feedback. Finally, do a "walk-through" rehearsal, where you work out where everyone will sit, how they will move about the room, where they will stand to present and how the visual aids will be positioned. Clumsy situations with people tripping over each other can be an enormous distraction for the client.

7. *Pay attention to emotions and politics:*

Once you've done your homework on the client, you should know the interpersonal dynamics of the people in the room. Be sure you understand their hot buttons, the issues they feel defensive about, statements that might potentially offend them. A small personal slight to the wrong person can kill an otherwise winning presentation.

8. *Go the extra mile:*

Competition in pitches among consultants is fierce. Doing just enough to satisfy the requirements set by the prospective client will almost never win the day. Think about how to stretch the brief, go beyond what's expected, and bring something extra to your presentation. If you don't, you can be sure your competition will.

9. *Present to the individual:*

Make sure you connect with each and every person in the room. Make good eye contact. Look carefully for signals of boredom or concern, and respond to them. Move around to keep them focused on you as well.

10. *Rehearse the Q&A:*

You should anticipate every question the client will ask and develop a plan for answering. Make sure everyone on the team gets a chance to speak during the Q&A. Rehearse their answers. Be careful about building on each other's points. One amplification is fine. Two begins to get risky. Three, and you may as well have said, "What that dummy meant to say was …"

A relentless approach to preparation will pay great dividends in your new business effort. Be a "slave to structure." Listen, and ask the right questions. Always allow time for rehearsal. Learn to stop editing the presentation in an effort to make it "perfect," and spend the time instead on the critical factors for success.

> A relentless approach to preparation will pay great dividends in your new business effort.

ETHICS IN PUBLIC RELATIONS CONSULTING

Companies like Johnson & Johnson have "credos" or statements of "values." The public relations profession, too, has codes of conduct. But consulting offers unique challenges for consultants and their firms.

The trade associations, including the Council of PR Firms in the US and the International Communications Consultancy Organisation, ICCO, offer guidelines specifically tailored to consulting. They establish behavioral guidelines and uniform standards to guide professional behavior. See Chapter 2, Ethics.

THE ICCO STOCKHOLM CHARTER

Public Relations consultancies are professional service firms that help clients influence opinions, attitudes and behaviour. Along with this influence comes responsibility to our clients, our people, our profession and society at large.

Objective Counsel and Advocacy

Public relations consultancies may not have interests that might compromise their role as an independent consultant. They should approach their clients with objectivity, in order to help the client adopt the optimum communication strategy and behaviour.

Society

An open society, freedom of speech, and a free press create the context for the profession of public relations. Consultants operate within the scope of this open society, comply with its rules, and work with clients that share the same approach.

Confidentiality

Trust is at the heart of the relationship between a client and a public relations consultancy. Information that has been provided in confidence by a client and that is not publicly known should not be shared with other parties without the consent of the client.

> Trust is at the heart of the relationship between a client and a public relations consultancy.

Integrity of Information

Public relations consultancies should not knowingly mislead an audience about factual information, or about the interests a client represents. Consultancies must make their best efforts to strive for accuracy.

Delivering Promises

Consultancies must work with clients to establish clear expectations in advance about the output of their efforts. They must define specific goals for communication actions and then work to deliver on their promises. Consultancies must not offer guarantees which are not supportable, or which compromise the integrity of the channels of communication.

Conflicts

Consultancies may represent clients with conflicting interests. Work may not commence for a new and conflicting interest without the current client first being offered the opportunity to exercise the rights under any contract between the client and consultancy.

Representation

Consultancies may refuse or accept an assignment based on the personal opinions of the firm's management or the organization's focus.

> Consultancies may refuse or accept an assignment based on the personal opinions of the firm's management or the organization's focus.

Governance and Business Practices

Public relations consultancies are committed to ethical behavior and implementation of best business practices in dealing with all audiences.

■■■

While the association codes are a helpful beginning, they have their weaknesses. They apply only to members, and are usually too general for any kind of enforcement. Also, association members are unwilling to criticize their peers and avoid getting involved in the process.

So, consultants are often on their own in defining what's ethical and what's not. They must consider ethics in terms of their relationships with clients, with the media, and in the firm itself.

Knowing the difference between right and wrong is generally pretty easy. It's the gray areas that cause problems. Consultants are well advised to pursue their clients' interests in an ethical manner both in counseling the client and representing them in public.

With the client, be sure you clearly understand what is being asked of you. Advise your client to do the right thing. Show the client how your advice can resolve the problem and help them reach a solution.

With the media, act ethically as the client's representative. Remember that reporters don't share your client's interests. Understand the client's vulnerabilities as you advocate on their behalf. While you're putting the client's best foot forward with the

> While you're putting the client's best foot forward with the media, always tell the truth and always be on your best professional behavior.

media, always tell the truth and always be on your best professional behavior. Assume nothing is "off the record."

Avoid innuendoes, and claims that are misleading. Never misrepresent your identity or motives. And remember not to burn bridges with a reporter—you'll have other clients to advocate for in the future.

Choosing Clients to Represent

A consultant's clients define who they are. Ask yourself if this is really a client for whom you want to work. Is the client doing the right thing? Will you have an impact? Will you be proud to present the client's point of view?

Often, a consultant's personal values can conflict with the client's agenda. That's especially true on broad public policy issues like abortion, contraception, guns, tobacco, liquor, or equal rights. Employees of a consultancy *must* be able to decline to work on client accounts that conflict with their personal values. If a subject makes them uncomfortable, for whatever personal reason, they have to know that they can "opt out" without fear of penalty or retribution.

Ethical decisions can be tricky, and often the right answer is elusive. But consultants can be guided by one simple piece of advice from Spike Lee, "Do the Right Thing."

BEST PRACTICES

See pages 369 and 374.

 ## RESOURCES FOR FURTHER STUDY

Ongoing developments in the public relations industry are available by visiting the following Web sites:

PRWeek magazine, http://www.prweek.com
Paul Holmes' newsletter, http://www.holmesreport.com
Jack O'Dwyer's Newsletter, http://www.odwyerpr.com
Public Relations Society of America, http://www.prsa.org
Council of Public Relations Firms, http://www.prfirms.org
Institute for Public Relations, http://www.instituteforpr.com

Suggested additional reading materials available online include:

"Hiring a Public Relations Firm: A Guide for Clients," prepared by the Council of Public Relations Firms, http://www.prfirms.org
"Careers in Public Relations Firms: Opportunities in a Dynamic Industry," prepared by the Council of Public Relations Firms, http://www.prfirms.org
"Working with Your Public Relations Firm," prepared by the Council of Public Relations Firms, http://www.prfirms.org

"Standards for Conducting a PR Firm Search, Principles and Practices," prepared by the
   Council of Public Relations Firms, http://www.prfirms.org

Perspectives on firm management can be gained from:

Gitlow, Howard, *Quality Management Systems, a Practical Guide* (Boca Raton: St. Lucie
   Press, 2001).
Maister, David, *Managing the Professional Services Firm* (New York: Free Press, 1997).

QUESTIONS FOR FURTHER DISCUSSION

Negotiation Exercises

EXERCISE #1

As a consultant at a public relations firm, you receive a request from your client for
support. He tells you he has a great piece of news about a groundbreaking new business-to-business technology his company has developed and is about to introduce to
the marketplace. You and your team have analyzed the story, and have concluded that
it will only appeal to a business audience. Your client, though, insists that you pursue
broad consumer media. "I want you to get the CEO on Oprah," he insists. You know
you'll be lucky to get coverage in general business magazines.

   Work in teams, with one team playing the role of the client, the other the consultant. Then switch roles.

EXERCISE #2

Your consulting firm has written copy for a client brochure, and the client has rejected
it. She said the work was so bad that she had someone on her staff rewrite it, and she
refuses to pay your bill. As the senior manager on the client account, you review the
situation and conclude that the original instructions from the client were wrong.

   Again, have one team play the role of the client, the other the consultant, and then
switch.

Exercise in Ethics

A reporter contacts your firm, asserting that you could save lives by giving out details
about a client's research on a life-saving medicine. The client has shared the information with you on a strictly confidential basis, since the public launch of the drug is six
months in the future. You know the information is not for public release, but lives
hang in the balance.

   What should you do?

It's not easy, ProCom. But you're on the right road.

The greatest challenge of communication
is the illusion that it has taken place.

— *George Bernard Shaw*

15 CHALLENGES AND OPPORTUNITIES IN CORPORATE AND ORGANIZATIONAL COMMUNICATION

■ ■ ■

An organization's reputation is the sum of how its various stakeholders view it. But all too often companies leave such stakeholder perceptions to chance.

Enlightened companies know that an effective corporate or organizational communication process can both enhance and protect its reputation. And they also know that the reputation, while an intangible asset, provides a number of tangible benefits to the company.

Fordham University Business School professor Kevin T. Jackson describes the benefits of a strong reputation in his book *Building Reputational Capital*:

> A critical mass of credible evidence is showing a link between superior corporate reputations and financial performance ... Companies with above-average overall corporate reputation scores demonstrate greater ability to sustain or attain an above-average return on assets.[1]

Professor Jackson also elaborates some of the benefits such a reputation provides, noting that firms gain sustainable competitive advantage by cultivating intangible and inimitable assets, based on their ability to maintain the confidence of key stakeholder groups:

> Companies compete for clients, customers, investors, partners, employees, suppliers, and the support of local communities. A good reputation erects an intangible barrier that rivals stumble to get over. You can cut marketing expenses, command top dollar for your services, erect barriers to competition, and enjoy expanded latitude in decision-making. By itself, this competitive advantage ensures stronger long-run returns to better-reputed firms.[2]

Firms gain sustainable competitive advantage by cultivating intangible and inimitable assets, based on their ability to maintain the confidence of key stakeholder groups.

A significant challenge for those who run corporate or organizational communication functions is to manage the ways the organization engages its key stakeholders. Because an organization competes for the positive attention of the groups who matter to it, how it engages those stakeholders has meaningful bottom-line impact. As Professor Jackson notes, effective

Effective engagement with stakeholders and a strong reputation create a barrier to competition.

engagement with stakeholders and a strong reputation create a barrier to competition. But ineffective engagement and weak reputation make it easier for competitors to penetrate those barriers.

Chapters 2 through 14 focused on tangible ways to organize and manage the various forms of corporate and organizational communication, including communication intended to engage particular stakeholder audiences.

A further challenge is to exercise leadership to align all the functions with each other and with the operational, legal, financial, and administrative functions that collectively define the work of any organization.

A related challenge is for the communication function to be a respected participant in corporate deliberations, not an afterthought. Leaders of enlightened companies include reputational considerations—and the input of those whose primary job is to protect and enhance reputation—at the table when they make decisions. But that doesn't mean that the communication function is entitled to be at the table. It must earn the right to contribute.

> The communication function is not entitled to be at the table. It must earn the right to contribute.

■ ■ ■

EARNING A SEAT AT THE TABLE: DEFINING THE PROFESSIONAL COMMUNICATOR'S ROLE

> Leaders listen to advisors whose views they think they need, not those who insist on a hearing because of the organizational chart.

Former U.S. Secretary of State Henry Kissinger—who knew a thing or two about bureaucratic infighting—observed that leaders listen to advisors whose views they think they need, not those who insist on a hearing because of the organizational chart.

As public relations becomes increasingly important to senior executives, many professional communicators find themselves marginalized, as CEOs take advice from lawyers, friends, and others rather than from their chief communication officers. Professional communicators who aspire to work at the top levels of their organizations need the grounding necessary to become trusted advisors to their senior-most executives.

There are several reasons the communication function gets marginalized. Sometimes the marginalization is self-inflicted; often it is imposed by other functions such as corporate law, finance, or even by the CEO. But whether self-inflicted or imposed by others, the marginalization typically is grounded in how the communication function—and hence the leaders of that function—are defined. These include:

- Being cast as an implementer: the head of communication is seen as a doer rather than as a leader.
- Being cast as a tactician: whether the head of communication is implementing

or managing the function, communication is seen solely as a tool or tactic, and not as part of the strategic focus of the enterprise.

* Being cast as part of a functional area: the head of communication is seen as a writer, or as a media person, or as a technology person, and not as having enterprise-wide standing to offer advice beyond the narrow functional area.

There are a number of ways to overcome this marginalization. At the very least, professional communicators need to learn the objective and subjective factors that leaders use to choose whom to listen to, and develop the skills and temperaments necessary to become trusted advisors to management. Three skills, or areas of expertise, are especially necessary.

> A communicator must have a thorough knowledge of the organization's operations and of finance, product development, marketing and human resources.

First, in order to speak for the organization, and to have standing to advise on how the organization should communicate, a communicator must have a thorough knowledge of the organization's operations and of finance, product development, marketing and human resources.

Second, the communicator must have a worldview that includes knowledge of issues that affect the company, its industry, the marketplace in general, and emerging social trends.

> The communicator must have a worldview that includes knowledge of issues that affect the company.

And third, the communicator must possess the art of giving advice and of building trust, everything from thinking problems through from the perspective of senior executives to offering insights that would not otherwise occur to a senior management team.

> The communicator must possess the art of giving advice and of building trust.

But these three approaches, while necessary, are not sufficient. Part of the challenge to be overcome is the very word, communication. Unlike the skill-set needed for nearly every other business function, communication is a skill that every executive thinks he or she possesses. Because non-communication executives often assume that communicators' key competence is speaking and writing, they assume that the function is something anyone could do well if only they had the time. After all, they've been speaking since they were young children, and reading and writing since at least first grade. The same cannot be said of manufacturing, engineering, finance, or law.

> Executives who wouldn't dream of micromanaging the work product of the engineering department or the corporate law department have no problem micromanaging the work product of professional communicators.

As a result, executives who wouldn't dream of micromanaging the work product of the engineering department or the corporate law department have no problem micromanaging the work product of professional communicators. Or of bypassing the professional communicators until it's time to distribute what has been drafted (often poorly) by others.

There are several ways to overcome this perception. The first is for the professional communicator to model communication excellence in everything he or she does. The top communicator in the company needs to be demonstrably the most gifted communicator in any meeting of senior executives.

> The top communicator in the company needs to be demonstrably the most gifted communicator in any meeting of senior executives.

But the bigger challenge is to frame the communication role as something more than words on paper or in electronic format; as more than the simple transmission of information from the company to its audiences. The key is to define the communication role in terms of the stakeholder groups who matter to executives. The primary value of a senior communication executive is less about transmitting information—the typical definition of communication—than about predicting how the stakeholders who matter to senior management are likely to behave.

> The primary value of a senior communication executive is less about transmitting information than about predicting how the stakeholders who matter to senior management are likely to behave.

One of the most important roles of the professional communicator is to provide a perspective on constituency behavior that an organization would not otherwise have access to. In this sense, the professional communicator's role is like a lens: to provide a corrective perspective to bring into focus what may be unclear to the executive team (see Figure 15.1).

The corrective perspective works in both directions: the professional communicator helps a management team understand how any given constituency is likely to think, feel, and behave in any given circumstance; the communicator also helps bring a company's desired perception into focus for the constituency.

> Professional communicators, when we do our best work, function as applied anthropologists.

We have long believed that professional communicators are valued not because of our communication skills, but rather because of our ability to predict how groups who matter to management are likely to behave, and further to predict how to get those groups to behave in more beneficial ways. In this sense professional communicators, when we do our best work, function as applied anthropologists.

Like any anthropologist, the best communicators undertake rigorous observation of the behavior of individual groups. Such groups could include any or all of the following:

- Customers
- Employees
- Investors
- Regulators
- Legislators and federal and state executive branch officials

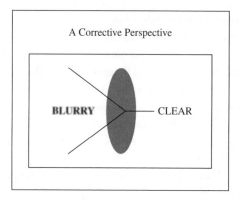

Figure 15.1   *(Illustration by Lisa Wagner)*

- Business partners
- Lenders
- Suppliers and vendors
- Communities in which a company does business
- Competitors
- Academics and other thought leaders such as think tanks and industry experts
- Industry associations
- Contract sales force, such as agents, brokers, and dealers
- The news media
- Society at large
- Any subset of any of the above

The best communicators further diagnose the values systems, social relationships, and power relationships within any given group, and among various groups. They understand what drives behavior within those groups, and understand how particular decisions are triggered and how the group's behavior plays out.

They can advise on how any given action or communication is likely to be interpreted by the group in question and how the behavior of any one group is likely to influence the behavior of the others.

Finally, professional communicators help mobilize the resources of their organizations to affect the behavior of those groups in ways that are more beneficial; that enhance the groups' relationship with the organization and that affirmatively contribute to a better reputation.

So the knowledge base of professional communicators is not just the mechanics of communication, or the industry or sector of the organization. Rather, like any anthropologist, the knowledge base involves understanding how to influence the groups that matter to the organization. Most of the chapters of this book address ways to assure the most effective engagement of these groups.

In most organizations there are structures to deal with each specific constituency. So the sales force deals with customers; human resources deals with employees; finance deals with bankers and investors; corporate law with regulators and legislators, and so on.

But the only standing structure whose mandate includes understanding all of these stakeholder groups, and the links among them, is the corporate or organizational communication function. Those who preside over corporate or organizational communication need to understand these links, and to be able to harvest the best knowledge about any given constituency. So the professional communicator needs to be able to diagnose behavior and prescribe a response beyond the individual silos that create artificial barriers between functional areas in a company. This cross-silo insight is a core competence, and one of the keys to reversing the marginalization of the function.

The ability to see patterns early, and to help a company influence the way a pattern plays out, can be greatly valued by a company's management team. The ability to engage management with

> The only standing structure whose mandate includes understanding all stakeholder groups, and the links among them, is the corporate or organizational communication function.

> The ability to see patterns early, and to help a company influence the way a pattern plays out, can be greatly valued by a company's management team.

a discussion of patterns and predictions of group behavior allows a professional communicator to argue persuasively in favor of taking difficult business decisions, even decisions that are contrary to the advice of other members of management who have their own expertise, such as lawyers, finance officers, or scientists.

| The professional communicator should generally avoid discussion of communication tactics and implementation with senior management. |

Finally, to overcome the marginalization of the function, and to demonstrate value beyond what is otherwise seen as the tactical practice of communication, the professional communicator should generally avoid discussion of communication tactics and implementation with senior management. Rather, the focus should be more strategic, on the outcomes that are desired among the constituencies who matter: what do we want our customers, employees, investors, communities, and other core constituencies to think, feel, know, and do? What do we need to do or not do, to say or not say, to cause them to think, feel, know, and do these things? Only after reaching agreement on desired end states should discussion focus on the mechanics of making that happen: on the tactics of communication. (More on being strategic follows later in the chapter.)

HISTORICAL PERSPECTIVE: EDWARD L. BERNAYS AND THE ROOTS OF APPLIED ANTHROPOLOGY

The seminal thinking about public relations as applied to anthropology dates to the 1920s. The father of modern public relations is Edward L. Bernays, who worked on the U.S. government committee that shaped U.S. public opinion during World War I, and who was the first person to call himself a public relations counselor. In 1923 Bernays taught the first university course in public relations—at New York University, where Fred and John and many of this book's contributors now teach. And that year he also published the first book on modern public relations, *Crystallizing Public Opinion*, to which the book you are reading is a successor. Bernays described public relations as "the vocation of the social scientist who advises clients on social attitudes and on the actions to take to win support of the public upon whom the viability of the client depends."[3]

Bernays writes, "The public relations counsel is first of all a student ... [whose] field of study is the public mind. His textbooks for this study are the facts of life ... He brings the talent of his intuitive understanding to the aid of his practical and psychological tests and surveys."[4]

Bernays adds:

The public relations counsel must discover why it is that a public opinion exists independently of church, school, press, lecture platform, and motion picture screen—how far this public opinion affects these institutions and how far these institutions affect public opinion. He must discover what the stimuli are to which public opinion responds most readily. To his understanding of what he actually can measure he must add a thorough knowledge of the principles which govern individual and group action. A fundamental study of group and individual psychology is required before the public relations counsel can determine how readily individuals or groups will accept modifications of viewpoints or policies.[5]

Bernays' description of public relations has direct bearing on professional communication for many reasons, not least of which is that it doesn't mention the mechanics of communication at all. Rather, it focuses on how those who matter to a company think and feel, and how to get them to think and feel differently. It focuses on social attitudes and on the actions a company must take to win support. It describes the public relations counselor as a social scientist—essentially 1923 vocabulary for an applied anthropologist. Even the title of his book, *Crystallizing Public Opinion*, focuses not on the mechanics of communication but on the outcome.

Bernays' description also recognizes that the most effective way to change groups' perception is to act in certain ways; that communication needs to be grounded first in the action a company takes. He says that a public relations practitioner is

> as much an advisor on actions as he is the communicator of these actions to the public ... He acts in this capacity as a consultant both in interpreting the public to his client and in helping to interpret his client to the public. He helps to mould the action of his client as well as to mould public opinion.[6]

> Bernays' description recognizes that the most effective way to change groups' perception is to act in certain ways; that communication needs to be grounded first in the action a company takes.

Bernays also recognized that groups—in modern vocabulary *stakeholders* such as those listed above—behave in predictable, if shifting, ways:

> The public relations counsel works with public opinion. Public opinion is the product of individual minds. Individual minds make up the group mind. And the established order of things is maintained by the inertia of the group. Three factors make it possible for the public relations counsel to overcome even this inertia. These are, first, the [overlapping] group formation of society; second, the continuous shifting of groups; third, the changed physical conditions to which groups respond. All of these are brought about by the natural inherent flexibility of individual human nature.[7]

And finally, Bernays notes that the interaction between a company and its critical constituencies isn't a one-time event, but rather continues over time, and each interaction is shaped by prior interactions and reactions:

Action and interaction are continually going on between the forces projected out to the public and the public itself. The public relations counsel must understand this fact in its broadest and most detailed implications. He must understand not only what these various forces are, but he must be able to evaluate their relative powers with fair accuracy.[8]

Bernays recognizes that the value of the public relations counselor—and today the value of the any professional communicator—is the ability to advise on the ongoing engagement between a company and its critical constituencies, and in particular how a company's engagement is likely to influence how that constituency is likely to think, feel, and behave across a number of scenarios.

Bernays' description of public relations—as a vocation applied by a social scientist who advises a client on actions to take in order to win support of the public on whom the client's viability depends—is a good way for a professional communicator to see his or her role.

■ ■ ■

THE FUTURE OF CORPORATE AND ORGANIZATIONAL COMMUNICATION AND PUBLIC RELATIONS

Fortune magazine, drawing on U.S. Bureau of Labor Statistics figures, projects that public relations will be among the 10 fastest growing professions in the U.S. through 2016.[9]

This growth is due mainly to three trends, according to John Paluszek, senior counsel to Ketchum Public Relations and past president of the Public Relations Society of America:

- PR is important today to every major institution: for-profits, not-for-profits, governments, and religions.
- Increasingly, institutions recognize that they practice many kinds of communication with many constituencies, and that they must all be coordinated, which is the proper role of public relations or its subset corporate communications.
- Public relations is being practiced around the globe.

Paluszek, at a Professional Development Seminar sponsored by the M.S. Degree Program in Corporate Communications and Public Relations at New York University, said that the profession is at its pinnacle, in terms of challenges and opportunities, and that his only regret is "that I am not starting out now."

SIX CHALLENGES FACING THE PUBLIC RELATIONS PRACTITIONER TODAY

By Judy Voss, APR, Director of Professional Development for the Public Relations Society of America, the world's largest organization for public relations professionals (http://www. prsa.org)

Successfully conquering today's challenges will give you the experience and perspective you need to secure your company's reputation, and keep you employed for a long time to come. From my point of view, these six challenges are the most critical to address first.

"TELL THE TRUTH. PROVE IT WITH ACTION"

Ethics is at the top of my list of challenges. I'm quoting two Arthur Page Society principles in the subhead above.[10] Page, a pioneer in the practice of public relations, served as the first vice president of public relations for AT&T beginning in 1927. He set the standards for the position as it related to strategic public relations in corporate management. He counseled corporations and several U.S. presidents, always managing their reputations supported with ethical conduct. The Page persona is missing today.

I asked a colleague, Tom Vitelli, APR, Fellow PRSA, Assistant Vice President, Communications for Intermountain Health Care, Salt Lake City, UT, about challenges he sees in the field. Ethics is also at the top of his list. He comments: "Ethics are a foundation for credibility, and credibility is a foundation of business development. It should be possible for PR firms and professionals to deliver their services on the basis of ethical advocacy as well as effectiveness in the achievement of business goals."

Public relations professionals who aspire to sit at the management table, to develop policy and participate in strategic planning to meet business goals must choose to demonstrate ethical behavior. You must think ethics, feel ethics, communicate ethics. That is your challenge.

Your CEOs and CFOs must be counseled to do the right thing in all cases at all times. Period. Corporate leaders read newspapers and watch CNN. They see dishonest corporate leaders getting caught and going to jail. So those leaders who dare to think or act without considering ethics should be prepared for a downfall with no sympathy from their publics. Or their public relations counselor after the fact. Period.

> Leaders who dare to think or act without considering ethics should be prepared for a downfall with no sympathy from their publics. Or their public relations counselor after the fact. Period.

NEW COMMUNICATIONS TECHNOLOGIES

Second on my list of challenges facing the PR practitioner today is how to keep up with changes in the new communications technology field. As a professional, you must pay attention to technology *plus* experience it yourself in order to learn just how powerful the new tools are. You obviously have to know the media habits of your publics. In today's segmented markets you may choose to reach them using Twitter, blogs, wikis, RSS feeds, or pod casting to get your company's message to them. After all, in this day of participative journalism, new technology is how your publics are reaching you, talking about your company, offering their opinions about your company's reputation.

Mixing the new technology with the "old fashioned" television and radio broadcasting, print advertising, and direct mail continues to be a challenge. I never thought I'd consider faxing as a type of direct mail, but today I do.

GLOBALIZATION

> Our friends are closer—
> so are our enemies.

Third on my list is the globalization of companies. The fact that corporations buy or partner with their counterparts in other countries means having to understand language and culture barriers. Certainly technology has shrunk the world. Our friends are closer—so are our enemies.

As much as the practice of public relations emphasizes working things out—solidifying relationships and building a better community—not everyone is listening. Americans are finding out just how much some of the world hates us. The process of globalization is where we have the most to learn and gain. Globalization, in the long run, will impact individuals, jobs, our economy, security, and power base.

THE MEDIA

Another colleague I turned to for the challenges she faces is Melissa May, APR, International Communication Consultant for the Population Council, New York, NY. Journalists show up prominently on her list. She cites such media challenges as journalists' failure fully to explore topics and their focus on titillating news. She goes on to mention media spinning and says, "I've been troubled by the habit of some journalists to print ideological language and concepts as if they are reality, using the language of extremists and incorporating it into journalistic lexicon ... lending the terms credibility by repeating them."

Her examples include the media "describing a judge whose political leaning is different from theirs as a 'judicial activist'" or "the purposeful confusion over ... emergency contraception and how reporters continue to discuss EC as if it were abortion when the research shows that it prevents pregnancy, thus actually reducing the numbers of abortions."

She points out that "Some terms used by reporters today may have started out as quotes by people on one side of an argument, but they soon were incorporated into coverage as standard language, skewing the perception of these issues by readers, listeners, and viewers. It seems more and more that reporters come into interviews with their minds made up and are simply looking for quotes to reinforce the story they have already written," says May.

BUILDING TRUST

Closely tied to all other challenges, building trust just may be the most difficult. Post-election re-counts demonstrate continuing distrust with voting systems and the people behind them. Ongoing religious wars and hard economic times also cultivate mainstream distrust. So where do you start? As Tim McMahon states in this book's Chapter 10, "Integrated Communication," "Relations are built on trust. To be trusted, be trustworthy." Start with yourself. Expanding trust and trustworthiness to your friends can be a strong framework for building trust with colleagues and communities, both online and in-person.

SURVIVAL

The guidance you're receiving while reading this book will help prepare you to meet the challenges listed above. In addition, I see the list of character traits below as "must-haves" for the new millennium public relations professional. To acquire them is an additional, very personal challenge.

- *Ambition*: Searching for opportunities to showcase your strengths and move up in the world
- *Knowledge*: Keeping up with changes, and wanting to participate with the new technology tools and whatever the future holds
- *Energy*: Eating, sleeping, and staying fit. Doing what you have to do to be proactive and responsive at work
- *Joy*: Liking what you do; enjoying your job while helping others carry out their own jobs
- *Curiosity*: Being inquisitive not only about work but also your entire environment; developing your perspective
- *Caring*: Having integrity and sincerity as a base for coming into the public relations profession in the first place; staying in touch with these feelings as you grow in your career

Back to the Arthur Page Society for one more principle, "Conduct public relations as if the whole company depends on it." We continue to see from today's headlines and the practitioner's capabilities to manage their company's reputation, that indeed, the whole company does depend on it.

■ ■ ■

BECOMING TRULY STRATEGIC IN MANAGING CORPORATE AND ORGANIZATIONAL COMMUNICATION

The most enlightened companies see communication as a strategic asset; as what in the military is known as a "force multiplier." Effective communication can help a company meet its business goals faster and better; ineffective communication can be a drag on performance.

One key to success is for those who run the communication function to organize communication strategically: focused on accomplishing defined business and communication goals.

> Many communication people default to the tactical. But enlightened communicators at all levels default to the strategic—to the goals that communication is intended to accomplish, and the most effective ways to accomplish those goals.

Many communication people default to the tactical—to discussion of press releases, or e-mails, or of other tools of the trade, leading to self-marginalization. But enlightened communicators at all levels default to the strategic—to the goals that communication is intended to accomplish, and the most effective ways to accomplish those goals. Over time this strategic emphasis can become habitual, and can lead to even greater contribution to an organization's success.

> Being habitually strategic means making judgments based on the goals to be accomplished, as one's first resort and not as an afterthought.

Being habitually strategic means making judgments based on the goals to be accomplished, as one's first resort and not as an afterthought. It means conditioning one's behavior to resist the temptation to leap to tactics but rather to consider consequences of various forms of action and communication. And because, as Aristotle taught us (see Chapter 2), we are what we habitually do, we become strategic by deliberately and persistently behaving in goal-oriented ways, and remaining focused on a specific outcome.

Individuals become habitually strategic when they persistently weigh alternative courses of action against desired outcomes, and act on the choices that most clearly lead to those outcomes. Organizations become habitually strategic when their leaders insist that all parts of the organization act strategically as a first resort. This means encouraging strategic thinking by, among other things, rewarding strategic decisions even if they sometimes fail, and discouraging immediate defaults to the tactical even when they sometimes succeed.

Habitually strategic organizations set clear goals and hold managers accountable for reaching those goals; they persistently reinforce those goals. The classic contemporary example of a corporation behaving strategically is General Electric, which, under the tenure of Chief Executive Officer Jack Welch, had very clear goals and strategies and held managers accountable for meeting those goals and fulfilling those strategies. Tactical execution that advanced those strategies was encouraged; tactics that distracted from the fulfillment of the strategies were discouraged, even when they were otherwise incrementally attractive. The best-known General Electric strategy during that period was to be number one or two in each of its areas of business, or to exit that sector.

Jack Welch's successor as General Electric CEO, Jeffrey Immelt, told *Fast Company* magazine the most important lesson he learned from Welch. Immelt said, "Every leader needs to clearly explain the top three things the organization is doing. If you can't, you're not leading well."[11]

Habitually strategic organizations also establish a culture of accountability, insisting that their values be lived and not merely posted on bulletin boards. And, not surprisingly, these companies find it easier to survive significant setbacks with minimal reputational, operational, and financial harm. Because all players in a company know what is expected, they manage to avoid many of the crises and much of the self-inflicted damage that plague companies who have not developed these habits. And when the inevitable negative event happens, the company is able to respond quickly and effectively, to take responsible action, and to communicate in ways that restore or maintain the confidence and trust of its core constituencies.

> Habitually strategic organizations also establish a culture of accountability, insisting that their values be lived and not merely posted on bulletin boards.

Those who head corporate and organizational communication can contribute to an organization's strategic success in two ways: first, they can use communication as a strategic tool that allows all stakeholders to understand what the organization's mission, vision, and values are. Second, they can establish a strategic focus for each of the elements of corporate and organizational communication: employee communications, community relations, media relations, investor relations, and so forth. They assure alignment of the various functions in support of a corporation's larger corporate goals.

What Is Strategy?

The word "strategy" is much-used and misunderstood in business and in communication. Its origins lie in warfare: the skills necessary to command an army. The English word "strategy" comes from the ancient Greek verb στρατηγεω (strategeo), to be a general or to command a military force. That verb, in turn, derives from the noun for army, στρατοσ (stratos), and the verb to lead, αγειν (agein). So the classical meaning of a strategist is a leader of a military force, what we would call a general. The word carried that meaning for much of Western history, from the Greeks to the Romans to the nineteenth century in Europe.

Not surprisingly, then, the first prominent modern use of the word was by a military officer writing about warfare. It appeared in the classic volume on military affairs, *On War*, by the Prussian general and head of the Prussian War College, Carl von Clausewitz. His 1832 book, ostensibly about the qualities necessary to conduct a military campaign, has become a classic of military strategy, governing much U.S. war planning (with the exceptions of the Vietnam war and the war in Iraq). But *On War* is useful not merely as a book about warfare. It is in many ways the seminal book on strategy itself, both military and civilian, and can provide valuable insights into business management and leadership in general and into the leadership of communication in particular.

Indeed, the Strategy Institute of the Boston Consulting Group argues that the principles elaborated upon in *On War* are essential to understanding contemporary business strategy:

> Clausewitz' *magnum opus* … deserves, now more than ever, the full attention of the modern business strategist for accomplishing the unlikely feat of offering new ways to order thinking in disorderly times and provides steadiness in charting strategy in an unstable environment.[12]

In Clausewitz, the Boston Consulting Group finds a kind of thinking that is not restricted to military matters, but rather is an integral part of leadership—leadership that applies to business management, and also leadership as it applies to those who run communication. The key is "ordered thinking"—that is, thinking that proceeds in a certain sequence and is directed toward certain outcomes. In a time of rapid social and technological change, the more unstable the environment, the greater the need for such ordered thinking.

Too often communication is seen as soft—as sentimental, and as intended to make people feel good. But using ordered thinking to help an organization accomplish tangible goals can help change the perception of the communication function internally. A strong leader can cut through the misperception, emotion, and clutter, and can use Clausewitz' principles to guide his or her communication organization to more closely resemble the hard science of management.

The Boston Consulting Group notes:

> It is the true strategist … who can benefit most from the work of Carl von Clausewitz because *On War* is quintessentially a philosophy of strategy that contains the conceptual seeds for its constant rejuvenation. It is a philosophy that fuses logical analysis, historical understanding, psychological insight, and sociological comprehension into an encompassing exposition of strategic thought and behavior. It is a philosophy that effectively prevents strategy from ever degenerating into dogma.[13]

The Boston Consulting Group describes why Clausewitz' way of organizing thinking and courageous behavior is so important:

> In its ultimate consequence, the philosophy of Clausewitz demands that commanders and executives not merely think when formulating strategy but that they arrive at a stage where they literally think strategy.[14]

In other words, by following Clausewitz one can learn to become *habitually strategic*. Over the years coauthor Fred Garcia has found that following Clausewitz holds one of the keys to effective stewardship of the organizational communication function. Clausewitz' principles can help professional communicators think clearly and organize their activities in ways that predictably help enhance an organization's reputation, operation, financial performance, and enterprise value. The ordered thinking, and the rigor that it represents, also appeals to executives and begins to neutralize the objection that communication is soft or sentimental.

Among the strategic principles Clausewitz lays out that have particular relevance to the communication function are the following:

ENDS AND MEANS: EYES ON THE PRIZE

Clausewitz' most famous utterance is the observation that *war is the continuation of policy by other means*. It is part of a continuum, a tool in the service of a much broader process. But it is only a tool. Clausewitz writes:

> The political object is the goal, war is the means of reaching it, and means can never be considered in isolation from their purpose.[15]

Means can never be considered in isolation from their purpose. This is the essence of habitual strategic thinking. This is Clausewitz' breakthrough concept that informs contemporary business leadership, and that can inform leadership of organizational communication.

The corollary to Clausewitz' observation that war is the continuation of policy by other means is that effective communication is merely the continuation of business by other means. The specific ways to communicate with constituencies are tools in a continuum of tools, all in the service of some clearly articulated business goal. And just as war is not the goal but the means, communication is not the goal, but simply the means to some other end. And since means can never be considered in isolation from their purpose, this view sees communication as the continuation of business, not as something separate from business—and in particular not as an afterthought.

> Effective communication is merely the continuation of business by other means.

> Communication is not the goal, but simply the means to some other end.

The principle of the objective, as Clausewitz' principle is called, helps the habitual strategic thinker to avoid impulsive—and self-indulgent—rushes to the tactical. Rather than doing what feels good, or what has always been done, the enlightened communication leader considers the situation as it presents itself and as it is likely to evolve, identifies a clear goal or end state toward which the resources of the enterprise will be directed, and prescribes the means that are most likely to accomplish the goal or end state.

The leader further evaluates tactical options based on the likelihood that they will contribute to the achievement of the goal, not because they make the leader feel good, or defer short-term pain or embarrassment. The test of whether any given tactical response should be taken is its alignment to the goal. Means can never be considered in isolation from their purpose.

So one begins to manage communication by understanding a business goal: either a desired business outcome, or a change in the business environment. This may include enhancing employee productivity, selling more products, changing a regulatory requirement that impairs organizational performance, and so forth.

Communicating effectively, in turn, begins with a clear communication goal: a change in the emotional, intellectual, or behavioral predispositions of target constituencies. This may include improving employee morale, increasing demand for a company's products, changing regulators' minds, and so forth.

Focusing on how those who matter to management—employees, customers, investors, regulators, adversaries—think and feel, and how they are likely to think and feel in the future, is a critical part of habitual strategic thinking in communication.

It is all too common for communication professionals to measure output: the number of employee meetings held, the number of press releases issued, the number of stories published. But these are measures of process, not of the goals. They are at best a weak proxy for effectiveness. Rather than focus on process, a more meaningful measure of communication impact is the degree that the communication goals—changes in constituencies' attitudes and opinions—have been accomplished.

ACTION AND REACTION

> Communication is an act of will directed toward a living entity that reacts.

A second Clausewitz concept that informs contemporary business leadership and communication is his observation that war is less like art and more like commerce; he calls it an "act of will directed toward a living entity that *reacts*."[16]

Communication is also an act of will directed toward a living entity that reacts. That living entity is the group of stakeholders who matter to management; the reaction is how that group is likely to think and feel and what it is likely to do in any given post-communication scenario.

> The effective communicator grounds all planning and implementation on the desired reaction among critical constituencies.

The effective communicator grounds all planning and implementation on the desired reaction among critical constituencies. Communication is not merely the transmission of information, but the predictable reaction to that information by the audience to which it is directed.

BUILDING IN FLEXIBILITY

The third principle of Clausewitz that informs communication is his notion of *friction: the innumerable small barriers to effective implementation of a strategy.* As Winston Churchill observed, "You'll never get to your destination if you stop to throw a rock at every dog that barks along the way." Clausewitz takes account of the inevitable distractions that interfere with the implementation of a plan:

> Everything in strategy is very simple, but that does not mean that everything is very easy. Once it has been determined, from the political conditions, what a war is meant to achieve and what it can achieve, it is easy to chart the course. But great strength of character, as well as great lucidity and firmness of mind, is required in order to follow through steadily, to carry out the plan, and not to be thrown off course by thousands of diversions.[17]

Similarly, in communication, the important principles are very simple. (Many are described in Chapters 2 through 14.) But implementing the simple principles can be complicated, especially in an environment of instantaneous linked communication, where all constituencies have near-simultaneous access to information about a company, both positive and negative. It can be very difficult to keep the various communication disciplines aligned with each other and with the communication and business goals, especially as each discipline works to respond to issues that arise with the constituency over which it has responsibility.

The "thousands of diversions" Clausewitz speaks about can be a defining part of many communication tasks. For example, in many large corporate media relations departments, a common complaint is that the media relations staff spend so much of their time fielding incoming press inquiries that they rarely get the opportunity to think strategically and affirmatively to shape stories. One of the challenges for communication leadership in such circumstances is to create structures that are immune from the day-to-day crush of incoming inquiries and to focus intently on self-generated media visibility.

Being strategic in communication involves recognizing that there will always be real internal and external obstacles to implementing any communication plan effectively. But that shouldn't deter one from developing the plan and being diligent in its implementation. Rather, recognizing the likelihood of obstacles allows the leader to plan for the inevitability of distraction, and to build processes to overcome, ignore, prioritize, or otherwise manage through those distractions. To use the Churchill analogy, the leader needs to recognize the likelihood that dogs will bark along the way, and build a plan that permits the organization not to allow the barking dogs to deter it from the most productive course.

Clausewitz' successor in the development of Western military strategy was Helmuth von Moltke, who served as Chief of Staff of the Prussian (and after unification, the German) General Staff for 30 years in the mid-to-late nineteenth century. He famously observed that *no plan survives its initial implementation*. Rather, each plan needs to be continuously adapted to take account of individual tactical encounters that modify what is possible and what is likely to be accomplished in the short term. But this observation does not minimize the importance of planning. Rather, it places a premium on having a clear and powerful set of goals and strategies, and recognizes that individual tactics will change as the plan is implemented. The goals and strategies, however, are unlikely to change; only the tactics, which will need to be adapted to reflect the situational reality. But the tactics are merely means, and means can never be considered in isolation from their purpose. So if the planned tactics should become ineffective in accomplishing their goals, they should be discarded in favor of other, more promising tactics.

Moltke writes:

> No plan of operations extends with certainty beyond the first encounter with the enemy's main strength. Certainly the commander in chief will keep his great objective continuously in mind, undisturbed by the vicissitudes of events. But the path on which he hopes to reach it can never be firmly established in advance. Throughout the campaign he must make a

series of decisions on the basis of situations that cannot be foreseen. The successive acts of war are thus not premeditated designs, but on the contrary are spontaneous acts guided by military measures. Everything depends on penetrating the uncertainty of veiled situations to evaluate the facts, to clarify the unknown, to make decisions rapidly, and then to carry them out with strength and constancy.[18]

> The communication leader needs to develop a robust plan that clearly manifests the goals and strategies, but remains sufficiently flexible to deal with mid-course corrections based on results of the initial tactical implementation of the plan.

So the communication leader needs to develop a robust plan that clearly manifests the goals and strategies, but remains sufficiently flexible to deal with mid-course corrections based on results of the initial tactical implementation of the plan. He or she needs to develop structures to penetrate the uncertainty of veiled situations, to evaluate facts, and procedures to make tactical decisions quickly.

■ ■ ■

> The key to successful corporate and organizational communication is to have clarity about the destination – the reputation that will help a company better accomplish its goals – and of the best path by which to get there.

The key to successful corporate and organizational communication is to have clarity about the destination—the reputation that will help a company better accomplish its goals—and of the best path by which to get there. That path typically includes assuring that all of the communication functions of an organization are strategically grounded, well-managed, and aligned with each other and with the broader activities of the enterprise. When they are, the destination is reached faster and more effectively; and the journey is considerably more enjoyable.

NOTES

Preface

1 James E. Grunig and Todd Hunt, *Managing Public Relations* (New York: Holt, Rinehart and Winston, 1984), p. 7.

Chapter 1

1 David W. Guth and Charles Marsh, *Public Relations, A Values-Drive Approach* (Needham Heights, MA: Pearson Education, Allyn and Bacon, 2000), pp. 292–4.
2 Charles J. Fombrun, *Reputation: Realizing Value From the Corporate Brand* (Boston: Harvard Business School Press, 1996), p. 376.
3 Ibid., p. 9.
4 George Cheney, *Rhetoric in an Organizational Society* (Columbia, SC: University of South Carolina Press, 1991).
5 Starbucks, "Sneak Peek at New Ad Campaign," http://blogs.starbucks.com/blogs/customer/archive/2009/04/30/sneak-peek-at-new-ad-campaign.aspx.
6 Lehman Brothers e-mail regarding suspending executive compensation, at Committee on Oversight and Government Reform, http://oversight.house.gov/documents/20081006141219.pdf.
7 Homily by Archbishop Sean P. O'Malley, July 30, 2003, at Archdiocese of Boston Web site, http://www.rcab.org/News/homily030730.html.
8 Ernie Grigg, "The Immigration Debate and the Catholic Church in the United States: The Archdiocese of New York" (MS capstone, New York University, 2008), p. 20.
9 Kurt Eichenwald, *Conspiracy of Fools: A True Story* (New York: Broadway Books, 2005), p. 590.
10 Hugh Lofting, *The Story of Doctor Dolittle* (A Yearling Book, May 1988), p. 76.
11 Harris Interactive, *The 10th Annual RQ: The 60 Most Visible Companies*, http://www.harrisinteractive.com/services/pubs/HI_BSC_REPORT_AnnualRQ2008_SummaryReport.pdf.
12 Rob Cox, "Too Small to Bail Has a Nice Ring to It," *New York Times*, September 28, 2009, http://www.nytimes.com/2009/09/29/business/29views.html.
13 Matt Taibbi, "Inside the Great American Bubble Machine," *Rolling Stone*, July 2, 2009, http://www.rollingstone.com/politics/story/28816321/inside_the_great_american_bubble_machine.
14 Johnson & Johnson Credo at http://www.jnj.com/our_credo/index.htm.
15 Booz & Company, "CEOs Hold Steady in the Storm," May 12, 2009, http://www.booz.com/global/home/what_we_think/reports_and_white_papers/article/45574145.
16 Carter Dougherty, "A Happy Family of 8,000, But For How Long?," *New York Times*, July 11, 2009, BU1.
17 Brent D. Ruben, Linda Lederman, and David W. Gibson (eds.), *Communication Theory: A Casebook Approach* (Dubuque, IA: Kendall Hunt, 2000), pp. 173–201.
18 Paul Watzlawick, Janet Beavin Bavelas, and Donald D. Jackson, *Pragmatics of Human Communication* (New York: Norton, 1967).

Chapter 2

1 Edward L. Bernays, *Propaganda*, with an introduction by Mark Crispin Miller (New York: IG Publishing, 1928 and 2005), p. 69.

2 "Enforcement and Communication of the IABC Code for Professional Communicators," *International Association of Business Communicators Code of Ethics for Professional Communicators*, http://www.iabc.com/members/joining/code.htm, p. 2.

3 *International Association of Business Communicators Code of Ethics for Professional Communicators*, http://www.iabc.com/members/joining/code.htm.

4 Interview with James E. Lukaszewski, APR, Fellow, PRSA, and member of PRSA Board of Ethics and Professional Standards, July 22, 2005.

5 Interview with Lukaszewski.

6 "A Message from the PRSA Board of Ethics and Professional Standards," PRSA *Member Code of Ethics* (New York: PRSA, 2000), p. 6.

7 Ibid., p. 11.

8 Ibid.

9 Ibid.

10 John Stauber and Sheldon Rampton, *Toxic Sludge is Good for You: Lies, Damn Lies and the Public Relations Industry* (Monroe: Common Courage Press, 1995), p. 14.

11 Ibid., pp. 203–4.

12 Ibid., pp. 205–6.

13 Ibid., p. 4.

14 Ibid., p. 192.

15 David Barstow and Robin Stein, "Under Bush, A New Age of Prepackaged TV News," *The New York Times*, March 13, 2005, http://www.nytimes.com/2005/3/13/politics/13covert.html.

16 "FCC Warns Broadcasters on Sourcing Video News Releases," *Reuters*, April 14, 2005, http://www.nytimes.com/reuters/politics/politics-television-videonews.htm

17 Quote from Michael Copps, FCC Commissioner, ibid.

18 Radio-Television News Directors Association, *RTNDA Guidelines for Use of Non-Editorial Video and Audio*, 2005, developed by the RTNDA Ethics Committee, as found on the organization's Web site, http://www.rtnda.org.

19 Ibid.

20 Sheldon Rampton, "Fake News? We Told You So, Ten Years Ago," *PR Watch*, vol. 12, no. 2, http://www.prwatch.org/prwissues/2005Q2/toldyouso.html.

21 Greg Toppo, "Education Dept. Paid Commentator to Promote the Law," *USA Today*, January 7, 2005, at http://www.usatoday.com/news/washington/2005-01-06-williams-whitehouse_x.htm.

22 Statement by Tribune Media Services, in Poynter Institute, *Poynter Forums, PoynterOnline*, http://poynter.org/forum/view_post.asp?id=8580.

23 Ben Feller, "Senators Probe Administration-Paid Journalist; Pundit Paid By Education Department Calls Move a 'Witchhunt'," Associated Press, January 13, 2005.

24 Howard Kurtz, "Propaganda Wars," *Washington Post*, January 27, 2005.

25 PRSA *Member Code of Ethics*, p. 11.

26 Larry Tye, *The Father of Spin: Edward L. Bernays and the Birth of Public Relations* (New York: Owl Books, 1998), p. 7.

27 Ibid.

28 Ibid.

29 Ibid., p. 58.

30 PRSA *Member Code of Ethics*, Approved by the PRSA Assembly, October 2000, p. 13.

31 Ibid., p. 14.

32 IABC *Code of Ethics for Professional Communicators*.

33 PRSA *Member Code of Ethics*, p. 15.

34 IABC *Code of Ethics for Professional Communicators*.

35 PRSA *Member Code of Ethics*, p. 15.

36 IABC *Code of Ethics for Professional Communicators*.

37 Unattributed article, "Omnicom Unit Settles on Overbilling Suit," *The New York Times*, April 21, 2005, http://www.nytimes.com/2005/04/21/business/media/21addes.html. (Full

disclosure: at the time of writing coauthor Helio Fred Garcia held shares of Omnicom Group, the parent company of Fleishman-Hillard.)

38 Ted Rohrlich and Ralph Frammolino, "PR Exec to Plead Guilty in Fraud; Steve Sugerman Will Cooperate in the Probe of Overbilling of DWP by Fleishman-Hillard," *Los Angeles Times*, June 10, 2005, http://www.latimes.com/news/local/la-me-fleishman-10jun10,1,5463756.story?coll=la-headlines-california.

39 Unattributed article, "Former Ogilvy Executives Sentenced for Overbilling," *The New York Times*, July 15, 2005, p. C5.

40 PRSA *Member Code of Ethics*, pp. 6, 7.

41 Bernays, *Propaganda*.

42 IABC *Code of Ethics for Professional Communicators*, ibid.

43 IPRA *Code of Athens*, http://www.ipra.org/detail.asp?articleid=22.

44 PRSA *Member Code of Ethics*, p. 15.

45 Tye, *The Father of Spin*, p. 49.

46 *CBS 60 Minutes*, January 19, 1992.

47 John R. MacArthur, *Second Front: Censorship and Propaganda in the Gulf War* (New York: Hill and Wang, 1992), pp. 51, 53.

48 *Integrity: The Spirit & Letter of Our Commitment*, General Electric, http://www.ge.com.

49 *Boeing Code of Conduct*, January 26, 2004, http://www.boeing.com.

50 Dan Richman, "Analysis: Boeing Conduct Code Worked Properly, Expert Says," *Seattle Post-Intelligencer*, March 8, 2005, http://seattlepi.nwsource.com/business/214916_ethics08.html.

51 Alan Murray, "Citigroup CEO Pursues Culture of Ethics," *Wall Street Journal*, March 2, 2005, p. A2.

52 *Enron Corp. Code of Ethics*, July 2000, http://www.thesmokinggun.com, p. 4.

53 *Enron Corp. Code of Ethics*, p. 2.

54 Barbara Ley Toffler with Jennifer Reingold, *Final Accounting: Ambition, Greed, and the Fall of Arthur Andersen* (New York: Broadway Books, 2003), p. 7.

55 Ibid., p. 124.

56 Ibid., pp. 124–6.

57 Ibid., p. 60.

58 Ibid., p. 8.

59 MacArthur, *Second Front*, p. 49.

60 Jack O'Dwyer, "PR Opinion/Items," *Jack O'Dwyer's Newsletter*, January 22, 1992, p. 4.

61 *CBS 60 Minutes*.

62 MacArthur, *Second Front*, p. 58.

63 Ibid., p. 61.

64 Ibid., p. 58.

65 Ibid., p. 68.

66 Ibid., p. 65.

67 As recounted in *O'Dwyer's PR Services Report*, vol. 6, no. 2 (1992), p. 1, and *Jack O'Dwyer's Newsletter*, February 26, 1992, p. 1.

68 On September 9, 1992 Fred Garcia contacted Hill & Knowlton about the CFK controversy and was referred to Thomas Ross, head of the media services group. Garcia told Ross that he was about to launch a communication ethics class at New York University; that he was assigning MacArthur's book, and that MacArthur would be a guest-speaker in the class. Garcia told Ross that in fairness to H&K, he wanted to give H&K the opportunity to tell its side of the story, and would make available time either before, during, or after MacArthur's talk. Ross said he was not interested in debating MacArthur, whom he described as a self-defeating alarmist. Garcia reiterated that he was inviting H&K to speak before, during, or after MacArthur. Ross said that H&K had probably spent too much time addressing MacArthur's views already, and would be reluctant to commit more resources to address the class. Garcia noted that he intended to continue to include MacArthur's allegations in his writing and teaching. H&K was invited to send documents outlining their point of view on the scandal. Ross said that H&K had been vindicated and declined to discuss the matter further. Source: Contemporaneous notes taken after phone call between Helio Fred Garcia and Thomas Ross, September 9, 1992

69 *Inside PR*, July/August, 1992, p. 30.

70 *O'Dwyer's PR Services Report*, vol. 6, no. 8, August, 1992, p. 1.

71 PRSA *Member Code of Ethics*, p. 13.
72 Interview with Lukaszewski.
73 Edward L. Bernays, *Crystallizing Public Opinion* (New York: Boni and Liveright, 1923), p. 12.
74 Aristotle, *Rhetoric*, I, 2, 1, in John Henry Reese (ed.), *The "Art" of Rhetoric with English Translation*, vol. 22 of *Aristotle in Twenty Three Volumes*, Loeb Classical Library (Cambridge, MA: Harvard University Press, 1982), p. 15.
75 Ibid.
76 Cicero, *Brutus*, xxii, 46, in J.S. Watson (trans.), *Cicero on Oratory and Orators* (Carbondale and Edwardsville: Southern Illinois University Press, 1970), p. 273.
77 Ibid., p. 274.
78 Plato, *Gorgias*, 452e, in W.R.M. Lamb, *Lysis, Symposium, Gorgias with an English Translation*, vol. 3 of *Plato in Twelve Volumes* (Cambridge, MA: Harvard University Press, 1983), p. 279.
79 Ibid.
80 Ibid., 455a, p. 287.
81 Ibid., 458e–459c, pp. 299–301. Note: the translator alternates his translation of *ho rhetor* between "rhetorician" and "orator." For the sake of consistency, we translate it as "rhetorician" three times in this quotation, and shall do so in all subsequent quotations.
82 Ibid., 463a, p. 313.
83 Ibid., 463d, p. 315.
84 Ibid., 465b, p. 319.
85 Ibid., 465c, p. 321.

Chapter 3

1 2000 Merck & Co. Inc. Annual Report, p. 22.
2 James E. Grunig and Todd Hunt, *Managing Public Relations* (Orlando, FL: Harcourt Brace Jovanovich, 1984), pp. 49, 399.
3 Ibid., p. 13.
4 Gina Kolata, "Pharmacists Help Drug Promotions," *The New York Times*, July 29, 1994.
5 Letter from *The New York Times* news editor William Borders to John Doorley at Merck, August 17, 1994.
6 Juan Forero, "Merck Pays $127,500 In Fines For Cuba Deal," *The Star Ledger*, October 25, 1995.
7 1995 Merck & Co., Inc. Annual Report, p. 51.
8 Erik Eckholm, "River Blindness: Conquering An Ancient Scourge," *The New York Times Magazine*, January 8, 1989.
9 Herb Schmertz with William Novak, *Good-bye To The Low Profile* (Boston: Little, Brown, 1986), p. 73.

Chapter 4

1 http://www.oreillynet.com/pub/a/oreilly/tim/news/2005/09/30/what-is-web-20.html
2 http://interactive.linuxjournal.com/article/8549
3 danah boyd, http://www.danah.org/papers/talks/MSRTechFest2009.html.
4 Charlene Li and Josh Bernoff, *Groundswell: Winning in a World Transformed by Social Technologies* (Boston: Harvard Business Press, 2008), p. 9.
5 Rick Levine, Christopher Locke, Doc Searls and David Weinberger, *The Cluetrain Manifesto* (Cambridge, MA: Perseus Books2000), p. xxii.
6 http://www.engagementdb.com/downloads/ENGAGEMENTdb_Report_2009.pdf.
7 http://www.awpagesociety.com/images/uploads/2007AuthenticEnterprise.pdf.
8 Don Tapscott and David Ticoll, *The Naked Corporation* (New York: Free Press, 2003), p. xi.
9 Ibid., p. xii.

10 http://www.edelman.com/trust/2009/.

11 Shel Holtz and John C. Havens, *Tactical Transparency* (San Francisco: Jossey-Bass, 2009).

12 danah boyd and Nicole Ellison, "Social Network Sites: Definition, History, and Scholarship," *Journal of Computer-Mediated Communication*, vol. 13, no. 1 (2007), article 11.

13 http://en.wikipedia.org/wiki/Search_engine_optimization

14 http://en.wikipedia.org/wiki/Wiki.

15 http://blogs.starbucks.com/blogs/customer/archive/2009/03/19/happy-birthday-msi.aspx.

16 For more information on the spread of news information online, see the research report, "Meme-tracking and the Dynamics of the News Cycle," http://www.cs.cornell.edu/home/kleinber/kdd09-quotes.pdf.

17 http://www.pr-squared.com/2008/04/social_media_release_template.html.

18 http://socialmediareleases.x.iabc.com/2008/03/01/iabc-assumes-social-media-release-leadership-role/.

19 http://shankman.com/some-fun-haro-stats/.

20 For a fairly complete list of social media crisis examples, see Jeremiah Owyang's post, "A Chronology of Brands that Got Punk'd by Social Media", http://www.web-strategist.com/blog/2008/05/02/a-chonology-of-brands-that-got-punkd-by-social-media/.

21 For more on the Target case, see http://www.nytimes.com/2008/01/28/business/media/28target.html. For more on the Domino's Pizza case, see http://www.nytimes.com/2009/04/16/business/media/16dominos.html.

22 http://industry.bnet.com/advertising/1000404/pepsi-apologizes-on-twitter-for-suicide-ad-by-bbdo/.

23 http://www.youtube.com/watch?v=H_jhLGxH-m4.

24 http://www.ipressroom.com/pr/corporate/document/ipr_2009_Digital_Readiness_final.pdf.

25 http://www.nytimes.com/2007/07/12/business/12foods.html.

26 http://womma.org/ethics/code/.

27 http://www.ftc.gov/opa/2008/11/endorsements.shtm, http://www.ftc.gov/os/2008/11/P034520endorsementguides.pdf.

28 See Charlene Li's "Corporate Blogging Policy Examples" for links to a few sample policies, including large corporations like IBM and Sun Microsystems, as well as academic institutions and non-profit organizations, http://www.socialtext.net/charleneli/index.cgi?corporate_blogging_policies.

29 Debbie Weil, *The Corporate Blogging Book* (2006), p. 10.

30 http://www.ethanzuckerman.com/blog/2009/07/07/activist-media-and-selective-amplifiers/.

31 http://blogs.harvardbusiness.org/cs/2009/08/will_the_real_myspace_users_pl.html#1.

32 For more on this topic, also see danah boyd's talks, "The Not-So-Hidden Politics of Class Online," http://www.danah.org/papers/talks/PDF2009.html and "MySpace Vs. Facebook: A Digital Enactment of Class-Based Social Categories Amongst American Teenagers," http://www.danah.org/papers/talks/ICA2009.html.

33 http://www.buzzmachine.com/archives/2005_06_21.html.

34 http://www.businessweek.com/bwdaily/dnflash/content/oct2007/db20071017_277576.htm?chan=top+news_top+news+index_top+story.

35 http://www.thefordstory.com/our-plan-progress/ford-is-first-among-major-manufacturers-to-report-sales-increase-in-2009/.

36 http://www.businessweek.com/autos/autobeat/archives/2009/07/ford_tops_quali_2.html.

37 http://virtue.com/blog/2009/01/29/the-virtue-100-top-social-brands-of-2008/.

38 http://www.sun.com/communities/guidelines_v1.jsp.

Chapter 5

1 Herbert A. Simon, "Designing Organizations for an Information-Rich World," in Martin Greenberger (ed.), *Computers, Communication, and the Public Interest* (Baltimore: The Johns Hopkins Press, 1971), pp. 40–41.

2 John M. Darley and C. Daniel Batson, "From Jerusalem to Jericho: A Study of Situational and Dispositional Variables in Helping Behavior," *Journal of Personality and Social Psychology*, vol. 27 (1973), pp. 100–108.

3 Jon Hanson and David G. Yosifon, "The Situation: An Introduction to the Situational Character, Critical Realism, Power Economics, and Deep Capture," University of Pennsylvania Law Review, no. 152 (2003–4), p. 129.

4 Wikipedia, "Rule of Thumb," http://en.wikipedia.org/wiki/Rule_of_thumb.

5 Lisa Endlich, *Goldman Sachs: Culture of Success* (New York: Touchstone, 1999), pp. 18–19.

6 Ibid.

7 Nick Paumgarten, "The Death of Kings," *New Yorker*, May 18, 2009, p. 40.

8 Andrew R. Sorkin, "Goldman Regrets 'Market Euphoria' That Led to Crisis," *DealBook*, June 16, 2009, http://dealbook.blogs.nytimes.com/2009/06/16/goldman-regrets-market-euphoria-that-led-to-crisis/?ref=business.

9 Chip Heath and Dan Heath, *Made to Stick: Why Some Ideas Survive and Others Die* (New York: Random House, 2007), pp. 25–7.

10 Ibid.

11 James Carville and Paul Begala, *Buck Up, Suck Up ... and Come Back When You Foul Up* (New York: Simon and Schuster, 2003).

12 Kelly Lambert, "Depressingly Easy," *Scientific American Mind*, August (2008), pp. 30–37.

13 Robert B. Cialdini, *Influence: The Psychology of Persuasion* (New York: William Morrow, 1993).

Chapter 6

1 The lobbying firm formerly known as Wexler, Reynolds, Fuller, Harrison and Schule, founded in 1981, is now known as Wexler & Walker Public Policy Associates.

2 Ohio Edison is now part of the First Energy Corporation.

3 United States Constitution, First Amendment.

4 Web site of Intercontinental Willard Hotel, http://www.washington.intercontinental.com.

5 The United States Senate, http://www.senate.gov/legislative/Public_Disclosure/FAQs.htm.

6 The White House, http://www.whitehouse.gov/the_press_office/Memorandum-for-the-Heads-of-Executive-Departments-and-Agencies-3-20-09/.

7 Bob Burke and Ralph Thompson, *Bryce Harlow, Mr. Integrity*, Oklahoma Heritage Assocation, 2000, Foreword by Dr. Henry Kissinger, p. 14.

8 Speech by Vice President Dick Cheney, given at Bryce Harlow Awards Dinner on March 16, 2005, in Washington, D.C., http://www.bryceharlow.org.

9 Bryce Harlow, "Corporate Representation," published by the Bryce Harlow Foundation, Washington, D.C., 1984, http://www.bryceharlow.org.

10 "Code of Ethics," American League of Lobbyists (ALL), http://www.alldc.org.

Chapter 7

1 Walter "Buzz" Storey, "Uniontown and Fayette County: Another Look," *Herald-Standard* (Uniontown Newspapers, 2001).

2 John Doorley interviews with Mr. Joe Hardy on May 11 and May 25, 2005.

3 Edmund M. Burke, *Corporate Community Relations: The Principle of the Neighbor of Choice* (Westport, CT: Praeger, 1999), pp. 15–16.

4 Ibid., p. 16.

5 Ibid., pp. 17–18.

6 Ibid., p. 10.

7 Ibid., p. 28.

8 Charles J. Fombrun, *Reputation, Realizing Value from the Corporate Image* (Boston: Harvard Business School Press, 1996), p. 195.

9 Burke, *Corporate Community Relations*, p. 25.

10 Ibid., pp. 47–50.

11 Ibid., p. 19.
12 David W. Guth and Charles Marsh, *Public Relations: A Values-Driven Approach* (Needham Heights, MA: Allyn & Bacon, 2000), pp. 424–7.
13 Erik Eckholm, Cover Story, "River Blindness, Conquering An Ancient Scourge," *The New York Times Magazine*, January 8, 1989.
14 2005 Merck Corporate Responsibility Report.
15 John Doorley's old notes verified by Dr. Vagelos in November 2005.
16 Facts via e-mail from Ken Gustavsen, Merck's manager of global product donations, December 1, 2009.
17 Burke, *Corporate Community Relations*, p. 54.
18 Ibid., pp. 21–3.

Chapter 8

1 Share price adjusted for later stock splits.
2 TSC Industries, Inc. v. Northway, Inc., 426 U.S. 438 (1976).
3 17 CFR 240.10b5.
4 Securities and Exchange Commission. Release 34-21138, July 12, 1984.

Chapter 9

1 Case study by Bonnie Rothenstein and Katja Schroeder, October 1, 2009.
2 Michael Morley, *How to Manage your Global Reputation: A Guide to the Dynamics of International Public Relations*, 2nd edition (New York: New York University Press, 2002), p. 24.
3 Robert I. Wakefield, "What's wrong with multinational public relations?" *Public Relations Strategist*, Spring (2000), http://members.prsa.org/ ScriptContent/resources/pdfpull. cfm?prcfile=6K-010034 pdf, 7/15/2005.
4 International Monetary Fund, http://www.IMF.org.
5 Fraser Seitel, *The Practice of Public Relations*, 9th edition (Upper Saddle River, NJ: Pearson Education Inc, 2004), p. 378.
6 Thomas L. Friedman, The World is Flat (New York: Farrar, Straus & Giroux, 2005).
7 Dennis Wilcox, Dennis, Phillip Ault, Warren Agee, and Glen Cameron, *Essentials of Public Relations*, (Harlow: Addison-Wesley, 2001), p. 283.
8 *BusinessWeek,* September 28, 2009.
9 2009 Edelman Trust Barometer, http://www.edelman.com/trust/2009/docs/Trust_Book_ Final_2.pdf.
10 Anthony P. Ewing, *Understanding the Global Compact Human Rights Principles*, and *Implementing the Global Compact Human Rights Principles*, in United Nations Global Compact and the Office of High Commissioner for Human Rights, *Embedding Human Rights Into Business Practice* (2004), available at http://www.unglobalcompact.org.
11 See, e.g., Norms on the Responsibilities of Transnational Corporations and Other Business Enterprises with Regard to Human Rights (Aug. 26, 2003), U.N. Commission on Human Rights, Subcommission on the Promotion and Protection of Human Rights, U.N. doc. E/CN.4/Sub.2/2003/12/Rev.2, preamble (noting that transnational corporations "have the capacity to foster economic well-being … and wealth as well as the capacity to cause harmful impacts on the human rights and lives of individuals … ").
12 Alan K. Freitag and Ashli Quesinberry Stokes, *Global Public Relations. Spanning Borders, Spanning Culture* (London and New York: Routledge, 2009).
13 R. Robertson, "Mapping the Global Condition. Globalization as the Central Concept," in M. Featherstone (ed.), *Global Culture: Nationalism, Globalization and Modernity*, pp. 15–30.
14 P. Lesly, "Public Relations in the Turbulent New Human Climate, " *Public Relations Review*, vol. 17 (1991), pp. 1–8.

15 D.W. Brinkerhoff and M.D. Ingle, "Integrating Blueprint and Process: A Structured Flexibility Approach to Development Management," *Public Administration and Development*, vol. 9 (1989), pp. 487–503; qtd by Wakefield in H. Culbertson and N. Chen, *International Public Relations: A Comparative Analysis*, ed. H. Culbertson and N. Chen (Hillsdale, NJ: Lawrence Erlbaum Associates, 1996), pp. 17–28, p. 25.

16 J.B. Manheim and R.B. Albritton, "Changing National Images: International Public Relations and Media Agenda Setting," *The American Political Science Review*, vol. 78 (1984), pp. 641–57, cited in Cutherbertson and Chen, *International Public Relations*, pp. 25–6.

17 R.E. Hiebert, "Global Public Relations in a Post-Communist World: A New Model," *Public Relations Review*, vol. 18 (1992), pp. 117–26, p. 126

18 J.E. Grunig and J. White, "The effect of Workviews on Public Relations Theory and Practice," in J.E. Grunig (ed.), *Excellence in Public Relations and Communication Management* (Hillsdale, NJ: Lawrence Erlbaum Associates, 1992), pp. 31–64; qtd by Wakefield in Culbertson and Chen, *International Public Relations*, p. 20.

19 G. Anderson, "A Global Look at Public Relations," in B. Cantor (ed.), *Experts in Action: Inside Public Relations*, 2nd edition (New York: Longman, 1989), pp. 412–22, p. 413.

20 Ibid.

21 It is not uncommon for nonprofessional workers around the world to have limited literacy in their native language. Companies must make verbal communication available as needed. Truck drivers, factory workers, maintenance staff, and others may also have limited access to computers. Provision must be made to get these employees the information they need.

22 Edward Trissel, personal interview, June 28, 2005.

23 Bonin Bough, personal interview, June 28, 2005.

24 Bough, personal interview.

25 *BusinessWeek*, September 28, 2009.

26 Ruder Finn Case Study 2002.

27 Schroeder, interview, May 2005.

28 Bough, personal interview.

29 Anderson, "A Global Look at Public Relations," p. 421.

30 Krishnamurthy Sriramesh and Dejan Vercic, "A Theoretical Framework for Global Public Relations Research and Practice," in K. Sriramesh, and D. Vercic (eds.), *The Global Public Relations Handbook* (Hillsdale, NJ: Lawrence Erlbaum Associates, 2003), pp. 1–17, p. 16.

31 Ibid.

32 Mike H. He, *Public Relations Tactics* (May 2003).

33 Schroeder, 2005.

34 Burns, Barbara, personal interview, July 15, 2005.

35 http://www.CNNMoney.com.

36 2009 Edelman Trust Barometer, http://www.edelman.com, 9/30/2009.

37 Frank Vogl, "International Corporate Ethics and the Challenges to Public Relations," *Public Relations Strategist*, Spring (2001), http://members.prsa.org/ScriptContent/resources/pdfpull.cfm?prcfile=6K-020119.pdf, 7/15/2005.

38 CokeFacts.org, http://cokefacts.org/citizenship/ cit_in_environmental_p.shtml, 7/20/2005.

39 *Wall Street Journal*, 6/7/2005, http://livesinfocus.org/aids/files/2008/11/wsjhow_a_global_web_of_activists_gives_coke_problems_in_india.pdf.

40 Ibid.

41 Geoff Colvin, "A Powerful Asset," *Fortune*, March 2, 2009.

42 United Nations Global Compact, December 1999, http://www.unglobalcompact.org/portal/default.asp, 7/20/2005.

43 Sylvia Ciesluk, "Where Does Corporate Citizenship Belong?" *Boston College Center for Corporate Citizenship*, March 2008.

44 Brundtland Commission, 1987, http://www.worldinbalance.net/intagreements/1987-brundtland.php.

45 John Elkington, *Cannibals with Forks: The Triple Bottom Line of 21st Century Business* (Oxford: Capstone Publishing Ltd. 1999).

46 PepsiCo, Environmental Sustainablity, http://www.pepsico.com/Purpose/Sustainablity/Environmental-Sustainability.html and http://www.pepsico.com/Purpose?Environment/Water.html.

47 *Newsweek*, September 21, 2009.

48 HP Power to Change Web site, http://h30470.www3hp.com/en-index.aspx and http://hp.com/hpinfo/globalcitizenship/gcreport/globalcitizen/managinggc.html.

49 Ibid.

50 *Newsweek*, September 21, 2009.

51 Burns, Barbara, personal interview, July 15, 2005.

52 Bonnie Rothenstein, September 29, 2009.

Chapter 10

1 Waggener Edstrom, "Thriving during a communications cataclysm," http://waggeneredstrom.com/influence/influence-manifesto/default.aspx, 6/16/2009, p. 2.

2 *Journal of Integrated Marketing Communication*, http://jimc.medill.northwestern.edu/JIMCWeb site/site.htm.

3 R. Ettenson and J. Knowles, 'Don't Confuse Reputation with Brand," *MIT Sloan Management Review*, vol. 40, no. 2 (2008), pp. 19–21, p. 19.

4 F. Reichheld, *The Loyalty Effect* (Boston: Harvard Business School Publishing, 1996), p. 19.

5 F. Reichheld, *The Ultimate Question: Driving Good Profits and True Growth* (Boston: Harvard Business School Publishing, 2006).

6 C. Fombrun, *Reputation: Realizing Value from the Corporate Image* (Boston: Harvard Business School Press, 1996), p. 9.

7 J. Welch and S. Welch, *Winning* (New York: HarperCollins, 2005), p. 53.

8 R.B. Hayes, *Public Relations and Collaboration: The Role of Public Relations and Communications Supporting Collaboration in a Complex, Converging World* (2008), http://www.lulu.com/content/paperback-book/public-relations-and-collaboration/4602019, 7/11/2009, p. 15.

9 J.E. Grunig, "Two-way Symmetrical Public Relations: Past, Present, and Future," in R. Heath (ed.), *Handbook of Public Relations* (Thousand Oaks, CA: Sage, 2001), pp. 11–30.

10 R. Heifetz, A. Grashow, and M. Linsky, *The Practices of Adaptive Leadership* (Boston: Harvard University Business Press, 2009) p. 3.

11 W.F. Drath, *The Deep Blue Sea: Rethinking the Source of Leadership* (San Francisco: Jossey-Bass, 2001), p. 18.

12 Arthur W. Page Society, "The Authentic Enterprise" (2007), http://www.awpagesociety.com/site/members/page_society_releases_the_authentic_enterprise, p. 7.

13 T. Levitt, *The Marketing Imagination* (New York: Free Press, 1983), p. 7.

14 M.E. Porter, *Competitive Advantage: Creating and Sustaining Superior Performance* (rev. ed.) (New York: Free Press, 1998 [original work published 1985]), p. 3.

15 P.F. Drucker, *The Practice of Management* (New York: Harper Business, 1993 [original work published in 1954]), p. 35.

16 A.J. Silk, *What is Marketing?* (Boston: Harvard Business School Press, 2006), p. vii.

17 D. Sutton and T. Klein, *Enterprise Marketing Management: The New Science of Marketing* (Hoboken, NJ: John Wiley & Sons, Inc., 2003), p. 23.

18 N. Rackham, *SPIN Selling* (New York: McGraw Hill, 1988), p. 85.

19 M. Moser, *United We Brand* (Boston: Harvard Business School Press, 2003), p. 136.

20 Grunig, "Two-way Symmetrical Public Relations."

21 P.M. Senge, *The Fifth Discipline: The Art and Practice of the Learning Organization* (rev. ed.) (New York: Currency Doubleday, 2006), pp. 183–6.

22 J. Swartz, "More Marketers Sign on to Social Media," *USA Today*, August 28, 2009, pp. B1–2.

23 D. Creevey, "'A Person Like Me' Now Most Credible Spokesperson for Companies; Trust in Employees Significantly Higher Than in CEOs, Edelman Trust Barometer Finds," January 23, 2006, http://www.edelman.com/news/showone.asp?id=102, 7/4/2009.

24 Heifetz, Grasho, and Linsky, *The Practices of Adaptive Leadership*, p. 169.

25 J.C. Rost, *Leadership for the 21st Century* (Westport, CT: Praeger, 1993), p. 102.

26 A. Zaleznik, "Managers and Leaders: Are They Different?" *Harvard Business Review*, vol. 82, no. 1 (2004), pp. 74–82.

27 J.A. Conger, "The necessary art of persuasion," *Harvard Business Review*, vol. 76, no. 3 (1998), pp. 84–96.

28 K.J. Gergen and M. Gergen, *Social Construction: Entering the Dialogue* (Chagrin Falls, OH: Taos Institute, 2004), p. 48.

29 S.A. Deetz, S.J. Tracy and J.L. Simpson, *Leading Organizations through Transition* (Thousand Oaks, CA: Sage Publications, Inc., 2000), p. 102.

30 G. Lakoff and M. Johnson, *Metaphors We Live By* (Chicago: University of Chicago Press, 2003), pp. 3–6.

31 Deetz, Tracy, and Simpson, *Leading Organizations through Transition*, p. 67.

32 N. Kumar, *Marketing as Strategy* (Boston: Harvard Business Press, 2004), p. 6.

33 Moser, *United We Brand*, p. 15.

34 K. Freiberg and J. Freiberg, *Nuts! Southwest Airlines' Crazy Recipe for Business and Personal Success* (Austin, TX: Bard Books, 1996), p. 125.

35 D. Coletti, D., "How Do Companies Measure Success?" (2002), http://www.instituteforpr.org/research_single/measure_prs_contribution/.

36 D.W. Stacks, "Best Practices in Public Relations Research," (2002), http://www.institute-forpr.org/research_single/best_practices_in_pr_research/.

Chapter 11

1 M. Taylor et al., *Public Relations Review*, vol. 29 (2003), pp. 257–70.

2 James E. Grunig and Todd Hunt, *Managing Public Relations* (New York: Harcourt Brace Jovanovich, 1984).

3 *The Art of War*, by Sun Tzu, translated by Thomas Cleary, (Boston: Shambhala, 1998), p. 82.

4 "GE's Jeff Immelt on the 10 Keys to Great Leadership," *Fast Company*, April (2004), p. 96.

Chapter 12

1 Rory F. Knight and Deborah J. Pretty, *The Impact of Catastrophes on Shareholder Value: A Research Report Sponsored by Sedgwick Group*, The Oxford Executive Research Briefings (Oxford: Templeton College, 1997).

2 Knight and Pretty, *The Impact of Catastrophes*, p. 7.

3 "Time for Exxon to Pay," Editorial, *The New York Times*, January 30, 2004, p. A24.

4 *Time* magazine, September 19, 2005 issue, published on-line on September 11, 2005, at http://www.time.com/time/magazine.

5 Todd S. Purdum and Marjorie Connelly, "Support for Bush Continues to Drop, Poll Shows," *The New York Times*, September 15, 2005, at http://www.nytimes.com/2005/09/15/politics/15poll.html.

6 Tamotsu Shibutani, *Improvised News: A Sociological Study of Rumor*, by Tamotsu Shibutani (Indianapolis: Bobbs Merrill, 1966), p. 172. Note: Shibutani uses the gender-specific words "man" or "men" to refer to people in general. Throughout, I will quote him using the gender-neutral "person" or "people."

7 Steven Fink, *Crisis Management: Planning for the Inevitable* (New York: American Management Association, 1986), p. 15.

8 Ibid., pp. 15–16. (Italics in original.)

9 Ibid., p. 16.

10 Ronald J. Alsop, *The 18 Immutable Laws of Corporate Reputation: Creating, Protecting, and Repairing Your Most Valuable Asset*, A Wall Street Journal Book (New York: Free Press, 2004), p. 220.

11 For historical roots of the phrase "Golden Hour" in emergency medicine, see Robert Locke, "New Techniques Developed for Treatment of the 'Epidemic'," *Associated Press*, January 18, 1982.

12 Carol Hymowitz and Joanne S. Lublin, "McDonald's CEO Tragedy Holds Lessons," *Wall Street Journal*, April 20, 2004, p. B1.

13 Ibid.

14 *Boeing Code of Conduct*, 1/26/2004, http://www.boeing.com.

15 Alsop, *The 18 Immutable Laws*, p. 218.

16 For more on these behaviors, how to recognize them, and how to prevent them, see also Helio Fred Garcia, *Avoiding Crisis Mis-Steps*, Logos Crisis Monograph Series (2004), http://www.logosconsulting.net.

17 Jonathan Harr, *A Civil Action* (New York: Random House, 1995), p. 295.

18 Shibutani, *Improvised News*, p. 62.

19 http://www.ruralfire.qld.gov.au/level2/M06/introduction.htm.

20 Gordon W. Allport and Leo Postman, "An Analysis of Rumor," *Public Opinion Quarterly*, vol. 10 (1946), pp. 505–06 (italics in the original).

21 Jean-Noël Kapferer, *Rumors: Uses, Interpretations, & Images* (New Brunswick: Transaction Publishers, 1990), p. 12.

22 Ibid., p. 108 (italics in the original).

23 Ibid., p. 9.

24 Gordon W. Allport and Leo Postman, *The Psychology of Rumor* (New York: Henry Holt & Co., 1947), p. ix.

25 Ibid., p. x.

26 Ibid., p. 1.

27 Ibid., p. 44 (italics in the original).

28 Ibid., p. 2.

29 Ibid., p. 3.

30 Ibid., pp. 33 and 34 (italics in the original).

Chapter 13

1 Nike press release, June 6, 1996.

2 Nike, Inc., FY05-06 Corporate Responsibility Report (2007), p. 7.

3 Nike, Inc., FY04 Corporate Responsibility Report (2005), p. 11.

4 *Social Responsibility or "Telescopic Philanthropy": The Choice is Yours*, remarks by Harold Burson, Founding Chairman, Burson-Marsteller, Columbia University, Graduate School of Business (March 20, 1973).

5 Cf. Milton Friedman, "The Social Responsibility of Business is to Increase its Profits," *The New York Times Magazine*, September 11, 1970; Peter Drucker, "The New Meaning of Corporate Social Responsibility," *California Management Review*, vol. 26, no. 2, (Winter 1984).

6 Few consumers today equate corporate philanthropy and corporate responsibility. In a survey of U.S. consumers, most defined corporate responsibility as a commitment to employees or communities. Fleishmann-Hillard/National Consumers League, Rethinking Corporate Social Responsibility (2006), available at http://www.csrresults.com/FINAL_Full_Report.pdf.

7 General Electric Company, *Our Actions: GE 2005 Citizenship Report* (2005), p. 4.

8 Communicating financial performance is covered in Chapter 8, "Investor Relations."

9 John Ruggie, *Business and Human Rights: Mapping International Standards of Responsibility and Accountability for Corporate Acts*, UN doc. A/HRC/4/035 (February 9, 2007).

10 The CERES Principles address protection of the biosphere, sustainable use of natural resources, reduction and disposal of wastes, energy conservation and product safety. CERES Principles (1989), available at http://www.ceres.org/coalitionandcompanies/principles.php.

11 See, for example, John Elkington, *Cannibals with Forks: The Triple Bottom Line of 21st Century Business* (Oxford: Capstone, 1997).

12 See, for example, Michael E. Porter and Mark R. Kramer, "The Competitive Advantage of Corporate Philanthropy," *Harvard Business Review*, (December 2002).

13 *The Case for Social Responsibility*, Presentation to the Annual Conference of Business for Social Responsibility, Boston, USA, November 10, 1998.

14 General Electric Company, Our Actions: GE 2005 Citizenship Report (2005), p. 3.

15 See, for example, World Economic Forum, *Values and Value* (2004).

16 Edelman Trust Barometer (2009), available at http://www.edelman.com/trust/2009/.

17 The fair trade movement seeks to improve living standards for small farmers worldwide by

creating a market for agricultural products purchased at fixed prices directly from farmer cooperatives. See generally, FairTrade Labeling Organizations International, http://www.fairtrade.net.

18 See, for example, "Special Report on Corporate Social Responsibility," *The Economist*, January 17, 2008.

19 NGOs engaged in the corporate responsibility debate include human rights organizations, environmental groups, labor unions, and development organizations. International organizations including the United Nations, the International Labor Organization (ILO), the World Bank and the Organization for Economic Cooperation and Development (OECD) are active in the corporate responsibility field.

20 *The New York Times*, "Citizen Shell," March 31, 1997, p. A14.

21 For a list of corporate codes that reference human rights standards, see Business & Human Rights Resource Centre, http://www.business-humanrights.org/Documents/Policies.

22 The mining company Freeport-McMoran has released an independent human rights assessment of its mining operations in Indonesia that found questionable links among company security personnel and the Indonesian military. Aaron Bernstein, "Freeport's Hard Look at Itself," *Business Week*, October 24, 2005, p. 108.

23 Fair Labor Association, *Widespread Overtime and Why It Doesn't Work* (2009), available at http://www.fairlabor.org/images/WhatWeDo/SpecialProjects/scope_how_may09.pdf.

24 Allen L. White, *New Wine, New Bottles: The Rise of Non-Financial Reporting* (Business for Social Responsibility, June 20, 2005).

25 Mandatory non-financial reporting is increasingly common in Europe. In the United Kingdom, the 2006 Companies Act requires companies listed on the London Stock Exchange to report on the potential materiality of social and governance issues, and in Denmark, the largest companies will need to report on their corporate responsibility efforts beginning in 2010. Ben Cooper, "Non-financial Reporting—Learning from Denmark," *Ethical Corporation*, March 10, 2009.

26 KPMG, *International Survey of Corporate Responsibility Reporting 2008* (2008) p. 4.

27 Global Reporting Initiative, *Sustainability Reporting Guidelines, Version 3.0* (2006).

28 *Oxford English Dictionary* (1999). See BSR and Futerra, *Understanding and Preventing Greenwash: A Business Guide* (July 2009).

29 e-mail from Unocal Director of Information Carol Scott to Unocal Media Contact and Spokesperson David Garcia, cited in *Doe I v. Unocal Corp.* (9th Cir., filed September 18, 2002).

30 Robert M. Reese, Senior Vice President of Hershey Foods, quoted in Bob Fernandez, "Hershey 'Shocked' by Report," *The Times Union* (Albany, NY), June 24, 2001, p. A7.

31 *The New York Times*, "Shell Game in Nigeria," December 3, 1995, p. E14.

32 Royal Dutch/Shell, *Statement of General Business Principles*, March 17, 1997.

33 Human Rights Watch, *Colombia: Concerns Raised by the Security Arrangements of Transnational Oil Companies* (April 1998).

34 See generally, Bennett Freeman, "Drilling for Common Ground," *Foreign Policy Magazine*, (July/August 2001).

35 Amnesty International UK, *Human Rights On the Line* (May 2003).

36 Jay Pearson, Regional Coordinator, BP plc, UN Global Compact Learning Forum, Nova Lima, Brazil (December 2003).

37 Human Rights Watch, *Turning a Blind Eye: Hazardous Child Labor in El Salvador's Sugarcane Cultivation* (June 2004).

38 Lynn Paine et al., "Up to Code," *Harvard Business Review*, (December 2005).

39 The UN Global Compact is a voluntary corporate citizenship initiative that calls on companies to integrate into their core business operations ten principles on human rights, labor rights, environmental protection, and transparency.

40 See, for example, Michael Liedtke, "Gap Inc. Says Some of its Factories are Sweatshops," *Associated Press*, May 13, 2004.

41 See, for example, Sheila Bonini, David Court, and Alberto Marchi, "Rebuilding Corporate Reputations," *The McKinsey Quarterly*, June (2009).

42 Examples of industry corporate responsibility initiatives include the Fair Labor Association Workplace Code of Conduct, the International Council of Toy Industries Code of Business Practices, the Common Code for the Coffee Community, the Cocoa Industry

Protocol, the Electronics Industry Code of Conduct, the Equator Principles (project finance) and the Global Network Initiative.

43 Nike, Inc., FY05-06 Corporate Responsibility Report (2007), p. 24.

44 Global Network Initiative, *Principles on Freedom of Expression and Privacy* (October 2008), p. 5, n. 12.

45 Eric Schlosser, "A Side Order of Human Rights," *The New York Times*, April 6, 2005.

46 "CSR - A Religion with Too Many Priests?," *European Business Forum*, issue 15 (Autumn 2003).

47 *Associated Press*, "Goldman to Spend $100M Educating Women," March 5, 2008.

48 *Kasky v. Nike, Inc.* (Cal. S087859, May 2, 2002).

Chapter 15

1 Kevin T. Jackson, *Building Reputational Capital: Strategies for Integrity and Fair Play That Improve the Bottom Line* (Oxford: Oxford University Press, 2004), p. 12.

2 Ibid.

3 Glenn Rifkin, "At 100, Public Relations' Pioneer Criticizes Some of His Peers," *The New York Times*, December 30, 1991, p. D6.

4 Edward L. Bernays, *Crystallizing Public Opinion* (Boni and Liveright, 1923), p. 52.

5 Ibid., pp. 96–97.

6 Ibid., p. 57.

7 Ibid., p. 139.

8 Ibid., p. 77.

9 *Fortune*, May 21, 2005.

10 The Arthur W. Page Society can be found at http://www.awp.society.com/.

11 "GE's Jeff Immelt on the 10 Keys to Great Leadership," *Fast Company*, April (2004), p. 96.

12 *Clausewitz on Strategy: Inspiration and Insight from a Master on Strategy*, ed. with comm. Tiha von Ghyczy, Bolko von Oetinger and Christopher Bassord (Boston: John Wiley & Sons, 2001), p. 2.

13 Ibid., p. 4.

14 Ibid., p. 37.

15 Carl von Clausewitz, *On War*, ed. and trans. Michael Howard and Peter Paret (Princeton: Princeton University Press, 1976), p. 87.

16 Ibid., p. 81 (italics in the original).

17 Ibid., p. 178.

18 *Clausewitz on Strategy*, p. 55.

INDEX